The Cold War and Asian Cinemas

This book offers an interdisciplinary, historically grounded study of Asian cinemas' complex responses to the Cold War conflict. It situates the global ideological rivalry within regional and local political, social, and cultural processes, while offering a transnational and cross-regional focus.

This volume makes a major contribution to constructing a cultural and popular cinema history of the global Cold War. Its geographical focus is set on East Asia, Southeast Asia, and South Asia. In adopting such an inclusive approach, it draws attention to the different manifestations and meanings of the connections between the Cold War and cinema across Asian borders. Many essays in the volume have a transnational and cross-regional focus, one that sheds light on Cold War-influenced networks (such as the circulation of socialist films across communist countries) and on the efforts of American agencies (such as the United States Information Service and the Asia Foundation) to establish a transregional infrastructure of "free cinema" to contain the communist influences in Asia.

With its interdisciplinary orientation and broad geographical focus, the book will appeal to scholars and students from a wide variety of fields, including film studies, history (especially the burgeoning field of cultural Cold War studies), Asian studies, and U.S.-Asian cultural relations.

Poshek Fu is Professor of History at the University of Illinois at Urbana-Champaign. His research focuses on media history, Cold War cultures, and U.S.-China relations. He is the author of *Between Shanghai and Hong Kong: The Politics of Chinese Cinemas* (Stanford University Press, 2003) and *Passivity, Resistance, and Collaboration: Intellectual Choices in Occupied Shanghai* (Stanford University Press, 1993). He is also the editor of *China Forever: The Shaw Brothers and Diasporic Cinema* (University of Illinois Press, 2008), and co-editor of *The Cinema of Hong Kong: History, Arts, Identity* (Cambridge University Press, 2002).

Man-Fung Yip is Associate Professor of Film and Media Studies at the University of Oklahoma. He is the author of *Martial Arts Cinema and Hong Kong Modernity: Aesthetics, Representation, Circulation* (Hong Kong University Press, 2017) and co-editor of *American and Chinese-Language Cinemas: Examining Cultural Flows* (Routledge, 2015). His work has also appeared in *Cinema Journal*, *Chinese Literature Today*, and numerous edited volumes.

The Cold War and Asian Cinemas

Edited by
Poshek Fu and Man-Fung Yip

Routledge
Taylor & Francis Group
NEW YORK AND LONDON

First published 2020
by Routledge
605 Third Avenue, New York, NY 10017

and by Routledge
2 Park Square, Milton Park, Abingdon, Oxon OX14 4RN

Routledge is an imprint of the Taylor & Francis Group, an informa business

British Library Cataloguing-in-Publication Data
A catalogue record for this book is available from the British Library

Library of Congress Cataloging-in-Publication Data
A catalog record has been requested for this book

ISBN: 978-1-138-35381-7 (hbk)

Typeset in Sabon
by codeMantra

Contents

Acknowledgments

This book is a joint effort. We would like to thank all of our contributors for the joy of working together to make this book happen. Without them, the book would not have even existed. We also express our gratitude to the enthusiasm and ideas of friends and colleagues—I-In Chiang, Tom Cunliffe, Qiliang He, Kwok-wai Hui, Christina Klein, Grace Mak, Senjo Nakai, Jinhee Park, and especially Priscilla Tse and Shuk-ting Kinnia Yau. Thanks are due to the Office of the Vice President for Research at the University of Oklahoma, which provided a grant to help cover indexing and other costs. Finally, we are grateful to the editors at Routledge, especially Suzanne Richardson and Felisa Salvago-Keyes, for supporting this project and offering expert guidance at various stages of publication.

Introduction

The Cold War was a momentous era in global history. The confrontation between capitalism and communism functioned as a macro-historical structure that shaped ideological conflicts and organized international relationships for much of the latter half of the twentieth century. According to conventional wisdom, the end of the Cold War can be dated to the late 1980s and early 1990s, when the fall of the Berlin Wall, the shredding of the Iron Curtain, as well as the ousting of the communist regime in the Soviet Union and the eventual disintegration of the Soviet empire brought about the collapse of the Communist Bloc. But just as scholarly inquiry always blossoms after the event, Cold War scholarship, spurred by newly declassified archival materials across the world in recent years and by the different insights opened up by other fields (notably cultural history), has continued to grow and be enriched over the last 30 years or so, as evidenced by new journals such as *Journal of Cold War Studies* and *Cold War History*[1] and by a proliferation of research monographs that have brought a wide range of new materials and perspectives to our understanding of the global conflicts.

A significant shift in the recent Cold War research has been an expansion of geographical scope beyond Euro-America and an adoption of a more local, non-totalizing, and culturally specific frame of analysis (Ang 2018; Chamberlin 2018; Chen 2001; Masuda 2015; Reynolds 2014). This means, on the one hand, conceptualizing the Cold War not simply in relation to the heightened state of hostility and rivalry between the United States and the Soviet Union, but as a global conflict fought as much between the two superpowers as between their allies and proxies across the world. Asia in particular, a region that witnessed the rise of communist China, the partition of Korea and the subsequent civil war, the Vietnam War, and so on, was a major battleground where the Cold War conflict was played out. On the other hand, concerted efforts have also been made to localize the Cold War experience by examining it in relation to other key trends and developments such as decolonization, nation-building, and other local processes and movements. In highlighting the local experiences of and responses to the Cold War, such an approach provides a more complex picture of the global Cold War and helps reimagine what has long been ignored or taken for granted.

At the same time, recent Cold War scholarship has also developed a broader focus that goes beyond its traditional preoccupations with military or political confrontations or with high diplomacy and interstate relations. The Korean War, the Cuban missile crisis, the Vietnam War, the détente, the Soviet invasion of Afghanistan—all these were major incidents of the Cold War and merit close attention. But the Cold War struggle involved also, and perhaps above all, ideological warfare—a battle fought with words and images, that is, in the cultural realm. It is thus imperative not to lose sight of what has been called the "cultural Cold War" and "Cold War culture"—a rapidly growing field that investigates the multifaceted ways in which art, literature, media, and other cultural sectors partook in, responded to, and were shaped by the Cold War dynamics (e.g., Cummings 2009; Day and Liem 2010; Doherty 2005; Klein 2003; Saunders 2000). The cinema in particular offers special insights into these processes, given that the medium, with its mass popularity and cultural salience in the mid- to late twentieth century, was seen by both sides of the ideological divide as a potent vehicle for creating and mobilizing support for their causes.

There is certainly much more to be studied about the Cold War, particularly from a non-Western cultural perspective, and it is this belief that has guided this collection on the intersection of the Cold War and Asian cinemas. While a sizable literature exists that investigates American and other Western (especially British, German, and the Soviet Union) cinemas within the context of the Cold War (e.g., Moine 2018; Shaw 2006; Shaw and Youngblood 2010), attempts to study Asian cinemas through a similar lens have emerged only relatively recently (Hee 2020; Hughes 2014; Wong and Lee 2009). There is no doubt a need for more research on the subject and greater attention to the complex issues involved. Driven by this observation, this collection sets out to offer an interdisciplinary and historically grounded inquiry into the nature and extent of the Cold War's connections to Asian cinemas. It builds on the premise that Asian cinemas during the Cold War—their films, their film industries, their film cultures, and the interconnections between all of these—were constituted at the juncture of a number of forces: the global ideological rivalry of the era was one of them, but no less crucial were a set of regional historical imperatives (decolonization, modernity, search for national identity) and local film-industrial demands (market pressures, the aspirations of building a national cinema). This suggests that Asian cinemas' responses to the Cold War were more fluid and intertwined than is generally thought; Cold War ideologies were often mingled with ideas and identities associated with local political, social, and cultural processes, while for many film companies and filmmakers, allegiance to the "left" or to the "right" was not a mere ideological issue but also a tactical means toward industrial or individual goals. The use of the Cold War as an analytical framework, then, does not mean seeing it as a deterministic influence, but rather as one among many forces driving Asian cinemas in the period.

On the other hand, the fact that many Asian films of the period were intertwined with Cold War ideologies or confronted with political pressures does not necessarily mean that they were mere propaganda or kitsch lacking artistic or entertainment values. The binary opposition between propaganda and art, ideology and entertainment, is too simplistic and fails to recognize the creative and cultural energy that can be observed even in films, such as Sergei Eisenstein's *Battleship Potemkin* (1925) and Charlie Chaplin's *The Great Dictator* (1940), with clear intention to serve political causes. The same is true with some of the most ideologically invested Asian films in the Cold War context: from Chinese model opera films and Thai's anti-communist actioners to South Korean and Vietnamese war movies, Cold War-inflected Asian cinemas created new ways of communication and engagement as filmmakers drew upon their own national cultures and various cinematic traditions (Hollywood, socialist realism, Soviet montage, etc.) and creatively deployed narratives, styles, and genres to assert their ideological commitments.

This collection also strives, as best as we could, for a more inclusive treatment of Asian cinemas during the Cold War; its geographical focus is set on East Asia (China, Taiwan, Hong Kong, Japan, Korea), Southeast Asia (Indonesia, Singapore, Vietnam), and South Asia (India). In adopting such an inclusive approach, we aim to bring an interdisciplinary and comparative perspective to the book, drawing attention to the different forms and meanings of the "cinematic Cold War" across the region. More generally, many chapters in the collection take on a transnational and cross-regional focus, one that sheds light on Cold War-influenced networks (such as the circulation of socialist films across communist countries) as well as on the efforts of American agencies (such as the United States Information Service or the Asia Foundation) to establish a transregional infrastructure of "free cinema" (e.g., the Asia Film Festivals) to contain the communist influences in Asia. This emphasis toward the transnational will further open up our understanding of the cinematic Cold War in Asia.

This collection consists of three parts. The first part, *Transnational Connections*, focuses on a variety of border-crossing formations and practices that can be observed in Cold War-influenced Asian cinema. Man-Fung Yip explores Vietnamese revolutionary films of the 1960s and 1970s and argues that the films, despite their clear didactic intent, are marked by a richly expressive style derived in part from the Soviet avant-garde cinema of the 1920s as well as from the "thaw" films in the immediate post-Stalin years. Namhee Han's chapter takes as its object of study the military newsreels made by the South Korean army in Vietnam and examines how these news films used images, sounds, and the compilation format to control the narrative about South Korea's military involvement in the Vietnam War. The last two chapters in this part both deal with issues of transnational film circulation and reception. Drawing on the memories of moviegoers, Li Jie retraces the reception of foreign films—primarily those from fellow socialist countries—in China during the Cold War era. Their use as propaganda notwithstanding, Li argues that there was "considerable grassroots heteroglossia and creativity" in the ways how these film imports were appropriated and refunctioned to meet the particular needs of the Chinese viewers. Lanjun Xu discusses the different ways in which the mainland Chinese film *Third Sister Liu* (*Liu Sanjie*, 1961) was received in Singapore and Hong Kong. She attributes the film's huge success in Singapore to the leftist labor and anti-colonial movements in the territory during the period, while in Hong Kong, the film and two locally made adaptations were locked in a fierce competition for audiences in which landscape and folk songs, as politically contested elements in representing Chinesesness, played a key role.

The second part, *Global Conflicts, Local Formations*, includes six chapters that explore how the macro structures and effects of the Cold War were refracted and mediated by local processes. Mitsuyo Wada-Marciano delves into the educational films of post-WWII Japan and argues that they did not simply reflect but actually created an emerging national ideology known as "postwar"—an ideology that was profoundly shaped by the unequal power relationships between Japan and the United States during the Allied Occupation and in the post-Occupation, Cold War era. Focusing on the topos of land and on the reflexive yet ambivalent appropriation of the discourse of revanchist cultural nationalism in the Nikkatsu studio's *Wataridori* series (1959–62), Michael Raine proposes cinema as part of Japan's Cold War cultural infrastructure, not so much a conduit for political messages as the environment in which audiences experienced and resolved the desires, resentments, and anxieties generated by Japan's subordination to the American government's shifting goals of (anti-communist) security and economic development in Asia.

In her chapter, Jessica Tan situates writer-director Evan Yang's MP&GI films within the context of Shanghai's literary modernism of the 1930s, and explores, through the interconnected motifs of the automobile and the modern woman, the modern sensibilities of the films in the Cold War film culture of 1960s Hong Kong. Calvin Hui, using Wang Ping and Ge Xin's *Sentinels under the Neon Lights* (*Nihong dengxia de shaobing*, 1964) as a case study, examines how leisure and consumption, rather than being accepted as part of everyday life, were frequently repressed and displaced as mere symptoms of bourgeois capitalism in communist China. Hye Seung Chung utilizes recently declassified archival materials and makes a convincing case that film censorship in South Korea during the Cold War era, unlike what many people think, was not a mere tool for political repression but worked, in a less draconian way, to boost public morale by instilling a "cheerful" sensibility into

Korean films. Rini Bhattacharya Mehta's chapter concludes the second part by exploring the elusive connections between Indian cinema and the Cold War. The evolution of Indian cinema, according to Mehta, was shaped, to a large extent, by the Indian nation-state's simultaneous espousal of democracy and a regulated "quasi-socialist" economy, while a clear apportioning along the Cold War geopolitical divide marked the global reception of Indian films, with the state-subsidized art films gaining more access in the capitalist "First World" and the commercial Hindi films being more popular in the socialist "Second World" (as well as many developing nations in Asia and Africa).

The focus of the third part, *Struggle for Hearts and Minds*, touches on one of the central aspects in the cultural Cold War—that is, using cultural practices and products as a tool to propagate opposing ideological positions in order to win the allegiance and support of the public. For Michael G. Vann, the 1984 Indonesia film *Pengkhianatan G 30 S/PKI* was made to do just that, a tool used by the Suharto government to cultivate a collective anti-communist memory surrounding the historical events associated with the failed 1965 coup d'état. Poshek Fu considers in his chapter postwar Hong Kong Mandarin cinema and explores the "cinematic containment" strategies promoted by the U.S. and Nationalist Taiwan psychological war agents and the so-called "Free China" studios to draw audiences away from communist influence. Man-Fung Yip's chapter explores the complex reasons for the waning of Hong Kong leftist cinema in the late 1960s and 1970s. Going beyond mere political factors (i.e., the heightened political and ideological control that came in the wake of the Cultural Revolution in China), Yip takes a close look at the leftist studios' struggle to adjust to a Hong Kong society marked by accelerated processes of modernity and modernization and by major demographic changes. Finally, Hang Sang Kim considers the propaganda films made by the United States Information Service in South Korea during and after the Korean War, and examines the mechanisms and structures of the gaze through which South Korean audiences were positioned in the films.

Taken together, we hope, the chapters in this collection bring a broader, deeper, and more nuanced understanding of the complex responses of Asian cinemas to the Cold War conflict. In doing so, they attest to this collection's goal to further the ongoing effort to extend discussions of the Cold War to the cultural realm and, more specifically, to help contribute to a global history of the cinematic Cold War.

Note

1 *Journal of Cold War Studies*, associated with the Harvard Project on Cold War Studies (HPCWS), was established in 1999, followed a year later by *Cold War History*, based in the Cold War Studies Program at LSE IDEAS, the Centre for International Affairs, Strategy and Diplomacy at the London School of Economics and Political Science.

References

Ang, Cheng Guan. 2018. *Southeast Asia's Cold War: An Interpretive History.* Honolulu, Hawaii: University of Hawai'i Press.

Chen, Jian. 2001. *Mao's China and the Cold War.* Chapel Hill, N.C.: The University of North Carolina Press.

Chamberlin, Paul Thomas. 2018. *The Cold War's Killing Fields: Rethinking the Long Peace.* New York: Harper.

Cummings, Richard H. 2009. *Cold War Radio: The Dangerous History of American Broadcasting in Europe, 1950–1989.* Jefferson, N.C.: McFarland & Company.

Day, Tony, and Maya H. T. Liem, eds. 2010. *Cultures at War: The Cold War and Cultural Expression in Southeast Asia.* Ithaca, New York: Southeast Asia Program, Cornell University.

Doherty, Thomas. 2005. *Cold War, Cool Medium: Television, McCarthyism and American Culture.* New York: Columbia University Press.

Hee, Wai-Siam. 2020. *Remapping the Sinophone: The Cultural Production of Chinese-Language Cinema in Singapore and Malaya before and during the Cold War.* Hong Kong: Hong Kong University Press.

Hughes, Theodore. 2014. *Literature and Film in Cold War South Korea: Freedom's Frontier.* New York: Columbia University Press.

Klein, Christina. 2003. *Cold War Orientalism: Asia in the Middlebrow Imagination, 1945–1961.* Berkeley and Los Angeles, CA: The University of California Press.

Masuda, Hajimu. 2015. *Cold War Crucible: The Korean Conflict and the Postwar World.* Cambridge, Mass.: Harvard University Press.

Moine, Caroline. 2018. *Screened Encounters: The Leipzig Documentary Film Festival, 1955–1990.* New York and Oxford: Berghahn.

Reynolds, Jonathan T. 2014. *Sovereignty and Struggle: Africa and Africans in the Era of the Cold War, 1945–1994.* Oxford: Oxford University Press.

Saunders, Frances Stonor. 2000. *The Cultural Cold War: The CIA and the World of Arts and Letters.* New York and London: The New Press.

Shaw, Tony. 2006. *British Cinema and the Cold War.* London: I. B. Tauris.

Shaw, Tony, and Denise Youngblood. 2010. *Cinematic Cold War: The American and Soviet Struggle for Hearts and Minds.* Lawrence, Kans.: The University Press of Kansas.

Wong, Ain-ling, and Lee Pui-tak, eds. 2009. *Lengzhan yu xianggang dianying* (Cold War and Hong Kong Cinema). Hong Kong: Hong Kong Film Archive.

Part I

Transnational Connections

1 Art in Propaganda

The Poetics and Politics of Vietnamese Revolutionary Cinema

Man-Fung Yip

With few exceptions, Vietnamese revolutionary cinema has received virtually no attention in English-language scholarly literature. This dearth of interest is due in part to lack of access: with the exception of a few art-house hits by Tran Anh Hung or by overseas Vietnamese such as Tony Bui and Nguyễn Võ Nghiêm Minh, Vietnamese films, and those from the 1960s and 1970s in particular, have not been widely available outside of Vietnam and thus have been ignored by historians and film scholars alike.

But there are perhaps deeper reasons for the critical disregard for the films. For many people, Vietnamese revolutionary cinema, operating under the control of a socialist regime and identifying closely with its policies and ideologies, is mere propaganda not worthy of study. More broadly, there is also a lack of interest in Vietnam as a sovereign nation with its own history and cultural distinctiveness. For a long time, Vietnam had been taken simply as a mirror to the international threat of communism and/or American failure. It is true that in the United States, copious films have been made about the Vietnam War—or the American War rather, as the conflict is known in Vietnam—and much has been written and discussed about these films. Yet this seeming attention to the conflict has never been much about Vietnam or about the war per se. Instead, it is first and foremost about the United States, specifically its Cold War fantasy of American exceptionalism or, contrarily, its ideological crisis following a long and traumatic war experience. In this context, the "Vietnam" represented in the films, often reduced to a dense primitive jungle and to a set of stereotypical Vietnamese characters (vicious soldiers, beautiful prostitutes, hapless villagers, etc.), figures not as a subject but as an imagined construct that serves as a ploy for America's self-reflection. And with the apparent end of the Cold War and the fading away of the Vietnam conflict from the American and global consciousness, even this deceptive interest has started to disappear.

My goal in this essay is to provide a preliminary study of Vietnamese revolutionary cinema (with special emphasis on the period of the 1960s and 1970s) and to make a case for its historical and aesthetic significance. Such an endeavor is important for a number of reasons, not least to restore Vietnamese subjectivity by drawing attention to and exploring narratives and images that present Vietnamese people and life from a local perspective. Moreover, a better understanding of the revolutionary films of Vietnam, not just at a politico-ideological level but at the level of aesthetics, also helps bring a more nuanced view of socialist cinema beyond its alleged status as mere propaganda. Widespread as it is, the notion of propaganda as aesthetically banal and uninteresting seems to me fundamentally flawed. The binary opposition between propaganda and art is too facile and fails to recognize the creative energy that can be found in even some of the most ideologically invested films—including, as will be clear, Vietnam's revolutionary cinema, which developed novel techniques of communication and engagement as filmmakers drew on their national cultures as well as a host of different cinematic traditions (socialist realism, yes, but also the Soviet avant-garde cinema of the 1920s and the cinema of the Thaw, among others) and inventively deployed narratives, styles, and genres to assert their ideological positions.

Before developing the aforementioned and other points further, I would like to point out some caveats in this study. First, due to the issue of access mentioned earlier but also to lack of space in this essay, my discussion focuses only on fictional films and leaves aside documentaries, even though the latter had played a major role in Vietnamese cinema and were produced in much greater quantity than any other types of film (save for newsreels) throughout the 1960s and 1970s. Second, and more importantly, I am not a Vietnamese studies scholar, nor do I speak or read the Vietnamese language. This definitely puts some limits to this study. Still, in concentrating my discussion on issues of form and style and illuminating in the process the unique aesthetics of Vietnam's revolutionary cinema, I believe that I can contribute something to our knowledge and understanding of this long-neglected film tradition.

Vietnamese Cinema: A Brief Historical Review

Cinema was introduced to Vietnam at the turn of the twentieth century. Over the next few decades, film production and exhibition were almost exclusively under French control—by the colonial authorities who commissioned films to propagate images of the colony in France, instituted censorship law to impose restrictions on film content, and legislated controls that espoused protections for French film imports; and by French businessmen who owned most of the distribution companies and movie theaters in Vietnam (Wilson 2007). But despite this monopolization, the 1920s and 1930s did see a number of indigenous attempts to make films with Vietnamese actors/actresses and, with the advent of sound film, in Vietnamese. These films, however, were hampered by inadequate material and technical resources, and none of them was able to compete with the foreign imports from France, the United States, and Hong Kong, which dominated movie theaters (mostly in Saigon, Hanoi, and other urban areas) throughout the interwar years (Phạm 2001, 60–1).

Not surprisingly perhaps, little emphasis is placed on the colonial era in state-sanctioned narratives of Vietnamese film history. In official accounts, the first important films—that is, important to the development of a free revolutionary cinema in socialist Vietnam—are traced to the documentaries made by guerrilla filmmakers during the resistance war against the French from 1946 to 1954, including *The Battle of Moc Hoa* (*Trận Mộc Hóa*, 1948) and *The Battle of Dong* (*Khe Trận Đông Khê*, 1950). According to Thong Win (2017), these documentaries, shot in combat zones and shown in clandestine screenings across rural areas along the Mekong Delta, served as a way to mobilize support from disparate, and largely neglected, rural communities and bind them into a resistant political body under a new communist Vietnamese nationalism. Later on, as Việt Minh, the national independence coalition set up by the Indochinese Communist Party in 1941, consolidated power and began to anticipate victory in the anti-French struggle, the state monopolization of culture started to take shape. It can be observed, for instance, in the attempts to structure the artists and intellectuals into a more vertical, top-down arrangement through the development of professional creative organizations under a state umbrella. In the case of cinema, Hồ Chí Minh, then president of the Democratic Republic of Vietnam (DRV) or North Vietnam, signed decree 147/SL in 1953 to establish the State Enterprise of Cinematography and Photography, thereby marking the official nationalization of the Vietnamese film industry. Following this was the establishment of the Vietnam Cinema Department, placed under the Ministry of Culture, in 1956, while the Vietnam Cinema School was founded three years later in 1959 (Phạm 2001, 64–5).[1]

From the focus on newsreels and documentaries in the late 1940s and much of the 1950s, the DRV moved on to make its first fictional feature—Nguyễn Hồng Nghi and Phạm Hiếu Dân (Phạm Kỳ Nam)'s *Along the Same River* (*Chung một dòng sông*)—in 1959, followed by the same directors' *The Memento* (*Vật kỷ niệm*) in 1960 and Mai Lộc's *A-Phu Couple* (*Vợ chồng A Phủ*) in 1961. But with the country getting into another long and fierce military conflict (with the United States) while still recovering from the anti-French resistance war,[2] the conditions of filmmaking were extremely difficult at the time, and only a few feature films were able to be made each year. In fact, the newsreel and documentary format continued to form the bulk of film production in communist-controlled areas of Vietnam. According to one researcher, 463 newsreels and 307 documentaries were produced in the DRV between 1965 and 1973, compared to just 36 fictional films made in the same period (Nguyen 2014).

One major feature of Vietnamese revolutionary cinema in the 1960s and 1970s is its persistent focus on the subject of war, specifically the anti-French and anti-American resistance as well as the conditions of life in wartime in general. Given the country's constant military struggle for independence and later unification, this choice of emphasis is no surprise. Indeed, it is in the war film genre that we can find some of the most acclaimed Vietnamese movies of the period, from Nguyễn Văn Thông and Trần Vũ's *The Passerine Bird* (*Con chim vành khuyên*, 1962) and Phạm Kỳ Nam's *Mrs. Tu Hau* (*Chị Tư Hậu*, 1963) to Hải Ninh's *Little Girl of Hanoi* (*Em bé Hà Noi*, 1974). In addition to the war theme, another key area of attention pertained to the construction of a new society and the new woman/man under socialism. Examples in this category include Trần Vũ's *Floating Village* (*Làng nổi*, 1964), which extols a woman's efforts in bringing the peasants together to maintain the dike and protect the village from floods, and Nguyễn Đỗ Ngọc's *The Echo of the River* (*Dòng sông âm vang*, 1974), a film about the collective work involved in building a hydroelectric plant.

With the reunification of North and South Vietnam in 1975, Vietnamese cinema entered a new stage of development. For one thing, film production saw a dramatic increase, with the annual number of fictional features skyrocketing from three to five during wartime to an average of 15 to 20 in the late 1970s and early 1980s. War as a subject continued to inform numerous films, albeit often in new and different ways. A good case in point is Đặng Nhật Minh's *When the Tenth Month Comes* (*Bao giờ cho đến tháng Mười*, 1984): in telling the story of a widow who asks a teacher to write letters in her late soldier husband's name so that her frail father-in-law will find the strength to live, the film eschews the simplistic glorification of soldiers found in earlier films, offering instead a nuanced picture of the sufferings and losses of war while also affirming the resilience of the people. Other films looked into the new social reality of peacetime, such as the problems encountered by soldiers returning from war to civilian life (e.g., Trần Vũ's *The People We Met* [*Những người đã gặp*, 1979]) and the wounds incurred to families by years of war separation (e.g., Huy Thành's *Back to the Sand Village* [*Về nơi gió cát*, 1981] and *Far and Near* [*Xa và gần*, 1983]). The film industry was confronted with new challenges from the late 1980s onward, after it had shifted from a state subsidy system to a market-oriented one in keeping with the country's economic reform policy known as *đổt mọi*. The result was an influx of private capital into the film industry and an explosion in low-budget and often sloppily made commercial films (especially video films), although the relatively liberal climate also facilitated works—by Đặng Nhật Minh, Lưu Trọng Ninh, and Lê Hoàng, among others—with innovative content and daring viewpoints (Phạm 2001, 76–80; Ngo 1998, 93–6). Entering into the twenty-first century, as Vietnam further opened up and became economically more buoyant, the trend toward privatization and commercialization intensified while attempts were also made to modernize the outdated filming equipment and poorly equipped film theaters. International cooperation has also been on the rise. Despite its many problems, then, Vietnamese cinema has been growing over the last decade or so, albeit in a markedly different direction from its revolutionary past.

Between Propaganda and Art

As can be seen from above, Vietnamese revolutionary cinema was born and developed in an era when the country was continually at war fighting for liberation, independence, and national unification. It was also an exclusively state-run enterprise, constituting part of a national cultural front that advocated the mobilization of all art forms in the service of the revolution and the socialist state. Such a politicized conception of the arts was spelled out clearly in two important documents—"Theses on Culture" from 1943 and the more substantial "Marxism and Vietnamese Culture" from 1948—written by Trường Chinh, the chief theoretician among the communist leaders in Vietnam. For Trường Chinh, artistic and cultural work in a free socialist Vietnam was to be based on three guiding principles: nationalization, popularization, and scientific orientation. The first principle, nationalization, entailed the search for a new Vietnamese identity, one that eschewed not only centuries of Sinicized classical culture privileging a literati elite, but also a modern Vietnamese culture tainted by French and Chinese influences. Going beyond this nationalist focus, popularization, the second principle, embraced a class standpoint in its emphasis on the people, insisting that artists must create for and serve the interests of the masses, that is, workers, peasants, and soldiers. Lastly, scientific orientation was marked by a rejection of traditional practices and stressed a sense of progress through rational thought and discussion (Ninh 2002, 28–34; 39–45). What we see in Trường Chinh's recommendations for a cultural front, then, is a prescriptive account of a new Vietnamese culture defined in the context of a mass-based, rational, and progressive national identity, which could only be achieved after a victorious national liberation. And this liberation, in turn, would only be possible under the guidance of the political party with the strongest organizational capacity and the most scientific vision about the direction of the country's future—that is, the Vietnamese Communist Party.

According to this framework proposed by Trường Chinh, a revolutionary cinema in socialist Vietnam was to be a "mass cinema" that would not only appeal to the people and reflect their daily lives, but also gain and galvanize their support for the state's social, political, and economic objectives (e.g., the anti-colonial/anti-imperialist struggle against France and the United States; the building of a new socialist society). This was precisely the direction in which the emergent revolutionary cinema of Vietnam would be heading; when the State Enterprise of

Cinematography and Photography was founded in 1953, for example, it was tasked with four major goals:

> 1 Propagating the policies and guide-lines of the Government;
> 2 Highlighting the feats of arms of the Vietnamese army and people in their heroic struggle;
> 3 Acquainting our people with the life and successes in struggle and construction of the peoples of fraternal countries; and
> 4 Instilling cultural knowledge and political consciousness into our population
>
> (Trinh 1983, 4).

With the onset of military conflict with the United States, these initial aims were revised to give primacy to the "education of opposition to the American invaders and their servants, in the promotion of patriotism and in the teaching of revolutionary heroism" (Tran 1990, 202). But for all the shifts in emphasis, what remained unchanged was the political utility of cinema: the conception of cinema as a fighting front, a weapon that was driven by the revolutionary goals set forth by the communist leadership, acting in the interests of the people.

Indeed, given a largely illiterate peasant population (the peasants made up about 90% of Vietnam's population at the time), the importance of cinema (and other forms of visual and audio media) in supporting the revolutionary causes of the state was clear and hardly escaped the communist leaders. For example, long-time Prime Minister Phạm Văn Đồng once quoted Lenin in saying that "Film is an artistic genre of great significance and impact as it penetrates the masses directly and at their most sensitive point" (as quoted in Tran 1990, 202). But it was not just the audiovisual nature of cinema that rendered it such a promising agitprop and educational tool. The fact that cinema was a young and emerging art form (especially true in Vietnam), whose aesthetic and social properties had not yet been fully formed and were thus open to maneuvering, can also be said to enhance the medium's political efficacy. As Thong Win (2017) rightly points out, "If Vietnamese intellectuals were in the process of defining a modern Vietnamese character both politically and within the arts, the emergence of a new popular art form as separate from centuries of traditionalism was undoubtedly appealing, since the production and reception of film could be tailored to meet Party demands during wartime. As an art form whose formal and aesthetic qualities were still being negotiated, cinema was granted a privileged position within the Party in a cultural struggle against colonial and imperial forces" (177).

While Thong Win's focus is on the underground documentary film practices (especially the clandestine screenings in the rural areas along the Mekong Delta) in the early years of Vietnamese revolutionary cinema, his point about negotiating and developing a new aesthetic commensurate with the state's political and ideological goals applies to later Vietnamese films as well. A crucial idea to consider in this connection is socialist realism. First institutionalized in the First Soviet Writers' Congress in 1934, socialist realism was the official cultural ideology and aesthetic paradigm of Stalinism. Central to this doctrine was a condemnation of formalism and modernism and their attendant philosophy of individualism: artists were expected to relinquish their individualistic selves so as to entirely devote themselves to fulfilling the ultimate end of history, that is, socialism (Robin 1992, 25–31). Anticipating in many ways Trường Chinh's proposed framework of artistic and cultural production in socialist Vietnam noted earlier, the three basic properties of socialist realism as formulated by the Soviets included "people-ness" (the relationship between art and the popular, defined simultaneously in relation to the masses and to the nation—the spirit of the people—as a whole), "class-ness" (the class characteristics of art), and "party-ness" (the identification of the artist with the Communist Party) (James 1973, 1–14). In a way that reflected the polarizations in the Cold War era, socialist realism had little impact in the capitalist world, where it was widely condemned as a totalitarian means of imposing state control over individual artists, but exerted a major influence in the Soviet Union and was widely adopted across socialist countries, including the DRV.[3]

Like its counterparts in other socialist countries, then, socialist realism provided a set of guidelines shaping Vietnamese revolutionary cinema (Nguyễn 2007). Specifically, as a method of practical filmmaking (rather than general aesthetic principles), the doctrine manifested itself in a number of interconnected features. First among them was simplicity of form and content—a clear-cut, unambiguous narrative with strong ideological closure, conveying easily accessible messages that conformed to the goals of the state. While this generally meant emphasizing what has been accomplished or won (such as a triumphant battle or successful efforts in building socialism), it did not preclude the depiction of events less immediately positive or promising. What was important were not the events per se, but the representation of reality in its inexorable evolution toward a better (socialist) future. As Trường Chinh ([1948] 2012) pointed out:

> We can, of course, describe a lost battle, but in doing so, we must see to it that people realize how heroically our combatants accepted sacrifices, why the battle was lost, what our gains were, and, notwithstanding the defeat, that our combatants never felt demoralized because all were eager to learn and draw the appropriate lessons in order to secure victories in future battles. We can describe a local defeat while showing that the war is going our way.
>
> (526)

It is from this perspective that we can understand films such as Nông Ích Đạt's *Kim Đồng* (1964) and Bùi Đình Hạc and Lý Thái Bảo's *Nguyễn Văn Trỗi* (1967), where the historically based protagonists lose their lives fighting for the revolutionary cause. Despite—or rather because of—their sacrifices, the tone of the endings of the films is one of affirmation rather than defeat; what is expressed is an orientation, a goal, an objective; a clear and unmistakable sense of the direction in which the future is headed.

Also indispensable in the method of socialist realism are the conventions of the positive hero or heroine, a figure of the masses who, with a high degree of revolutionary fervor and passion, exemplifies the new man or woman in a socialist society. In Vietnamese revolutionary cinema, such an ideal figure can be observed in many war films where the protagonists are imbued with the spirit of heroic patriotism: a soldier during the anti-French resistance war who, despite being assigned the job of cook at the beginning, teaches himself to read and write as well as to use a gun, and in the end manages to destroy an enemy's tank (Hải Ninh and Nguyễn Đức Hinh's *The Young Soldier* [*Người chiến sĩ trẻ*, 1965]); a young woman who, along with her father, guards a supply trail for the Vietnamese People's Army (VPA) and organizes the building of a makeshift but workable bridge in short order after a bomb crater and an unexploded bomb block the trail (Hải Ninh's *Miss Tham's Forest* [*Rừng O Thắm*, 1967]). On the other hand, there were also films about men and women devoting themselves to the building of a new society in socialist Vietnam. In stressing the valiant efforts of individuals to sacrifice one's self-interest for the collective good (Trần Vũ's *The Story of the Luc Couple* [*Truyện vợ chồng Anh Lực*, 1971]) or to fight against poverty and backwardness in the country's mountain areas inhabited by ethnic minorities (Nông Ích Đạt's *Teacher of the Highlands* [*Cô giáo vùng cao*, 1969]), such films served to energize the population to participate in the intense efforts of economic and social transformation in Vietnam's march toward socialism.

A variation of this positive hero or heroine convention pertains to protagonists who, impulsive and politically immature in the beginning, undergo a transformation, often through the guidance of an experienced party cadre, in the course of the film. The eponymous character in the Vasilyev brothers' *Chapaev* (1934), a quintessential socialist realist film from the Soviet Union (and a favorite of Josef Stalin), is a prototypical example of this type of "flawed" hero. In Vietnamese revolutionary cinema, a similar character can be found in Phạm Văn Khoa's *Fire on the Middle Line* (*Lửa trung tuyến*, 1961): Dũng, platoon leader of an artillery section, is disappointed and becomes hot-tempered after he is ordered to withdraw from the frontline and to be in charge of an ammunition store. It is only later that he comes to realize, through the heroic actions of the people when the ammunition store is hit by enemy's fire, that the frontline is everywhere, and that every mission is important to the final victory. In depicting this change in attitude, the film presents the protagonist as a model of the "spontaneity" of the individual that needs to be enlightened by the "consciousness" of the masses.

There is no question that the adherence of Vietnamese revolutionary films to socialist realism made them a propaganda tool to spread the state's revolutionary message to the public. A more contentious issue resides in the commonly held assumption that these films, precisely due to their status as state propaganda, are formulaic and simplistic and thus not worthy of serious study. Yet it is a mistake to write these films off out of hand; for one thing, such a dismissive stance overlooks the fact that the films, despite their ideological purpose and content, offer a glimpse of Vietnamese life and people through local lenses and render perceptible many aspects that are systematically excluded in Western (and especially American) images of the country. In *Little Girl of Hanoi*, set (and partially shot) in the United States' fierce bombings of Hanoi in December 1972, a little girl is seen wandering through the rubble of the city, looking for her father. In many ways, the film may be taken as just another propaganda effort (even though the focus here is not so much on demonizing Americans as on emphasizing the resilience and solidarity of the Vietnamese people), but the bombings, and the piles of debris and ruined buildings, were real and extracted from reality, giving a palpable sense of civilian sufferings and losses. On the other hand, in Hồng Sến's *The Wild Field* (*Cánh Đồng Hoang*, 1979), we see a couple's mundane family life—fishing, gathering wood, repairing the house, cooking, eating, taking care of the baby son, relaxing, sleeping—interspersed with war activities (such as serving as a contact for the liberation forces in South Vietnam and protecting themselves from American helicopter gunfire). For a people who had been at war for decades, they had come to learn to live a normal life in the midst of war, and this is precisely what was captured so poignantly in the film.

No less importantly, the propagandistic nature of Vietnamese revolutionary cinema does not mean that it was entirely bound by political and ideological shackles and had no artistic value. On the contrary, compared to their Soviet and Chinese counterparts, Vietnamese films of the 1960s and 1970s are, in many cases, aesthetically more interesting. John Charlot (1991), for instance, speaks of the "handsome black-and-white camera work" in both documentaries and fictional films, and compares the chiaroscuro effects in nighttime sequences to traditional Vietnamese lacquer art. The sinuous lines and atmospheric effects of many outdoor scenes are also said to evoke ink paintings on silk (48). While I am not completely convinced of this kind of culturalist reading, the larger point of Charlot's argument—that is, the relatively high aesthetic quality of Vietnamese revolutionary films—is not to be disputed. Indeed, considering the limited resources (lack of funding, equipment, trained personnel, etc.) and exceptionally challenging working conditions (a poor country constantly in the midst of wars), the artistic excellence of the films is nothing short of amazing.

What makes Vietnamese revolutionary cinema so fascinating from an aesthetic point of view is in part its highly expressive use of film techniques, especially those—composition, staging, lighting, cinematography—that pertain to the visual construction of the shot. Here, the Vietnamese films show an obvious affinity to Soviet avant-garde cinema of the 1920s, which, as noted by Philip Cavendish (2013), has "a strong commitment to maximize the expressive potential of filmic images through recourse to innovative compositional mechanisms" in order to convey the extremes of revolutionary experience (7).[4] Much the same may be said of the Vietnamese films of the 1960s and 1970s (and beyond); in them, one sees a strong propensity for striking and expressive images, which manifest themselves in a number of different forms and serve a number of different purposes. In some cases, highly stylized images are utilized as a means for character delineation: close-up shots of the protagonist's radiant face angled up toward the sky, for instance, emphasize the vision and determination of a revolutionary heroine or hero (Figure 1.1), whereas the use of cast shadows and a perspective-distorting high-angle shot makes the oppressors look sly and devious (Figure 1.2).

In other instances, the goal is to amplify the dramatic tension of a scene. In Vũ Sơn's *Two Soldiers* (*Hai người lính*, 1962), the clash between a Việt Minh soldier and a local villager over the fate of a French prisoner of war is vividly captured by a bold composition that pits the close-up faces of the Vietnamese characters against one another in the foreground, with the French captive anxiously watching

Figure 1.1 A proud, confident revolutionary heroine in *Miss Tham's Forest* (1967).

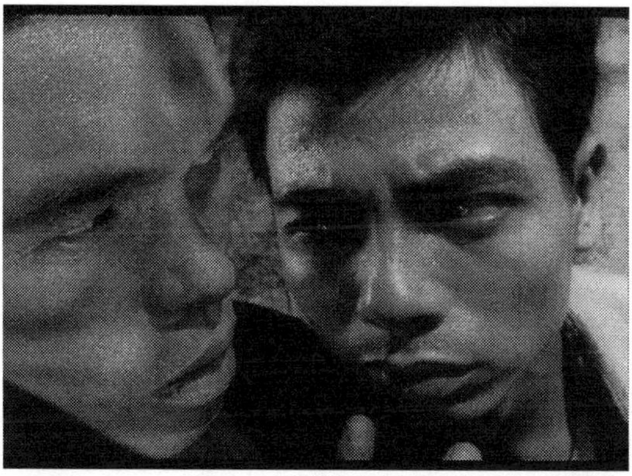

Figure 1.2 Sly and devious oppressors in *The Passerine Bird* (1962).

Figure 1.3 *Two Soldiers* (1962).

the confrontation from behind (Figure 1.3). Tension can be heightened in other ways as well: in an early scene from *Mrs. Tu Hau* where the female protagonist is assaulted by a Vietnamese collaborator and ultimately raped by a French soldier, the director makes use of set design (a small hut crammed with dried fish hung from the ceiling) and atmospheric, almost expressionistic lighting effects (casting light through the bamboo wattle) to create an oppressive ambiance and sharpen the tense situation (Figure 1.4). On the other hand, the last image of *The Wild Field*—a wide shot of a woman, with a baby in the arms and a rifle on the shoulder, walking off slowly after shooting the American helicopter gunner who has killed her husband—achieves its stunning effect by juxtaposing two markedly contrasting elements through the principle of internal montage (Figure 1.5).

Figure 1.4 *Mrs. Tu Hau* (1963).

Figure 1.5 *The Wild Field* (1979).

In addition to manipulating the content within the shot, Vietnamese filmmakers also paid much attention to the relationship between shots—in other words, editing—in their attempts to heighten the expressivity of their works. This can be especially seen in battle scenes—a staple in war films—where fast cutting, often coordinated with sharp alternations in camera angle, generates an impression of agitation, urgency, and kinetic energy. (The inclusion of actual battle footage further augments the experiential veracity of the scenes.) But like Sergei Eisenstein and other Soviet pioneers in the 1920s, who are usually associated with a "montage" approach to filmmaking, Vietnamese revolutionary films also resort to more abrupt, disjunctive forms of editing. At the end of the first part of Bạch Diệp's *The Holy Day* (*Ngày lễ thánh*, 1976), the wedding of Ái, a Catholic sister who breaks with the moral code of the Church in remarrying, is disrupted by her disloyal (ex-)husband and her devoutly religious sister. Tension mounts as Ái's sister is confronted by the village cooperative chairman (in a composition very much similar to the example from *Two Soldiers* discussed earlier). Then the film abruptly cuts to a close-up of an oil lamp, whose glass ruptures suddenly. And we see, in the next shot, the cooperative chairman suffer a serious wound in his head (Figure 1.6). In presenting the attack in such a terse and elliptical

Figure 1.6 The Holy Day (1976).

manner, the film not only accentuates its impact by making it appear so unexpected and quick, but also adds a sense of mystery by not revealing who the culprit is for the attack. Only later, after we see someone squeezing a rock into the hand of Ái's sister in the ensuing chaos, do we know that she is *not* to blame.

Another, and even more remarkable, example can be found in a combat scene near the end of Trần Vũ and Nguyễn Thụ's *Smoke* (*Khói*, 1967). The scene opens with a medium shot of a bugle-playing soldier, followed by a series of extremely brief and highly fragmented shots of Vietnamese fighters getting out of the dugouts and charging forward. These shots may seem confusing because the way in which they are edited is not totally bound by plot requirements, but rather serves to create a perceptual and affective impact that highlights the importance of the moment (i.e., the onset of the Vietnamese counterattack). As the bugle song gives way to rousing orchestral music, the scene's focus shifts to the charging soldiers in open field, and here the editing dynamizes the action by making the vectors of the soldiers' movement "clash" between shots. The scene escalates to a new pitch of intensity during the actual combat; the film's protagonist, an intelligence officer of the VPA, is shown lurching forward toward the camera, and the next shot shows an American soldier falling on his back, away from it. Then comes a rapid succession of shots, filmed almost exclusively with a handheld camera and in close-up, that underscore the utter chaos of the fighting. In all of this, the scene evinces a style of editing that builds up a dramatic action out of many short and fragmented pieces. In fact, the average shot length of the scene is an astounding 1.3 seconds, and this exceptionally fast cutting rate, together with the often disjunctive ways in which the shots are put together, establishes a nervous, vibrating rhythm and intensifies the sequence's force of impact.

So far we have looked at how the revolutionary cinema of Vietnam, influenced to a large extent by the tension-based montage aesthetic of 1920s Soviet avant-garde films, developed a dynamic expressive style that utilized various resources of the cinematic medium to accentuate the perceptual and emotional impact of the viewing experience. Yet there existed a different form of expressivity in the Vietnamese films—not as dramatic or intense and more inclined toward the lyrical and the poetic, with strong emphasis on nature, on pastoral beauty and peasant traditions, as well as on the simple but charming details of daily life. Indeed, this poetic and lyrical dimension is, more than anything else, what distinguishes Vietnamese revolutionary films from their socialist counterparts. It is to this very aspect, particularly as it pertains to the use of landscape, that I will turn my attention to in the next section.

The Landscape in War

To speak of a poetic sensibility in Vietnamese cinema is not something new. "Poetry," as Charlot (1991) contends, "is at the center of

Vietnamese culture and sensibilities, and cinema cannot be divorced from it. This poetic sense separates their creations clearly from conventional socialist realism" (46). Similarly, Irina Miakova (2007) argues that the passion for poetry goes deep into the minds of the Vietnamese people at all levels of society, from political leaders (it is well known that many Vietnamese leaders, including Hồ Chí Minh, wrote poems themselves), soldiers, to even those who are illiterate and cannot read or write (as attested to by the folk poetry known as *ca dao*). From this, she concludes that "The popularity, long development, and broad functions of poetry in Vietnamese society have greatly influenced the Vietnamese people's perceptions and personalities as well as other forms of art, including the cinema" (478). In fact, paradoxical as it may sound, this "poetic touch in the national character," as a critic puts it, is such a deep and enduring feature that it can be observed in every Vietnamese film even during wartime, in the midst of all the fighting ("Images of the Land," 15).

Most critics thus take the long and rich poetic tradition of Vietnam as the root for the expressive poeticism in Vietnamese cinema. While this is certainly true, it is possible to identify other sources of influence. The films of Alexander Dovzhenko are a case in point. Considered to be part of the revolutionary cinema of the Soviet Union, Dovzhenko's films, according to Vance Kepley Jr. (1986), are some of the most lyrical works of Soviet cinema, deriving "much of their beauty from a Ukrainian pastoral tradition and from an abiding faith in peasant custom" (3). In his films, particularly his acclaimed masterpiece *Earth* (*Zemlya*, 1930), one can find an abundance of images of nature and rural landscape—cloudy skies and misty rivers, wind blowing across immense wheat fields, a solitary tree against a large expanse of sky, rain-drenched apples hanging from the trees and lying on the ground—that manifest a strong lyrical impulse. The Vietnamese revolutionary films, too, are rife with similar natural and pastoral imagery: a clouded sky broken by sun rays (Hoàng Thái's *Stories of my Homeland* [*Câu chuyện quê hương*, 1963]; *Smoke*), solar glare through the tree foliage (*The Passerine Bird*; *Stories of My Homeland*), peasants laboring in a wind-blown rice field (*The Memento*), images of the forest (*Miss Tham's Forest*) and the ocean (Nguyễn Tiến Lợi and Nguyễn Ngọc Trung's *Call of the Sea* [*Biển gọi*, 1967]), a tree-lined river flowing idyllically (*Stories of my Homeland*), a small boat gliding across a marsh full of lotuses/water lilies (Nguyễn Thụ's *Portrait Left Behind* [*Bức tranh để lại*, 1970]; *The Wild Field*), and so on. As in the films of Dovzhenko, the concerted efforts to capture the beauty and wonder of pastoral nature impart to the Vietnamese films an intense lyricism and poetic expressivity.

However, for a predominantly agricultural country such as Vietnam in the 1960s and 1970s, trees, rivers, marshes, rice fields, and so forth were among the most typical forms of landscape. It is thus no surprise that they would frequently appear, and become the major poetic elements, in the country's cinema and culture. So as far as Dovzhenko's influence is concerned, the choice of subject matter—that is, the emphasis given to the rural natural world—is less important than the poetic manner in which this world is rendered into the visual construction of the films. Both Dovzhenko's works and the revolutionary films of Vietnam display a high level of compositional originality. Indeed, they share some strikingly similar strategies of framing and shot design: for example, radically decentered compositions in *The Passerine Bird* and Mai Lộc and Trần Vũ's *Remarriage* (*Đi bước nữa*, 1963), placing the human/animal figures along the lower edge of the frame and reducing them to tiny silhouettes against the immense billowing cloudy sky, bear a strong resemblance to some of the shots in *Earth* (Figures 1.7–1.9). Similarly, the image of a lone tree against the sky in Huy Vân and Hải Ninh's *A Day in Early Autumn* (*Một ngày đầu thu*, 1962) (Figure 1.10) evokes a similar shot in Dovzhenko's *Zvenigora* (1928) (Figure 1.11), while both Dovzhenko and Vietnamese filmmakers like to resort to reflections (of trees, human figures, etc.) in the waters of a stream or river (Figures 1.12 and 1.13). These similarities suggest a different aspect of Soviet influence on the Vietnamese revolutionary films beyond the montage aesthetic. Embracing the painterly and the poetical, this alternative style imbues the images with such richness and suggestiveness that they achieve the emotional depth and complexity of lyric poetry.

Another point of reference is the so-called "thaw" films that first emerged and came into prominence during the liberalization in Soviet politics and, by extension, artistic productions following Josef Stalin's death in 1953. During the "thaw" period, as Josephine Woll (2000) points out, Soviet cinema revived from the stultifying political shackles in the previous decades and exploited the growing opportunities available in the new milieu. Film production increased markedly, and

Figure 1.7 The Passerine Bird (1962).

Figure 1.8 Remarriage (1963).

Figure 1.9 Earth (1930).

Figure 1.10 A Day in Early Autumn (1962).

Figure 1.11 Zvenigora (1928).

Figure 1.12 Reflections on a river in *Remarriage* (1963).

Figure 1.13 Reflections on a river in *Zvenigora* (1928).

a new generation of filmmakers—Grigorii Chukhrai, Marlen Khutsiev, and others—emerged and were responsible for making *Spring on Zarechnaia Street* (Khutsiev 1956), *Ballad of a Soldier* (Chukhrai 1959), and other landmark films of the 1950s. These films—and the new efforts made by veteran directors, such as Mikhail Kalatozov's *The Cranes Are Flying* (1957) and *Letter Never Sent* (1959)—broke with the norms of socialist realism and reclaimed some of Soviet cinema's earlier avant-garde tradition. While not usually associated with the rubric of poetic cinema, some of these "thaw" films are nonetheless notable for their poetic touch and sensibility. *Ballad of a Soldier*, for instance, is called a "lyrical tale, a poem in black-and-white" (Youngblood 2007, 123), and Neia Zorkaia, the doyenne of Soviet film historians, raves about *The Cranes Are Flying* as a film marked by "the entire wealth of the metaphor, composition, and rhythms of cinematic poetry" (as quoted in Woll 2000, 212). There is no doubt that Vietnamese filmmakers were aware of, and had high regard for, these "thaw" films. *The Cranes Are Flying*, for instance, was as much appreciated as the works of Eisenstein (Charlot 1991, 41), while Đặng Nhật Minh (2017) talks about the ways in which the "thaw" films were like "a new wind that brought a vital breath to the old Soviet cinema" and left a "deep imprint" in his mind (29). One can point to more specific connections as well: the rape scene in *The Cranes Are Flying*, with its expressionistic close-ups, skewed camera angles, and dynamic lighting, had likely exerted an influence on a parallel sequence in *Mrs. Tu Hau* discussed earlier. And it is not unreasonable to think that the stylistic boldness of the "thaw" films, especially as it pertains to the poeticized treatment of natural/rural landscape (Figures 1.14 and 1.15), would be drawn upon by the Vietnamese filmmakers.

Figure 1.14 Ballade of a Soldier (1959).

Figure 1.15 Letter Never Sent (1959).

It is clear from the above discussion that the poetic propensity of Vietnam's revolutionary cinema, derived from the country's venerable tradition of poetry and mediated through the works of Dovzhenko and Soviet "thaw" films of the 1950s, is centrally grounded in the depiction of natural landscape. Yet it is important to point out that such landscape representations not only serve a poetic or aesthetic purpose but also have an essential ideological function. This latter point has been noted by Lan Duong (2014), who argues that landscape in Vietnamese films "serves as an affective site for a gendered construction of nationalism within key moments in Vietnamese history" (258). This tendency, she goes on to say, was particularly evident during the era of revolutionary filmmaking.

In what follows, I will take a deeper look at the use of landscape as an ideological tool in Vietnamese revolutionary films of the 1960s and 1970s. To begin with, let me call attention to a recurrent feature in the Vietnamese films (especially war films)—that is, the ways in which they use landscape shots or scenes to establish a lyrically poetic tone and to conjure up a sense of tranquility, harmony, and wholeness, and put them in juxtaposition with the more dramatic sequences such as the combats, which are characterized by an impression of turmoil and violence. Consider, for instance, *The Wild Field*; as a war movie, the film has its moments of exciting action (a particularly memorable scene depicts an attack by American helicopters, whose broad undersections are seen as menacingly lowering down on their targets, thanks to the use of an extremely low-angle shot), but it also spends a good amount of time focusing on the natural terrain and the ordinary everyday life of the protagonists in it. These lyrical interludes, however, are not meant to simply poeticize the film, create a sense of rhythm, or even add realism to the representation of wartime life. All this is true, but what need emphasizing here are the larger symbolic meanings at stake: in stressing the proximity and connectedness of the Vietnamese characters—or, more generally, Vietnamese people—to the natural world, the scenes make clear the profound unity and identification between the two. In this sense, the violence of the combat sequences is manifested not so much in the number of casualties—of which there are not many—but in the wide destruction caused to the space of nature and, by extension, to the spirit and identity of the Vietnamese people intrinsic to it.

This idea of nature as an allegorical site for articulating an authentic Vietnamese identity can be further explored by taking a deeper look at some of the more specific ways in which the identification between space (landscape) and identity (Vietnameseness) is established in the revolutionary films of Vietnam. In *Remarriage*, a film about a peasant woman's struggle to defy traditional feudal thinking and get remarried, this identification is brought about through a process of focalization: early in the film, we see the heroine walking back home from work. She stops and looks back, and the next shot shows what she sees: an idyllic image of a tree-lined river with a small boat in the background. The film then returns to the heroine, who smiles, turns around, and walks away. Another cut takes the viewer back to the river, now in much closer range, and the boat can be seen gliding through the water along the upper part of the frame. The camera pans with the boat for a while, then stops, and the boat eventually goes out of frame. Lasting less than two minutes and seemingly unrelated to the rest of the film, this sequence is nonetheless important in forging a link between the lyrical landscape and the heroine. To be specific, the link is first established (in the first shot of the river) by the latter's optical point of view. The connection, however, is not simply visual; the ensuing half-smile of the heroine, and her apparent sense of peace and calm, indicate a deep emotional identification and projection. And once this emotional or affective relationship is formed, the point-of-view structure can become more flexible. The second (and more extended) shot of the river, for instance, is not from the heroine's optical perspective, but it is still imbued with her subjectivity—the subjectivity of a new socialist woman, of a new socialist Vietnamese nation indeed, in total harmony with the serene and wholesome natural world.

The Passerine Bird, on the other hand, uses a different technique to get the point across. At the end of the film, Nga, a little girl who lives with her father and helps him with boating Việt Minh revolutionaries across the river, is shot by French soldiers as she tries to warn a group of revolutionaries of a planned ambush. As she dies, she releases her pet bird to the sky. The film then cuts to a shot of Nga's head floating on the river's rippling waters. The image gradually brightens, effecting in the process a certain "merging" of Nga and the river (Figure 1.16), before it finally dissolves into a bright open sky where a bird—ostensibly the one set free by Nga—is seen flying in the distance. All this time, we hear not only a stirring song intoned by a women's chorus but also the

Figure 1.16 The Passerine Bird (1962).

sound of a chirping bird. With this ending, *The Passerine Bird* succeeds in reinforcing a central ideological point that it has set out to make from the beginning; like *The Wild Field*, the film puts a lot of emphasis on creating a poetic space that takes its source in nature and has a harmonious relationship with the (Vietnamese) characters, but it is not until the last images discussed earlier, with the gradual merging of Nga's face with the waters of the river and then both dissolving into the open sky, that the fusion between Nga and landscape (nature) is completed. Nga may have sacrificed her life, but the image of the open sky with a free flying bird conjures up freedom and hope—a symbol of rebirth not only for Nga but for the entire nation she epitomizes.

Other examples can be enumerated. In the case of *Miss Tham's Forest*, even the title suggests a connectedness between character (Thắm) and landscape (forest). And harking back to the ending of *The Passerine Bird*, a dissolve leading up to the film's final sequence, after the successful effort to reopen a supply trail to Vietnamese soldiers thanks to Thắm's determination and bravery, superimposes the heroine's face and the trees of the forest together in an iconic shot, thus further underscoring their profound unity. Also important is the fact that the film both opens and closes with a tracking shot through the trees of the forest, which gives rise to the perception of a symbolic circularity: in spite of the American bombings and other adversities, the idyllic natural world, which serves as a metonymic symbol of the heroine and the Vietnamese people at large, will persist and triumph in the end. A similar cyclical structure can also be found in *Portrait Left Behind*, which tells the story of a painter who, at the risk of his life, paints portraits of Hồ Chí Minh in U.S.-controlled South Vietnam. In this instance, it is two wide tracking shots of a river covered with lotus flowers and leaves that serve as bookends to the film. Again, a powerful sense of continuity, both visual (the blissful landscape) and allegorical (the revolutionary spirit of Vietnam), is invoked. Also worth mentioning is the gender dimension of the landscape: in contrast to the examples discussed earlier (and in Lan Duong's essay [2014]), the landscape in the film is gendered male instead of female. It is linked not just to the (male) painter protagonist but to Hồ Chí Minh himself: at a key moment in the film, ethereal shots of lotus flowers and their reflections on the river are juxtaposed with the flashback of an old man about his—and other villagers'—epiphanic experience of seeing a huge portrait of Hồ painted by the protagonist. Not coincidentally, the film was made to commemorate the 80th anniversary of Hồ Chí Minh's birth.

The ideological function of landscape in Vietnamese revolutionary films is significant in the larger sociopolitical context of Vietnam where the peasants were often granted a special status. For one thing, the fact that the success of the Việt Minh and the continuing American War depended to a large extent on the contributions of peasants led to the idea of the latter as the lifeblood of the revolution. But the appeal of the peasants went beyond that; in many ways, they constituted the central term linking nationalization and popularization, the two basic principles in Trường Chinh's framework of artistic and cultural work in socialist Vietnam. In other words, the peasants were seen—by party leaders, intellectuals, cultural workers—as the epitome of the nation and the people: on the one hand, Vietnam in the 1950s and 1960s, despite some degree of urbanization, was still primarily an agricultural society. The majority of the Vietnamese (i.e., the masses) were villagers who spent much of their lives working in the fields. On the other hand, in contrast to the "high" cultural traditions, the folk culture of peasants was relatively free from Chinese and French influences and thus more unequivocally "Vietnamese." As Patricia M. Pelley (2002) argues:

> In a schematization that contrasted the purity of rural traditions with the hybridity of urban ones, the village—not any village in particular but "the village" as a composite, ideal type—appeared as the hearth of authentic Vietnamese tradition. Villagers, far removed from the effects of Chinese occupation and uncorrupted by a century of French colonial rule, figured as the custodians of authentic culture.
>
> (132)

This is arguably a major reason why Vietnamese filmmakers, in an attempt to develop a tradition of authentic Vietnamese films that spoke and appealed to the people, placed peasants and the rural traditions at the center of many of their films. This meant a heightened emphasis on the daily lives of peasants (tilling the soil; planting, transplanting, and harvesting rice; repairing dikes) as well as on their intimate relationship with the land (or nature in general)—hence the importance given to rural natural landscape. But ironically, the foregrounding of peasants did not entail that they, as a group, became an autonomous subject. This becomes evident from the fact that an issue of great importance to them—the bungling and chaos that characterized the land reform (1953–56)—was completely ignored in Vietnamese films of the revolutionary period, even though a formal critique on the government's mishandling of the matter was officially launched in September 1956. The behavior and subjectivity of peasants depicted in Vietnam's revolutionary films reflected not so much on the peasants themselves but on the state; what the films sought to show is the peasants' heightened sense of commitment to the revolution and their affection for the Communist Party leadership.

Conclusion

Vietnamese revolutionary films, like their socialist counterparts from around the world, are didactic works. Yet creating propaganda is not necessarily incompatible with achieving powerful aesthetic effects. As I have tried to argue in this essay, many Vietnamese films of the 1960s and 1970s are aesthetically complex and engaging; working within the broad framework of socialist realism, Vietnamese filmmakers drew upon various currents in Soviet cinema as well as the venerated poetic tradition of their own country, and developed a richly expressive style marked not only by moments of high tension and dynamism but also by a strong poetic vein of lyricism. Since the reunification of the country in 1975, Vietnamese films have become less overtly propagandistic and more open to depicting issues that cropped up in the new social reality. And the turn to a market system from the late 1980s onward has created many challenges for the hitherto state-sponsored film industry. But despite all the changes, the expressive power of Vietnamese cinema, especially its rich and evocative poeticism, has persisted in some of its best recent films, such as *When the Tenth Month Comes*, Việt Linh's *Travelling Circus* (*Gánh xiếc rong*, 1988), and Nguyễn Thanh Vân's *Sandy Lives* (*Doi cát*, 1999), all of which are powerfully haunting and represent valuable contributions to world cinema. The expressive and poetic tradition of Vietnamese cinema deserves more exposure and attention; I would be pleased if this chapter helped contribute to this end.

Notes

1 After the French were defeated at Điện Biên Phủ, a peace agreement negotiated at the Geneva Conference in 1954 resulted in the (supposedly temporary) division of Vietnam into two nations: the Democratic Republic of

Vietnam (DRV), a socialist state established in the North, and the United States-backed Republic of Vietnam (RVN) in the South. As a result, there also emerged two separate Vietnamese film industries: one centered in Hanoi and focused on agitprop/educational filmmaking, and the other centered in Saigon and associated primarily with commercial films.

2 Planned elections for a unified Vietnam were rejected by the South Vietnamese government. A bitter civil war ensued, and the conflict would further intensify with the deployment of American combat forces to South Vietnam in 1965.

3 In his important document "Marxism and Vietnamese Culture" discussed earlier, Trường Chinh ([1948] 2012) already mentioned socialist realism as a "method of artistic creation that portrays the truth in a society evolving toward socialism according to objective laws" (526).

4 This affinity to the Soviet avant-garde films of the 1920s comes hardly as a surprise, considering the pervasive Soviet influence on the DRV at the time. In fact, many Vietnamese filmmakers, including Trần Đắc, Bùi Đình Hạc, Nguyễn Khắc Lợi, Nguyễn Thu, and Lê Đăng Thực, were sent to study their craft at the Soviet film school (All-Union State Institute of Cinematography or VGIK), while the courses in the Vietnam Cinema School, at least in the late 1950s and early 1960s, were often taught by experts from the Soviet Union and socialist bloc countries (Đặng 2017, 29; 35). The noted director Đặng Nhật Minh, who had studied Russian as a young teenager, worked as a translator at the Vietnam Cinema School in the late 1950s. One of his responsibilities was to translate film books and articles written in Russian for the direction and scriptwriting students. He recalled doing "some research to find the right texts to translate" and becoming "deeply interested in the writings of Eisenstein, Pudovkin, Vertov and other great directors and theorists of Russian cinema" (Dang 1990, 10).

References

Cavendish, Philip. 2013. *The Man with the Movie Camera: The Poetics of Visual Style in Soviet Avant-Garde Cinema of the 1920s*. New York and Oxford: Berghahn.

Charlot, John. 1991. "Vietnamese Cinema: First Views." *Journal of Southeast Asian Studies* 22 (1): 33–62.

Đặng Nhật Minh. 2017. *Mémoires d'un cinéaste vietnamien*. Aix-en-Provence: Presses universitaires de Provence.

Dang Nhat Minh. 1990. "In the Realm of Darkness and Light." *Cinemaya* 7 (April–June): 12.

Duong, Lan. 2014. "Gender, Affect, and Landscape: Wartime Films from Northern and Southern Vietnam." *Inter-Asian Cultural Studies* 15 (2): 258–73.

"Images of the Land." In *30 years of Vietnam's Cinema Art*, edited by Trinh Mai Diễm, 13–7. Hà Nội: Vietnam Film Archives.

James, C. Vaughan. 1973. *Soviet Socialist Realism: Origins and Theory*. New York: St. Martin's Press.

Kepley, Vance, Jr. 1986. *In the Service of the State: The Cinema of Alexander Dovzhenko*. Madison: University of Wisconsin Press.

Miakova, Irina. 2007. "Vietnamese Cinema: Characteristics of Realism." In *Vietnamese Cinematography: A Research Journey*, 471–90. Hà Nội: Thế Giới Publishers.

Ngo Phuong Lan. 1998. "The Changing Face of Vietnamese Cinema during Ten Years of Renovation 1986–1996." In *Mass Media in Vietnam*, edited by David Marr. Political and Social Change Monograph 25. 91–6. Canberra: Department of Political and Social Change, Australian National University.

Nguyễn Đức Dương. 2007. "Method of Social Realism in Việt Nam Movies." In *Vietnamese Cinematography: A Research Journey*. Hà Nội: Thế Giới Publishers.

Nguyen Trinh Thi. 2014. "Vietnam Documentary Film: History and Current Scene." *DocNet Southeast Asia*. www.goethe.de/ins/id/lp/prj/dns/dfm/vie/enindex.htm.

Ninh, Kim N. B. 2002. *A World Transformed: The Politics of Culture in Revolutionary Vietnam, 1945–1965*. Ann Arbor: University of Michigan Press.

Pelley, Patricia M. 2002. *Postcolonial Vietnam: New Histories of the National Past*. Durham, NC and London: Duke University Press.

Phạm Ngọc Truong. 2001. "Vietnam: A Brief History of Vietnamese Films." In *Films in Southeast Asia: Views from the Region*, edited by David Hanan, 59–82. Hanoi: SEAPAVVA, in association with the Vietnam Film Institute, and the National Screen and Sound Archive of Australia.

Robin, Régine. 1992. *Socialist Realism: An Impossible Aesthetic*. Translated by Catherine Porter. Stanford, CA: Stanford University Press.

Tran, John. 1990. "Vietnamese Cultural Production during the American War." In *The Vietnam Era: Media and Popular Culture in the US and Vietnam*, edited by Michael Klein, 199–211. London and Winchester, MA: Pluto Press.

Trinh Mai Diễm, ed. 1983. *30 years of Vietnam's Cinema Art*. Hà Nội: Vietnam Film Archives.

Trường Chinh. (1948) 2012. "Marxism and Vietnamese Culture." In *Sources of Vietnamese Tradition*, edited by George E. Dutton, Jayne S. Werner, and John K. Whitemore. Reprint. New York: Columbia University Press.

Wilson, Dean. 2007. "Film Controls in Colonial Vietnam: 1896–1926." In *Vietnamese Cinema/Le cinéma vietnamien*, edited by Philippe Dumont and Kirstie Gormley, 75–85. Lyon: Asiexpo Edition.

Win, Thong. 2017. "Screening the Revolution in Rural Vietnam: Guerrilla Cinema across the Mekong Delta." In *The Colonial Documentary Film in South and South-East Asia*, edited by Ian Aitken and Camille Deprez, 171–85. Edinburgh: Edinburgh University Press.

Woll, Josephine. 2000. *Real Images: Soviet Cinema and the Thaw*. London and New York: I. B. Tauris Publishers.

Youngblood, Denise J. 2006. *Russian War Films: On the Cinema Front, 1914–2005*. Lawrence: University Press of Kansas.

2 Incomplete Pictures

Mediated Immediacy in the South Korean Newsreel, *The Frontline in Vietnam*

Namhee Han

The Forty-Year History of Army Filmmaking, published by the Public Relations Department of South Korea's Armed Forces, includes rarely known but significant reflections of filmmakers, producers, cameramen, and technicians who were dispatched to Vietnam from the mid-1960s to the early 1970s. Among them, producer Pak Chŏngsu's essay (1992) stands out. The title, "Shooting Film in Vietnam Was as Arduous as Fighting the War," literally refers to his physically and psychologically challenging experience of making the film, Kim Muk's *Heroes of An Khê* (*Angk'eŭi yŏngungdŭl*, 1973), amid the war (126). Despite the short length of the essay, he enumerates six episodes of life-threatening moments in Vietnam. Pak's comparison of filming with fighting seems inappropriate, but considering that he, in South Korea, had never been well informed about what the Vietnam War actually was, his sheer terror expressed in the essay is understandable. During the period of South Korea's participation in the Vietnam War from 1965 to 1973, domestic newspapers and TV news usually provided limited and sporadic coverage of the war. Most news was about local political debates on whether South Korea should dispatch its combat troops to Vietnam. After the government's decision to participate in the war, the main focus of news coverage moved to South Korean troops' successful military operations, the peaceful economic development projects toward South Vietnamese civilians, and the meetings between Korean politicians and Vietnamese leaders. Domestic news media did not show the brutal battlefields as described in Pak's memoir.

Pak's feeling of terror, moreover, was not shared by his colleagues in the Army Film Studio, who might have similar experiences in Vietnam. In their writings, they mainly recollected their honorable past of making army films—or *kunyŏnghwa* in Korean—for their country. It seems that they wanted to ensure the morality of South Korea's military involvement and to control the official narrative of what the Vietnam War was to South Korea even almost 20 years after the end of the war. As I shall discuss in this chapter, most filmic works that the Army Film Studio made in Vietnam are not entirely different from what Pak's colleagues attempted to remember in their memoirs. The films often called the Vietnam War "the war against communists" and carefully chose footage that was not too disturbing or shocking for viewers. In this regard, Pak's memoir, imbued with his personal agony and terror, is indeed exceptional, constituting a rare testimony about war violence which the South Korean general public was not aware of in the 1970s.

This chapter illuminates Cold War filmmaking practices in South Korea by investigating the production of the military newsreel series *The Frontline in Vietnam* (*Wŏllam chŏnsŏn*, 1966–75), and, more specifically, by analyzing its form of compilation and audiovisual style through the concept of "mediated immediacy." The newsreel series was made by the Army Film Studio under the Ministry of Defense, and it was mainly used for the military's internal purposes, such as education of military personnel and recruitment. The series can be considered as an official cinematic document of South Korea's first overseas deployment of its military forces. Moving images vividly captured in the series open up a critical space for looking into how the South Korean military authority attempted to represent its participation in the Other's war by using the newsreel format. Historian Charles K. Armstrong (2001) claims that just as the Korean War was forgotten by the United States, the Vietnam War was forgotten by South Korea in the sense that accounts of wartime atrocities committed by South Korean soldiers against civilians were forcibly suppressed. *The Frontline in Vietnam* shows that in making national history, forgetting does not merely refer to one's willful act of not remembering; rather, it entails the act of limiting personal narratives or interpretations of historical events. The newsreel shows South Korea's precarious sub-imperial gaze and invites us to explore the following questions: how did South Korean army cinema approach the Vietnam conflicts? What geopolitical order of the global Cold War did *The Frontline in Vietnam* project as a translocal work? And what cinematic form and style did the newsreel series develop with the intention of providing, but at the same time controlling, public information about the war?

The main focus of my discussion is not on the propaganda function of *The Frontline in Vietnam*, but on the cultural and aesthetic implications of the newsreel series. Seeking a fresh approach to the military newsreel, I define it as an expressive as well as an informative medium. We cannot entirely deny that *The Frontline in Vietnam*, made under the control of Park Chung Hee's authoritarian regime, served to shape public understanding of South Korea's participation in the Vietnam War and to maintain the support of the public. However, it is also an expressive audiovisual document through which we can access what the military authority wanted the public to see and hear of the war. As an informative and expressive work of Cold War South Korea, the newsreel series commented on the global power structure and reimagined South Korea's place within it. Its multiple sequencing of events and its series of disoriented moving images demonstrated that military filmmaking, including newsreels, is as much a cinematic and cultural practice as it is a political practice.

This chapter consists of three parts. It first examines major approaches to newsreels and army films and proposes a threefold meaning of "incomplete pictures" in relation to the material, representational, and aesthetic aspects of *The Frontline in Vietnam*. Second, it investigates how the Vietnam War facilitated the development of South Korean military film production by briefly tracing the long-standing relationship between wars and cinematic works produced by state-owned film studios. Finally, it closely analyzes *The Frontline in Vietnam*, focusing in particular on the period between 1971 and 1972, when the South Korean government decided to pull out its troops from Vietnam. I argue that the initial status of *The Frontline in Vietnam* as the state's information medium was challenged by the "mediated immediacy" inherent in the newsreel series' compilation form and its heterogeneous images of the war.

The Frontline in Vietnam as Incomplete Pictures

There are two analytical categories that we should consider in investigating *The Frontline in Vietnam*: the newsreel and the army film. In cinema and media studies, the newsreel is a marginalized subject, and the historical and political context in which this particular kind of film was produced and consumed has led researchers to emphasize its function as state propaganda. Newsreels—whether conservative or progressive—have had a long-lasting relationship to the state, as we see in Dziga Vertov's avant-garde works of the 1910s and 1920s and numerous newsreels of the First and Second World Wars. Previous historical surveys, thus, often tie the emergence and popularity of the newsreel to its political purpose set by the state during wartime. Marcel Huret (1984) claims that after the introduction of sound technology in the 1920s, the newsreel became an attractive mass medium for nationalist discourses. It was used as a means of indoctrination during the World Wars and sometimes even as a tool of war itself. Peter Baechlin and Maurice Muller-Strauss (1952) state that the wide international appeal of newsreels started from the 1910s, along with printed photojournalism. Meanwhile, Mark D. Harmon (2010) notes that the heyday of newsreels was roughly between 1911 and 1945, and the interim wars generated a typical form and style for newsreel films. Although these pioneer works have contributed to restoring the newsreel to the place it deserves in the history of international filmmaking, they trace more or less monolithic historical paths and focus on the ideologically heightened moments in which newsreels mainly served as vehicles of state propaganda. Consequently, what is emphasized are the ways in which newsreels manipulated the public, and less attention is paid to the cinematic elements that individual newsreels might have developed, or to the discrete institutional contexts that affected the aesthetic decisions of newsreel filmmakers, cameramen, and technicians.

The second category—the army film—broadly refers to cinematic works produced under the guidance or control of military authorities. It encompasses a range of forms and styles, not just the newsreel but also fiction film, feature-length documentary, short film, and even experimental work. Despite their differences, the institutional context in which these diverse forms are produced and consumed justifies them being called army films. Most studies on military cinema do not readily abandon mistrust or suspicion toward it because of an ideological assumption underpinning the assessments of the history and aesthetics of films sponsored by military institutions. Challenging this tendency, revisionist works have recently emerged. Alice Lovejoy's *Army Film and the Avant-Garde* (2014), for instance, shows that army films should be examined within contemporary international film culture and across institutional boundaries between civilian and military filmmaking. According to Lovejoy, there are two principal practices in army filmmaking. The first practice considers army film to be essentially different from civilian cinema; examples include interwar British documentary films, which had clear political purposes and developed a pedagogical style rarely taken in mainstream commercial cinema. The second practice is more cinematic and can be seen in newsreels of the Stalinist period. These films sought to dissolve the boundary between army and civilian cinema and attempted to create greater prestige for military films. In addition to these two dominant historical practices, Lovejoy considers another approach—one exemplified by the exceptional aesthetic and political dimensions of Czech army films, which resist the binary paradigms of military versus civilian filmmaking, of state-controlled production system versus market-based one, and of fiction versus non-fiction.

Korean-language studies on newsreels and army films have also centered on the state's dominant role in shaping and controlling these productions. Most works illuminate the social functions of the films to control public understanding of the state's economic policies and political decisions. For example, Pak Sŏnyŏng (2015) examines a range of works from military newsreels to the commercial films made by the national film studio called *Kungnib yŏnghwajejakso*. She aptly points out that in term of production, the boundary between military and civilian filmmaking was usually blurred during periods of authoritarian governments. However, she does not consider possible slippery from or resistance to intended political purposes. Her approach, following the ideological assumption noted earlier, puts emphasis on the long-lasting tradition of the military's involvement in shaping national film culture during the era of political repressions in modern Korea. Cinema had been used for state propaganda since the colonial period, and the military was a prime agent to promote the state's ideology and politics until the late 1980s. Although South Korean authoritarian governments did not pursue strict censorship and cultural policies toward the film industry as much as the colonial regime had done, they strategically maintained the overall structure of using newsreels and army films as propaganda tools. All newsreels were produced by the national film studio, and some of them were obligatorily shown in movie theaters before the feature films the audience came to see. While the business of newsreel films declined in the United States after the 1950s, when television news emerged as the major medium for audiovisual journalism, South Korean newsreels continued being produced and consumed until the early 1990s, and the political and cultural institutions of army cinema, television, and radio still exist. This historical tradition stigmatizes South Korean newsreels and army films for their suspicious status as state media and often leads researchers to highlight their potential propaganda effects. Although this dominant approach has increased Korean-language studies on state-produced or state-sponsored films and media, it runs the risk of binding our intellectual imaginations to a narrow framework that emphasizes the films' political functions.

The wide range of state-produced films in South Korea impels us to offer more nuanced readings that would enable us to see the uniqueness of individual newsreels and army films as creative works. In fact, the Army Film Studio was not strictly controlled by any particular military authority from the mid-1960s to the early 1970s, and members of the studio were thus given certain autonomy in creating films that considered the public's cultural interests. They also developed distinct cinematic aesthetics and had flexible relationships with their civilian counterparts. Filmmakers, cinematographers, and technicians in the Army Film Studio sometimes joined the production of mainstream commercial films. In addition, the established processes of the production, distribution, and exhibition of army films allowed the army filmmakers to become free from the market logic of the film industry. They were neither concerned with box office results nor did they compete with civilian films. South Korean newsreels and army films were, in short, more than ideological products.

I propose here the idea of "incomplete pictures" and use it as a tool to explore the possibility of a multilayered reading of *The Frontline in Vietnam*. "Incomplete pictures" have a threefold meaning. First, the term pertains to the material aspect of the newsreel series. We can hardly tell what makes the series a complete cinematic work. Footage of South Korean troops in Vietnam was shot on location and edited into the different issues of the series. At the same time, the footage remained "incomplete" insofar as it constituted a rare historical document to be recycled in future filmic or media works about the Vietnam War. Actually, some footage shot for *The Frontline in Vietnam* was reused for a feature-length documentary film, *The Crusade for Freedom* (*Chayuŭi sipchagun*), which was widely released to movie theaters in 1973. The footage was given a new significance within an entirely new political and historical context—a moment of forceful public celebration of the achievement of South Korean military forces in the Cold War and the memorialization of the end of the Vietnam War.

Second, "incomplete pictures" refer to the partial representations of the global ideological and military conflicts in Vietnam found in *The Frontline in Vietnam*. The newsreel series did not aim at a full and complete coverage of the war. Two-thirds of each issue is usually dedicated to presenting South Korean troops' peaceful economic development projects, their medical services, and their education projects for South Vietnamese civilians. Although one can easily see the progress of the war by chronologically tracing each issue of the newsreel series, the individual issue as a discrete unit is uninterested in informing the viewer of the political and military conflicts in depth. Surprisingly, there are no images of America and its allies losing the war or failing in their military operations. And the newsreel series ambiguously ends, without informing the viewer of the result of the war.

Finally, "incomplete pictures" refer to the cinematic aesthetics of mediated immediacy, which entails a particular temporality that *The Frontline in Vietnam* explores through its compilation form and heterogeneous audiovisual style. Specific film technologies and techniques were of interest to newsreel filmmakers as they tried to develop effective forms and styles of newsreels. According to Raymond Fielding (2011), sound technology made newsreels take a more cinematic form; the Nazi German newsreels of the late 1930s were a case in point. The Nazi newsreel filmmakers skillfully edited battle footage from current military campaigns rarely seen in a traditional information medium such as newspaper. Nazi newsreels consisted of multiple sequences, but they managed to give a sense of unity among the different subjects by means of fades, dissolves, music bridges, and voiceover narration. Most significantly, compared to other cinematic forms, newsreels evince a distinctive temporality in that they "swiftly [bring] spatially and temporally distant events into the here and now through the moving photographic image" (Hoffmann 2016, 81). In using cinematic languages that generate a sense of mediated immediacy, *The Frontline in Vietnam* turned historical events distant from the local audience into a present viewing experience. Each issue of the series highlighted the recent military operations of South Korean troops and displayed vividly shot and edited moving images of the war. The vibrant images give viewers a sense of witnessing the battlefields here and now, but they remain incomplete in their open-ended temporality, offering instead what may be called a sense of perpetual presence.

Taken together, these three meanings of "incomplete pictures" address the uniqueness of *The Frontline in Vietnam*, whose form, style, and subject matter were imbricated with South Korea's sub-imperial view on the Vietnam War on the one hand, and with the national filmmaking practices of army films during the Cold War period on the other hand. As I shall discuss later, the incompleteness and mediated immediacy of the newsreel series allowed the viewer to witness possible contradictions among sequences within the same issue or between issues in the entire series, and thereby to challenge the military authority's initial intention to produce state propaganda.

The Cold War and South Korean Army Film

Cold War geopolitics was reflected not only in the political and military endeavors of a state but also in its visual culture, including the production of newsreels. During the transitional period of the 1950s, from the end of the Second World War to the early Cold War, newsreels were criticized for their stereotypical form and style, but they were still widely used as a medium for delivering information. The 1952 UNESCO report on the worldwide newsreel industry expressed concerns about the impression of objectivity and the authoritative voice that newsreels generated. According to the report, "the sameness of coverage, unified perspective, and lack of dissenting voices" heightened the impression that newsreels offered a definitive account of events (Baechlin and Muller-Strauss 1952, 46). It warned about the quality of conviction that newsreels deployed as a mode of rhetoric. The authority, the report argued, came from the interplay between image and sound, wherein the narrator used moving images captured on film to illustrate the version of events he or she submitted to the audience. The authoritative tone of the voice-over and the assumed evidentiary value of moving images combined to create the appearance that the newsreel depicted "events as they [had] actually happened," as opposed to an edited version of events reported by a news agency (47). Although Bill Nichols (1992) sees the impression of objectivity in newsreels as the "great value of the expository mode" in that it offers a "frame of reference that need not be questioned or established but simply taken for granted" (35), the UNESCO report was concerned that this "frame of reference" might lead the viewer to uncritically accepting newsreel information as fact.

Despite UNESCO's critique, newsreels continued to take a prominent place in media culture during the early Cold War. While newsreel-producing agencies moved to civilian film studios after the end of the WWII, they continued to turn out weekly or biweekly newsreels and ten- to twenty-minute features, which greatly impacted the audience's understanding of recent political events. For example, Fox's commercial newsreel company, Movietone, claimed that its newsreels were seen by approximately 8% of the world's population every week in 1946 (Lawrenson 1946). The UNESCO report also remarked that a total of 1.7 billion people or about two-thirds of the estimated global population saw weekly newsreels in 1950. The estimated weekly newsreel exposure figures showed that 5–11% of the combined population of all 48 countries surveyed was exposed to a domestic-language newsreel every week in 1950 (Baechlin and Muller-Strauss 1952, 73–91). Interestingly, in both communist and anti-communist countries, newsreels were used to shape the public's views and to highlight the superiority of one's own values and morals over those of the other camp in the bipolar world. Especially, in the former fascist countries, the allied forces led by the United States strategically used information media for a comprehensive ideological reorientation as part of the larger Marshall Plan, and newsreels played an integral role in this process (Mäder 2016). In West Germany, newsreels covered a wide range of topics—politics, scientific, and technical innovations, cultural and art-related events, sports, fashion, and other entertainment or consumer goods—all of which were relevant to building an anti-communist developmentalist country in the period of "economic miracle" (Schwarz 2016).

The development of South Korean army films, including newsreels, was deeply integrated with the cultural politics of the global Cold War. The Film Unit of the Armed Forces was first established in South Korea on July 4, 1950, amid the Korean War, and turned into the Army Film Studio on February 17, 1953. During the Korean War, it completed the documentary films *Advance of Justice I* (*Chŏngŭiŭi chin'gyŏk I*, 1951) and *Advance of Justice II* (*Chŏngŭiŭi chin'gyŏk II*, 1952) by compiling newsreel footage that recorded the major military operations of the United Nations and South Korea's Armed Forces. In addition, it produced 66 issues of the newsreel series *Defense News* (*Kukpang nyusŭ*) from June 22, 1952 to May 18, 1956. Military units also functioned as film distributors and released education and culture films as well as newsreels. After the Korean War, the production of army films decreased, but some filmmakers, cameramen, and technicians who had been members of the Film Unit of Armed Forces joined the civilian film studios and contributed to building the postwar film industry.

The government's decision in 1964 to dispatch its troops to Vietnam marked a major transition in South Korea's army film practices, as it reactivated the Army Film Studio and increased its production, including its first overseas work, *The Frontline in Vietnam*. From September 1964 to March 1973, South Korea sent more than 300,000 troops to South Vietnam. The South Korean Army, Marine Corps, Navy, and Air Force all participated as an ally of the United States and comprised the units of the Tiger Division, the White Horse Division, and the Blue Dragon Brigade. For purposes of indoctrination and recruitment, the military authorities needed newsreels as a mass information medium. The Public Relations Department of the Armed Forces characterized the period of the Vietnam War as an era of tremendous growth for army cinema. The task of making newsreels in Vietnam, most of all, enhanced the Army Film Studio's technical, financial, and professional resources because making overseas works commanded a large arsenal of technological resources and skilled people. From 1966 to 1972, a total of 32 cameramen were sent to Vietnam to record South Korean troops' military operations and economic development projects for South Vietnamese civilians. In addition, the studio was allowed to purchase new modern film equipment, including four 35 mm Aimo cameras, four 35 mm Ariflex cameras, fifteen 16 mm Filmo cameras, eight tungsten lighting kits, two Nigra sound recorders, and one 16 mm and one 35 mm black and white and color film developer.

Besides military newsreels, the Ministry of Defense was interested in producing or sponsoring commercial civilian films. It encouraged collaborations between the Army Film Studio and civilian film studios in an attempt to publicly display South Korean soldiers' achievements in Vietnam and to seek the public's continued support for the government's international political decisions. Members of the Army Film Studio joined the production of commercial feature films and culture films set in the Vietnam War, and the Ministry of Defense sponsored works of civilian film studios, including 13 fictional films and seven education films, all of which were widely released to movie theaters. Among them, prominent auteur Yi Manhŭi's work, *The Boy Who Returned* (*Toraon sonyŏn*, 1970), is worthy of mention. It garnered critical acclaims and won several awards at major local film festivals even though the film was a government-sponsored work, which local film critics usually dismissed. Also remarkable is the fact that the film was permitted to be shot on location in South Vietnam and was helped by the Tiger Division unit. Its narrative follows the political conversion of a Vietnamese boy whose father is a Viet Cong, and shows the changing relationships between South Korean soldiers who help reconstruct a village and Vietnamese civilians who suffer from military and ideological conflicts. The film satisfied military authorities because it was a well-made commercial film that could promote government sponsorship of civilian films about the Vietnam War and introduce South Korean troops' peacemaking role to the general public. Intriguingly, *The Boy Who Returned* consciously appropriated the recurring opening sequence in *The Frontline in Vietnam* as if to underline its status as a sponsored work. Like the opening sequence that introduces each issue of the newsreel series, the film begins with a full shot emphasizing giant tanks and dashing soldiers who make their way through the jungle, accompanied by the victorious music of a military march.

The Frontline in Vietnam was, without doubt, the Army Film Studio's major work about the Vietnam War. It offered the local audience a firsthand perspective of the global Cold War, which was not possible in other contemporary domestic media. The entire newsreel series was made between 1966 and 1975, comprising a total of 125 issues. Each issue comprises three to four sequences of discrete events and lasts eight to ten minutes. Although the series was not aimed toward the general public, it was widely shown to soldiers in both South Korea and Vietnam. Most significantly, the series was the only national audiovisual record of South Korean troops' combat missions and their economic development and education projects in South Vietnam. Unlike domestic television news or newspaper coverage, which rarely showed images of actual combats, every issue of the newsreel series produced in 1971 and 1972 included major battles South Korean troops participated in, thus allowing the audience to immediately access information about the war in progress.

As a visual work produced by and for the military, *The Frontline in Vietnam* provides a privileged point for examining the optical unconscious of the gaze that sub-imperial South Korea attempted to project. Paul Virilio (1989) and Friedrich Kittler (1999) argue for the significance of military technology and people's perception of war in investigating the developments and aesthetic expressions of visual media. Virilio argues that films and other visual works have long been central to the process of military mapmaking, and they serve as tools that sharpen our perception of the world. Building on Walter Benjamin's insight into the alliance of war and cinema, Kittler also demonstrates how cinematic imagery becomes an instrument of military deception and persuasion. Both Virilio and Kittler convince us that we should place the military at the vanguard not only of cinematic or media technology but also of visual aesthetics in order to make sense of the social and political implications of optical tools, techniques, and expressions.

The Frontline in Vietnam, in making visible the sub-imperial gaze of South Korea and articulating the idea of "Korea's Vietnam," opens a critical space to explore South Korea's anxious, in-between position within the power structure of the global Cold War. In studies on the Korean experiences of the Vietnam War, it is often claimed that the war led South Korea to practice its military power as a sub-empire following the United States. Jin-Kyung Lee (2009) insists that like powerful countries in the postcolonial era, South Korea invented new ways of controlling people and places beyond the nation's territorial boundaries with a minimum of colonial commitments, and the Vietnam War was a critical event to perform this sub-imperialism. By redrawing the geopolitical map in a way that shifts its focus to South Korea, *The Frontline in Vietnam* suggested what the Vietnam War could be for South Korea and for its own political and cultural purposes. In most issues of the newsreel series, the presence of the United States in Vietnam was intentionally diminished or invisible. Instead, South Korea's intimate, but not quite interactive, relation with South Vietnam was emphasized.

The gaze of sub-imperial South Korea presented in the newsreel was quite vulnerable. A state document written in July 1966 expressed some concerns regarding the public's perception of the newsreel in Vietnam. The first part of the document celebrated the achievement of the newsreel production, stating that a 35 mm version of the newsreel was about to be released at movie theaters in major cities in South Korea, and that a 16 mm version of it would be widely shown in rural areas. The second part, however, addressed the government's concerns regarding possible controversies that the newsreel could cause: "We are sending three release prints of the 16 mm version of this work to our troops and civilians who are striving in South Vietnam and wish for it to be shown. However, we ask that you target the viewing at specific South Vietnamese people after you carefully examine the content of the newsreel" (Kungnib yŏnghwajejakso 1966). The gaze of sub-imperial South Korea will be further examined in the next part, as I analyze how a sense of "mediated immediacy" addresses the cultural anxiety in representing the idea of "Korea's Vietnam," which refers to South Korean experiences with and imaginations of the Vietnam War. The newsreel, on the one hand, attempted to control the perception of people both within and outside of South Korea, but on the other hand, it exposed the national, gender, racial, and ethnic hierarchies among countries involved in the Vietnam War.

Mediated Immediacy and "Korea's Vietnam"

The idea of temporality offers a fresh way to examine newsreels beyond the framework of state propaganda and allows us to consider the aesthetic aspects of individual works. In particular, the sounds, moving images, and overall structure of *The Frontline in Vietnam* require our attention because they mediate the viewer's sense of temporality as well as its larger meanings. The newsreel is widely defined as a "historical audiovisual medium with specific combinatorics of reports in their rhetoric mix of sound—a usually male voiceover, spoken comments, music, noise—and moving images" (Imesch, Schade, and Sieber 2016, 9). This definition implies that the audiovisual elements of newsreels have meanings that are not immediately associated with their political functions. Previous studies on news media show that time is a major feature driving innovation in information media, from carrier pigeons, ships, and telegraph wires to faxes, satellite technology, and the Internet. Likewise, the information that *The Frontline in Vietnam* provided was time-based, marked with periodicity and immediacy. The newsreel series brought a physically distant event (i.e., the Vietnam War) to local audiences every week or every other week, which was a relatively short period, compared with news coverage of the war in other domestic media.

The issue of time distinguished *The Frontline in Vietnam* from other contemporary South Korean films about the Vietnam War. In the early 1970s, popular films dealing with South Korean experiences in Vietnam showed dramatic changes. The main genre moved from war action films to melodramas, and the narratives, in their focus on recently returning war veterans from Vietnam, considered the Vietnam War as a past historical event. Yi Sŏnggu's *Sergeant Kim's Return from Vietnam* (*Wŏllamesŏ toraon kimsangsa*, 1971) is a good example of this trend. The opening sequence suggests that the Vietnam War has become a past for South Korea. The war experiences of the main male characters are briefly mentioned, and once they arrive in Seoul, they are surprised by well-built highways and fast-moving cars. They soon realize that they are late for experiencing an economically transformed South Korea. The rest of the film then shows how the Vietnam veterans turn into industrious workers who support the economic developments of their country. In the 1970s, *The Frontline in Vietnam* was the only work that still reminded the viewer of the Vietnam War in progress.

The Frontline in Vietnam offers the viewer a sense of presence or immediacy, which is a unique aesthetic experience. Drawing on Hans Burger's work, Philip Auslander (1999) remarks that immediacy pertains to "the sense of a continuous perceptual experience unfolding in real time" (20). Nathan Rotenstreich (1991) discusses the experience of immediacy as featuring an instantaneous, spontaneous, and authentic connection with another being or event. Jay David Bolster and Richard Grusin (1999) demonstrate that to create a sense of presence, the media have shown a growing propensity to capture an immediate lived experience. But among scholars that explore the idea of immediacy, G.W.F. Hegel makes the most intriguing point, claiming that immediacy and mediation are inseparable (Wallace 2005). For my purpose here, mediation in a newsreel is defined in relation to the intervening role that the process of filmmaking and film-viewing plays in making meanings and generating a particular temporality of immediacy. It is significant to note that the immediacy of watching a war in progress in *The Frontline in Vietnam* is not the kind of immediacy that we see on live television news, but is rather mediated by the compilation of multiple sequences within a single issue and by a heterogeneous audiovisual style. Such mediated immediacy allows viewers to explore meanings beyond what is explicitly expressed in the newsreel.

The audiovisual elements that generate mediated immediacy in *The Frontline in Vietnam* offer viewers a guide to witness war violence and have them affectively connected to what is shown on screen. Aural elements of the newsreel series make graphic images more intelligible and reinforce their claim to "realism" at the expense of authentic reality. Unlike newsreels of WWI and WWII that heavily rely on voiceover narration, *The Frontline in Vietnam* uses a narrator to convey only geographical information of battlefields or of cities or villages where South Korean troops were serving Vietnamese civilians. Playing a more prominent role are the sounds of combat fields directly recorded in Vietnam. Battlefield sounds authenticate the images captured on the newsreel.

Although the sounds of gunfights, helicopters, and tanks are not refined because the Army Film Studio did not have the advanced equipment to record multiple sound tracks, they are vivid enough for audiences to imagine what battlefields sound like, not to mention that they also add an emotional force to the viewing experience. Raw location sounds of combats have the effect of engulfing the audiences and possibly intensifying their imagination of military conflicts in Vietnam.

Music is carefully used to maintain formal consistency of the newsreel series and sometimes to create dramatic effects, assuring that the viewer observes the war in progress from a temporal and spatial distance. Music punctuates the opening and ending of every issue of the series. In the opening sequence, marching music accompanies the scene in which camouflaged South Korean soldiers walk through the jungle. In the (usually open-ended) closing sequence, the music is full of suspense and gives an impression that the war against communists and the peace projects in South Vietnam should continue. The repetition of the same theme music in the opening and closing sequences gives consistency to the formal structure of the newsreel series and reminds the viewer that the war is in progress. Occasionally, dramatic music is used in the main sequences that show the military operations of the South Korean troops. For example, in issues 88 and 98, the audience witnesses the success of Operation Eagle 71-1 and the victory at the Battle of An Khê, respectively, and lively music celebrates South Korean troops' achievements in both cases. The compounding aural elements of direct sound and music generate a sense of mediated immediacy, allowing viewers to vividly observe combats from a temporal and spatial distance and thus transform the historical event of the war into an affective viewing experience.

Mediated immediacy is most explicitly visible in the compilation form, which assembles multiple sequences of discrete events into one issue of the newsreel and skillfully proposes a particular narrative of South Korean experiences in Vietnam. Although *The Frontline in Vietnam* is a military work produced during wartime, it shows not just combat operations but South Korean troops' economic development projects as well as medical and educational services for civilians. Most issues in 1971 and 1972 consist of three sequences—battlefields, economic reconstruction or cultural events, and services to civilians in South Vietnam. The multiple sequences compiled together shape and control the viewer's perception of the war and of the relationship between South Korean troops and Vietnamese civilians, recounting the war from the perspective of South Korea.

The compilation form proposes two main narratives of "Korea's Vietnam" in 1971 and 1972, integrating multiple sequences and mediating the relationship between South Korean troops and South Vietnamese civilians. First of all, it emphasizes the Vietnam War as a global war against communists rather than a national ideological conflict among the Vietnamese. Once South Korea decided to join the war, the government publicly claimed that Vietnam was the second frontline in that both South Korea and South Vietnam should work together to fight against neighboring communist countries. In *The Frontline in Vietnam*, the war is depicted as an ideological conflict between the global community of anti-communist developmentalist states and that of communist socialist states, but the newsreel series does not provide the overarching historical and political context or the strong overlay of nationalism, colonialism, and postcolonialism in modern Vietnam. The Viet Cong are usually called communists, and in contrast to them, South Korean troops are portrayed as competent forces managing major military operations on behalf of Vietnamese civilians.

Second, the compiled sequences connect national economic development projects with transnational anti-communism, which binds South Korea and South Vietnam to the transnational and transracial community of anti-communist Asia. The newsreel series shows South Korean soldiers working for the reconstruction and modernization of South Vietnam as much as they are fighting in battlefields. It is not uncommon to find two-thirds of an issue dedicated to Korean soldiers' peaceful interactions with Vietnamese civilians in hospitals and schools, and the Koreans are portrayed as modern, victorious, and well prepared to defend Vietnam from communists. For example, in issue 99 released in 1972, the audience is first introduced to a combat operation (Operation 3-1, Golden Bat) conducted by the White Horse Division. This is followed by a ceremony celebrating the sixth anniversary of the founding of the South Korean Crux in Vietnam, and the issue ends by showing the White Horse Division's medical services for Vietnamese children and elders. These multiple sequences give the impression that the Vietnam War was not only about long-lasting military conflicts but also about the developmentalist project to build a new modern nation-state and improve civilians' health and well-being in Vietnam. The overall compilation structure of the newsreel series attempts to persuade the viewer to see the war as part of a larger regional project of anti-communism.

Interestingly, the mediated immediacy that is emphasized by the compilation form and the heterogeneous moving images allows viewers to take note of and question contradictions in South Korea's peacemaking role, as it captures the immediacy of war violence and records the hierarchical relationship between South Korean troops and South Vietnamese civilians. In many issues of the series, the viewer is led to observe both grim battlefields and attractive, exotic cities under construction. South Korean troops are reliable and victorious but simultaneously appear intimidating to Vietnamese civilians, most of whom are children, women, and senior citizens. Suspicion is raised to its highest level when viewers watch the combat sequences and directly encounter the military conflicts and experience an intense sense of presence. Handheld and traveling camera shots accompanied with the sounds of combat strongly allude to war violence. These shots engulf the audience within the chaos of the battlefields. For example, in issue 101, which introduces the White Horse Division's Operation Sŏngma 72-1, aerial shots reveal smoky battlefields in the aftermath of gunfire and bombing. Traveling shots slowly pan across aligned helicopters waiting to carry the wounded and loads of guns and ammunition. The invisible violence suggested by the shots evokes disturbing imagination and presents a critical opportunity to question South Korean troops' participation in the global Cold War. Although the combat scenes are mainly taken from the South Korean soldiers' perspective and Vietnamese communists are not shown, the commotion of combat, murky air, and imagery of heavy weapons powerfully impact the viewer's perception of the war and the violence it entails.

The temporality of mediated immediacy invites the viewer to observe the vulnerability of the sub-imperial gaze, which *The Frontline in Vietnam* employs to claim South Korea's in-between position within the global Cold War. For example, issue 84 includes a sequence of the White Tiger Division's cultural project for the Vietnamese. The Division hosts a children's drawing competition and asks Vietnamese children to draw a picture of the South Korean navy. The sequence attempts to stage an amicable relationship between South Korea and South Vietnam, but the camera shows faces of children that demonstrate a lack of enthusiasm. Their pictures are full of typical images such as the national flag of South Korea or South Korean soldiers performing traditional Korean martial arts. Some of the children directly confront the camera, thus indicating that they are aware of the presence of South Koreans (and their authority over them).

It is significant to note that the mediated immediacy found in the newsreel series exposes limitations of South Korea's sub-imperial gaze. Not entirely totalizing, concentrated, or competent, this gaze is often disrupted by other gazes such as those of the United States and Vietnam, with the South Korean newsreel filmmakers caught in the in-between position of looking and being looked at. Although the filmmakers' sub-imperial gaze is upon South Vietnamese civilians, they do not overtly pursue the logic of conquest as previous European empires did. Mediated immediacy allows the viewer to be present in moments, not only of South Korea becoming a sub-empire following the United States in postcolonial Vietnam but also of South Korea's new global political role being looked at and responded to by Vietnam. The periods of 1971 and 1972 indicate that the sub-imperial gaze was more precarious and relational. The South Korean government had already decided to withdraw its military forces from Vietnam and might have been aware of its defeat by global communists.

Mediated immediacy in *The Frontline in Vietnam*, generated by the heterogeneous cinematic languages and compilation form of the newsreel series, demonstrates that military filmmaking is as much a cinematic and cultural practice as it is a political practice. It encourages viewers to practice intellectual autonomy, opening up the possibility of dismissing, if not undermining, the state-imposed narrative of South Korea's

Vietnam. Although the newsreel series emphasizes South Korea's central place in the global Cold War by drawing attention to its military and peacemaking endeavors in Vietnam, this attempt is traceable only through what may be called "incomplete pictures," which indicate the cultural anxiety in inventing a new visual mechanism to represent South Korea's in-between position, one that was below the United States but above South Vietnam.

Conclusion

The Frontline in Vietnam was more than a vehicle for state propaganda. The newsreel series, with its filmed immediacy mediated by the compilation form and heterogeneous moving images, demonstrates that military films are cultural as well as political works. I have argued that mediated immediacy, as a temporal logic and cinematic aesthetic, reflected South Korean experiences of the Vietnam War. On the one hand, it captured the moments of global ideological and military conflicts. On the other hand, it commented on the national, gender, racial, and ethnic hierarchies and war violence that sub-imperial South Korea partook in, thus adding to our understanding of the power structure of the global Cold War.

After producing the newsreel series, the Army Film Studio made more strategic use of film and mass media to maintain public support for South Korea's international relations and domestic political policies in the 1970s and the 1980s. Some staff members who had been involved in making *The Frontline in Vietnam* later joined the production of the television series *The Leader of the Korean* (*Paedarŭi kisu*, 1972–90). Most episodes of the series were set either in the Korean War or in the present when South Korea was threatened by North Korean espionage activities. The television series perpetuated anti-communist ideology by reminding the audience of the emergency state of South Korea. It seems that unlike *The Frontline in Vietnam*, *The Leader of the Korean* was able to come to a complete vision of what Cold War South Korea should look like. It eschewed the temporal logic of mediated immediacy in the newsreel series, favoring instead the past and the legacy of the Korean War. The Cold War filmmaking practices in South Korea of the 1970s and 1980s were more concerned with conveying historical events within a fixed temporality. The "incomplete" works that the Army Film Studio made in Vietnam might have shown that the past was much more controllable in addressing the state-led narrative and ideology of the Cold War.

Acknowledgments

This research project was made possible through the generous support of the Asian Modernities and Traditions (AMT) Research Fund at Leiden University.

Works Cited

Armstrong, Charles K. 2001. "America's Korea, Korea's Vietnam." *Critical Asian Studies* 33 (4): 527–39.

Auslander, Philip. 1999. *Liveness: Performance in a Mediatized Culture*. London and New York: Routledge.

Baechlin, Peter, and Maurice Muller-Strauss. 1952. "Newsreels across the World." UNESCO Digital Library. https://unesdoc.unesco.org/ark:/48223/pf0000030104.

Bolster, Jay David, and Richard Grusin. 1999. *Remediation: Understanding New Media*. Cambridge, MA and London: MIT Press.

Fielding, Raymond. 2011. *The American Newsreel: A Complete History, 1911–1967*. Jefferson: McFarland and Company.

Harmon, Mark D. 2010. "That is Not Goldfish Swallowing: Newsreels Encounter Protests against the Vietnam War." *Visual Communication Quarterly* 17 (4): 200–12.

Hoffmann, Hilde. 2016. "The Visual Memory of the Cold War: The Long Afterlife of the Fox *Tönende Wochenschau* Newsreels on the Building of the Berlin Wall." In *Constructions of Cultural Identities in Newsreel Cinema and Television after 1945*, edited by Kornelia Imesch, Sigrid Schade, and Samuel Sieber, 81–100. Bielefeld: Transcript.

Huret, Marcel. 1984. *Ciné Actualités: Histoire de la presse filmée, 1895–1980*. Paris: H. Veyrier.

Imesch, Kornelia, Sigrid Schade, and Samuel Sieber. 2016. "Introduction." In *Constructions of Cultural Identities in Newsreel Cinema and Television after 1945*, edited by Kornelia Imesch, Sigrid Schade, and Samuel Sieber, 7–20. Bielefeld: Transcript.

Kittler, Friedrich. 1999. *Gramophone, Film, Typewriter*. Translated by Geoffrey Winthrop-Young and Michael Wutz. Stanford, CA: Stanford University Press.

Kungnib yŏnghwajejakso (The National Film Production). 1966. "Wŏllam chŏnsŏn kirokyŏnghwa" (Documentary film, *The Frontline in Vietnam*). Korean Film Archive. Accessed 10 January 2019. www.kmdb.or.kr/history/pdfViewer.

Lawrenson, Harry. 1946. "Foreign Editions." *Journal of the Society of Motion Picture Engineers* 47 (5): 361–64.

Lee, Jin-kyung. 2009. "Surrogate Military, Subimperialism, and Masculinity: South Korea in the Vietnam War, 1965–73." *Positions* 17 (3): 655–82.

Lovejoy, Alice. 2014. *Army Film and the Avant Garde: Cinema and Experiment in the Czechoslovak Military*. Bloomington: Indiana University Press.

Mäder, Marie-Therese. 2016. "Between Migration and Integration." In *Constructions of Cultural Identities in Newsreel Cinema and Television after 1945*, edited by Kornelia Imesch, Sigrid Schade, and Samuel Sieber, 167–88. Bielefeld: Transcript.

Nichols, Bill. 1992. *Representing Reality: Issues and Concepts in Documentary*. Bloomington, IN: Indiana University Press.

Pak, Chŏngsu. 1992. "Chŏnjaengmank'ŭmina ŏryŏun ch'waryŏng" (Shooting film in Vietnam was as arduous as fighting the war). In *Kunyŏnghwa sashimnyŏnsa* (The Forty-Year History of Army Filmmaking). 126–8. Seoul: Public Relations Department of Armed Forces.

Pak, Sŏnyŏng. 2015. "Kukkaŭi p'ŭreimŭro kuhoektoen pet'ŭnamjŏnjaeng" (The Vietnam War captured in the frame of the state). *Sarim* 53: 57–90.

Rotenstreich, Nathan. 1991. *Immediacy and Its Limits: A Study in Martin Buber's Thought*. Abingdon, Oxon: Routledge.

Schwarz, Uta. 2016. "West German State Newsreels in the Period of the Economic Miracle, 1950–1954." In *Constructions of Cultural Identities in Newsreel Cinema and Television after 1945*, edited by Kornelia Imesch, Sigrid Schade, and Samuel Sieber, 55–80. Bielefeld: Transcript.

Virilio, Paul. 1989. *War and Cinema: The Logistics of Perception*. Translated by Patrick Camiller. New York: Verso.

Wallace, Robert M. 2005. *Hegel's Philosophy of Reality, Freedom and God*. Cambridge: Cambridge University Press.

3 Gained in Translation

The Reception of Foreign Films in Cold War China

Jie Li

Cold War's most direct and palpable impact on cinema in the People's Republic of China (PRC) was probably the expulsion of Hollywood from the early 1950s until the end of the 1970s (Xiao 2004). Nevertheless, audiences in Mao Zedong's China still had access to an impressive array of international films, thanks to Chinese cultural diplomacy with other countries in the Socialist bloc as well as non-aligned countries (Du 2015; Xu 2017). Besides many Soviet films dubbed into Mandarin with a Northeastern accent (Chen 2004, 2009), Chinese citizens could watch films from countries as diverse as Bulgaria, Czechoslovakia, Egypt, England, Hungary, India, Iraq, Italy, Japan, Mexico, and Poland, thanks to the many "film weeks" showcasing imported films in major cities in the 1950s and early 1960s (Ma 2016). With the souring of Sino-Soviet relations, Soviet and East European films gradually disappeared from Chinese screens after 1964. Yet within the Cultural Revolution decade, more foreign feature films were shown than domestic ones, albeit from a small number of countries that remained China's allies. Hence, in the 1970s, a popular saying circulated about the masses' cosmopolitan film diet: "Chinese films: documentary newsreels; Vietnamese films: airplanes and cannons; North Korean films: weep, weep, smile, smile; Romanian films: hugs and kisses; Albanian films: baffling and bizarre." The cultural Cold War, then, both delimited and expanded the gamut of films on Chinese screens; moreover, much as cinema was an important weapon in the ideological warfare, there was also considerable grassroots heteroglossia and creativity in the reception of cinema intended as propaganda.

This chapter studies the exhibition and reception of a few popular foreign titles as recounted in the cinematic memories of Chinese who grew up in China during the Cold War era. Specifically, it focuses on four case studies chosen for their wide release and enduring influence, thereby lending themselves to diachronic analysis. I begin with two Soviet films—Mikhail Romm's biopics *Lenin in October* (1937) and *Lenin in 1918* (1939)—because their reception in China lasted nearly four decades, from their first showings in the Communist base area in 1940, a nationwide release in the early 1950s, to repetitive screenings throughout the Cultural Revolution. I then discuss the Chinese reception of North Korean and Albanian films—especially Ch'oe Ik-kyu's *The Flower Girl* (1972) and Gëzim Erebara and Piro Milkani's *Victory Over Death* (1967)—which enchanted audiences with emotional and aesthetic elements missing in the domestic productions of the time. My last case study will be the evolving resonances of Raj Kapoor's *Awara* (*The Vagabond*, 1951) in China, first screened as part of an Indian "film week" in 1955 and later receiving a much wider release in the late 1970s. Although originating in altogether different historical and cultural contexts, all four films were widely and repeatedly shown during or, in the last case, around the Cultural Revolution decade, when Chinese feature film production slowed to a trickle but film projection units grew at an unprecedented rate. Over the decades and in special exhibition contexts, these foreign films turned into unexpected canonical classics for those growing up in China during the Mao era. Their accumulating and differentiated reception over time reveals the complexities and unintended ramifications of the cultural Cold War from a bottom-up perspective.

In the broader discipline of cinema studies, audience reception remains a neglected but emerging subfield. From the 1990s and 2000s, film scholars have challenged psychoanalytic conceptualizations of the spectator as a homogeneous mass with unified responses to film texts and given increasing attention to the audience as historically constructed and culturally specific subjects. Focusing on early cinema, stars/fans, and social demographics, the study of film reception has moved beyond the textually implied spectator to draw on published reviews and articles (critical reception studies, see Hansen 1991; Staiger 1992), on cultural or sociological context (historical or cultural reception studies, see Stacey 1994; Tsivian 1994), as well as on interviews with audience members (empirical reception studies, see Reinhard & Olsen, 2016). Joining a growing number of Chinese cinema studies that also highlight exhibition and reception over production history and textual analysis (such as Berry & Zhang 2013; Chen, 2004; Du 2015; Huang 2014; Ma 2016; Pickowicz & Johnson 2009; Xiao 2004, 2010), I seek to examine how Chinese audiences actively engaged with the foreign films they watched in a Cold War context.

This chapter draws on a variety of sources both official and unofficial, contemporary and retrospective—including newspaper articles, local film gazetteers, oral histories, memoirs, online blogs, and even fictional texts that synthesize collective memories. Some sources detail exhibition practices, such as how projectionists showed or censored films, while others recall various emotional, intellectual, aesthetic, and behavioral responses to foreign films: from laughter to tears, from catharsis to reflection, from emulation to mockery. No source gives unmediated access to "real audiences" as individuals or collectives. Whether writing a film review upon its release or answering a scholar's questions about their memories of a film four decades after seeing it, the historicity and intended audience of every recounting influence the construction of meaning. As Annette Kuhn (2002) suggests, interviews and other "memory texts" do not provide a "window on the past," but rather selected and performative recounting (9–10). While such hindsight "taints" memories, it can sometimes also provide trenchant commentary on both the past and present. Thus, while keeping in mind the mediated nature of these sources, I also ask readers of this chapter to be open to the illuminations emerging from the historical vicissitudes embedded in these "memory texts." Indeed, I contend that the sheer diversity of these personal, even idiosyncratic, accounts show us how a film's meanings could multiply with its audience members.

Extrinsic Meanings

Critical theorists have long drawn our attention to the agency of the reader/audience/consumer as an active producer of a text's plural meanings (Barthes 1974; Fiske 1986). While their theories inform my discussion of foreign films' reception in socialist China in this chapter, the huge cultural and temporal gaps these films leaped over—and never quite "bridged"—warrant a more nuanced look at specific historical conditions of the Cold War that contributed to transcultural meaning-making. I argue that, as the foreign films crossed national and even continental borders to meet with mass audiences for whom they were never intended, the radically different exhibition and reception contexts helped generate new meanings. Whether we speak of subtitles or dubbing, we usually assume that something of the original film is lost in translation, but here I would like to borrow from Salman Rushdie's (1991) claim that something can also be "gained in translation" (17). What is gained, I argue, lies with film reception. I use "translation" to refer not to linguistic translation of film dialogue but to cultural translation, or the transplantation of films into a different social, historical, and cultural context from their countries of origin. "Translation" here also refers to the "interpretation" of films, not just by critics and scholars who usually try to get at intended or symptomatic meanings, but by ordinary audience members who bring their personal sentiments, cultural repertoires, and historical circumstances to bear on cinematic meanings. Moreover, in cases of films shown not just in a given season or year, but repeatedly over many years and to different generations, focusing on their reception allows us to track the evolving and palimpsestic meanings they may have had for different audiences over time.

In *Making Meaning*, David Bordwell (1991) argues that we can construct four levels of meanings—referential, explicit, implicit, and symptomatic—in any film. To get a film's *referential* meaning, a spectator draws on prior knowledge of the real world to comprehend the film's characters and their actions in a literal and concrete sense. *Explicit* meaning is an abstract, usually thematic meaning often stated by a character in the film—providing its "moral," "message," or "point." *Implicit* meaning, not directly stated, is often allegorical and may be contested between different spectators. Whereas referential, explicit, and implicit meanings are usually intended by the film's creators, the spectator may also "construct *repressed* or *symptomatic* meanings that the work divulges 'involuntarily,'" either as "the consequence of the artist's obsessions" or "traced to economic, political, or ideological processes" (8–9).

Discussing film interpretation in Western journalistic and academic contexts, Bordwell's typology of meanings is also useful in thinking through the different ways Chinese audiences made sense of foreign films. Nevertheless, I argue that meanings gained in translation—which I call *extrinsic meanings*—often go beyond the intentions and repressions of a film's creators, thus presenting revisions of Bordwell's four categories; that is, through cross-cultural transplantation, a film's referential meaning can get lost or take on exotic valences; its explicit meaning or ideological message can be ignored or mocked; and audiences may construct implicit and symptomatic meanings of a foreign film that say more about their own historical experiences than the filmmakers or the film's production contexts. The extrinsic meanings constructed in this process are not so much *comprehension* and *interpretation* of what is intrinsic to a film text, but rather a matter of *appropriation* and sometimes *re-creation*. In addition to cognitive interpretations, this chapter will also delve into affective responses, hidden pleasures, and viewer identifications. Ultimately, as I will elaborate in the conclusion, studying foreign cinema's reception in Cold War China broadens the concept of "Chinese cinema" to include "cinema in China" with all of its socialist cosmopolitan connections, revises our assessment of the Cultural Revolution as a "cultural desert," and invites us to reconsider today's Chinese media ecology in light of its socialist, Cold War past.

Soviet Films from Revolutionary Model to Campy Nostalgia

Prior to the communist revolution, audiences in Chinese cities watched foreign films—mostly Hollywood films—with explanatory booklets, subtitles on lantern slides, or live interpretations through earphones in the best cinemas (Zhang 2009, 291–311). Linguistic barriers, literacy requirements, and expensive ticket prices limited Chinese audiences of Hollywood films to upper classes prior to communist takeover (Xiao 2010, 61–6). Yet from the late 1940s onward, the Cold War remapped what Tina Mai Chen (2009) calls "international film circuits," so that Soviet cinema replaced Hollywood's dominance of Chinese screens.

The dubbing of more than 400 Soviet films from 1949 to 1957—more than China's entire domestic feature film production of the 1950s—as well as the expansion of film exhibition to workers, peasants, and soldiers launched an unprecedented encounter between "proletariat" Chinese audiences and foreign cinema. As Tina Mai Chen (2004) has argued, Soviet films "provided socialist heroes and heroines through whom the Chinese could envision their future" (82).

Two particular Soviet films—*Lenin in October* and *Lenin in 1918*—should be singled out because their exhibition and reception in China spanned four decades from 1940 to the end of the 1970s. Although sneered upon as humdrum propaganda in North America (Nugent 1939), these two Lenin films caused quite a sensation in the Chinese Communist base area of Yan'an and were brought from the USSR by none other than the Chinese Communist Party (CCP) leader Zhou Enlai (Wu and Zhang 2008). After being dubbed into Mandarin in the early 1950s, the films also met Chinese rural audiences, many of whom nevertheless had trouble understanding even the films' basic "referential meaning"—such as telling which character was Lenin—making it necessary for projectionists to provide explanations during screenings ("Zuohao yingpian" 1953). As Sino-Soviet relations soured by the end of the 1950s, however, the number of new Soviet films imported into China dropped dramatically, and those screened in the 1960s tended to be Stalinist classics. Ironically, as Tina Mai Chen (2004) writes, "many of the same films shown in the 1950s under the byline 'The Soviet Union Is China's Tomorrow' now functioned to inspire self-sacrifice for the revolution" as well as "struggle against revisionism" (104).

During the Cultural Revolution decade, *Lenin in 1918* and *Lenin in October* became the only Soviet feature films openly and repeatedly screened in China starting in 1969 (Chen 1994, 155). The films became so ingrained in the public imagination that many lines became everyday speech. Instead of expressing the films' explicit messages, audiences playfully quoted film dialogue to attribute to them new extrinsic meanings. For example, the line "there will be bread" in the film refers to pre-revolutionary hardship and post-revolutionary bounty, but repeating the phrase in 1970s China became a wry commentary on the economic austerity of the post-revolutionary age and the eternal postponement of a fulfilling everyday life. Familiarity with the Lenin biopics also facilitated mockery and appropriation, as demonstrated in Jiang Wen's film *In the Heat of the Sun* (1994). During an open-air screening of *Lenin in 1918*, audiences off-screen shout in unison, "Careful, it's poison," before the camera tilts up to the screen where a villain utters the same line, provoking roaring laughter from the crowd. This is one clear instance where the exhibition and reception context radically transforms the meaning of the film text: from suspense into jadedness, from murder mystery into campy comedy.

Besides casual banter in more mundane contexts, the revolutionary heroism of these Lenin films also had an impact on their audiences. In the closing scenes of *Lenin in October*, for example, Lenin's speech to the proletariat masses with exaggerated gesticulations was especially memorable for Chinese orators, from middle school teachers to Red Guards, who imitated Lenin by putting their thumbs inside their vests while doing their own public speaking (Liu 2009; Lu 2008). Yet the favorite and most talked about scenes from *Lenin in 1918* were not about Lenin's heroism but a ballet performance of *Swan Lake* and an intimate exchange between Vasily and his wife. These erotically charged scenes conveyed important plot information and were thus never cut out of the film, but they were sometimes manually censored by the projectionists on orders from above. A military projectionist describes how he used his hands to "shield the lens to stop our soldiers from seeing the bare legs of ballet dancers or the kissing between Vasily and his wife. Every time I did this, audience members turned around and stared at me with resentment. As they imagined what was being blocked, sometimes I would open my fingers just a crack so that they could get a few glimpses of the forbidden images" (Wu 2001). Blocking out the images, then, could also have the opposite effect of enhancing their tantalizing eroticism, and even when audiences were denied the *sight* of the ballet, some rewatched *Lenin in 1918* again and again just to listen to Tchaikovsky's music (Li 2007, 2:182). It was also common for audiences who had already seen the film multiple times to leave the film in droves after the *Swan Lake* scene, and the noises of their flapping seats made quite a racket (Xie 1999, 441–2). Such "extradiegetic" noises and interruptions of the film-watching experience attributed rich extrinsic meanings to scenes that probably appeared unremarkable to Soviet audiences in the 1930s and to us watching them today.

Apart from deriving aesthetic or sensual pleasure from a revolutionary epic, Chinese audiences also "sinified" *Lenin in 1918* by assimilating it into local folk culture. Writer Mo Yan saw *Lenin in 1918* in his native village for the first time at the age of 16, and readily adapted it into a work of the Shandong folk opera Maoqiang: "Mr. Lenin faces an emergency. He dispatches people to find Vasily. There's food shortage in the city. Go get some food from the country" ("Mo Yan" 2012). More recently in 2011, the popular *xiangsheng* (comedic cross talk between two performers) master Guo Degang tapped into the collective memory of the film with a piece also called *Lenin in 1918*, which describes the plight of traditional Ping opera performers during the Cultural Revolution who "translated" highlights from the movie into a Ping aria to farcical effect.

Screened in China throughout the Cold War era, these Lenin biopics made in the Stalin era took on different connotations over time for their Chinese audiences: from a model for China's future to an object of campy nostalgia, from a glimpse of Western culture to an oft-repeated folktale subject, to indigenous adaptations. But whereas Soviet films constituted 49% of all translated cinema in the Seventeen Year Period (1949–66), North Korean films came to dominate Chinese screens from the early to the mid-1970s.

North Korean Melodrama and Chinese Catharsis

Whereas the Lenin biopics took on extrinsic meanings of humor, irony, and eroticism through repeated screenings over four decades, the release of North Korean films in China during the Cultural Revolution occasioned the emancipation of long repressed emotions. Of the 48 films Changchun Film Studios dubbed from 1966 to 1976, a total of 24 were from North Korea and consisted of "revolutionary films, films about constructing a new society, and anti-espionage thrillers" (Tan 2014, 61). Regardless of subject matter, North Korean films, with their vivid and expressive palette of emotions, filled a major affective and aesthetic gap in Chinese cinema at the time. Melodramas in the classical sense of *melos* (music) plus drama, these films might be considered in terms of what Linda Williams (1991) calls the "body genre," that is, a type of film that produces excessive and mimetic bodily sensations from audiences (2–13).

The best-known North Korean film to Chinese audiences and the most sensational film release of the 1970s was the musical melodrama *The Flower Girl*. As stated in the opening credits, the film is an adaptation of an opera script written by Kim Il-sung in the 1930s, and its production was overseen by Kim Jong-il (Kim 2016, 171–89). Set during Japanese colonization, the "flower girl" Kkot-bun sells flowers on the street to help her sick, dying mother and her younger sister, blinded by the landlord's wife. The landowner has killed her father, and Kkot-bun's only hope is the return of her imprisoned revolutionary brother. The heroine in *The Flower Girl* became an iconic figure pictured on North Korean currency and a model of emulation for North Korean farmers and factory workers (Martin 2004, 272), but not even Kim Jong-il could have anticipated the sensation the film was to become in China.

The Flower Girl was made in widescreen format, which, according to Kim Jong-il, allows fewer transitions between shots and longer duration of shots to depict the psychological and emotional development of characters (Yi 2003, 163–4). To accommodate this new aspect ratio, cinemas and projection units throughout China broadened their screens and installed widescreen lenses, further enhancing the film's aesthetic appeal and hype (Beijingshi wenhuaju 1996, 138–9; Lou 2016). Overcrowding incidents at screenings of *The Flower Girl* were reported throughout the country, often with fatalities. For example, an army unit stationed in Jiangjin got hold of a print of the film around Chinese New Year in 1973 and wanted to show it to its rank-and-file soldiers, but tens of thousands of local civilians who heard about *The Flower Girl* tried to enter the drilling ground where the film was being screened. After a wall collapsed, a stampede followed and ended with 15 deaths and many wounded (Luo 2002).

What made *The Flower Girl* such a *sensation* in 1970s China? Here I use "sensation" to refer both to the passionate crowds that flocked to this film and to the feeling of "overwhelming pathos in the weepie" (Williams 1991). As Ben Singer (2001) explicates, "melodramatic excess is a question of the body, of physical responses. The term tearjerker underscores the idea that powerful sentiment is in fact a physical sensation" (40). There are many exaggerated stories about the tears Chinese audiences shed for *The Flower Girl*. In Northeastern areas, it was said that women's tears turned into icicles (Li 2007, 3:13). Some recalled fellow audiences jumping up from their seats in tearful rage and waving their fists at the villain onscreen (Zhou 2007, 159). According to another viewer, the storm of emotions made her collapse on the ground, so that the morning after, her swollen eyes convinced all her friends that she had watched a great, bitter movie (Wang 2014, 67).

Why did Chinese audiences cry? Following explicit meanings in the film's song lyrics, the politically correct interpretation that schoolchildren wrote in essays was that the film reinforced a sense of international class solidarity: "The Korean people, like the Chinese people, are full of class revenge and national rancor. Crows all over the world are equally black"; "All over the world, the poor help the poor" (Beifangzhiyin 2016). Yet there was also a performative aspect to the shedding of tears for *The Flower Girl*: a Beijing viewer recalled that whoever did *not* cry at the movie was considered lacking in political consciousness, and that a neighbor of her watched it nine times and shed theatrical tears of class sympathy and outrage every time (Jing 2009, 89). Writer Mo Yan (2010) offers another interpretation of Chinese people's tears in the 1970s in response to a film "with so mediocre and formulaic a plot in hindsight": "For a very long time, people had not only lost their bodily freedom, but also their emotional freedom... The only Chinese films screened were model revolutionary works that were empty, didactic, otherworldly, and emotionless." By contrast, *The Flower Girl*'s lyrical and melancholic music, vibrant colors, a beautiful girl's desolate plight, and the "grand reunion" ending helped to "fill an emotional void of the Chinese people" and became an "outlet of their catharsis." In conclusion, Mo Yan wrote, "We were not crying for the Flower Girl. We were crying for ourselves" (220–4). The memories of many Chinese audiences support Mo Yan's views. A blogger put it bluntly: "The flower girl had a bitter fate? But my mother's fate is even more bitter" (Laomalasong 2013). Another viewer cried for a whole week after watching *The Flower Girl* because of her "shared plight" with the heroine: her own mother died when she was a child, and her father was imprisoned as a counterrevolutionary, leaving her and her siblings to look after themselves (Li 2007, 1:166–7). A former sent-down youth speculated that if the camera had turned to Chinese families who were poor, sick, or oppressed at the time, it would have found many tales even more tragic. Moreover, it was not possible to sell flowers—at once a "bourgeois good" and "capitalist venture"—in the Cultural Revolution (Wusi adu2 2016). "Translating" *The Flower Girl* into the early 1970s Chinese context, these audience members found even greater pathos in differences than similarities.

In addition to its cathartic effect, *The Flower Girl* appealed to Chinese audiences for aesthetic reasons. Many remembered the beauty of its songs, which had circulated beyond the film via radio and printed song books, whereas some others, such as my mother, appreciated its vivid colors and widescreen format; she even tried painting various shots from the film while attending an art college for "workers, peasants, and soldiers." Finding *The Flower Girl* less than impressive upon rewatching it in 2018, she reflected on the dearth of art books and other reproductions of masterpieces in the 1970s, a scarcity that turned films into an important resource for students of visual art, who often drew or painted film shots to hone their sketching skills and visual memory (Wang 2018).

Another kind of creative reproduction of *The Flower Girl* is fictionalized in Dai Sijie's autobiographical novel and film *Balzac and the Little Chinese Seamstress* (2002), in which a mountain village leader dispatches two sent-down youths to watch *The Flower Girl* in town and then retell the film to the rest of the village. Their ingenious storytelling, furnished with alternative details from European novels they have read, mesmerizes their listeners. Later, a village girl goes to see *The Flower Girl* and finds the "oral cinema show" to be much better. Her disappointment with the actual film speaks to the disjunction between Mao era's film texts, which may seem dull to today's audiences, and the enchanted cinematic memories of the period, indebted to the imaginations of the films' historical audiences. In other words, it is Chinese audience's "translation" of the North Korean films into the diversity and austerity of their own lives that turned them into such influential classics.

Albanian Cinema and Bourgeois Aesthetics

Alongside North Korea, Albania was one of China's only allies after the Sino-Soviet split and dubbed a "socialist bright lamp in Europe." From 1956 to 1977, a total of 28 Albanian films were translated and released in China (Tan 2014, 61–5), most of them featuring anti-fascist fighters during WWII and thus akin to Chinese revolutionary cinema about guerrilla resistance. Yet their attraction to 1970s Chinese audiences often lay more with their "bourgeois" sentiments and aesthetics—objects of criticism during the Cultural Revolution.

In particular, many young Chinese audiences received a sentimental education from the 1967 film *Victory over Death* (first released in China in 1969). Based on a true story from 1944, *Victory over Death* features two young female resistance fighters imprisoned and tortured by the Gestapo; rather than betray their comrades, the heroines walk unflinchingly to their deaths. Interspersed between their arrest and execution are nine flashbacks, mostly depicting one of the female fighters' memories of middle school days and a chaste romance with a guerrilla leader. In the film's most famous scene, she and her lover sing a melancholic song accompanied by his guitar: "Let's go up the mountain, warriors. Let's join the guerrillas this spring...." The revolutionary message in the lyric dissolves in the young man's grainy baritone voice and the slow leaning of the heroine's head on his shoulder. The guitar, once considered a "bourgeois" and "hooligan" instrument at the start of the Cultural Revolution, regained legitimacy and popularity through this film (Wang 2012). Furthermore, this film's release in China coincided with the sent-down youth movement to "go up the mountain and down to the countryside," and so the song lyrics also found special resonance with this cohort (Liu 2002, 198–9).

Long after the Cultural Revolution was over, *Victory over Death* remained so popular that Chinatown video store owners in California recall renting out the film on VHS and DVD well into the 2000s (Longo 2016). In Xiao Jiang's 2005 film *Electric Shadows*, the female protagonist and cinephile goes into premature labor during an open-air screening of *Victory Over Death*, which inspires her to stand up for herself and stay in town despite the disappearance of her lover. Despite its somewhat contrived plotting, *Electric Shadows* does resonate with other memoirs that consider the courageous heroine in the Albanian film an inspiring idol for young women and men alike in 1970s China (Cheng 2012, 135–45).

As for the reputation of Albanian films in 1970s China as "strange and bizarre," "headless and tailless," or "going back and forth," this referred to their nonlinear narrative structure and emphasis on visual storytelling. The film that confused a generation of Chinese was Viktor Gjika's *The Eighth Is Bronze* (released in Albania in 1970, and in China in 1973). Set in Nazi-occupied Albania between 1943 and 1944, the film shows the flashbacks of seven guerrillas carrying the statue of their deceased comrade. The *Rashomon*-like structure perplexed many Chinese viewers used to classical, clear, and didactic revolutionary narratives. Poet Yi Sha recalls it as a "war film from my childhood, but... had no idea who was fighting against whom" (as quoted in Zhao 1997: 80). Some audiences even speculated that the censors had cut out so many parts that the film no longer made sense. To borrow Roland Barthes' (1974) terminology, this film is not a "readerly text" that invites a narrow interpretation, but rather a "writerly text" that resists closure and coherence. When Chinese audiences were awash in propaganda films that imposed singular interpretations, encountering such a polysemic and ambiguous film such as *The Eighth Is Bronze* could be as baffling as it was refreshing. In hindsight, various audience members recalled the film as their first exposure to modernism, structuralism, and stream-of-consciousness (Chao 2017).

Even if viewers failed to comprehend a film's plot or characters, they still had aesthetic takeaways. Shanghai writer Cheng Naishan (2004) notes that, soon after the screening of *The Eighth Is Bronze,* Shanghai women began knitting the protagonist's black-and-white wool coat (87–9). And according to a widely circulated urban legend, a Shanghai woman invited her hair stylist to watch the film eight times to perfect the curly long hairstyle of its heroine (Zhou & Wu 2008, 181). As Chris Berry and Zhang Shujuan (2013) argue, since the 1970s was a time when people made their own clothes, they could easily add individuated fashionable touches after having a bit of inspiration. Likewise, a former audience member who had watched *Victory over Death* many times in the 1970s, recalled being most impressed by establishing shots of the protagonist's house with its elegant furniture, lamps, and other accouterments, because her own family was living at the time in a factory dormitory in Sichuan, with few things inside its four walls (Li 2016).

In 2017, the director of Albania's state-funded Institute for Communist Crimes planned to initiate legislation outlawing television broadcasts of communist-era films, calling them "a massive brainwashing tool" and "an ethical and aesthetic catastrophe" for the younger generation (Tsui 2017). He was clearly unaware that, for millions of Chinese audiences during the Cultural Revolution, these communist films from Albania were the very antithesis of propaganda and served as the most important window to Western sentiments and aesthetics—from romantic expressions to cinematic modernism, from guitar music to permed hairdos and "petit bourgeois" home décor.

Indian Film *Awara* and Evolving Chinese Resonances

In contrast to the many Soviet, North Korean, and Albanian films screened in socialist China, only eight Indian films were imported, translated, and released in the Mao era. Of these, *Awara* had immense emotional, intellectual, and aesthetic reverberations that lasted from the 1950s to the 1980s. Part of a broader cultural diplomacy between China and India, *Awara* was one of three feature films screened in the Indian Film Week of 1955, and a delegation of Indian filmmakers, including director and star Raj Kapoor, visited China at the same time. In a special issue of the Chinese magazine *Popular Cinema* in 1955, Kapoor wrote: "*Awara* is our small contribution to the creation of a good society that does not produce 'vagabonds'; I hope that the audience in China, rapidly advancing to a perfect socialist society, even though you do not need the revelations presented in the film, will nevertheless appreciate the main content and the moving conflict in the film" (as quoted in Van Fleit Hang 2013, 146). Indeed, both the Indian filmmakers and Chinese audiences assumed in 1955 that a "liberated China" had already solved the problems represented in the film, which were attributed to capitalist exploitation. Along these lines, Van Fleit Hang's (2013) study of the Chinese reception of *Awara* considers it a leftist text "that depicted a fellow third world nation also engaged in constructing an alternative to the western experience of modernity" (141–6). After contextualizing the import of Indian cinema in terms of Sino-Indian relations in the mid-1950s, most of her article is devoted to a comparison of *Awara* to left-wing Shanghai cinema of the 1930s and 1940s, which also frequently featured urban poverty and vagabonds. To address *Awara*'s reception in China head-on, the following discussion will draw on more empirical sources and discuss the Indian film's evolving meanings in China, which went far beyond the anticipations of its producers.

Awara's first Chinese audiences were cultural bureaucrats who watched the film in censorship screenings and wrote articles to guide its reception in terms of "socialist brotherhood" (Cai 2006, 220). After being released in cinemas in 20 Chinese cities, *Awara* became a huge hit, especially among students and intellectuals. Its theme song, "Vagabond's Ballad," had a catchy refrain that caught on immediately throughout big cities, circulating via radio, gramophone records, and collective singing practices (Ding 2015, 181). The film also had fans among CCP leaders such as Hu Yaobang, who, according to his daughter, considered the film "profound and moving." Hu's daughter, in middle school at the time, recalled how her classmates learned many of *Awara*'s songs and sang them to the accompaniment of accordion (Hu 2011).

Yet *Awara*'s popularity raised some alarm among Chinese critics, who cited confessions from juvenile delinquents who imitated the film's hero (Yuan 1956) or argued that the Chinese version of the "Vagabond's Ballad" turned "a song of remorseful indictment into a frivolous and flirtatious tune" (Zai 1956). Although not immediately censored, the "Vagabond's Ballad" took on new extrinsic meanings with the changing Maoist political landscape. Poet Ai Qing, who first met his wife Gao Ying at a 1955 screening of *Awara*, was labeled a "Rightist" in 1957 and banished to Xinjiang in 1959. The couple heard "The Vagabond's Ballad" on the westward-bound train and reinterpreted it as a song of exile for the wrongly accused (Gao 2012, 77–9).

Although *Awara* was no longer in cinemas by the 1960s, memories of its tragic plot resonated anew with audiences who suffered as a result of their "bad class backgrounds." In the film, what haunts and ruins the protagonist's life is his birth father's conviction that "the son of a judge will be a judge; the son of a thief will be a thief." This motto bears uncanny resemblance to the later "bloodline theory" distilled into a notorious 1966 Red Guard couplet: "If the father's a hero, the son's a great fellow; If the father's a reactionary, the son's a rotten egg" (Hu 2012). Yu Luoke, a young Beijing worker whose influential essays critiqued the bloodline theory in 1967, once recounted *Awara*'s plot to his younger brothers and sisters and added: "Who could have thought that such an absurd viewpoint, long criticized in foreign countries, is gaining ground in China today?" (Yu 2016, 43) For his heterodoxy, Yu Luoke was arrested and executed in 1968.

After the Cultural Revolution, *Awara* received a much wider rerelease in China, and one can hardly find any urban Chinese today over the age of 50 who has not seen this film. A 1978 comedic *xiangsheng* piece entitled "The Fate of the Vagabond" touches on various registers of the film's appeal: Performer A starts singing the theme song from *Awara* and encourages Performer B to dance along, telling him that "you have to move all your joints to Indian music so that it stimulates blood circulation, helps the muscles to relax, clears the mind, and helps digestion." Performer A then speaks of how the song made him think of his mother, who, like the protagonist's mother, was also a "victim of fascist dictatorship." Someone suspected and denounced her as a spy because she had a distant relative (her second aunt's mother-in-law's niece's husband's brother-in-law) in Taiwan. If it had not been for the fall of the Gang of Four, the *xiangsheng* goes on, the son would have been labeled "Little Spy" and been sentenced to at least 20 years of prison. No beautiful Rita (the protagonist's lover) would have waited for him, since their children would also be considered counterrevolutionaries following the bloodline theory (An 1979, 101–3). Such a hypothetical transplantation of the Indian film's plot into Chinese historical circumstances adds extrinsic meanings to the film that spoke to common injustices from the Cultural Revolution.

By the early 1980s, *Awara* became popular among a younger generation who grew their hair long or got it permed, wore bell bottom pants, and had the "Vagabond's Ballad" blasting from their cassette players. What resonated with this particular audience was the part about the protagonist looking for work, for the period saw many sent-down youths returning from the countryside and trying to find a place for themselves in urban society (Gold 1980, 757). The theme of vagabond youth also echoed through the works of celebrated filmmaker Jia Zhangke. His first feature film *Xiao Wu* (1997) centers on a thief who found innocence and redemption through romantic love, whereas his second film *Platform* (2000), an epic chronicle of a small-town performance troupe, pays explicit tribute to *Awara* by showing the young protagonists going on a double date to see the film around 1980. As the "Vagabond's Ballad" is shown onscreen, one young woman is pulled out of the cinema by her father, a policeman who does not want his daughter to go to the movies with a young man so much like the vagabond in the movie. Jia Zhangke emphasized the influence this Hindi film had on him at the 2016 Mumbai Film Festival: "I loved the Hindi film *Awara* as a child. Now I am also an 'awara' in the film world and shall continue to wander into the future" (as quoted in Hu 2016).

Conclusion

Jia Zhangke is not the only contemporary Chinese filmmaker to pay homage to foreign films that he had watched in his youth. As noted earlier, memories of many films discussed in this chapter are staged as meta-cinema in works such as Jiang Wen's *In the Heat of the Sun*, Dai Sijie's *Balzac and the Little Chinese Seamstress*, and Xiao Jiang's *Electric Shadows*. The frequent appearance of cinema itself in Chinese domestic features of the 1990s and 2000s serves as a kind of elegy for cinema not unlike the film-within-a-film structure in Italian cinema of the 1980s and 1990s, all "imbued with nostalgia for a lost golden age" (Parigi 2017, 513). In post-socialist China, foreign films have their own aesthetic afterlives in the creative responses of their audiences. Indeed, the original filmmakers could not have anticipated the diverse Chinese reception of their works, whose influences in China were sometimes broader, deeper, and more enduring than even in their countries of origin. If we recall Andrew Higson's (1989) call for "an exhibition-led, or consumption-based, approach to national cinema" (37), it would make good sense to include the reception of "translated" films in the study of *Chinese national cinema*.

Over the last two decades, the powerful paradigm of national cinema has been challenged through studies of transnational cinemas (Higbee & Lim 2010). But while attending to the crossing of national borders at the level of production and sometimes critical reception, few scholars have attempted to excavate how historical audiences encountered and made sense of foreign cinema beyond Hollywood. Methodologically, most scholarship has dealt with meaning-making at the level of intended meanings by the makers or with *our own* critical readings of film texts. By examining diverse extrinsic meanings attributed to films by audiences for whom the films were *not intended*, I have argued that cross-cultural exhibition and reception can transform the original meanings and add rich ambiguities to otherwise propagandistic film texts. Shifting from textual analyses and production histories to studies of exhibition and reception, I have experimented with an audience-centered methodology that broadens the field of what we call "Chinese cinema" to include "cinema in China" with all of its cosmopolitan connections.

The second intervention this chapter makes is to challenge the conventional wisdom that regards Maoist China—especially the Cultural Revolution decade—as isolationist and disconnected from the rest of the world. Analyzing literary exchanges and influences between the PRC and other socialist countries, Nicolai Volland (2017) defines "socialist cosmopolitanism" as "a set of attitudes and practices that appreciates a shared yet diverse socialist culture and promotes transnational circulation across the socialist world." Socialist cosmopolitanism, as conceived by Volland, is characterized by "valorization of the collective," the "reconciliation of the transnational and national," and a counterhegemonic "egalitarianism" (12–4). In the cinematic universe, the transnational circulation of films from China's "socialist brothers" also shared utopian models and represented class struggle, but Chinese audiences often appreciated foreign films precisely for their *differences* from the domestic fare, be it humor or pathos, romance or adventure, eroticism or exoticism. These audiences share the memory of a Spartan cultural life: either having no films to watch for months on end, or watching the same films over and over again. The repetition made them pay attention to formal elements—what Kristin Thompson (1977) calls "cinematic excess"—that had little to do with the films' intended ideological messages. Audience engagement with these films evolved from repetition and mimicry to appropriation and parody. Rather than being passively "brainwashed," audiences actively, creatively, and sometimes subversively poached everyday witticisms, political lessons, emotional catharsis, fashion tips, and hidden pleasures from these ostensibly didactic texts. These films thus constituted the unintended cultural canon anchoring the structure of feelings and collective memories of several generations.

Finally, the rejection of Hollywood and the import of foreign films as a part of China's cultural diplomacy created a special historical media ecology that introduced ordinary urban Chinese audiences to various films from the "Second" and "Third" Worlds. This alternative distribution network of "socialist cosmopolitanism," complemented with the state-sponsored dubbing of foreign films and expansion of projection units into industrial and rural areas, made it possible for national cinemas as "unknown" and "minor" as North Korean and Albanian cinema to find a mainstream, even mass audience in China. In this connection, I would like to close this essay with a thoughtful comment comparing cinema-going in the Cold War era to the media ecology of today's China. Digging out an old notebook that recorded all the movies he watched in 1962, Shanghai cinephile Ye Zhiguang wrote in 2011:

> My family should be considered ordinary working class, with all six of us living from my father's 80 yuan monthly salary.... In 1962, I watched 125 films, about one film every three days, [of which] 91 films (or 72%) were foreign movies from the Soviet Union, Czechoslovakia, Hungary, Poland, Romania, Bulgaria, East Germany, England, France, West Germany, Spain, Norway, Finland, Argentina, Colombia, Mexico, Korea, Cambodia, Thailand, and Egypt....

> [Let us compare all those choices to] today's ever more luxurious environment, ever bigger screens, ever more advanced technology, ever louder and flashier publicity, and ever more astronomical figures in the remuneration of stars. Yet audiences eating popcorn and sipping Coke face these pale, anemic films. Is this progress or retrogress? Are we living in the best of times or worst of times?

Acknowledgments

This chapter is a revised version of "Gained in Translation: The Reception of Foreign Cinema in Mao's China" published in *Journal of Chinese Cinemas* 13 (1) (2019): 61–75. Many thanks to the journal's editors for their feedback and for the reprint permission.

Works Cited

An, Guchen. 1979. "Liulangzhe de mingyun" (Fate of the vagabond). In *Quyi zhuanji* (Special Collection of Folk Performance Art), edited by Dalian Worker Palace. Dalian: Dalian Worker Palace.

Barthes, Roland. 1974. *S/Z*. Trans. Richard Miller. New York: Hill and Wang.

Beifangzhiyin. 2016. "Chongdu dianying *Maihua guniang*" (Re-reading the film *The Flower Girl*). *Xinlang boke*. http://blog.sina.com.cn/s/blog_ebbb2c060102vzxy.html.

Beijingshi wenhuaju (Beijing Cultural Bureau). 1996. *Beijing shi dianying faxing fangying danwei shi* (History of Film Distribution and Exhibition in Beijing). Beijing: Beijing Cultural Bureau.

Berry, Chris, and Zhang Shujuan. 2013. "Shanghai de dianying yu shishang: wenge shijian shenme (bu) neng chuan" (Film and fashion in Shanghai: what (not) to wear during the cultural revolution). *Yishu Guandian* (ACT Magazine), no. 54: 46–63.

Bordwell, David. 1991. *Making Meaning: Inference and Rhetoric in the Interpretation of Cinema*. Cambridge, MA: Harvard University Press.

Cai Chusheng. 2006. "Wei youyi yu heping huanhu—huanying yindu dianying zhou de juxing he yindu dianying gongzuozhe de guanglin" (Hurray for friendship and peace—welcome for the Indian Film Week and the arrival of Indian film workers). In *Cai Chusheng wenji* (Collected Works of Cai Chusheng). Vol. 2. Beijing: Zhongguo guangbo dianshi chubanshe.

Chao, Yuanyuan. 2017. Personal Interview. April 6, 2017.

Chen, Huan, ed. 1994. *Jilin dianying faxing fangying jishi 1907–1992* (Jilin Film Distribution and Exhibition Chronicles, 1907–1992). Changchun: Jilin Film Distribution and Exhibition Company.

Chen, Tina Mai. 2009. "International Film Circuits and Global Imaginaries in the People's Republic of China, 1949–57." *Journal of Chinese Cinemas* 3 (2): 149–61.

Chen, Tina Mai. 2004. "Internationalism and Cultural Experience: Soviet Films and popular Chinese understandings of the future in the 1950s." *Cultural Critique* 58 (1): 82–114.

Cheng, Naishan. 2004. *Haishang sakesifeng* (Shanghai Saxophone). Shanghai: Wenhui Press.
Cheng, Xiaoyin. 2012. *Yu qingchun youguan de nvren* (Women of My Youth). Shanghai: Wenhui Press.
Dai Sijie. 2002. *Balzac and the Little Chinese Seamstress*. New York: Random House.
Ding Yaping. 2015. "Kua wenming xiangyu: cong Yindu dianying dao Zhongguo dianying" (Encounter across civilizations: from Indian cinema to Chinese cinema). In *Tan Yunshan xianxiang yu 21 shiji zhongyin wenhua jialiu* (Tan Yunshan Phenomenon and Sino-Indian Cultural Exchange in the 21st Century), edited by Niu Genfu, 147–54. Beijing: Wenhua yishu chubanshe.
Du, Weijia. 2015. "Beyond the Ideology Principle: the Two Faces of Dubbed Foreign Films in PRC, 1949–1966." *Journal of Chinese Cinemas* 9 (2): 141–58.
Fiske, John. 1986. "Television: Polysemy and Popularity." *Critical Studies in Media Communication* 3 (4): 391–408.
Gao, Ying. 2012. *Wo he Ai Qing* (Ai Qing and I). Beijing: Renmin wenxue.
Gold, Tom. 1980. "Back to the City: The Return of Shanghai's Educated Youth." *The China Quarterly* 84: 755–70.
Hansen, Miriam. 1991. *Babel and Babylon: Spectatorship in American Silent Film*. Cambridge, MA: Harvard University Press.
Higbee, Will, and Song Hwee Lim. 2010. "Concepts of Transnational Cinema: Towards a Critical Transnationalism in Film Studies." *Transnational Cinemas* 1 (1): 7–21.
Higson, Andrew. 1989. "The Concept of National Cinema." *Screen* 30 (4): 36–47.
Hu, Deping. 2011. "Fuqin de yisheng hen zhi" (Father's life was very worthwhile). *Nanfang renwu zhoukan* (Southern People Weekly), April 29, 2011. http://news.sina.com.cn/c/sd/2011-04-29/114522381400_2.shtml.
Hu, Jian. 2016. "Jia Zhangke huo yindu mengmai guoji dianying jie jiechu yishu chengjiu jiang" (Jia Zhangke wins excellence in cinema award at Mumbai International Film Festival). *China News Net*. www.chinanews.com/yl/2016/10-21/8039491.shtml.
Hu, Wenqi. 2012. "Dianying *Liulangzhe* guanhougan" (Reflections after watching *Awara*). *Xinlang boke*, June 7, 2012. http://blog.sina.com.cn/s/blog_5fe93b290102dxkx.html?tj=1.
Huang, Xuelei. 2014. "The Heroic and the Banal: Consuming Soviet Movies in Pre-Socialist China, 1920s–1940s." *Twentieth-Century China* 39 (2): 93–117.
Jing, Fang. 2009. "Woshi liulinghou" (I was born in the Sixties). *Duku* 0901.
Kim, Jong Il. 2016. *Kim Chŏng-il chŏnjip* (The Works of Kim Jong Il). Vol. 15. Pyongyang: Chosŏn Rodongdang Ch'ulp'ansa.
Kuhn, Annette. 2002. *An Everyday Magic: Cinema and Cultural Memory*. London: IB Tauris.
Laomalasong. 2013. "*Maihua guniang* ye wu qing" (*The Flower Girl* elicits no feelings). *Hunan zhiqing wang*, November 1, 2013. http://2013.hnzqw.com/forum.php?mod=viewthread&action=printable&tid=75517.
Li, Aidong, ed. 2007. *Dianying: Women gongtong de jiyi* (Cinema: Our Common Memory). 3 vols. Beijing: Zhongguo dianying chubanshe. [Chongzhou Literary and Historical Materials].

Li, Rong. 2016. Personal Interview. November 10, 2016.
Liu, Hai. 2009. *Qingchun wuzhu* (Derelict Youth). Beijing: *Renmin ribao chubanshe.*
Liu, Jialing. 2002. *Jiyi xianhong* (Vivid Red Memories). Beijing: Zhongguo qingnian chubanshe.
Longo, Regina M. 2016. "The Albanian Cinema Project: Saving and Projecting Albanian Film Heritage for Global Audiences." *KinoKultura*, Special Issue 16. www.kinokultura.com/specials/16/longo.shtml.
Lou, Weihua. 2016. Personal Interview. November 17, 2016.
Lu, Gusun. 2008. "Wenge zhong kan dianying" (Watching Movies in the Cultural Revolution). *Nanfang zhoumo* (Southern Weekend), October 15, 2008. www.infzm.com/content/18469.
Luo, Xuepeng. 2002. "*Maihua guniang* yu shiwu tiao Zhongguo ren de shengming" (*The Flower Girl* and the lives of fifteen Chinese). Originally a blogpost on CND, archived at http://mjlsh.usc.cuhk.edu.hk/Book.aspx?cid=4&tid=3455.
Ma, Ran. 2016. "A Genealogy of Film Festivals in the People's Republic of China: 'Film Weeks' during the 'Seventeen Years' (1949–1966)." *New Review of Film and Television Studies* 14 (1): 40–58.
Martin, Bradley K. 2004. *Under the Loving Care of the Fatherly Leader: North Korea and the Kim Dynasty*. 1st ed. New York: Thomas Dunne Books.
Mo, Yan. 2010. "Kan *maihua guniang*" (Watching *The Flower Girl*). In *Sanwen xinbian* (New Collection of Essays). Beijing: Wenhua yishu chubanshe.
"Mo Yan: Wo meiyou xiangguo ziji youzhaoyiri hui gen dianying fasheng guanxi" (Mo Yan: I didn't think I would have anything to do with movies), 2012. *Fenghuang Wang* (Phoneix Web), October 11, 2012. http://culture.ifeng.com/huodong/special/2012nuobeierwenxuejiang/moyan/detail_2012_10/11/18166386_0.shtml.
Nugent, Frank S. 1939. "The Russians Continue Their Biography of a Revolutionist with 'Lenin in 1918' at the Cameo." *The New York Times*, June 27.
Parigi, Stefania. 2017. "The Screen in the Mirror: Thematic and Textual Reflexivity in Italian Cinema." In *A Companion to Italian Cinema*, edited by Frank Burke, 512–30. Chichester: John Wiley & Sons.
Pickowicz, Paul G., and Matthew Johnson, eds. 2009. *Journal of Chinese Cinemas* 3 (2). Special issue on "Exhibiting Chinese Cinemas."
Reinhard, Carrie Lynn D., and Christopher J. Olson, eds. 2016. *Making Sense of Cinema: Empirical Studies into Film Spectators and Spectatorship*. New York: Bloomsbury Publishing.
Rushdie, Salman. 1991. *Imaginary Homelands*. London: Granta/Viking.
Singer, Ben. 2001. *Melodrama and Modernity. Early Sensational Cinema and Its Contexts*. New York: Columbia University Press.
Stacey, Jackie. 1994. *Star Gazing: Hollywood Cinema and Female Spectatorship*. New York: Routledge.
Staiger, Janet. 1992. *Interpreting Films: Studies in the Historical Reception of American Cinema*. Princeton, NJ: Princeton University Press.
Tan, Hui. 2014. *Zhongguo yizhi dianying shi* (History of Translated Cinema in China). Beijing: Zhongguo dianying chubanshe.
Thompson, Kristin. 1977. "The Concept of Cinematic Excess." *Cine-Tracts* 1 (2): 54–63.

Tsivian, Yuri. 1994. *Early Cinema in Russia and Its Cultural Reception*. New York: Routledge.

Tsui, Clarence. 2017. "Why Albanian Films Are Big in China: Cultural Revolution Nostalgia." *South China Morning Post*, March 24, 2017.

Van Fleit Hang, Krista. 2013. "'The Law Has No Conscience': The Cultural Construction of Justice and the Reception of *Awara* in China." *Asian Cinema* 24 (2): 141–59.

Volland, Nicolai. 2017. *Socialist Cosmopolitanism: The Chinese Literary Universe 1945–1965*. New York: Columbia University Press.

Wang, Erliu. 2012. "Hebin dianyingyuan" (Hebin cinema). In *Guiyang wenshi* (Guiyang Literature and History), no. 1: 18–9.

Wang, Lichun. 2014. "Dadi dianyingyuan" (Big earth cinema). *Haiyan* (June): 64–9.

Wang, Yaqing. 2018. Personal Interview. January 20, 2018.

Williams, Linda. 1991. "Film Bodies: Gender, Genre, and Excess." *Film Quarterly* 44 (4): 2–13.

Wu, Hehu. 2001. "Liening zai yijiuyiba: zhifeng jian de dianying" (*Lenin in 1918*: movie between the fingers). http://culture.163.com/edit/010221/010221_46500.html.

Wu, Zhuqing, and Zhang Dai. 2008. *Zhongguo dianying de fengbei: Yan'an dianying tuan de gushi* (Monument of Chinese Cinema: Story of the Yan'an Film Group). Beijing: Renmin University Press.

Wusi adu2. 2016. "Dianying maihua guniang" (The film *The Flower Girl*). *Shanghai zhiqing wang*. www.shnczq.org/bbs-detail.php?bbsid=21&id=45889.

Xiao, Zhiwei. 2010. "American Films in China Prior to 1950." In *Art, Politics, and Commerce in Chinese Cinema*, edited by Ying Zhu and Stanley Rosen, 54–69. Hong Kong: Hong Kong University Press.

Xiao, Zhiwei. 2004. "The Expulsion of American Films from China, 1949–1950." *Twentieth-Century China* 30 (1): 64–81

Xie Chunchi, ed. 1999. *Gaosu houdai: Xiamen laosanjie zhiqing ren jishi* (For Posterity: Documenting the Lives of Xiamen's Sent-down Youths). Xiamen: Xiamen University Press.

Xu, Lanjun. 2017. "The Southern Film Corporation, Opera Films, and the PRC's Cultural Diplomacy in Cold War Asia." *Modern Chinese Literature and Culture* 29 (1): 239–282.

Ye, Zhiguang. 2011. "1962 nian: yige Shanghai yingmi de meihao shidai" (1962: a Shanghai cinephile's golden age). *Dongfang zaobao* (Oriental Morning Post). http://news.mtime.com/2011/02/23/1451796-2.html.

Yi, Yang-il. 2003. *Yŏnghwa ch'waryŏng* (Filmmaking). Pyongyang: Munhak Yesul Chonghap Ch'ulp'ansa.

Yu, Luowen. 2016. *Wojia: wo de gege Yu Luoke* (My Family: My Brother Yu Luoke). New York: World Chinese Publishing. ASHION.

Yuan, Shuipai. 1956. "Dianying gequ qingnian" ["Film, song, youth"]. *Renmin ribao*, December 27, 1956.

Zai, Yaomu. 1956. "'Daochu liulang' taiduo le!" (Too much 'wandering everywhere'). *Jiefang ribao*, November 8, 1956.

Zhang, Wei. 2009. *Tan ying xiao ji—Zhongguo xiandai yingtan de chenfeng yi yu* (Chats about Cinema—A Dusty Nook of the Modern Chinese Film World). Taipei: Xiuwei.

Zhao, Ning. 1997. *Qingrenjie de wuhui* (Dancing on Valentine's Day). Beijing: Zuojia chubanshe.

Zhou, Haibo. 2007. *Yongyuan de xiangshou* (Eternal Company). Haikou: Hainan Press.

Zhou, Shifen, and Wu Xiangdong. 2008. *Ningbo lao qiangmen* (Ningbo's old city gate). Ningbo: Ningbo Publishing House.

"Zuohao yingpian de xuanchuan jieshi gongzuo—duzhe laixin zongshu" (Take care to publicize and explain films—a summary of letters from readers). 1953. *Renmin ribao*, January 16, 1953.

4 Contested Chineseness and *Third Sister Liu* in Singapore and Hong Kong

Folk Songs, Landscape, and Cold War Politics in Asia

Lanjun Xu

In the early 1960s, there was a fever over Su Li's film *Third Sister Liu* (*Liu Sanjie*, 1961) in Singapore. With its focus on peasants' lives, its use of folk songs, and its beautiful scenery, the film became an instant sensation. It was continually screened in theaters for more than seven months, shattering all box-office records in Singapore during that time (Zhou 2014, 51). This chapter examines the circulation and reception of the *Third Sister Liu* phenomenon in Sinophonic communities of the 1960s by focusing on three films: *Third Sister Liu* and two of its adaptations, namely, Luo Zhen's *The Shepherd Girl* (*Shange lian*, 1963) and Yuan Qiufeng's *The Songfest* (*Shange yinyuan*, 1964). Based on recently declassified archival materials, oral histories, film studio records, press coverage, and government documents, this study first takes a close look at the fever over *Third Sister Liu* in Singapore and examines its relation with the period's radical political movements of laborers in Singapore, the issues surrounding identity politics among diasporic Chinese communities, and the transregional flow of leftist cultures and emotions between China and the Nanyang region.

Combining textual analysis and archival research, the second part of my paper compares the three films' uses of folk songs, crowds (especially in the group singing contests), love and romance, and landscape and asks the following questions: unlike *Third Sister Liu,* which was made and shot in mainland China, *The Shepherd Girl* was shot in Hong Kong and *The Songfest* was a Hong Kong production shot on location in Taiwan; how did the landscape and folk songs become politically contested elements in representing Chinesesness in the 1950s and 1960s? Did the political polarization of Cold War China clearly differentiate the two Hong Kong films from the mainland version, or were the boundaries between them more fluid and ambiguous? Generally speaking, in exploring the circulation and local reception of *Third Sister Liu* and its adaptations in Singapore and Hong Kong, my study treats the films as a Cold War structure of feeling and investigates how a sentimental narrative mode like the musical was closely intertwined with the local politics of decolonization in Southeast Asia, with the cultural diplomacy of the People's Republic of China (PRC), and with the transregional cultural nexus between Communist China and the diasporic Chinese communities in Cold War Asia.

Third Sister Liu and Anti-colonial Movements in Singapore

"The Shanghai-Hong Kong nexus" described by Poshek Fu (2003) continued to influence the filmic and other cultural connections between mainland China, Hong Kong, and the Nanyang region in the 1950s and 1960s. As I discuss in a separate article, the PRC adapted numerous local operas into films in the 1950s, which it exported throughout Asia and into Western countries in the hope of promoting friendship among neighboring nations and blurring the boundaries of the bamboo curtain. These opera films played a particularly significant role in overseas Chinese communities, especially those in Hong Kong and Southeast Asia. They could be imported more readily and find a warmer reception because of their seemingly apolitical themes, often adapted from traditional folklore. And as Lydia Liu (2003) suggests, these films could be considered as one part of "official popular culture" in the Mao era, and the combination of folk materials and mass media may give rise to "unintended meanings capable of rendering the official ideology irrelevant" (571). More importantly, these opera films revolve mainly around romantic love stories of scholars and beauties and as such are in a sentimental mode that emphasizes the forging of bonds and the creation of solidarity among lovers and family (Xu 2017). In Christina Klein's (2003) words, such a sentimental mode, as a Cold War structure of feeling, "is [...] a universalizing mode that imagines the possibility of transcending particularity by recognizing a common and shared humanity" (14). At the same time, in the case of the PRC's opera films, these sentimental human connections are characterized by a localism that is rooted in shared dialects or kinship ties with the ancestral homeland in mainland China, especially the coastal south and east. Sang Hu's 1954 film *Liang Shanbo and Zhu Yingtai* (*Liang Shanbo yu Zhu Yingtai*; thereafter *Liang-Zhu*) is a good example. It was the first opera film from the PRC to be introduced into Hong Kong after 1949, and held the box office record among all PRC-made opera films shown in the then British colony. Communist China also successfully used this romantic and sad love story to change its masculine and military image in the global community. After the excellent reception given to *Liang-Zhu*, more opera films were imported from the mainland; so it can be said that the success of the former opened up a market for mainland films in Hong Kong (Shu 2005, 34). The PRC produced 121 opera films between 1953 and 1966, and 47 of them were distributed to Hong Kong via Southern Film

Corporation (Nanfang yingye youxian gongsi; thereafter SFC), which was one of the most important distributors of Chinese films to Southeast Asia in the 1950s and 1960s.

Together with the opera films, the musical is another genre that could be more easily disseminated to the overseas Chinese community; some good examples are Wang Jiayi's *Five Golden Flowers* (*Wuduo jinhua*, 1959) and *Third Sister Liu*. Different from the classic structure of the "scholar and beauty" romance in most opera films, *Third Sister Liu*, made by China's Changchun Film Studio (Changchun dianying zhipian chang) in 1960, tells the story of *Third Sister Liu*, a legendary folk singer of the Zhuang minority in Guangxi Autonomous Region. She loves ordinary people and despises her vicious landlord, who tries unsuccessfully to prohibit her from singing. The landlord kidnaps her, but Third Sister Liu later escapes with the help of her lover and others. In the end, she travels to other places to inspire the people with folk songs. *Third Sister Liu* was the first musical film in China to be categorized as a "scenic musical" (*fengguang yinyuepian*). It featured young and popular performers, 109 folk songs of the Guangxi Zhuang minority, and, not least, the beautiful scenery of Guangxi. These were three main attractions behind the film's popularity, especially since most of its audiences were overseas Chinese who could not return to China easily. The film could assuage their homesickness.[1] Before the film was shown in Singapore for the first time in July 1962, it had been screened in Hong Kong two months earlier. Probably seeing the popularity of the film in Hong Kong and Southeast Asia, Shaw Brothers became interested in the genre of mountain-song musical and made two adaptations: *The Shepherd Girl* and *The Songfest*. The two Hong Kong adaptations were released in Singapore in 1963 and 1964, respectively. Both in Hong Kong and Singapore, *Third Sister Liu* underwent a few rounds of screening. During its second round of screening in Hong Kong, *The Shepherd Girl* was also being shown in theaters. The two films claimed to be the "authentic mountain-song film" and had a stiff competition for audiences.

Third Sister Liu had two main rounds of screening in Singapore: one in 1962 and 1963, and the other in 1978.[2] This essay focuses mainly on the earlier round of release. Singapore's two main Chinese newspapers, *Nanyang Siang Pau* and *Sin Chew Daily*, documented the enthusiastic responses of viewers in Singapore. When the film was in theaters in Singapore, its songs were broadcast by radio stations, and serial picture stories also came out. For instance, Radio Rediffusion, a private British-owned company, broadcast a recording of the mountain songs from the film during prime time. Based on memoirs, some audience members even wrote down the songs one by one and memorized them (Zhou 2014, 49). Quite a number of people watched the film multiple—even more than ten—times. All this information testifies to the popularity of *Third Sister Liu* in Singapore.

With respect to the relationship between mainland Chinese films and local politics in Cold War Asia, *Third Sister Liu* in Singapore is a typical case. At first, the British colonial government blocked the film from being shown in Singapore. Only with the help of Lee Khoon Choy (1924–2016), who was an important leader of the ruling People's Action Party (PAP) at the time and also a member of the first five Parliaments of Singapore, was the import made possible.[3] Then three local intellectuals, who worked mainly in local newspapers, established a short-lived firm called the New Century Company (Xin shiji gongsi) in 1962, and used their media resources to advertise the film. After importing *Third Sister Liu* and one other Chinese film, the company closed down.

Wang Ruming, one of the three intellectuals who established the New Century Company, in a personal interview with the author in 2018, said that they imported *Third Sister Liu* mainly because it was a "healthy film" compared with the sexually suggestive Hollywood films of the time. The term "healthy film" was closely related to the Anti-Yellow Culture Movement (*fanhuang wenhua yundong*), which happened in Singapore in the period of 1953–61. In 1953, a young girl was raped in Singapore, which sparked a campaign against imported, degenerate forms of culture that were said to corrupt the individual and lead to declining public morals. The left-leaning Chinese community of Singapore blamed such imported culture, such as the increasingly popular and sexually suggestive Hollywood films, pornographic picture books, and erotic shows in amusement parks, as the evils of British colonialism and capitalism. *Third Sister Liu*, especially the folk songs in it, became the shared language of political activism in the transition from the colonial to the postcolonial, as different parties contended for votes through the mobilizing language of anti-colonialism. Films made by Hong Kong's leftist companies such as Great Wall (Changcheng) Movie Enterprise and Phoenix (Fenghuang) Film Corporation, or those imported from the PRC, were considered as "healthy films" and used as important cultural resources to articulate visions of a fresh and robust Malaya culture as well as to mobilize support from the populace. It is not accidental that the Anti-Yellow Culture Movement emerged at a moment in Singapore's history "when a plethora of postcolonial imaginings was [sic] in competition, and the most direct strategy to capture the ground was through arguments of cultural morality" (Lau 2016, vi).

In this understanding, it is perhaps also no coincidence that the popularity of *Third Sister Liu* between 1962 and 1963 paralleled a period in which the entire Singapore was debating the issues of merger and independence. As Jennifer Lindsay (2010) explains in her discussion of Singapore's 1963 Southeast Asia Cultural Festival, the period between 1962 and 1963 was a critical historical moment in Singapore. It was a transitional period from the colonial to the postcolonial. With its internal self-government created in June 1959, Singapore faced a major choice: to claim independence or to merge into the new Federation of Malaysia (232–3). Within the PAP, "fighting between the non-Communist leftists and pro-Communist leftists resulted in the pro-Communists breaking away [...] to form the Socialist Party" (Liu and Wong 2004, 154). Noticeably, both the PAP and the Socialist Front (i.e., the Socialist Party mentioned earlier) used *Third Sister Liu* for their political needs. The ruling PAP, which supported confederation with Malaysia, engaged in a harsh debate with the Socialist Front, which supported independence. When *Third Sister Liu* was first screened in Singapore on July 12, 1962, the major news on the front pages of local newspapers was the debate between the two parties about the merger or confederation with Malaysia. As indicated by news reports of the time, including a newspaper article entitled "The War on Publicity for Referendum Has Entered the Decisive Stage" (*Quanmin toupiao xuanchuan zhan kaishi jinru bairehua jieduan*) on *Wartawan* on August 24, 1962, the two parties were locked in a tight contest for grassroots support through propaganda campaigns. Both the PAP and the Socialist Front chose to hold free screenings of *Third Sister Liu* in order to attract those audiences from the labor class to join their events. The PAP, for instance, held a few screening receptions for *Third Sister Liu* together with other political documentaries, including *Malaysia Week* and *The Agreement of Malaysia,* to raise money for its activities (Figure 4.1). Lee Khoon Choy was often the chairperson of these events, which may explain why he helped the New Century Film Company import *Third Sister Liu* to Singapore. One important part of these film receptions was to introduce the PAP policies as well as their achievements to the audience. To a certain degree, fundraising was not the main reason for the receptions as one may expect; rather, the PAP wanted *Third Sister Liu* to attract more audiences for the two documentaries, thereby mobilizing them in

Figure 4.1 Third Sister Liu in Singapore (photo courtesy of Shu Don-lok).

support of the party's policies and decisions, especially with regard to the confederation with Malaysia.

In the film, the legend of Third Sister Liu was adapted to "express gender awareness and class struggle. The artists aroused popular memory of social hierarchy differences, and they developed a homogenized collective memory of class conflict and class struggle" (Chen 2016). As a result, Third Sister Liu is both a talented singer and a model revolutionary heroine standing against social inequality. Her singing is a powerful tool of class struggle. For most ordinary Chinese audiences in Singapore, in addition to the film's charming landscape of Guangxi, the star power of Huang Wanqiu, who plays Third Sister Liu in the film, as well as the beautifully recreated folk music, the class struggle between the poor peasants and the rich landlords in the film also appealed to them as it spoke to their concerns in real life. In the 1960s, the radical political movements of laborers in Singapore were at their peak. As some scholars point out,

> the labor movements in Singapore in the first two decades after the Second World War were closely linked to its Chinese community, although not all strikes were initiated and led by Chinese workers... [A]s the Chinese made up of 75 percent of the total population, one can appreciate the importance of the Chinese workers and Chinese unions in Singapore.
>
> (Liu and Wong 2004, 169)

The poor laborers considered the folk songs in *Third Sister Liu* a powerful tool to fight against social injustice and an effective way of relieving their anxiety. For instance, the leftist newspapers often published poems written in the format of a mountain song, as can be seen in this example:

> The machines make noises all day and drown our laughter and happiness; we work so hard until we bleed, but are still hungry, yet our bosses are growing fat.... Thanks to Liu Sanjie, after listening to her mountain songs, we feel much relieved. Braving the storms, we sing mountain songs. We keep on singing, till the sun shines on our land Singapore.
>
> (*Fanxing Bao*, August 1, 1962)

It is worth noting that in the film, Third Sister Liu always stands together with the peasants, and a few episodes of the peasants' lives, such as picking tea leaves and catching fish, could bring audience members with connections to Nanyang closer to the film. According to a newspaper review, the film's story "is transformed from a romantic love story into an educational comedy of class struggle. The conflict between landlords and peasants is emphasized, while the love interest and the song competition are retained—although, of course, revolutionary sentiment becomes the foundation of the former and the latter is presented as a contest between the landlord class and the peasants" (*Minbao*, June 19, 1962). The film, then, keeps a balance between a mythical romance and a revolutionary story. On the reception of the film in Singapore, an essay entitled "What We Should Learn from Third Sister Liu" in *Zhen Xianbao*, the official newspaper of the Socialist Front, guided the audience to focus on the following three main aspects: Third Sister Liu's spirit of fighting for the poor peasants, her spirit of resistance, and her forthright personality. "Today," the essay argued, "we are also in a society of class struggle, so we should serve the class of the labors and workers. In order to get our people's support as Third Sister Liu receives, we must fight against the exploiting class, those British colonists and also their followers" (*Zhenxian bao*, December 23, 1962). It can be seen that the British colonialists, who were the common foe that both the PAP and the Socialist Front fought with, also became the main target when *Third Sister Liu* was used for political purpose.

The singing contest in *Third Sister Liu* features the opposition between the landlord and the peasants. In the film, the landlord wants to take Third Sister Liu as his concubine. Liu responds with a counterplot by proposing that they have a singing competition before she agrees to his wish. The landlord hires three scholars to compete with her. This subplot was added to the film version and became very controversial. One main criticism was the modernization of Liu from a mythical folk figure into a model revolutionary heroine. As some critics pointed out, Third Sister Liu looks more like a "Communist Youth League member" than a legendary folk singer (U 2010). Third Sister Liu fights against the landlord and the three scholars he invited for the contest. Whenever Liu finishes a song, the crowds of labors behind her burst into roaring laughter, which is extremely powerful due to its sense of collective solidarity. If we say that *Liang-Zhu* is a sentimental love romance based on individual feelings, *Third Sister Liu* transmits the radical power of collective laughter. I use the concept of "laughter" in terms of Mikhail Bakhtin's definition and emphasize its anti-authority function. The song contest in the film can be interpreted as a "carnival," full of qualities of inversion, ambivalence, and excess: "The carnivalesque principle abolishes hierarchies, levels social classes, and creates another life free from conventional rules and restrictions. In carnival, all that is marginalized and excluded—the mad, the scandalous, the aleatory—takes over the center in a liberating explosion of otherness" (Stam 1989, 86). In *Third Sister Liu*, the eponymous heroine uses folk songs to deride the landlord and the three scholars he invited as animals, thus arousing the laughter of the mass of peasants behind her. The collective singing in the film creates a powerful form of group consciousness, and the laughter becomes the form of a free and critical consciousness. According to a local film review in Singapore,

> the most impressive episode [of the film] was the singing contest between Third Sister Liu and the three scholars, which aroused the echoing songs of the crowds all over the mountains. It also made the audience laugh loudly and the theater resounded with applause during the screening.
>
> (*Sin Chew Daily*, July 1, 1962)

The advertising posts of the film in Singapore often claimed that it could make one "laugh for two complete hours" (*xiaozu liangdianzhong*). As a musical, *Third Sister Liu* transmits its meaning through its deployment of songs. The scenes of collective singing transmit radical passions of revolution, which perfectly fit the emotional needs of the audiences in Singapore at the time, most of whom belonged to the labor class. To a certain degree, we can say that the film mobilized the laborers to sharpen their political emotions and join in the prevailing decolonization sentiments.

More importantly, the major political parties used the format of antiphonal singing (*duichang*) in their political debates, in a play on the Guangxi songs featured in the film. For instance, the Socialist Front wrote a song entitled "All People Vote with Blanks," which appropriated the antiphonal songs of *Third Sister Liu* in its question and answer format, to criticize the PAP's position of merging with Malaysia: "Is so-and-so collaborating with the colonizers? Is so-and-so implementing the plan of the Great Malaya? How will their future be? What is their fate?"[4] The same song also criticizes the PAP leaders: "People have a mouth but cannot speak out, the radio does not have a mouth but speaks so loudly. The minister has feet but doesn't walk, and the truth doesn't have feet but can spread throughout the world." Christina Klein (2003), in her studies on the American musical *The King and I* (Walter Lang, 1956), treats the musical as an ideological genre, specifically a genre of integration (192). In comparison, *Third Sister Liu* seems quite different. It emphasizes opposition and class struggle rather than integration. At that important historical moment, both the PAP and the Socialist Front needed the masses to stay on their side and fought for their votes. *Third Sister Liu*, especially the sequences of the singing contest, brought fighting and debating to the forefront in popular thinking among the mass audience. On this point, despite their different political agendas, both the PAP and the left-leaning opposition shared a similar interest. In other words, identification with *Third Sister Liu* did not entail a preference for the communist camp. Rather, the aim was to mobilize the mass audience toward confrontation and competition of different kinds of political struggles.

The fever over *Third Sister Liu* suddenly died out in January 1963, with the end of the fight between the PAP and the Socialist Front and the arrest of the opposition's top leaders on February 2. The reason for the arrest was the claim that the leaders of the Socialist Front had connections with the communist camp, especially the Malaysia Communist Party. As Timothy Harper (2015) argues, the rhetoric of counterinsurgency deeply permeates the colonial documents on which the dominant narrative of the Singapore story is based, and "the very idea of a 'Communist United Front' is perhaps a misnomer: most of the groups caught up in leftist popular radicalism... were neither communist, united, nor a front for anybody but themselves" (13). In the case of *Third Sister Liu*, we find that both the PAP and the Socialist Front used this PRC-made film for constructing their arguments and promoting their activism.[5] I would argue that one main reason for the popularity of the film in Singapore is that it effectively expressed the masses' frustrations toward the social injustice under the colonial rule of the British government, and that it also contributed to creating a new vocabulary to interpret localized concerns.

In contrast to the great popularity of *Third Sister Liu*, the two Hong Kong adaptations were not very well received in Singapore. When *The Songfest* came out, it was praised as having "grand setting, attractive landscape, and also more than forty songs." The extended sequences of the song contest in the film were particularly recommended (*Nanyang Siang Pau*, August 1, 1964). Another review used the phrase "unique emotional appeal" to describe the film and categorized it as a "costume blockbuster" with beautiful landscape shot in Taiwan (*Nanyang Siang Pau*, July 1, 1964). Between *The Shepherd Girl* and *The Songfest*, the latter was a little more popular in Singapore. One review of the time criticized that the love triangle in *The Shepherd Girl* was not healthy, especially the part where the boatman and the hunter fight to decide who can get the bride. The author also was not satisfied with the mountain songs in the film. In his view, they were meaningless (*Nanyang Siang Pau*, March 18, 1964). Interestingly, the reviews of the time did not clearly connect the two films with *Third Sister Liu*. Based on my oral interview,[6] some leftist-leaning intellectuals of the 1960s directly used the term "fake" to describe the two adaptations. In their views, the two Hong Kong films simply copied the mainland version and could not represent the "true" mountain-song film.

The "Cold War" between *Third Sister Liu* and Its Adaptations in Hong Kong

As Poshek Fu (2018) points out,

> Dubbed by the press as the 'Cold War city,' Hong Kong had become after 1949 China's 'window' to the West and, at the same time, an American 'watchtower' to counter the expansion of Chinese Communism. It was also a major battleground of the unfinished civil war between New China and the Nationalist regime.
>
> (2)

As a result, Hong Kong also became the battleground for the conflicts between the so-called rightist films and leftist films. That mainland opera films survived in Hong Kong despite the censorship of the time was due to the colonial authorities' perception of the genre. In July 1949, before the establishment of the PRC, the British authorities considered it "the duty of the Hong Kong government to maintain a neutral attitude to the Kuomintang and Communist parties" ("Film Censorship" 1949–50). To help avoid exacerbating the political rivalry between the two parties in Hong Kong, the British government decided not to ban cultural products from Communist China outright. Rather, they preferred methods of censorship, "assuming the films came through commercial channels and not through organizations or individuals claiming to act as representatives of the Chinese Communist Party" ("Film Censorship" 1949–50). In other words, the British colonial authorities did not want to impose a complete ban on all communist films, but did want to control the number and type of Chinese film imports.

Partly due to the popularity of *Third Sister Liu* in Hong Kong, Shaw Brothers made two adaptations of it: *The Shepherd Girl* and *The Songfest*. Compared with *Third Sister Liu*, which emphasizes the theme of class struggle, the two Hong Kong adaptations mainly focus on the romance aspect and the beautiful landscape. The script of *The Shepherd Girl* introduces the main female character as follows: "Xiu Xiu is a happy village girl who does not know any sadness. She is innocent, capricious or even wild."[7] The film starts with a singing duel between Xiu Xiu in the mountains and Liu Dalong on a boat in the sea. They exchange their feelings for each other through songs before they meet in person. The actress who plays Xiu Xiu, Julie Yeh Feng, describes the film as "unconventional" because of its "simple and unpretentious tone of the fishing village, which makes people feel fresh and pleasant." She also mentions how the film's "beautiful mountain songs represent the pure folk style" ("The Shepherd Girl" 1964b). *The Shepherd Girl* was Yeh Feng's first film for Shaw Brothers. As an actress, she was described as "wild" and "sexy." A sexy film actress performing as a shepherdess was quite eye-catching and also stirred the audience's curiosity. Such casting against type also worked for Kwan Shan, the lead actor in the film, who was famous for his suit roles but played a simple fisherman this time ("The Shepherd Girl" 1964b). *The Songfest*, the second Shaw Brothers adaptation of *Third Sister Liu*, features a beautiful tea picker Sung Yulan and a handsome fisherman Li Chunyang, and they both love singing mountain songs. However, their sweet love is interrupted by the king's brother-in-law, Hu Sanbao, who is an ugly playboy and infatuated with Yulan's beauty. In order to avoid trouble, Yulan suggests choosing her mate through a song contest, and every young villager has a chance, including the king's brother-in-law. But Hu is rejected as expected since he cannot sing. On the wedding day of the young lovers, Hu and his associates try to stop the marriage and kidnap Li Chunyang. The plot fails, and the lovers get married in the end, thanks to Hu's upright father.

The onscreen personae of song girls in Hong Kong had been changing, and both *The Shepherd Girl* and *The Songfest* feature village girls as central characters. Regarding the songstress in Chinese cinema, Jean Ma (2015) traces the continuity between the emergence of the filmic songstress in pre-1949 Shanghai and its flourishing in Hong Kong during the postwar period. However, her analysis does not touch much on the interactions between musicals (including opera films) from the PRC and the development of musicals in Hong Kong. Did the PRC films also play a role in the rise of Hong Kong musicals in the 1950s and especially the 1960s? In the historiography of the postwar songstress in Hong Kong films, *The Shepherd Girl* and *The Songfest* have often been ignored. In the changing social context of the Cold War period, the important commonalities that the two films have with the mainland production *Third Sister Liu* may be one reason for their marginalized position in the history of Hong Kong-made musical films. Rather, scholars have often mentioned Wang Tianlin's *Songs of the Peach Blossom River* (*Taohua jiang*, 1956) and Inoue Umetsugu's Hollywood-style *Hong Kong Nocturne* (*Xianggang hua yue ye*, 1967), which are interpreted as implicating "an emerging complex of desire for and an imagination of modernity, transnationality, and local self-identity" (Li 2008, 77). The uniqueness of *The Shepherd Girl* and *The Songfest*, on the other hand, was their use of mountain songs. They copied the plot and the musical style of *Third Sister Liu*, but did not evoke "nostalgic nationalism in exile," which often came through in the costume dramas and historical epics made by Shaw Brothers. If those costume dramas and epics often projected a cultural China using "a visual style of the grand artificiality of studio shooting plus a meticulous attention to historical details, sets, and props" (Li 2008, 79), the two mountain-song musicals were noted for their shots of beautiful landscapes of Hong Kong and Taiwan. They did not completely erase "China" like the later musicals such as *Hong Kong Nocturne*, but they changed the geographical origin of the landscape.

Space becomes very important in the three mountain-song films discussed in this essay. As W. J. T. Mitchell (2002) argues, the moving cinematic landscapes are the "dynamic medium" for identity formation. From the very beginning, the local government of Guangxi Autonomous Region was closely involved in making *Third Sister Liu* together with the Changchun Film Studio. The government had two clear requirements: first, the film must be shot in Guangxi and showcase its beautiful landscapes; second, the film should include locals in the cast. The first requirement testifies that landscape is an essential part of the film, and this can clearly be seen in the way the film starts with a two-minute landscape sequence before the protagonist Third Sister Liu appears. More importantly, the film pairs the landscape sequence with the mountain songs sung by Third Sister Liu (Meng 2008, 22). Even though Third Sister Liu does not appear in the sequence, her acousmatic voice dominates the whole scene. The meaning of the mountain song Third Sister Liu sings, which mainly criticizes social inequality, creates a tension with the soft and lyrical landscape on the one hand, but on the other hand, the connection between songs and the mountains as well as rivers becomes organic. These songs become one part of the "landscape" and are naturalized. In the film, when the male protagonist A Niu and his father meet Third Sister Liu for the first time, the first question they ask is: what fairy are you? Though Third Sister Liu asserts that she is not a fairy, only a poor girl trying to escape a landlord's persecution, she is represented as a goddess in a few folk stories. Such a mythic tone is also manifested at the ending of the film, when Third Sister Liu successfully evades landlord Mo's hunt and disappears on the river. She returns back to "nature" together with her songs.

After the film came out, the beautiful landscape of Guilin became an important selling point. The advertisement of *Third Sister Liu* often quoted a Chinese saying to describe the beauty of Yangshuo: "The mountains and rivers of Guilin are the most beautiful in the world, and the scenery of Yangshuo is the best in Guilin." From the reception of the film among the audiences in Hong Kong and Southeast Asia, especially those immigrants from mainland China, it can be seen that the landscape of the remote southwest of China relieved their homesickness and also created a closer sentimental link with the homeland they left. When Shaw Brothers remade the film, it still emphasized the beautiful landscape. *The Shepherd Girl* was shot in Hong Kong and *The Songfest* was made completely in Taiwan. Such choices can be considered as one way of creating alternative political associations, which could provoke different identification among audiences and direct their emotions to another direction.

The Shepherd Girl was praised as "the first Hong Kong-made mountain-song musical" and as a new style of musical film. One important characteristic of its "newness" was its use of mountain songs: "The songs in this film are not huangmei tone or mandarin songs [*shidaiqu*], but the well-known mountain songs that are particularly popular among the people living in villages in the mountains or along the seaside. Among the audiences in Hong Kong, quite a number are Hakka from Huizhou [in Guangzhou province]. They show a great capacity in appreciating these mountain songs" (*The Kung Sheung Evening News*, July 13, 1964). To legitimize the connection between mountain songs and Hong Kong, one review emphasized that Hong Kong is an island, where there are fishing villages and farmers; mountain songs are used by those groups to express their feelings (*The Kung Sheung Evening News*, July 8, 1964). Despite Shaw Brothers' efforts to undertake new experiments with the mountain song, *The Shepherd Girl*'s similarity to *Third Sister Liu* led some to complain that it should not be allowed to be shown in Taiwan. Such complaints pushed the Taipei Film Censor Committee to review the film again and invite specialists to compare its songs with those in *Third Sister Liu* one by one. Though the final finding was that only a few of them were similar, and the film was still allowed in theaters, the need for the review shows that mountain songs were often perceived as being imbued with a leftist ideological stance (*The Kung Sheung Daily News*, March 23, 1964).

Another point deserving attention is the significant similarity between the SFC's marketing strategy for *Third Sister Liu* and that of Shaw Brothers for the two adaptations, though the two companies competed with each other tightly for the local audience's support. Some common tactics included stressing the box-office records in newspaper advertising, organizing mountain-song competitions, and publishing illustrated stories of the films. *The Shepherd Girl* received the best music award at the Asian Film Festival in 1964 and was screened in five cinema houses in Hong Kong, from the middle of July to late August of that year. *Third Sister Liu* also received a second round of screening at the same time and was lauded as "the king of the mountain-song musical," according to a newspaper advertisement. The same advertisement also stated, "Fire is the test of gold. Sanjie's singing gets louder and louder." And then, "How can your songs be more numerous than mine? Mine can fill up countless baskets. I came to Hong Kong to sing last year, and Hong Kong and Kowloon were both filled with songs" (Figure 4.2). The SFC also organized a mountain-song singing competition across Hong Kong and asked the audience to learn the mountain songs of the film. More than 200 people participated in the contest, and the distribution company held a large awards ceremony and invited some famous local film stars to attend.

The publicity materials for *The Shepherd Girl* emphasized the film's cast of beautiful girls, its more than 100 mountain songs, and its story of romantic love. To attract viewers, an illustrated story of the film was

Figure 4.2 An advertisement of *Third Sister Liu* on *Overseas Chinese Daily News*, July 12, 1964.

WAH KIU YAT PO

兩部山歌打起冷戰

周詩祿肝病呈惡化

熊雪妮臨急抱主脚

君麗下月返港

在星拍彩色片

鍾偉明介紹

山歌戀歌曲

Figure 4.3 "Two Mountain-song Musicals Started a Cold War" (*liangbu shange daqi lengzhan*), *Overseas Chinese Daily News*, July 15, 1964.

also serially published in a local newspaper, and the local TV station showed a special program about the film.[8] Also, in step with the SFC's strategy, Hong Kong Commercial Radio broadcast the film's mountain songs and organized a singing competition on them. More than 500 people registered for the contest. The two main performers of the film, Julie Yeh Feng and Kwan Shan, acted as judges together with some other film stars from Shaw Brothers. The final competition was broadcast on radio. All these events greatly contributed to the sensation surrounding the film in Hong Kong (*The Overseas Chinese Daily News*, July 22, 1964).

That both *Third Sister Liu* and *The Shepherd Girl* claimed to be the authentic mountain-song musical led to a confrontation. The media directly described their confrontation as a "cold war" (Figure 4.3), a notion also vividly manifested in the films' newspaper advertisements. For instance, one newspaper advertisement for *The Shepherd Girl* claimed that "The mountain songs spread across streets and lanes, and the old songs and operas are in decline. We should bring forth the new in a timely manner as the old songs are so wordy." Apparently, the "old songs" refer to the mountain songs in *Third Sister Liu*. *The Shepherd Girl* was also promoted as "the first mountain-song musical in Hong Kong, which most suits the local audience's taste" (Figure 4.4).

Both *The Shepherd Girl* and *The Songfest* build their love stories through lots of songs and dances. As an article in *The Southern Screen*, the official magazine of Shaw Brothers, described *The Shepherd Girl*:

> This is a story of love at first sound, not sight, between a long-legged shepherdess (Julie Yeh Feng) and a warm-hearted boatman (Kwan Shan). The young couple first learn of each other's existence through their singing and grow fond of each other later when they meet for the first time.
>
> ("The Shepherd Girl" 1964a)

Figure 4.4 An advertisement of *The Shepherd Girl* on *Overseas Chinese Daily News*, July 15, 1964.[9]

According to Eddy U (2010), "singing competitions, the activity in the most famous scene of *Third Sister Liu*, are a popular pastime in southern, southwest, and northwest China. During the contest, the opponents take turns asking and answering questions using folk-style singing. Because the subject matter is virtually unlimited, excellent skill in improvisation is necessary for maintaining superiority" (67). In other words, singing competitions emphasize improvisation and spontaneity. More importantly, it is a tradition of the Zhuang, as well as some of other minorities, for young people to come together to sing and find their marriage partners through songs. These mountain songs could add freshness and "wildness" to the musical film. The custom among some minorities of using songs to express love was viewed by traditional mainstream Confucian culture as barbaric, as something that was required to be reformed or even banned. In the PRC-made *Third Sister Liu*, such a wild and even subversive songfest was "reformed" to express class struggle, rather than transmitting love and spontaneous feeling. However, the custom of expressing love through singing competitions was retained in the two Hong Kong adaptations and was even represented as the climactic moment of the romance. *Songfest* is a typical example in this regard. It was a follow-up to *The Shepherd Girl* and, though inferior in both budget and casting, is

> distinguished by the exuberance of Zhou Lanping's music, which incorporates a wide spectrum of folk songs. The spectacular 'songfest' singing competition is particularly remarkable, attesting to [the director's] efforts to reform his musical vocabulary after his initial success with *huangmei diao* films.
>
> (Chen 2003, 65–6)

Very similar to *Third Sister Liu*, the singing contest is set on a hillside close to a river. Yulan and her female friends as a group stand on a hill overlooking the king's brother-in-law Hu Sanbao together with the guests he invited and also a crowd of villagers, who are all below. The two groups of people stage a spectacular "confrontation." Hu has hired a few singers with deformities to join the contest, including a dwarf, a hunchback, and a bald man. Yulan sings back at all of them and defeats them. Finally, Li Chunyang, the male protagonist of the film, appears and matches Yulan song for song. He wins Yulan's heart and also the crowd's blessings.

In the two Hong Kong adaptations, the issue of class struggle, which is the main theme of *Third Sister Liu*, almost disappears, but the fight against social inequality and the conflicts between the poor and the rich still exist. For instance, in *The Songfest*, Hu Sanbao intrudes on the two lovers' marriage and kidnaps the male protagonist on their wedding day. In the end, it is Hu's father, a high-ranking official, who corrects the son's wrongdoings. Notably, in one scene of the film, a crowd of fishermen with farming tools flocks into the official's house and tries to force the official's son to release the male protagonist. This scene is very similar to one in *Third Sister Liu* in which A Niu's father and a group of farmers rush into landlord Mo's house in an attempt to rescue Third Sister Liu. However, a major difference is that in *The Songfest*, it is the high official who helps solve the problem.

Conclusion

As Tony Day (2010) argues, "cultural expression of the Cold War in Southeast Asia in this period was primarily shaped by the long-standing search by Southeast Asians, begun in the colonial period, for national identity, modernity, and independence. It was also strongly influenced by the international context in which this search took place after 1945, by the global rivalry between the United States and the Soviet Union, with a third power, the People's Republic of China (PRC), emerging onto the scene in 1949 as a major Cold War contender for influence over Southeast Asian political and cultural affairs" (3).[10] The great popularity of *Third Sister Liu* was deeply imbricated with the anti-colonization movement in Singapore. As a vehicle for channeling their views as well as mobilizing support, the film was used by different political agents in the independence campaign. It exactly fit the specific moments of conflict and confrontation in Singapore in the 1960s and enjoyed great popularity among the Chinese community from the 1950s to the 1980s. Certainly, the term "left" remained contentious during this period of Singaporean history, and therefore we need to be careful when we analyze what the radical passion as embodied by the concept of "left" meant to the audience then. In the 1960s, different factions in Singapore wrestled to claim the nation.

The popularity of *Third Sister Liu* and its two adaptations made by Shaw Brothers captured the conflicts of identity uneasily negotiated by a Chinese community pulled in different directions by various agents, in particular the PAP and the Socialist Front. Despite the official containment of leftist interests after 1960, *Third Sister Liu* continues to have a following even today. It is hard to explain the continuing popularity of the film as simply stemming from nostalgia. Reflecting on the issue across a wider historical arc, it may be said that the contemporary popularity of *Third Sister Liu* in Singapore is related to the waning of the radical and youthful ideals of the 1960s; in this sense, the film's resonance may be better treated as a symptom reflecting a historical trauma for left-leaning intellectuals or leftist sympathizers who are still alive in Singapore today.

If we say that the "rivalry" rhetoric in *Third Sister Liu* mainly echoed the tensions within various streams of leftist activism in Singapore, such a structure of "confrontation" had a very different meaning in Hong Kong and resonated more with the commercial contest between *Third Sister Liu* and the two adaptations from Shaw Brothers. As discussed earlier, the SFC and Shaw Brothers both claimed their films to be authentic mountain-song musicals. *Third Sister Liu* and *The Shepherd Girl* were screened in theaters at almost the same time, and they used similar marketing strategies to compete with each other. However, such a confrontation was not necessarily or entirely political in nature. Shaw Brothers made the two adaptations mainly because the company saw the great popularity of *Third Sister Liu* in Hong Kong and wanted to capitalize on it. Also, despite the emphasis of *Third Sister Liu* on class struggle, the audiences in Hong Kong may not have paid much attention to the radical political messages in the film. Rather, they probably enjoyed more the film's beautiful landscape, the beauty of its young actress, and the fresh rhythms of its mountain songs. Indeed, the SFC also emphasized those "soft" characteristics of the film in the advertisements in order to avoid censorship from the British government.

More broadly, through a study of the circulation and reception of *Third Sister Liu* in Hong Kong and the Southeast Asian region, the unfolding interactions and contentions between the film industries in Hong Kong and Singapore during the 1950s and 1960s can also be mapped out (Mak 2018). The triumph of the communists in the Chinese Civil War divided the film industries in the Sinophone world, and the ensuing Cold War in the region pushed the new communist regime to spare no efforts in competing for the support of the overseas Chinese community. As a major form of mass culture at the time, cinema became an important tool to win the hearts and minds of overseas Chinese, especially those in the geopolitically significant locations such as Hong Kong and Singapore. In this light, a transborder history of the China-Hong Kong-Singapore (the diasporic Chinese community in Southeast Asia) filmic linkages during the Cold War period needs to receive further studies.

Notes

1 Several film reviews mentioned these three main attractions. These reviews were collected in *Liu Sanjie zai xinjiapo yingchu teji* (Collections of Newspaper Reports on *Third Sister Liu* in Singapore), created by the New Century Film Company in 1963. According to Shu Don-lok, the collection was given to SFC as a gift to show how popular *Third Sister Liu* was in Singapore.

2 *Third Sister Liu* started screening in Singapore on July 12, 1962. It lasted for 186 days till January 14 the following year. Half a year later, it was released again briefly, twice. The first time the film was screened in six cinemas for 25 days from June 28 to July 22. The second time was at the year's end. Taking advantage of the long school-term break, film companies started screening the film on November 25, and the run lasted for five days. This first round of screening that spanned 1962 and 1963 totaled 216 days (over seven months). Sixteen years later, *Third Sister Liu* was screened again for 60 consecutive days in the 13 cinemas belonging to the Chong Gay Theatres Ltd.

3 The information is from an interview between Shu Don-lok and the author in 2015. Shu also mentioned that because the film was used by the Socialist Front to fight against the PAP, Lee Khoo Choy was impeached out of the Parliament and became Singapore's ambassador in Egypt.

4 This verse is also from *Liu Sanjie* (1963).

5 I also agree with Lau Yuqing's (2016) observation in her study of the Anti-Yellow Culture Movement of postwar Singapore: "While the political climate of the vocal nationalists in post-war Singapore was already left-leaning and receptive to communism, the pervasiveness of socialist ideology was dependent on its ability to offer an attractive alternative to British rule, and its appeal was real to many of its adherents" (11).

6 I did an oral interview with some leftist intellectuals on December 8, 2018, about their impressions of *Third Sister Liu* and its two Hong Kong adaptations.

7 The original scripts of *The Shepherd Girl* and *The Songfest* are in the central library of National University of Singapore and were donated by Chua Boon Suan.

8 The illustrated story of the film was also serially published in *The Overseas Chinese Daily News* from July 9, 1964 onward.

9 The following is written at the top left-hand corner of the advertisement: "The film is here finally! Eagerly awaited by many during the school holidays. Awesome songs, awesome show with a fresh style. The first mountain-song musical from Hong Kong, a sure hit among the local audience."

10 Tony Day's book covers mainly the period from 1948 to the late 1970s, which is often considered as the start and end points of the Cold War in Southeast Asia. For more information, see also Hack and Wade (2009).

Works Cited

Chen, Edwin W. 2003. "Musical China, Classical Impressions: A Preliminary Study of Shaws' *Huangmei Diao* Film." In *The Shaw Screen: A Preliminary Study*, edited by Wong Ain-ling, 51–73. Hong Kong: Hong Kong Film Archive.

Chen, Yunqian. 2016. "Bursting with Mountain Songs: Gender Resistance and Class Struggle in Liu Sanjie." *Frontiers of History in China* 11 (1): 133–58.

Day, Tony. 2010. "Cultures at War in Cold War Southeast Asia: An Introduction." In *Cultures at War: The Cold War and Cultural Expression in Southeast Asia*, edited by Day Tony and Maya H.T. Liem, 1–20. Ithaca, NY: Cornell University Press.

"Film Censorship: Hong Kong." 1949–50. CO 537/6570, Kew-Colonial Office, Commonwealth and Foreign and Commonwealth Offices, the National Archives, London.

Fu, Poshek. 2018. "More than Just Entertaining: Cinematic Containment and Asia's Cold War in Hong kong, 1949–1959." *Modern Chinese Literature and Culture* 30 (2): 1–55.

Fu, Poshek. 2003. *Between Shanghai and Hong Kong: The Politics of Chinese Cinema.* Stanford, CA: Stanford University Press.

Hack, Karl, and Geoff Wade. 2009. "The Origins of the Southeast Asian Cold War." *Journal of Southeast Asian Studies* 40 (3): 441–8.

Harper, T. N. 2015. "Lim Chin Siong and the 'Singapore Story.'" In *Comet in our Sky: Lim Chin Siong in History*, edited by Tan Jing Quee and K. S. Jomo, new ed., edited by Poh Soo Kai, 2–55. Petaling Jaya: Strategic Information and Research Development Centre.

Klein, Christina. 2003. *Cold War Orientalism: Asia in the Middlebrow Imagination, 1945–1961. Berkeley: University of California Press.*

Lau, Yuching. 2016. *The Anti-Yellow Culture Movement, 1953–1961: Morality and the Language of Decolonising Singapore.* Master's Thesis, NUS.

Li, Siu Leung. 2008. "Embracing Glocalization and Hong Kong-Made Musical Film." In *Forever China: The Shaw Brothers and Diasporic Cinema*, edited by Foshek Fu, 74–94. Urbana, Ill.: University of Illinois Press.

Lindsay, Jennifer. 2010. "Festival Politics: Singapore's 1963 Southeast Asia Cultural Festival." In *Cultures at War: The Cold War and Cultural Expression in Southeast Asia*, edited by Day Tony and Maya H.T. Liem, 227–46. Ithaca, NY: Cornell University Press.

Liu, Hong, and Sin-Kiong Wong. 2004. *Singapore Chinese Society in Transition: Business, Politics & Socio-Economic Change, 1945–1965.* New York: Peter Lang.

Liu, Lydia H. 2003. "A Folksong Immortal and Official Popular Culture in Twentieth-Century China." In *Writing and Materiality in China: Essays in Honor of Patrick Hanan*, edited by Judith T. Zeitlin, Lydia H. Liu, and Ellen Widmer, 553–612. Cambridge, Mass.: Harvard University Asia Center.

Liu Sanjie zai xinjiapo yingchu teji (Collections of Newspaper Reports on *Third Sister Liu* in Singapore). 1963. Singapore: New Century Film Company.

Ma, Jean. 2015. *Sounding the Modern Woman: The Songstress in Chinese Cinema.* Durham, NC: Duke University Press.

Mak, Yan Yan Grace. 2018. *Xianggang dingyian yu Xinjiapo: lengzhan shidai xinggang wenhua lianxi, 1950–1965* (Hong Kong Cinema and Singapore: A Cultural Ring between Two Cities, 1950–1965). Hong Kong: Hong Kong University Press.

Meng, Xiongqiang. 2008. "Dianying Liu Sanjie paishe de taiqian muhou" (The story of making *Third Sister Liu*), *Wenshichunqiu* 2: 20–7.

Mitchell, W. J. T., ed. 2002. *Landscape and Power.* Chicago: University of Chicago Press.

"The Shepherd Girl." 1964a. *The Southern Screen*, no. 76 (June).

"The Shepherd Girl." 1964b. *The Southern Screen*, no. 71 (January).

Shu, Don-lok. 2005. *Kenguang tuoying (Cultivating Light and Shadow).* Hong Kong: MCCM Creations.

Stam, Robert. 1989. *Subversive Pleasure: Bakhtin, Cultural Criticism, and Film.* Baltimore and London: The Johns Hopkins University Press.

U, Eddy. 2010. "Third Sister Liu and the Making of the Intellectual in Socialist China." *The Journal of Asian Studies* 69 (1): 57–83.

Xu, Lanjun. 2017. "The Southern Film Corporation, Opera Films, and the PRC's Cultural Diplomacy in Cold War Asia, 1950s and 1960s." *Modern Chinese Literature and Culture* 29 (1): 239–81.

Zhou, Weijie. 2014. "Bange shijie qian de shehui qinggan fuhao: Liu Sanjie zai xinjiapo (Emotional symbols of the society half a century ago: Third Sister Liu in Singapore)." *Yiheshiji* (Ee Hoe Century) 21: 48–53.

Part II

Global Conflicts, Local Formations

5 Educational Films in Postwar Japan

Traces of American Cultural Policies in the Cold War Period

Mitsuyo Wada-Marciano

Introduction

Documentaries in Japan continued to be produced by the same filmmakers throughout the transwar period—as can be seen with the career of filmmaker Kamei Fumio, who managed to keep creating documentary films in both wartime and postwar Japan. However, the end of the war did, in a number of respects, bring transformations to the form and characteristics of the documentary genre. For one thing, a new term, "*kyōiku eiga*" (educational film), distinct from the prewar "*kiroku eiga*" (documentary film) and the wartime "*bunka eiga*" (culture film), came into use.[1]

It seems clear that these differences in terms are not mere pro forma relabeling but have genuine semantic significance, in that culture films of the wartime period were received very differently, and by different processes, than postwar educational films. Under the stipulations of the militarist regime's Film Law (1939–45), all ordinary cinemas were strictly required to add a culture film to every single screening program of fiction films, and as a consequence, market demand for culture films rapidly soared. In other words, documentary films made during the war, while always theatrical in nature, fulfilled a propaganda role entirely supportive of the will and ideas of the state. Postwar educational films, on the other hand, faced a much bleaker situation: the Film Law was abolished following Japan's defeat, and the film industry began operating according to the logic of capital, meaning that educational films could not compete with the much more popular fiction films and vanished from the cinemas. In short, the documentary film genre underwent a transition into a non-theatrical mode of exhibition and reception.

Here I must point out, however, that the disappearance of documentary films from movie theaters in postwar Japan does not mean that ordinary people were unable to see them, nor does it indicate that this sort of film stopped being produced. During the 1950s, educational films grew in presence, if anything. This is because, firstly, quite a few people involved in the creation of culture films had lost all such work after

Japan's defeat, and found a form of reemployment in the world of educational film production. Moreover, from a standpoint external to the film industry, the Occupation forces, in an effort to disseminate the idea of democracy nationwide, distributed more than 1,300 American-made Natco 16 mm film projectors and over 400 short documentary films (dubbed "CIE [Civil Information and Education Section] Films" and renamed to "USIS [United States Information Service] films" after 1952) to public libraries throughout Japan as well as to the American Centers that had been set up in major cities. The main goal of this distribution of documentaries was the social education of viewers, but the films and projectors were also intended for use in formal education in schools.

Postwar educational films, then, were made under circumstances that featured both continuity (in that the films were made by the same filmmakers) and discontinuity (their label was changed from "culture" to "educational" films, and the films were forced to coexist alongside American-made documentaries) with wartime film production. But considering these films as texts, to what extent can they be said to be connected to past documentary films on the level of content? Is it really the case that culture films of the wartime period, which after all were audiovisual texts designed to depict—and promote—the national ideology of the Japanese Empire, gave up that propagandistic function entirely after their name was changed to "educational films" in the postwar era?

It might well be true that scholars continue to focus their research on documentary films made in postwar Japan precisely in the hopes of finding evidence of a continuing propagandistic or political quality in such films. I am convinced that postwar documentaries did not merely *reflect* the national ideology of Japan in the Cold War period, which was intimately connected to and shaped by the unequal power relations between Japan and the United States during Allied Occupation of Japan and in the post-Occupation, Cold War era, but actually *created* this national ideology, fulfilling their role as the ideal medium in this process of ideological reorientation.

If this is the case, exactly what sort of form or image does postwar Japan within the Cold War regime take in such educational films? In this essay, the issue of "postwar Japan" is dealt with through close attention to the multiple subjects involved in the education process associated with the educational films; at stake, in other words, are the questions of who exactly was doing the educating, who was being educated, and what meanings this education held. I wish to consider carefully the indispensable relationship between educational films and the national ideology labeled "postwar," which took form in the 1950s, that is, the immediate postwar period under the influence of the Cold War structure. Moreover, the object of analysis here, namely, postwar Japanese documentaries, refers to two types of films: the pioneering educational films disseminated by CIE and their successors, and the educational films produced in greater numbers by Japanese filmmakers from the 1950s onward. Let us first examine the former category, CIE's educational films.

CIE Educational Films

The fact that Japan's postwar ideology, closely influenced by the Cold War political regime, was constructed immediately after its defeat by GHQ (short for "General Headquarters of the Supreme Commander of the Allied Powers") and was, in fact, a key policy of the Occupation, may seem blindingly self-evident. Research into the Occupation policies promulgated by GHQ, particularly the relationship between the cultural policies and Japanese film, has been analyzed by a number of scholars in recent years, including research projects in American history, the history of education, and film history. The CIE film project was launched in March 1946. At first, efforts were concentrated on introducing an initial crop of nine films intended to facilitate the dissemination of democracy in Japan, but from May 1948 onward, the steadily rising tensions of the Cold War system made CIE films an absolutely indispensable component of American cultural policies. As a result, the number of CIE films sent to Japan was greatly increased.

Tanaka Jun'ichirō, the noted scholar of Japanese cinema, wrote the following on the subject of CIE educational films:

> In February of 1948, CIE promised to donate 1300 Natco 16mm film projectors and 630 Beseler 35mm slide projectors to Japan's Ministry of Culture, with instructions to distribute them throughout the country and set up appropriate screening schedules in order to provide both adult education and social education to the Japanese. "Natco" is the name of a brand of American-made film projector with two portable trunks, one of which contains the projector itself and an amplifier, and the other a loudspeaker. The Natco projectors had been used as a tool for relaxation and pacification at various fronts and in occupied territories throughout the war in the Pacific, and now were bestowed upon the Japanese government with the surrender.
>
> (Tanaka 1979, 473)

CIE educational films were not simply an implement of propaganda by the U.S. army during the Occupation, as even after the Occupation ended in 1952, after their name was changed to "USIS educational films" and their jurisdiction transferred to the U.S. State Department (via the U.S. Embassy), the films had continued to "contribute" to Japan's society until the waning of 16mm film's popularity in the early 1970s. Under Tanaka's definition, the CIE films were intended for "adult education and social education," a phrase which might well convince the reader that those who watched these films were all adults. But according to magazine articles of the time, viewership of CIE films extended to children as well, considering that the films were also used in the classroom as part of school education (Ochiai 1949, 6–8).[2] CIE headquarters requested that the educational films, in principle, be loaned out free of charge and for 20 days per month. In fact, the films and projectors were loaned out at such a furious pace, to a great number of non-profit organizations such as community centers and schools, that they suffered significant wear and tear, and even damage. Regarding the question of where and with what frequency CIE educational films were screened, as well as what sort of people watched them, Tsuchiya Yuka, a scholar of American history, has offered the following details:

> CIE films had little impact in major cities, where from long before the war films had enjoyed popularity as a medium of entertainment, but in rural areas, where entertainment was scarce, they received an enthusiastic welcome.... (T)here were, however, cases where CIE films were shown in cities alongside fiction films in set programs, yet the audience could not have realized that they were watching a CIE film. According to the statistics produced by the Occupation forces on audience size, statistics based on data submitted by all the prefectures in Japan, a total of 945,053,007 Japanese persons had attended screenings of CIE films through July, 1951, and the number continued to climb thereafter. Given that the population of Japan in 1950 was about 83 million, it is a simple matter to calculate that each and every Japanese citizen watched at least 10 CIE films *every year.*
>
> (Tsuchiya 2010, 155–81)

This fact—that every Japanese watched ten or more CIE films every year—makes clear just how widely disseminated these films were and is an important clue when we consider the intimate relationship between CIE educational films and other postwar Japanese documentaries. But I will say no more on this here, as this topic will be addressed in greater detail later.

Although the subject matter of the more than 400 CIE educational films is extremely varied, it is possible to identify a number of major trends by examining the film index that was regularly distributed by the U.S. Embassy to all the CIE film libraries in Japan. Specifically, we can count the number of films that fall under each of the content-based categories in the *1955 Index of USIS Films*. At this point, four key points seem especially worthy of close consideration.

The first point is that many CIE films appear to stress how very scientific American society was (with 33 films classified under the categories "science" or "engineering," and another seven indexed as "atomic power" films), and how modernized Americans' standard of living had become, thanks to the influence of democracy and utilitarianism—a portrayal that also amply shows a high degree of economic security in the United States (21 films were indexed as "political/administrative," while 14 fell under the heading "for ladies," a category that included films about "bright and happy home life"; 34 films were indexed under the "democracy" category). In other words, careful scrutiny of these films, which are full of praise for both American society, thoroughly permeated with democracy, and capitalism, the linchpin of American social structure, leads the viewer to realize that they must have been very carefully selected. The fact that depictions of societal problems like racism or the gap in earning power between men and women, which only worsened in postwar American society, are entirely absent from this group of films also suggests that their selection was anything but arbitrary.

Secondly, the types of rhetoric used in these filmic representations of American life are worthy of special attention. As we see with, say, *Genshiryoku* (*Atomic Power*, 1948), one characteristic of those films depicting science is that they did not simply talk about science; rather, they tried to visualize as much as possible invisible processes, like the splitting of an atom, in an effort to literally educate the viewers. This visualizing of science, one of the most significant "weapons" in the Cold War period, was to have a profound influence on the history of Japanese documentary films, which had heretofore been characterized by a preference for rather lyrical turns of phrase, as seen, for example, in Shimomura Kenji's *Aru hi no higata* (*One Day in the Tidelands*, 1940). In a way, one might even say that this sort of visualization presented Japanese documentary filmmakers with a new "syntax" for filmmaking (more on this later).

Thirdly, CIE films are characterized by a thorough degree of politicization. This feature is especially stark in the group of works that depict the Red Purge—the movement to discharge people regarded as "Communists and their sympathizers" in early 1950s Japan—which occurred under the auspices of the Cold War system. Titles that give off an unmistakable odor of propaganda are relatively few, but as one can see with a film like *Heiwa e no ishi* (*The Will for Peace*, 1951), which appears to stress that peace is something achievable only through the American global economic policies of the Marshall Plan, the political principles underpinning CIE films are often clearly pro-America and anti-communist. From our vantage point in the twenty-first century, the extraordinarily narrow-minded presentations of ideology in these films cannot help but invite disbelief in that ideology. However, to Japanese viewers back in the 1950s, before television—the medium which crosses borders and allows people all over the world to see all manner of news simultaneously—became widespread, films like *Soren wa kō kangaeru* (*As Russia Sees It*, 1950) or *Aka no inbō* (*The Communist*

Conspiracy, 1952), which visualized the actual situation in Moscow (even if they did so through an anti-communist lens), must have held great significance in letting viewers "see" the world. During the war, the actual situation in the world, especially the social circumstances in the United States and Europe, was kept well out of sight from Japanese audiences. For this reason, the visualization of the outside world in CIE films would have value even if what was shown was a carefully selected, self-serving compilation of images.

Lastly, a fourth key point deserving attention is that films connected to Japan, as well as films produced in Japan by CIE, are surprisingly numerous. Among the more than 400 CIE educational films, 59 works were categorized under the heading "Japan: including films about Japan and films produced in Japan." Among this group of films, some were indeed made by Japanese film production companies, though, in some cases, no production company is indicated in the credits at the express request of CIE or its later incarnation, the USIS office. We may speculate the reason for this "no identity" policy as CIE/USIS's desire to be politically transparent, while the offices saturated their Cold War ideology in Japan through those films. Given their role in commissioning the films and providing lavish amounts of capital and the ever scarce raw film stock, CIE/USIS would feel justified, as in the case of Shū Taguchi's *Sunadoru hitobito* (*Men Who Fish*, 1950), in interrupting the production of the films in order to let them convey the political meanings which they wanted to add on. There were also cases in which CIE/USIS arranged to purchase ready-made films—those that seemed to align best with their own ideas and ideologies—from Japanese film companies. One such example is *Koshi no magaru hanashi* (*Bent with the Years: Women and the Agricultural Cooperative*, 1949), which was one of the more popular of CIE educational films.

Although the CIE educational films made in Japan did not all follow the same production course, investigating some of the processes by which these films were made can provide a fascinating glimpse into the behind-the-scene world of documentary film production in Japan in the late 1940s and the early 1950s. For instance, these films did not come into being simply as the product of the relationship between CIE, itself a branch of GHQ, and Japanese film studios. Instead, central organizations of the Japanese national government then in power also mediated the relationship between CIE and the film studios. Furthermore, clearly the relationship between CIE and the Japanese government was also involved in supporting, if indirectly, the production of a number of documentary films that cannot be labeled "CIE films" at all. In other words, CIE certainly poured some of the capital earmarked for film production into the hands of these central governmental organizations, but the source of that capital was kept murky, and so, on the surface, films made with that funding were presented to the general viewing public of Japan simply as films that had earned an endorsement by the Japanese government. From all this it is clear that, to CIE/the Occupation authorities, films were considered perhaps the most critically important medium for enacting their cultural policies in Japan during the Cold War period.

"Adaptation" and Collusion

CIE educational films were produced not only with Japan in mind. They were also shown in various countries in Europe, including Italy and Germany, as well as in the Philippines—all countries where, in the Cold War climate, Americans felt it especially critical to present the United States in the best possible light. To cater to the diverse audiences, adaptation—dubbing the films into the native languages of the countries in which they were distributed, duplicating prints, and reorganizing the films into a form that aligned better with local cultures—was necessary. This process of adaptation is critically important when considering not just those CIE educational films made in Japan but CIE educational films in general and the relationship they had with other postwar Japanese documentaries. The reason for this is that the adaptation process provided, in a direct form, much-needed economic support to film production companies of the period. At the same time, the process also provided these corporations, or rather the people working for them, with the opportunities to make, essentially, their own films. As filmmakers of the day watched and rewatched CIE educational films during this process of adaptation, they became receptive to the storytelling style and the representational forms used in the films. The question facing us, then, is why this causal relationship, and the fact that CIE educational films and other postwar documentaries made in Japan coexisted in the same sociocultural space, has gone almost completely unmentioned in the established narrative of Japanese film history.

It was through their educational films that CIE carried out what the United States considered at the time to be absolutely essential cultural policies of the Cold War regime in Japan.[3] I must point out, however, that we should not simply dismiss this body of CIE educational films as monolithic, one-sided propaganda from the United States targeting Japan. As I mentioned earlier, Japanese film companies were hired to dub these films from English into Japanese, an instance of "collusion" which nonetheless provided a massive infusion of capital into the Japanese film industry, then teetering on the brink of bankruptcy. Moreover, Tsuchiya Yuka, the aforementioned expert in American history, has pointed out that the CIE film project itself was quite polysemous, and that the CIE films exhibited a wide variety of uses and benefits, including political indoctrination, propaganda, education, enlightenment, and entertainment. She divided the CIE films into two periods—early and late—and showed that films of the late period, in particular, from the late 1951 onward, do not simply feature American narrators who explain things from an American perspective from start to finish. However, some CIE films include a format in which Japanese narrators comment on American society, and can therefore be seen as an instance of "complicity"; in other words, those Japanese narrators took on the roles of sympathetic "translators" and/or American "agents" (Tsuchiya 2010, 151–81).

Research on CIE Educational Films: The State of the Field

In this section, I will first discuss and evaluate what scholars have hitherto said about CIE educational films—which, in many ways, perfectly illustrate the political relationship between Japan and the United States at that time—before considering in more detail the "purge" of theories which posit a causal relationship between CIE films and postwar Japanese documentaries.

CIE educational films have heretofore been researched from a wide variety of viewpoints. However, it is only very recently, after vestiges of the films—previously thought to have been returned en masse to America—were unexpectedly discovered in various schools, libraries, and archives in Japan, that it has become possible for scholars to actually view the films, thereby triggering a new wave of scholarly interest. Moreover, it was only in the mid-1990s that a series of American archival documents from GHQ dating from the Occupation started to be declassified and entered the public domain. This opening of the archives has spurred on research into CIE educational films as well. Since the early 1980s, education scholar Abe Akira (1983) has been working to situate CIE films within the history of regional educational systems and policies in postwar Japan. Other scholars of education working from an angle similar to Abe's include Shiba Kazumi (2001) and Misaki Tomeko (2008). Shiba's work considers the significance of CIE educational films from a science education viewpoint, while Misaki analyzes CIE films in the context of efforts to improve daily life in agricultural communities—particularly the space of "dining room"—and the films' relationship to postwar home economics education. Tanikawa Takeshi (2002), on the other hand, approaches the films within the context of the historical role of American films in Occupation policy, while the work of sociologist Nakamura Hideyuki (2002) examines *Eiga kyōshitsu* (Film Classroom), a specialized trade journal devoted to educational films, for evidence of how CIE films were received by Japanese society at the time.

Within the multidirectional field of CIE educational film research is the work of two scholars of American history, Fujita Fumiko and Tsuchiya Yuka, who seek to situate CIE films in the larger political context of American cultural policy toward Japan, and to evaluate the significance and uses of the films in that context. Regarding CIE films vis-à-vis American cultural policy toward Japan in the post-Occupation period of the 1950s, Fujita (2003) writes:

> In addition to providing an influx of commercial American culture, the films also served the purpose of increasing the feeling of affinity with the United States among the Japanese, and helped to weaken Japanese opposition to the American military presence in Japan. (14)

But at the same time, she also points out that the U.S. cultural policies did not operate on a monolithic national level, from America to Japan; analyzing several CIE educational films, she makes a case that these policies unfolded through a complex series of negotiations on the level of actual foreign policy, on the level of the participating organizations, and even on the level of individuals.[4] Tsuchiya (2010), by contrast, resituates American cultural policy toward Japan within a framework of educational policy, thereby drawing our attention to the fact that the educational project of CIE films was first and foremost intended to benefit the United States. But like Fujita, Tsuchiya also argues that the subject position of Japanese viewers of CIE films was not merely one of passive reception; rather, the dissemination of CIE films prompted Japanese viewers to engage proactively in the process of education and thereby to seek self-betterment.[5]

The work of Fujita and Tsuchiya can be seen as an example of research on CIE educational films that seeks to draw attention to the process by which the Japanese collaborated with the cultural policies of the United States. Seen in this light, CIE films were specific instantiations of this process of collaboration, which is a topic explored by journalists Alex Dubro and Matsui Michio. From November 1994 to May 1995, Dubro and Matsui published a seven-part report entitled "Panel-D-Japan hajimete veil wo nugu Amerika tai-Nichi sennō kōsaku no zenbō" (Panel-D-Japan: The complete story of America's brainwashing operations against Japan) in *Views*, a monthly magazine. Despite the inflammatory title, the approach these two journalists took was more straightforward than one might expect; they steadily gathered evidence from among the official documents declassified at the National Archives in Washington D.C., describing the particulars of the U.S. government's "brainwashing operation" in the 1950s and showing their effects on the increase in pro-American—and anti-Communist—sentiment in Japan. Their work is based on a simple hypothesis: "As a symbol of freedom, wealth, and cheerfulness, American culture... was accepted by the Japanese... but what if we assume the influx of American culture into Japan as a strategy deliberately deployed by certain individuals in an effort to control and shape Japanese culture?" (Dubro and Matsui 1994, 1:38). They then proceed to provide proof that such a strategy did, in fact, exist. As part of its use of psychological warfare tactics—under the code-name "CLOVEN" in France and "DEMAGNETIZE" in Italy, for example—the U.S. government launched in Japan "PANEL-D-JAPAN," a top-secret cultural project manifesting itself in a wide variety of areas and fields. Dubro and Matsui's report describes the many political and economic ways in which this "PANEL-D-JAPAN" project affected Japanese society from the end of the Occupation through the Anpo protests of 1960. It sheds light on how individuals (like Kishi Nobusuke, Nakasone Yasuhiro, and Shōriki Matsutarō) and institutions (like Waseda University, Kyoto University, the Daily Yomiuri, and NHK) were involved in the process of promoting pro-American and anti-communist sentiment in Japan. In addition to this, Dubro and Matsui's report also reveals the stunning fact that these "brainwashing operations" by the United States permeated many levels of postwar Japanese society in a surprising range of permutations. For example, such efforts included information operations on the political level; ideological schemes on a cultural level via mass media like film, radio, newspaper, and television; and brainwashing—to use their term—against intellectuals, especially famous authors, as well as college professors and students. These various efforts were expected to have a tremendous influence over the general population, in particular on the issue of atomic energy, the public opinion on which was manipulated via newspapers and speeches of certain politicians to produce a situation more favorable to the United States. In their report, Dubro and Matsui forcefully assert that "the raison d'être of USIS films [the name given to CIE films after 1952, after jurisdiction over the films was transferred from GHQ to the U.S. State Department and the American Embassy] was their role as anti-Communist propaganda" (44).

Rendering Influence Invisible

The aforementioned summary of the research on CIE educational films based on declassified materials brings into view the extent to which, throughout the Occupation and post-Occupation 1950s, American cultural policies deployed in Japan both expanded in scope and surreptitiously advanced toward their goals. However, when we examine the current narratives of postwar Japanese film history, especially those pertaining to the history of documentaries, we are likely to get the impression that no such American cultural policies were deployed in Japan. For example, in his 1977 work, *Nihon kiroku eizōshi* (A History of Japanese Documentary Moving Images), Satō Tadao, perhaps Japan's most prominent film scholar and today the president of Nihon Eiga Daigaku (The Japan Institute of the Moving Image), seems to argue that the influence of those at GHQ and CIE on the Japanese film industry was extremely limited.

Several excerpts from Satō's claims about GHQ and/or CIE are given in the following text. For example, he asserts that "D. Conde, the person in charge of film matters during the Occupation, apparently suggested to Japanese documentary filmmakers that they make films similar to *March of Time*, a film produced in the United States during the war" (138). And regarding Maruyama Shōji's *Kodomo kaigi* (*Children's Conference*, 1947), Satō describes it as a "democratically enlightening film... which the Occupation army promoted for use in postwar education as a classroom tool to foster discussion" (144), but notes that the film's true interest lies in how contrived and artificial the children's discussions are. For Satō, then, the film "encapsulates the paradox of 'democracy' in Japan, an ideal which winked out of existence at the very moment, in postwar Japanese education, when it was being hailed as just about to make a glorious entrance" (147). *Children's Conference* was not shown to viewers under the CIE educational film label, but it was produced and screened during the same period when CIE educational films were being distributed throughout Japan. In any case, the references Satō makes to CIE or the cultural policies of GHQ fail to illuminate the direct relationship between CIE educational films (documentaries "borrowed" from the United States) and works like *Kodomo kaigi* (postwar Japanese documentaries), although he does drop hints at American influence.

Moreover, the indiscernibility of the influence CIE films had on the development of postwar Japanese documentary is not limited to works of film scholarship (like that of Satō Tadao) published in the 1970s at the height of the Cold War, when American cultural policies toward Japan were still in effect. In May 2012, a collaborative research volume, entitled *Iwanami eiga no ichi oku furēmu* (100 Million Frames of Iwanami Film) and devoted to the study of Iwanami Eiga Seisakusho (Iwanami Film Studio), was published by the Kiroku Eiga Archive Project (Documentary Film Archive Project). Iwanami Film Studio was founded in 1950 with the financial backing of Iwanami Shoten, a publishing company which had already won the trust of many intellectuals in Japan, thanks to its endorsement of Kōzaha ("Lecture School") socialism via prewar book series like Iwanami Bunko and Iwanami Shinsho. The newly founded studio soon launched various projects—mainly science education films but also several excellent works of the "industrial film" genre (i.e., public relations or PR films)—in support of the key industries being targeted as vital to Japan's postwar economic revitalization.[6] But despite the fact that most Iwanami productions were educational films like their CIE counterparts and were made and shown during the same time period as the latter, most of the articles in the volume published by the Documentary Film Archive Project do not touch at all on the relationship between the two groups of films but rather treat them as entirely separated. Can the seeming affinities between the films really be a mere coincidence?

Although the book in large part gives the impression, not only that there was no interaction at all between Iwanami films and CIE films but that they constituted two entirely separate paradigms, one contributor, namely Okada Hidenori, curator of the National Film Archive of Japan, does make several pertinent remarks. Firstly, he points out that "there have been almost no attempts to approach the topic of *kyōzai eiga* (films used for teaching) from the perspective of film history" (Okada 2011, 210). He then argues that the main reason why Iwanami Film Studio, with its science educational films, succeeded in winning over audiences so quickly after its founding was that "they took great care to show that their films were… not made under a '*bunka eiga*' [culture film] outlook" (206). As Okada explains, the concept of "culture film" originated in a series of short films, which were referred to as "Kulturfilm(e)" in German, made by the German company UFA in the 1930s. The concept was popularized in Japan by way of the translation (entitled *Bunka eiga-ron* [On Culture Films] in Japanese) of Paul Rotha's book *Documentary Film*, a work which had tremendous influence on Japanese documentary filmmaking from 1938 onward. Okada defines *bunka eiga* as any film which shows the influence from the documentary film movement in 1930s United Kingdom—in other words, any film which embraces the moral cause of improving society. He argues that Iwanami films sought to distance themselves from this moral mission of culture films, "the majority of which were 'documentaries' only in the sense of being records of the didactic message at their core, which meant that they were prone to conversion into propaganda" (206). As such, he asserts, Iwanami films "were the first signs of a full-blown 'postwar' in the field of documentary filmmaking" (206). According to Okada, the trademark feature of this sort of recognizably "postwar quality" in Iwanami films is that, although these films were made under a system of sponsorship by corporations and government agencies, the filmmakers were not content merely to throw together films haphazardly, but rather endeavored to create high-quality work. Indeed, in some cases, Iwanami films "refused to kowtow to the sponsors' desires," instead showing resistance against them. The result, Okada points out, was that Iwanami films became the foundation on which subsequent development of the short film format occurred (207).

It is certainly true that from the 1950s onward, Japanese documentary films, including PR films and films with sponsors, deliberately differentiated themselves from culture films, whose very reason for existence was their political messages. But is it really the case that the only source of influence on postwar documentaries—including Iwanami films—and the only type of film from which they tried to differentiate themselves, was the culture film? When we examine postwar documentaries from a diachronic viewpoint, it is true, as Okada points out, that they offered an intentional contrast with wartime culture films. But when looked at synchronically, it seems to me that these films also consciously sought to distinguish themselves from the American-made CIE educational films then being pervasively shown throughout the nation. Indeed, one can see the concerted effort made by postwar Japanese documentaries to separate themselves from CIE films as their very raison d'etre and their fundamental characteristic—at least initially. In the next section, I would like to continue this line of inquiry and illuminate the connection between CIE films and postwar documentaries with more specific examples.

The Impact of CIE Films on Japanese Educational Films

It is thought that Japan's postwar "educational film" system was first established in 1951 (Yoshihara 2011, 177). The main reason that this system emerged in 1951 was the merger in that year of Dai Nihon Eiga Kyōikukai (Greater Japan Film Education Association), an educational organization, with Kyōiku Eiga Seisaku Kyōgikai (Education Film Production Convention), an association of filmmakers, to form Nihon Eiga Kyōiku Kyōkai (Japanese Film Education Society). It is said that this society was created in order to engage in activities that only a brand-new educational organization could do. On the other hand, as I noted earlier, the CIE film project started in March 1946. The fact that CIE set these films up to be watched on a permanent basis throughout Japan, especially at prefectural libraries and American Centers, meant that they remained in circulation in Japanese society for over 20 years after the end of the Occupation in 1952.

What, precisely, was the relationship between CIE films and postwar Japanese documentaries? How, and how much, did the CIE films influence postwar documentaries? There are three key elements in this story of influence I would like to focus on: first, the benefits CIE films brought to the infrastructure of the film industry in Japan, raising the production level of subsequent postwar documentaries; second, the definition of the "educational" in educational films—in other words, the question of who was being educated and how; and third, similarities on the level of visual and representational style.

The CIE film project had a major role to play in laying the infrastructural groundwork on which postwar Japanese documentaries were produced. Most prominently, there is the issue of filmic technology and equipment. CIE had lent 1300 Natco 16mm synch-sound ('talkie') film projectors to Japan for free since 1946, which revolutionized independent film culture in Japan, where the standard technology was 8mm film for amateurs and 16mm silent film for "small scale" films. Indeed, one might say that this influx of Natco 16mm projectors was responsible for making the talkie the new standard in the world of independent filmmaking. As I have already pointed out, this new technology is what moved postwar documentaries out of traditional movie theaters and into new exhibition spaces. It goes without saying that this change of screening (and therefore viewing) environment had a tremendous impact on how these films were received. Indeed, this change was nothing less than a radical transformation—or transplantation—of Japan's documentary film culture, which, up until that point, had been centered on regular movie theaters and concentrated in large urban areas, into a diffused, peripheral, and, above all, local film culture which thrived in libraries, community centers, and schools. Incidentally, this shift away from movie theaters is doubtless a major reason documentaries were later able to enter the cultural sphere of television with comparative ease.

Another key area in which CIE films provided the infrastructure for later documentary film production was in the economic boost they brought to the film industry in Japan. As mentioned earlier, all the CIE films shown in Japan were first reedited and dubbed into Japanese, and major film companies in Japan, namely, Tōa Hassei, Nichiei, Shōchiku, Tōhō, and Daiei, were the ones that got paid by the CIE office to produce the Japanese-language versions of these films (Yoshimi 2011, 94). After remaking the films into Japanese versions, these companies would make quite a number of duplicate copies for each of the films, which generated a good amount of extra income for the companies. It is clearly thanks to these oft-repeated processes of reediting CIE films and making duplicate prints that many Japanese film studios were able to stay afloat financially. In addition, not only did CIE, via this regular reediting and dubbing work, passively ensure that Japanese film studios would be able to make films continuously, it also took on the role of producer commissioning films from Japanese companies.

Here I would like to point out an intriguing aspect of this process of CIE film "adaptation." As Yoshihara Junpei (2011), quoting a 1949 work by education specialist Takahagi Ryūtarō,[7] says, "Japanese companies were hired to complete the task of reediting these [CIE] films sent from the United States in a manner Japanese people would understand. Therefore, the Japanese versions of these films should be easier for the Japanese to understand than the original versions (94).[8] Yet in my viewings of over 30 CIE films, I actually found few films that seem to have been reedited for easier understanding, leading me to wonder whether such cases were comparatively rare. One example of a film that clearly was reedited is *Hi no yōjin* (*Beware of Fire*, released June 17, 1948; 18 min.). This work reuses some footage from the American-made film *The Chemistry of Fire* (released June 10, 1948; 43 min.), but it also adds new scenes on educational instruction featuring Japanese actors. The film was clearly reedited in an effort to make it a more practical and easy-to-use educational tool in classroom settings.[9] Similarly, Misaki Tomeko (2012) analyzes the film *Shōrai no sekkei* (*Design for the Future*, 1948), pointing out that while it was originally a British production, the second half of it used footage taken from *Nijūnen go no Tōkyō* (*Tokyo in Twenty Years*), a Japanese film produced by Nihon Kankō Eigasha in 1946 (213–41). At this point in my research, the number of films I have been able to locate and examine is still limited, which means that much work remains to be done in order to uncover the true story of this critical element of "reediting" in the adaptation process.

Next, let us consider the relationship between CIE films and postwar Japanese educational films from an educational perspective. The CIE film project heavily influenced the nature of the educational film—in other words, the nature of audiovisual education, or how films should be used for educational purposes—in postwar Japan. Yoshihara Junpei (2011) has the following to say about the double meaning of "educational film":

> The term "educational film" was used to convey two different meanings. There was the extremely wide sense of "educational film" as the realization, for filmmakers in the immediate postwar period, of the dream of "reviving culture films once more"; in this sense, the term encompassed a wide range of non-entertainment films, and this body of films hoped to rely on the then flourishing industrial films for financial support.... [I]n the "general education" category, which was eventually added to education film festivals, industrial films won quite a number of prizes. Unsurprisingly, the highly regarded "education film" category at such education film festivals had a much narrower, stricter definition: those educational films which proved to be effective instructional tools in school or social education settings received financial support and sold well, whereas those whose effectiveness was in doubt did not.
>
> (184–5)

In other words, the educational film in postwar Japan was initially very broadly defined and treated as a synonym for "documentary," but the definition gradually grew narrower with the passage of time until the term came to apply only to "instructional films" suitable for use in educational settings. The statements made by Yaguchi Shin—an educationalist who relocated in those days from a major citizen-owned research institute to a national education research institute—are very much in line with this shift in how educational films were defined. In 1949, Yaguchi criticized what was called the "film classroom" system in which schoolchildren were brought to movie theaters in the morning, before they opened to the general public, to see whatever random films happened to be shown. For Yaguchi, the main problem with this system was that "the contents [of such randomly chosen films] almost never had any connection to what was being taught in the classrooms" (as quoted in Yoshihara 2011, 140). Yaguchi instead advocated a new approach to "educational films," calling for wider proliferation of 16 mm film projectors, development and maintenance of film libraries at each and every school in the nation, and, finally, both qualitative and quantitative improvements to those film collections.

To Yaguchi, therefore, "educational film" should and did refer to instructional materials useful in audiovisual education, which led him to introduce a new term, *kyōzai eiga* (instructional film). His conception of the educational film would later earn the endorsement of the Japanese Film Education Society, an organization at the very center of the postwar educational film world in Japan. Concurrently, commercial film companies clearly began to support—or be complicit in—this philosophy of film education. In the 1950s, three film studios, namely, Iwanami Film Studio, Gakushū Kenkyūsha (Gakken Co., Ltd.), and Tōei Kyōiku Eizōbu (Tōei Educational Film Co., Ltd.), produced and sold compendiums (*taikei*) of instructional films in social studies, science, and Japanese geography, gambling with the companies' futures on the success of these compendiums. And they were not disappointed: by the end of the 1950s, a boom of compendium-style instructional films began to sweep the film world.

Undoubtedly, the idea about the essence of the new educational/instructional film, and the plan to create film libraries, both originated in the legacy of CIE films, which had been sent to every prefecture in Japan and were required to be stocked at Japan's public libraries in the form of "CIE film collections." Nor was the influence of CIE films on instructional films limited to these structural features; it can also be seen in the spread of the attitude that viewed films as tools, as mere containers for the information one wished to convey. In the magazine *Shichōkaku kyōiku* (Audiovisual Education), Yoshihara Junpei provides an account of a fascinating debate between Yaguchi Shin and filmmaker Tanikawa Yoshio. To Yaguchi's assertion of films as mere instructional tools, Tanikawa objected:

> We may call them instructional films, but films are truly comprehensive and have many roles to play. It is for this reason that films must be artistic creations. Filmmakers must not simply haphazardly gather materials for a film. You claim that educators require pure instructional materials, and such works need not possess artistic sensibilities. But speaking from the filmmaker's perspective, I would emphasize the fact that we filmmakers simply cannot make effective instructional materials under those circumstances. Mr. Yaguchi Shin has said, "It is a problem when films are too film-like," but what, I ask, shall films become if they cease to be "film-like"?
>
> (As quoted in Yoshihara 2011, 141–2)[10]

This challenging retort by Tanikawa—what will films become if they are no longer film-like?—was made in 1958, but I suspect it did not cause as much trouble as one might expect, partly because, at the time, those potentially disturbing "no longer film-like" films were numerous. The widespread acceptance of the notion that educational films remain not-film-like can be attributed to the pattern of educational filmmaking established by CIE films, which had been spread very widely and used as instructional films all over Japan. When seen in retrospect, it might be possible to replace the various oppositional binaries—Yaguchi versus Tanikawa, educationalists versus filmmakers, moving images as instructional materials versus moving images as artistic creations—with a single binary, namely, the opposition of CIE films (films as a mere tool for propaganda, not art) versus postwar Japanese documentaries (films with artistic impression, at least in the Japanese filmmakers' mind).

The aforementioned Okada Hidenori from National Film Archive of Japan gives the following concise account of the filmmaking policy at Iwanami Film Studio:

> Kobayashi Isamu, Iwanami Film Studio's managing director, foresaw that if the company devoted itself solely to making independently planned science films, they would soon exhaust the limits of that genre. So he formulated several principles: the recruiting of sponsors, a focus on creating very high quality works, and the avoidance of becoming a yes-man for the corporate sponsors. This "sponsor-centric" model was not limited to Iwanami Film Studio, but rather became the very foundation on which the then contemporary world of short films based its development.
>
> (Okada 2011, 206–7)

We can easily see this attitude Okada emphasizes, the attitude of not becoming a "yes-man" for the sponsors, as evidence of the filmmakers' resistance against those films—and CIE films had been like this from the beginning—which placed great importance on the views of the sponsors (i.e., whoever was doing the educating in the film). It comes as no surprise that this "resistance" is, in the end, what contemporary Japanese filmmakers utilized to identify and maintain a distinction between their body of work and CIE films. In other words, while all acknowledge that postwar educational films in Japan were heavily influenced by CIE films, there was a feeling among the Japanese creators that their films were very much different from the latter.

Here it behooves us to turn our attention once more to Nakamura Hideyuki's work (2012) concerning those CIE films made in Japan. Nakamura provides several counterexamples to the binary opposition of CIE films versus postwar Japanese documentaries. First, he points out that "there is very little theoretical affinity… [between] 'propaganda and education' [and] 'films'" (250). He then goes on to talk about several CIE films made in Japan, calling attention to the fact that they have "an ambiguity which thwarts attempts to reduce them to their supposedly unified message as educational films" (251). Of these works, Nakamura also says that they were made in a way that made the most of their nature as films. In some ways, we might well say that this characteristic resonates well with the "resistance" filmmakers considered indispensable to the filmmaking process at Iwanami Film Studio.

Now I would like to turn to the third element of analysis, namely, the similarities on a visual level between CIE films and postwar Japanese documentaries. Earlier I explained how one characteristic feature of CIE films is their tendency to depict and explain easy-to-understand scientific processes that are in actuality quite difficult to visualize, such as the nuclear fission process in atomic energy. The rhetorical style of such visualizations of science, or alternatively of processes of thinking, was passed on to many postwar Japanese documentaries. For example, under the instruction of the physicist Nakaya Ukichirō, Iwanami Film Studio completed a film called *Totsu renzu* (*Convex Lens*, 1950), which, as the title suggests, illustrates the properties and functions of convex lenses through a series of experiments. The film depicts how light is refracted when it passes through a convex lens. Regarding this film, Maki Makoto (2011) recounts a fascinating episode, noting how he pointed out the contradictions of the film in the entrance examination of Iwanami Film Studio, which eventually got him admitted to the company:

> I was shown *Convex Lens* on the occasion of joining Iwanami Film Studio, and told to write my impressions of it.... [T]he fact is that, as they admit in the film, in order to conduct experiments with light rays one must have parallel beams of light. This film was made according to a concept of strict experimental physics, and yet in it they used a system of lenses to create parallel beams of light. When I heard that this was an educational film for middle school students, I responded that it was absurd. After all, if you want to do an experiment with parallel beams of light, sunlight is ideal. And indeed, virtually all such light ray experiments are conducted using sunlight, so I wrote how strange I thought it was that they decided to use such large-scale lenses instead. Creating a system of lenses like that is a painstaking task.
>
> (166–7)

Maki's reflections bring into relief the fact that, when *Convex Lens* was made, the film crew deliberately chose to use a system of lenses to create parallel beams of light, despite the fact that using sunlight would have been much easier. And I think we can see this choice not as the result of a careless oversight by the film staff—which included physicist Nakaya Ukichirō—but rather as a desire on their part to show just how scientific this lens-based process of creating light was. Put otherwise, the film is a visualization of science itself.

We should bear in mind that this sort of visualization of science, which, as we have seen, contains some inconsistencies, also appears in the aforementioned CIE film *Atomic Power*. I said earlier of *Atomic Power* that via the film's attempt to make visible, to the extent possible, the invisible and unvisualizable process of splitting an atom, the audience was being literally "educated." However, the visualizations occurring in the film—such as its depiction of the way in which atoms are bound together, are stimulated, and lose stability to produce atomic energy, with the film footage based on substitute images of the process—are in actuality not sufficient for the average viewer to completely understand nuclear power per se. Rather, the "education" the viewers receive is, if anything, about science itself, a statement about the manner in which one should rationally understand science. Alternatively, we might say that the film suggests that atoms are just like other objects: they can be split. In other words, the film depicts science as just another thing under the dominion of humans. In this sense, the fact that *Convex Lens* uses a system of lenses to create parallel light beams, and the visualizations of science on display in CIE films in general, can be interpreted as conveying a deep belief of human mastery over science.

In Lieu of an Epilogue

To conclude this essay, I would like to discuss the things that were not able to be shown, and thus had to be made invisible, in those films shown in Japan during the Occupation period. One of the major contradictions of the Allied—in reality, American—Occupation was that despite the oft-repeated mantra about democratizing Japan, the Americans were conducting severe speech control via GHQ's press code and censoring a wide range of cultural media. And to prevent this contradiction from being exposed and becoming a problem, GHQ also planned and executed a policy that suppressed, via media censorship, any mention of the very fact that Japan was being occupied. For example, in films it was forbidden to show any of the English-language signs which were ubiquitous throughout Japan during the Occupation, and the visual depiction of American GIs, who in those days were crammed into every city, town, and village, was totally suppressed. As for the CIE films, their political message, or indeed their very identity as vehicles of American cultural policy, was suppressed. This nicely illustrated the entire censorship situation, and the contradictions of GHQ in particular, in the period. And given the existence of the abovementioned anti-Japanese brainwashing operations, "PANEL-D-JAPAN," it was also necessary to render invisible this aspect of CIE films. In other words, we might say that the political mission of CIE films, namely, to foster pro-American sentiment and anti-communist ideology in the viewers, was hidden under, and within, the larger mission of spreading democracy in Japan.

When watching postwar Japanese educational films, I sometimes get the sense that they are consciously avoiding politics. When we recall that CIE films also feature this sense of distance from politics (i.e., the art and finesse of rendering politics unseen), can we say that the postwar educational films put a strain on viewers' powers of imagination as well? In his analysis of Tokieda Toshie's 1957 Iwanami film *Machi no seiji* (*Town Politics*), Yoshimi Shun'ya (2011) discusses how, within this work, those people who might be "inconvenient" are erased from view or rendered invisible. The "town" in *Town Politics* is actually Kunitachi, a city in western Tokyo, and the film depicts its postwar growth and development in its dual guises as a college town and as a center of culture and learning. The film also displays the gatherings of women, dubbed "studying moms," in this area, and the decision by these women to involve themselves in town politics. Yoshimi points out that in contrast with its depiction of civic political participation of these women, the film consciously renders invisible the true political crisis that Kunitachi then faced:

> This film leaves some things unsaid. It shows the "mothers" hard at work "studying" the structure of the town's budget and striving to improve the educational conditions for the children of the area. But what this film does not show—or oppose—is the fact that, right next door to the college town of Kunitachi, in the neighboring town of Tachikawa [which had a U.S. military base], the occupation continued, day after day. The beginning of the film does refer to Kunitachi's relations with Tachikawa, but only to show that it is resisting "Tachikawa-ification" and does not go any further than that. Moreover, despite the fact that in Sunagawa, the other town adjacent to Kunitachi, repeated anti-base expansion rallies and protests were being held right as the film was being made, no connection is drawn, at least on the surface, between the women opposing the American bases and the "studying moms" of Kunitachi.... [I]n other words, the "women of the night" and "protesting ladies" of the adjacent towns are treated as phenomena that remain entirely outside the "town" being depicted.
>
> (300–1)

The participation of these women in the political governance of their town, and their progressive advancement in society and their ability to express themselves, all exemplify the storytelling elements favored by and emphasized in CIE films. Clearly, these elements are symbolic of the emancipation of women, historically discriminated against in Japan, from the bonds of the feudal system; as such, they constitute the perfect image to symbolize the spread of democracy in Japan. And it is no leap to suggest that *Town Politics*, like many of the CIE films that came before it, uses these idealized images to hide from view the fact that the United States occupied Japan—in this case by rendering invisible the issue that the mothers of Kunitachi were most deeply concerned about, namely, that their town would become a base town like Tachikawa and fall under the negative influence of the United States.

However, it is incumbent upon me to point out here that not all postwar Japanese documentaries were shaped in the political mold derived from CIE films. For example, Kamei Fumio, who made his directorial debut in 1935 and continued to make movies right through the war and into the postwar period, created several films in the 1950s—namely, *Kichi no ko* (*Children of the Base*, 1954), *Ikiteite yokatta* (*It's Good to be Alive*, 1956), *Ryūketsu no kiroku: Sunagawa* (*Record of Bloodshed: Sunagawa*, 1957), and *Ningen mina kyōdai* (*Men Are All Brothers*, 1960). These films took up such subjects as the hypocrisies of the Occupation and the sufferings arising from the atomic bomb, and cast a critical eye on the ostensibly democratic education in postwar Japan in order to expose the intractable problem of deeply rooted class prejudice in Japanese society. In addition, Tsuchimoto Noriaki, a director who emulated Kamei in eventually leaving Iwanami Film Studio to begin producing independent documentaries, worked from the late 1960s into the 1970s on *Minamata: kanja-san to sono sekai* (*Minamata: Patients and Their World*, 1971), a film which uses the issue of pollution and its victims to bring the hypocrisies of Japanese society to the surface.

As the examples of Kamei and Tsuchimoto make clear, the world of postwar Japanese documentary film, and the educational film in its midst, cannot be defined by, or reduced to, a single standout characteristic. Moreover, we must not lose sight of the fact that the American cultural policies carried out in postwar Japan did not vanish with the cessation of the Cold War, but rather continue to be reproduced, for instance, in the academic paradigm of Japanese film studies. In order to rid ourselves of this Occupation legacy once and for all, a great deal more investigation, built on a foundation of transdisciplinary cooperation, still needs to be done.

Notes

1 In the *Eiga nenkan sengohen 1950 nenban*, the term "kyōiku eigakai" (the world of educational films) was used as the subject heading for documentary films. It is in the *Eiga nenkan sengohen 1951 nenban* that this subject heading was first changed to "tanpen/kyōiku eigakai" (the world of film shorts/educational films), which thereafter became the standard term in the *Eiga nenkan*, though in 1955, the term was reworded to "educational/short films." It also bears mentioning that the subgenre of "kyōzai eiga" (films for classroom use), which I discuss later, first appeared in the 1951 edition of *Eiga nenkan*. This is not meant to suggest, however, that the expression—and genre—of "educational film" did not exist in prewar Japan. According to Tanaka Jun'ichirō (1979), several live-action films, including one produced

by the Yoshizawa Shōten company on the Boxer Uprising, had been shown under the heading "kyōiku katsudō shashinkai" (educational moving picture society) on September 1–4, 1901, at the Kinkikan cinema in the Kanda district of Tokyo (28). Moreover, in this essay, I am using "documentary" as a kind of broad, catch-all expression, but changes in terminology, to the specific terms in use for this genre in wartime and postwar Japan, reflected and helped bring about alterations to Japan's film culture. For example, Atsugi Taka's translation of Paul Rotha's *Documentary Film* (1936) was published in 1938 as *Bunka eigaron Pōru Rūta cho* (Kyoto: Daiichi geibunsha), making use of the contemporary term "culture film" for "documentary film," but in the postwar reprinting, the title was changed to *Dokyumentari-eiga Pōru Rōsa cho* (Tokyo: Misuzu shobō, 1960).

2 Specifically, Ochiai has the following to say: "From the start, CIE educational films were provided in order to aid in accomplishing the adult educational goals of the Occupation, but because school-appropriate teaching materials for democratic education were extremely scarce, the Natco film projectors, which had been deployed in order to help disseminate democratic ideals, were not used solely for adult education, but also in classrooms" (8).

3 Moreover, the films CIE used to spread their propagandistic messages were not limited solely to the category of educational films. During the 1950s, CIE was involved in the production of fiction films even though the office refused to reveal its involvement by not listing itself as producer. This fact only came to light after the investigation launched by two journalists, Alex Dubro and Matsui Michio (Dubro and Matsui 1994–95). Six secretly CIE-produced fiction films actually reached the screen, namely, Abe Yutaka and Shimura Toshio's *Watashi wa Siberia no horyo datta* (*I Was a POW in Siberia*, 1952, produced by Shū Taguchi and distributed by Tōhō), Nakata Haruhisa's *Tetsu no hanataba* (*The Iron Bouquet*, 1953, produced by Nakata Prod. And distributed by Hokusei), Shimura Toshio's *Arashi no seishun* (*Storm's Youth*, 1954, produced by Nakai Prod. and distributed by Shintōhō), Shimura Toshio's *Dotō no kyōdai* (*Brothers of the Surging Waves*, 1957, produced by Shintōhō), Kobayashi Tsuneo's *Jettoki shutsudō dai 101 kōkūkichi* (*The Jet Takes off from Airbase 101*, 1957, distributed by Tōhō), and Hara Takumi's *Korosareru no wa gomen da* (*I'd Rather You Didn't Kill Me*, 1960, produced by Sakura Prod. and distributed by Shintōhō). Thus, it is safe to say that the films secretly produced by CIE were not always with the same company or director but rather spread out. Only one of these films—*Iron Bouquet*—is currently viewable at the National Film Archive of Japan, but it is possible to get information about some of the other films from various sources. For example, according to Ōki Fukue, who worked as a production assistant on *The Jet Takes off from Airbase 101,* that film contains a scene where Takakura Ken—still a brand new actor when the film was made in 1957, the period just before the Anpo (U.S.-Japan Security Treaty) protests—has the line "What is wrong with having a Self-Defense Force?" Moreover, all the fighter jets used in that film were the property of the U.S. Air Force (Dubro and Matsui 1994, 1:42). The impetus for the Japan Self-Defense Force (JSDF), established on July 1, 1954, can be traced back to the outbreak of the Korean War in 1950. During the Occupation, Police Reserve Corps had been formed by order of GHQ, which was itself based upon the terms of the Potsdam Agreement. It changed its name to the Security Corps in 1952, and then transitioned into the Ground Self-Defense Force. In this same period, the last vestiges of the Imperial Navy were following quite a similar path, initially renamed into the Japan Coast Guard and then the Defense Corps before being incorporated into the JSDF. Thus, one can clearly make out, in the background, American insistence on Japan's

rearmament because of the perceived necessity of a Japan that could and should possess national armed forces, a perception shaped by the Korean War as well as by the communist takeover of China in 1949. It is difficult to see the pro-JSDF figure of the Japanese pilot (Takakura Ken) who appears in one of these CIE-sponsored films, then, as anything other than a mouthpiece for American cultural policy.

4 See also Fujita (2009), which could be considered a sequel to her aforementioned work.

5 See also Tsuchiya (2005, 2006, 2009).

6 For more on this topic, see Niwa Yoshiyuki (2012). Iwanami Film Studio also nurtured several exceptionally talented filmmakers, including Hani Susumu, Haneda Sumiko, Tokieda Toshie, Kuroki Kazuo, and Ogawa Shinsuke, who are all invariably mentioned in accounts of postwar Japanese documentary film. Although Iwanami Film Studio closed its doors in 1998 due to financial hardship, the masterpieces these directors completed while working there help ensure that its name will remain ever prominent in histories of Japanese documentary film.

7 Nakamura Hideyuki (2012) makes the following statement about Takahagi Ryūtarō's standpoint in those days, and uses Takahagi as an example of the "continuity in personnel" with which the Japanese film industry weathered the transition from wartime into the postwar years: "CIE educational film policies, by relying on Japanese producers to complete [the reediting work], led to the reviving and reshuffling of the same filmmaking organizations which had been in operation since prewar Japan. Naturally, this meant not only the continuing survival of the filmmaking organizations themselves, but also a considerable degree of continuity in personnel from the prewar into the postwar. Perhaps the best example of such continuity is the aforementioned Takahagi Ryūtarō. Takahagi was born in 1916, graduated in 1936 from Tokyo-fu Aoyama Shihan Gakkō [Tokyo Prefecture Aoyama Teacher-Training School, currently Tokyo Gakugei University], and became a teacher at the Minamiyama Elementary School in Azabu Ward. He poured considerable effort into film-based education. His efforts, which extended from the prewar period through to the war years, apparently included making use of Tokyo's libraries, organizing meetings of the Kōdō Eigakai [a film society active at elementary schools around Japan], and leading students in field trips to movie theaters" (245).

8 Takahagi Ryūtarō's original article, "CIE kyōiku eiga kara nani wo manabi toru ka" (What can we learn from CIE educational films?), appears on p. 38 of the June 1949 edition of *Eiga kyōshitsu*. Note the remarkable way in which this article by Takahagi begins: "*I do not have detailed knowledge* of *the ways CIE educational films* were *produced* in *Japan*, but it seems that, firstly, Japanese companies were hired to revise the films sent over from the United States in order to make them easier for Japanese people to understand" (italics mine).

9 Shiba Kazumi (2001) compares these two works in considerable detail, so those wishing for more information on this topic are urged to consult it.

10 The original article by Tanikawa, entitled "Kyōzai eiga ni tsuite" (About teaching material films)," was published in the May 1958 issue of *Shichōkaku kyōiku*.

Works Cited

Abe, Akira. 1983. *Sengo chihō kyōiku seido seiritsu katei no kenkyū*. Tokyo: Fūkan shobō.

Dubro, Alex, and Matsui Michio. 1994–95. "Panel-D-Japan hajimete veil wo nugu America tai-Nichi sennō kōsa no zenbō." 7 parts. *View* 4.13–5.5 (November 1994 thru May 1995).

Fugita, Fumiko. 2009. "1950 nendai Amerika no tai Nichi bunka seisaku no kōka." *Tsuda juku daigaku kiyō*, no. 41: 19–43.

Fujita, Fumiko. 2003. "1950 nendai no Amerika no tai Nichi bunka seisaku—gaikan." *Tsuda juku daigaku kiyō*, no. 35: 1–18.

Maki, Makoto. 2011. "Iwanami no kagaku kyōiku eiga: sono denjū to shisō." In *Iwanami eiga no ichi oku furēmu*, edited by Tanba Miyuki and Yoshimi Shun'ya. 165–82. Tokyo: Tokyo Daigaku Shuppankai.

Misaki, Tomeko. 2012. "Eisei kazoku no tanjō: CIE eiga kara USIS eiga he, renzoku sareru kazoku no shōzō." In *Senryō suru me, senryō suru koe: CIE/USIS eiga to VOA rajio*, edited by Tsuchiya Yuka and Yoshimi Shun'ya, 213–41. Tokyo: Tokyo Daigaku Shuppankai.

Nakamura, Hideyuki. 2012. "Haisha ni yoru haisha no tame no eizō: CIE eiga kyōiku to Nihon sei CIE eiga ni tsuite." In *Senryō suru me, senryō suru koe: CIE/USIS eiga to VOA rajio*, edited by Tsuchiya Yuka and Yoshimi Shun'ya. 243–63. Tokyo: Tokyo Daigaku Shuppankai.

Nakamura, Hideyuki. 2002. "Senryōka beikoku kyōiku eiga ni tsuite no kansho—*Eiga kyōshitsu* shi ni miru Natoko (eishaki) to CIE eiga no juyō ni tsuite." *CineMagaziNet* 6. Accessed 19 October 2018. www.cmn.hs.h.kyoto-u.ac.jp/CMN6/nakamura.htm.

Niwa, Yoshiyuki. 2012. "Eizō de miru sengo Nihon no kagaku gijutsu, shakai, bunka." In *Iwanami eiga no ichi oku furēmu*, edited by Niwa Yoshiyuki and Yoshimi Shun'ya, 1–17. Tokyo: Tokyo Daigaku Shuppankai.

Ochiai, Kyōichi. 1949. "Special Report on the Present Stage of Education through Film: What Level Have Films for Education Reached in Postwar Japan?" *Eiga kyōshitsu* 3(3): 6–8.

Okada, Hidenori. 2011. "Eigashi no naka no Iwanami kagaku eiga." In *Iwanami eiga no ichi oku furēmu*, edited by Niwa Yoshiyuki and Yoshimi Shun'ya. Tokyo: Tokyo Daigaku Shuppankai. 203–215.

Satō, Tadao. 1977. *Nihon kiroku eizōshi*. Tokyo: Hyōronsha.

Shiba, Kazumi. 2001. "Sengo rika kyōiku kankei shiryō no kenkyū (I): rika kyōiku no tame no CIE eiga ni tsuite." In *Hiroshima Daigakuin kyōiku kenkyū kiyō*, no. 50: 91–100

Tanaka, Jun'ichirō. 1979. *Nihon kyōiku eiga hattatsushi*. Tokyo: Kagyūsha.

Tanikawa, Takeshi. 2002. *Amerika eiga to senryō seisaku*. Kyoto: Kyoto Daigaku Shuppankai.

Tsuchiya, Yuka. 2010. "Senryōki no CIE eiga (natoko eiga)." In *Fumikoeru dokyumentarii*, edited by Kurosawa Kiyoshi et al., 155–81. Tokyo: Iwanami shoten.

Tsuchiya, Yuka. 2009. *Shin bei Nihon no kōchiku: Amerika no tai Nichi jōhō, kyōiku seisaku to Nihon senryō*. Tokyo: Meiseki shoten.

Tsuchiya, Yuka. 2006. "'Paburikku dipuromashii' no shuppatsuten to shite no Amerika senryōgun: CIE eiga." *Interijensu* 7: 60–70.

Tsuchiya, Yuka. 2005. "Amerika tai Nichi senryōgun 'CIE eiga': kyōiku to puropaganda no kyōkai—(2. Kan) Nihonjin ni yoru juyō to kaishaku." *Ehime Daigaku hōgakubu ronshū: sōgō seisaku gakkahen* 19: 27–54. Yoshimi, Shun'ya. 2011. "Benkyō suru okāsan to senryō suru tasha." In *Iwanami eiga no ichi oku furēmu*, edited by Tanba Miyuki and Yoshimi Shun'ya. 300–1. Tokyo: Tokyo Daigaku Shuppankai.

Yoshihara, Junpei. 2011. *Nihon tanhen eigashi: bunka eiga, kyōiku eiga, sangyō eiga*. Tokyo: Iwanami Shoten.

6 The Cold War as Media Environment in 1960s Japanese Cinema

Michael Raine

The Cold War in Asia was warmer than in Europe. Hot wars and massacres in China, Korea, and Southeast Asia kept the whole region unstable. In Japan, the Cold War was less extreme but also ubiquitous, the fundamental military-political-economic-cultural fact that underpinned postwar Japanese society. Previous studies have focused on the interference of American Cold War institutions in Japanese cinema or the critique of the Cold War in Japanese films; however, this chapter argues more broadly that cinema was part of Japan's Cold War cultural infrastructure, not so much a conduit for political messages as the environment in which audiences experienced and resolved the desires, resentments, and anxieties generated by Japan's subordination to the American government's shifting goals of (anti-communist) security and economic development in Asia.

One means of bringing those feelings into focus on film was the topos of land: land that is occupied, expropriated for military bases, or threatened with economic exploitation. After the protests against the U.S. military bases and the renewal of the Treaty of Mutual Cooperation and Security Between the United States and Japan (*Anpo*) that came to a head in 1960, that topos was intensified if also rendered more ambiguous. Land stood for the sovereignty that was threatened by modernity and Americanization, but at the most crucial turning point of the Cold War in Japan it was the fundamentally unserious treatment of that topic and the conflicted emotions that it allowed audiences to experience, rather than any particular message, that made up the Cold War "structure of feeling" in popular Japanese cinema. After reviewing the more direct ways in which the Cold War intervened in and was addressed by Japanese cinema, this chapter argues that the Nikkatsu studio's *Wataridori* series (1959–62) cites a contemporary discourse of revanchist cultural nationalism while allowing ambivalence about that feeling by patterning the films after the syntax and semantics of popular Hollywood genre cinema. Although other studio films were more straightforward, the divided significance of "native place" in films that are usually regarded as popcorn cosmopolitanism anticipates later "new wave" films that questioned the appeal to indigeneity of both progressive and conservative politics in 1960s Japan.

The Cultural Cold War

Anti-communism long preceded the Cold War in Japan. Japanese counterrevolutionary armies were the last to withdraw (in 1922) from the USSR, and the militarist government signed the Anti-Comintern Pact with Nazi Germany in 1936. Communist organizing before 1945 was met with arrest and torture, as well as with a highly effective moral coercion that converted leftist resistance into ideological obedience to the state. That cultural aspect to the anti-communist policy extended to the cinema: exhibition spaces were subject to police surveillance, scripts were censored before production, and each print was inspected before it could be shown. It was a commonplace of wartime policy that films were bullets in the "cultural war" (*bunkasen*; see Tsumura 1943) even as filmmakers were regarded with suspicion as cosmopolitan intellectuals (Yamamoto 1998, 265). Defeated by an incendiary and atomic bombing campaign that destroyed 40% of urban Japan and killed hundreds of thousands of people, Japan was stripped of its colonial territories and subordinated to a U.S.-led military Occupation that fell hardest on Okinawa. The Supreme Commander for the Allied Powers (SCAP) first focused on the "democratization" of Japan, but as the iron curtain descended on Europe and the civil war in China turned in Mao's favor, U.S. policy embarked on a "reverse course" toward Cold War containment. Japan was vital to that goal, seen as both a staging post for the projection of U.S. military power and as the leader of economic development in Asia that would bring other Asian nations into the Western capitalist fold.

Driven by the domino theory, the Eisenhower and Kennedy administrations engaged in a "total Cold War" against the USSR and China that had military, political, economic, and cultural dimensions (Osgood 2006). Even after the Occupation ended (except in Okinawa) in 1952, Japanese subordination continued through an unequal Security Treaty that guaranteed American freedom of military action from bases throughout the archipelago. After "losing" China and reaching a stalemate in the Korean War, the U.S. intervened in Japanese domestic politics, using slush funds to smooth the merger of the two main conservative parties into the Liberal Democratic Party (LDP), ensuring an electoral dominance that has continued almost unbroken until today. Those LDP politicians, many active in the wartime government, played off America's Cold War concerns, avoiding rearmament but granting military bases, and rejecting trade with China in return for money and access for Japanese exports (Prados 2009; Samuels 2001; Schaller 1997). Culture, too, was an essential component of American policy. According to Kenneth Osgood, the United States Information Agency (USIA, also known as the United States Information Service [USIS]) spent over a third of its budget on anti-communist propaganda in East and Southeast

Asia. Its surreptitious propaganda operation in Japan was the third largest in the world (after Germany and India). Much of that money was spent on translation and publishing aimed at students and intellectuals, or on exhibitions of high art to demonstrate that the United States was not only a materialist culture. But the USIA also targeted mass media, providing music and discussion programs for radio and television broadcast, placing "message clips" into newsreels distributed by Paramount and Universal, and sponsoring the production of feature films (Osgood 2006, 115–7).

Cinema as Cold War Strategy

Although divided between progressive and conservative wings, SCAP's thinking on the utility of cinema in shaping public opinion mirrored that of the Japanese authorities, so there was much continuity between the wartime and postwar censorship systems. Against a prewar background of studies of propaganda and "media effects", both sides sought to block harmful influences and inject positive messages into the populations they administered. In the first years of the Occupation, the Civil Information and Education (CIE) section of SCAP proscribed "feudalism" and prescribed "democratization and enlightenment," even encouraging the production of anti-militarist films such as the unreleased *Nihon no higeki* (1946) directed by Kamei Fumio (Hirano 1994, 105–46).[1] Film studio unions were often quite militant, especially at Toho, the most modern studio and the center of wartime propaganda filmmaking. However, the reverse course empowered the military authorities over the civilian "New Dealers." In 1948, a new management team at Toho attempted to fire almost 300 union members, sparking the third, last, and longest of a series of strikes (Hirano 1994, 205–40). Rather than simply withdraw their labor, the union engaged in "production control"—it occupied the space of the studio between April and August and continued to produce films, aiming to show that management was unnecessary and to influence the political orientation of Japanese cinema (Dower 1999, 254–75). The cinema was seen as crucial to Cold War communications, so SCAP supported the studio in obtaining an injunction against the union occupation. The strikers, led by weeping actresses, paraded from the studio under the supervision of 1,800 members of the new Police Reserve and a platoon of U.S. soldiers from the First Cavalry Division, supported by five tanks and six armored cars. As criticism of this extraterritorial show of force had it, the Americans brought "everything but a battleship" (Hirano 1994, 312).

Information on the CIA-sponsored feature films is quite sparse, but Osgood and Prados claim that five or six films were produced by Japanese studios between 1953 and 1959, including Kobayashi Tsuneo's *Jet Vapor Trails in Dawn* (*Jetto-ki shutsudo*, 1957) starring a pre-stardom

Takakura Ken. Agency reports trumpeted that this pro-rearmament film was seen by 15 million people (Osgood 2006, 117; Prados 2009, 165). The CIA also worked through front organizations such as the Asia Foundation to produce sympathetic films and to sponsor the Asian Film Festival, open only to anti-communist nations, while American film companies took advantage of the tense climate to make topical films set in Japan with anti-communist themes (Baskett 2014; Lee 2014, 2017; Kitamura 2009). Senior left-wing critic Iwasaki Akira (1958a) saw SCAP film policy in a Cold War light: America needed Japan to rearm, so it imported many Hollywood war films to create in Japan not nationalism (*aikokushin*) but Americanism (*aibeishin*) (186). Film historian Yamada Kazuo (1970) even argued that cinema bankrolled American Cold War policy—profits from the screening of Hollywood films that could not be repatriated because of currency restrictions were instead diverted to CIA slush funds, or intervened in Japanese culture by sponsoring Christian universities (152–4).

Seen from another perspective, however, these results are not particularly impressive. According to jmdb.ne.jp, about 3,000 feature films were produced in Japan between 1953 and 1959; six films constitute only 0.2% of the total. The claimed audience figure for *Jet Vapor Trails in Dawn* also seems like an exaggeration; the most successful film for Toei in that period was an all-star version of the *Mito Komon* story, which had an audience of approximately 11 million.[2] Left-wing critics complained that featuring Japanese Self-Defense Forces (JSDF) in Honda Ishiro's *Godzilla* (Toho, 1954) promoted the remilitarization of Japan (Tsurumi 1959, 128), but even films such as Makino Masahiro's *Pure-Hearted Army Squad* (*Junjo butai*, Toei, 1957) that appealed to audience nostalgia for the warm camaraderie of military life never promoted Japanese war aims, and very few postwar films endorsed Japan's role in America's Cold War policy. Rather than instrumentalist views of the cinema as a conduit for ideological messages, we would benefit from thinking more carefully about the role cinema played in the Cold War struggle for the future of Japan.

Independent Production and the Cinema of Cold War Resistance

There was a clear divide between principals and agents in the postwar Japanese film industry—the owners were often anti-communist, even right-wing, with ties to organized crime as well as the Japanese business community that supported the LDP and its Cold War bargain with the U.S., but most of the filmmakers were part of a more or less cosmopolitan and intellectual class. Films that made politics the subject of their narratives were generally on the left. The Japanese Communist Party (JCP) emerged from the war with an enhanced reputation, so many intellectuals and cultural workers, including filmmakers, were members even if they had not been sympathetic before the defeat. The leaders of the Toho strike and others "purged" by SCAP in 1950 formed the nucleus of the "independent production" (*dokuritsu puro*) sector that was sponsored by trade unions, film societies, and study groups to produce films that were often shown in union halls as well as in commercial cinemas. In the 1950s, these low-budget films were critically highly regarded, often listed in the "best ten" poll by the largest film magazine, *Kinema junpo*. The independent films included documentaries as well as feature films that employed a "semi-documentary" aesthetic derived from the authority of Soviet and Maoist-inspired socialist realism and reportage. At the same time, as the deployment of weeping actresses at the end of the Toho strike might indicate, the films relied heavily on melodramatic tropes of victimization and overwhelming emotion rather than solely on political argument. Direct criticism of the United States was veiled or absent: the villains were usually militarists or corrupt politicians, while the victims were the good-hearted masses (*taishu*) or ordinary people (*shomin*).

There were even efforts to establish a circuit of independent cinemas for the exhibition of independently produced films. However, that potential for an alternative infrastructure to film exhibition faded when the Nikkatsu studio, which had been distributing Hollywood films, restarted production in 1954 (Kitamura 2007, 37). Nikkatsu contracted with many of those independent film workers and cinemas to make and show the studio's films, including the films discussed in this chapter. Despite the purge, there was no blacklist in Japan: the introduction of a double-bill system in 1956 created a demand for product; so, as opportunities for independent production and exhibition faded, leftist directors worked on a contract basis or released independently produced films through the studios. Although there were some protests against films that were seen as anti-American (Howard 2016), after the Occupation had ended it was relatively common to see films in commercial Japanese cinemas that criticized capitalism or militarism, and were sympathetic to the contemporary Non-Aligned Movement. Shindo Kaneto's *Sea Bastards* (*Umi no yarodomo*, Nikkatsu, 1957), for example, featured rising star Ishihara Yujiro in an allegorical critique of Japan's comprador status between West and East. Yujiro plays a foreman who mediates between corrupt white officers and the multiethnic crew of a cargo ship in Tokyo. In a crisis modeled on Eisenstein's *Battleship Potemkin*, the crew mutinies against their exploitative living conditions and the film intercuts their celebrations with newsreel footage of North African independence celebrations.

In the same year, Imai Tadashi directed *Story of Pure Love* (*Jun'ai monogatari*, Toei), a film about a pickpocket and a delinquent who is dying of radiation sickness caused by the atomic bombing of Hiroshima.

The film won the director's prize at the Berlin International Film Festival. Imai was also the most highly regarded filmmaker of the late 1950s in Japan, when great masters such as Ozu Yasujiro and Naruse Mikio were seen as old-fashioned and before the "new wave" filmmakers had made their mark (Togawa 1960). As with other areas of Japanese cultural and intellectual life, the tenor of Japanese film criticism was strongly on the left. *Story of Pure Love* was voted by critics in *Kinema junpo* as the second-best film of 1957, after Imai's *Rice* (*Kome*, Toei), which focuses on the hard lives of villagers who fish and grow rice in and around Kasumigaura Lake in Ibaraki, northeast of Tokyo. The film follows a family over the course of a growing season as they are treated badly by their landlord and penalized by an unsympathetic police force. *Rice* was a popular melodrama (the film came in ninth at the box office for the year), but it was also the first postwar film to focus on the everyday lives of farming families caught in a network of social and economic inequalities. At the end of the film, after Mochizuki Yuko, star of many "mother film" melodramas about the sacrifices mothers make for their children, has been indicted and humiliated, a pan across the ripened rice crop leads to Mochizuki at the lake, where she drowns herself in silent protest against the system that is about to dispossess her of the land she farms.

Land, particularly the agricultural land of rural Japan, figured large in left-wing protests against Cold War modernity in Japan. After the JCP Central Committee was purged by SCAP in 1950, Tokuda Kyuichi and other leaders went into exile in China, from where they directed Mountain Village Operation Units (*sanson kosakutai*) that attempted to foment a Maoist revolution in Japan, centered in mountain villages. The JCP "soldiers" were often university students who offered medical care and education, along with propaganda, to local people and at the same time attacked government-mandated infrastructure in the territory such as police boxes, train lines, and dam construction sites. The Mountain Village Operation Unit insurgency was a total failure, rejected by local people and collapsing the JCP electoral share from 10% to 2.5%, but there was a more popular register in which appeals to land resonated. Yanagita Kunio had already developed folklore studies (*minzokugaku*) in prewar Japan, and in the postwar established a research group from which his disciples began publishing his collected works (Naoe 1953, 218). *Minzokugaku*'s attention to the landscape of the non-metropolitan margins (Christy 2012, 37–85) and to ordinary Japanese society appealed to many across the political spectrum as a way to register resistance toward Japan's subservience to the U.S., and the modernization project that it entailed (Morse 1990, 179; Naoe 1953, 217). Referring to this period, filmmaker Imamura Shohei wrote: "I started to approach Japanese society from the perspective of indigenous [*dochaku*] culture and customs. During the season of politics the only thing I was interested in was Yanagita Kunio and folklore studies. How did the Japanese create today's society and sense of values? It wasn't the democracy forced on us by America but folk beliefs and rules passed down from ancient times" (Imamura 2004, 105).

The biggest protests in the 1950s were over Japanese land—the expansion of military bases to accommodate the jet fighters and bombers that were part of the U.S. force projection during the Cold War. The largest of those protests was known as the Sunagawa Struggle, after the village that would have been partly obliterated to expand the Tachikawa air base west of Tokyo. Starting in 1955 and continuing through 1957, students and trades unionists joined local farmers in resisting the expropriation of their land. Further incidents, such as the shooting of a scavenger at a firing range by an off-duty soldier in 1957, made the extraterritoriality of the bases, and of the laws that governed Americans in Japan, central to the resistance to Japan's Cold War subordination (see Osgood 2006, 244, for an account of the incident). The Sunagawa Struggle was also a media battle. The CIA-sponsored *Jet Vapor Trails in Dawn* was made explicitly to justify the expansion of the runways (Osgood 2006, 117). On the opposite side, documentary filmmaker Kamei Fumio made a series of three films in support of the protests, shown in cinemas that specialized in Western films, while independent filmmaker Sekigawa Hiroshi made a feature film with the Toei studio, *Airplane Roar and the Land* (*Bakuon to daichi*, 1957), that focused on the resistance to the attempts to survey the farmers' land. The images of the pitched battles in the Sunagawa documentaries established a tropology of land, occupation, and sovereignty that highlighted the violence of the American Occupation and influenced the direct action of radical students in the struggle against the U.S.-Japan Security Treaty (*Anpo*) in 1959 and 1960.

Anpo and Cold War Media

Japanese Socialist Party (JSP) Chair Asanuma Inejiro had visited China in 1959 and denounced U.S. imperialism as a common enemy, but few Japanese could look past the deaths of Japanese prisoners of war in the U.S.S.R. or the long-standing ideology of superiority toward China to want to switch sides in the Cold War (Packard 2010, 166; Schaller 1997, 148). However, Japan had attended the 1955 Bandung Conference that sparked the Non-Aligned Movement, albeit to make reparations in the form of overseas development deals, and the opposition to the Security Treaty called for Japan to adopt a similar stance. The LDP government, led by wartime bureaucrat and strong anti-communist Kishi Nobusuke, planned to ride Japanese nationalism to rearmament and a more active role in the Cold War by renegotiating the terms of the original Security Treaty. Kishi had come to prominence by emphasizing territory and sovereignty, arguing that Japan could not be an independent nation until it could defend its own land (Samuels 2001). The U.S. side, more concerned by Japanese neutralism than by Japanese nationalism, was happy to accept the changes and to commemorate the event with a visit to Japan by President Eisenhower, the first by a sitting U.S. president. A combination of radical student protests against the renewal, recalcitrant LDP rivals, and the U2 crisis of May 1960 threatened to derail Kishi's plans. The arms race to develop larger hydrogen bombs and the launch of the Soviet Sputnik satellite caused popular anxieties about Japan's place in the U.S.-led Cold War to explode. Being "America's unsinkable aircraft carrier in the Pacific" no longer seemed like such a good idea (Packard 2010, 158). As Justin Jesty (2012) has argued, the U.S.-Japan alliance that was a precondition of ending the Occupation in 1952 was initially quite popular, but by 1960, only 14% supported it, and 59% supported a policy of neutrality. In response, Kishi pushed approval of the treaty through the lower house of the Japanese parliament using unorthodox means, and then extended the parliamentary session until the agreement was automatically ratified. In May and June 1960, hundreds of thousands of ordinary Japanese protested that strategy—as Edwin O. Reischauer (1960) wrote in an influential article that led to his appointment as ambassador to Japan in 1961, "the vast majority of the demonstrators went out into the streets because they felt that Kishi, in his refusal to dissolve the Diet and in his ramming through of the treaty ratification, was trampling on democracy and leading Japan back to rearmament and war" (23; see also Schaller 1997, 147).

The Sunagawa and *Anpo* conflicts coincided with another conflict, one over the purpose and significance of audiovisual media. Shifts in media theory in late 1950s Japan produced tensions between different producers and critics. While the established parties and unions still supported the combination of reportage and melodrama to address mass audiences, they were challenged on the one hand by a younger generation of filmmakers and intellectuals who criticized the older cohort as insufficiently dialectical in their understanding of subjectivity and representation, and on the other by social psychologists who paid more attention to audience agency. Hanada Kiyoteru inspired what would come to be called the New Left with his criticisms of older filmmakers such as Kamei Fumio, helping to create among young filmmakers and critics such as Matsumoto Toshio (2012) a reflexive attention to the operations of realism that Yuriko Furuhata (2013) has called a "cinema of actuality." Although still clearly on the left, other groups such as *Shiso no kagaku* focused on popular culture, including the cinema that was increasingly dominated by Japanese films, and favored critics such as Sato Tadao who wrote "from the position of the audience" (Bronson 2016; Tsurumi 2005; see Ogi 1994, 815, for the comment on Sato). After an editorial split in 1955, the major film journal *Kinema junpo* published surveys and opinion polls by social psychologist Minami Hiroshi and his colleagues, normalizing that approach to film (Gerow 2014, 70; Inui and Minami 1994; Minami 1954). Even the senior left-wing critic in Japan, Iwasaki Akira, endorsed that methodology, claiming that political and economic developments in the 1950s had changed the Japanese audience. Iwasaki argued that while popular audiences had supported the anti-war films of the early 1950s, the political uprisings in Eastern Europe, along with the growth of popular weekly magazines and other aspects of mass communications, had caused audiences to lose faith and interest in history and become politically nihilistic. Iwasaki went on to claim that audiences were not interested in independent productions and that Toei executives were shocked by how badly films such as *Story of Pure Love* and *Airplane Roar and the Land* had done in the cinemas. Nikkatsu star Ishihara Yujiro was the new "idol" of the age, providing his young fans a vicarious experience of freedom in this conservative period of "relative stability" (*sotaiteki antei*). Iwasaki recognized that Yujiro's celebrity was constructed by the mass media, but insisted that was why entertainment films (*fuzoku eiga*) were tied to history and should be studied closely (Iwasaki 1958b, 20–1). When battles between police and students led to the death of an *Anpo* protester, posters asked if it was acceptable for Yujiro to be killed too (Packard 1966; "Suta ni kiku" 1960, 46). The cinema around 1960 was not only a Cold War cinema but a commercial cinema of high economic growth.

The *Anpo* crisis was defused by Kishi's replacement with Ikeda Hayato, who won the general election in November 1960 and followed an "income doubling" policy that was easily achieved after the Kennedy administration decided to emphasize economic ties with Japan to secure the military bases required for the Cold War (Schaller 1997, 160–2). As Yoshimi Shun'ya (2003) has argued, this pivot shifted the image of the U.S. in Japan, from the tense relation between "desire and violence" as the two sides of America (youth culture and military bases) before 1960, to a period in which American pop culture came to the fore while the military presence was deemphasized on the mainland and concentrated in Okinawa. Iwasaki was also clearly correct that Japan's media environment changed from the late 1950s. Film was rapidly being absorbed into a broader field of mass media made up of popular music, sports, and television, all synchronized by a growing publication culture. Mainstream jazz and country music were popularized by SCAP's Far East Network (FEN) radio broadcasts and covers by Japanese singers and musicians. Weekly magazines (*shukanshi*) and "film and movie entertainment magazines" such as *Heibon* boomed in the late 1950s (from 110 million copies per week in 1957 to 520 million in 1960), linking film and popular music and intensifying the celebrity culture around the new youth stars (Partner 1999, 250).

The 1950s was a golden age of Japanese cinema, but the celebrated art films were supported by series featuring stars characterized by ubiquity (they would appear in about one film per month), propinquity (they were rendered close through repeated viewings, personal appearances, and "star goods"), and pose (they were heavily typecast, to the point that they were known not only for their typical roles but their characteristic gestures and expressions).[3] Although average cinema attendance peaked at about 11 times per capita per year, the figures were higher in urban areas and for younger audiences, and film-going was amplified by a plethora of fan magazines, some published by the studios. Mass media in this sense were not separate channels into which messages could be inserted, but part of what John Durham Peters (2015) calls a "soft" cultural infrastructure (32). Dismissed as insignificant, those infrastructures stand underneath experience, taken-for-granted and withdrawing, like all media that "sacrifice their own visibility in the act of making something else appear" (34). The JCP Mountain Village Operation Units targeted the hard infrastructure of modern Japan, but it was the soft infrastructure of cinema (as well as radio, television, and other media) that reconciled Japanese people with their Cold War environment, not through messages encoded in specific texts but in the everyday practice of popular film viewing in the cinemas that rendered the tension between sovereignty and subordination absurd, and thereby livable.

Nikkatsu's *Wataridori* Series as Cold War Cultural Infrastructure

Young Japanese movie stars were almost invariably singers too. After an apprenticeship in youth films and as a sidekick to Ishihara Yujiro, Kobayashi Akira had been promoted to the "diamond line" of Nikkatsu's young male stars in early 1959. He now invariably played the lead and sang the film's theme song. With the success of Saito Buichi's *Leaving Tosa of the South* (*Nangoku tosa o ato ni shite*) in August 1959, in which he established the rootless character of Taki Shinji, Kobayashi appeared in *The Rambling Guitarist* (*Gita o motta wataridori*, 1959) two months later, and then in another episode of that *Wataridori* or "migratory bird" (that is, vagabond, wanderer, or rambler) series every three months, interleaved with two other popular series. In all, he starred in 47 films between 1959 and 1962, a number that Hiroshi Kitamura (2012) calls "astonishing" (36) but that was also typical of leading actors in the Japanese high-volume, low-budget production system. The *Wataridori* series, all but one directed by Saito Buichi, constitutes a multiverse rather than a universe (although there are some links, the central character, Taki Shinji, is not the same person in each of the films, and the films are also not part of the same timeline). That loose continuity is typical of cinema as a cultural infrastructure in which the basic unit was not the individual film but the series and the star, with the same actors playing similar roles to a regular audience in cinemas that were often contracted to specific studios. That intimacy between audiences and actors in the studios' repertory companies was the basis of the jokey "putting on a show" mood of the films that allowed them to tweak the sometimes anxiety-producing circumstances of Cold War Japan.

The *Wataridori* films are always set in modern tourist locations on the margins of Japan or, in the case of *The Rambler under the Southern Cross* (*Hato o koeru wataridori*, 1961), in Hong Kong and Thailand. Taki usually wanders into town and ends up working for a modern gangster who turns out to be oppressing a sympathetic local group. That oppression often involves the expropriation of land or treasure, and the narrative is resolved when Taki helps eliminate the gang, before leaving the town and a bereft love interest behind. The original story for a number of the *Wataridori* films was written by Hara Kenzaburo, the only LDP politician at the time actively writing for the movies. Hara represented a constituency on Awaji Island, a rural area between the main islands of Honshu and Shikoku, and his stories are sensitive to the power imbalance between center and periphery that often seems to extend to the power imbalance between Japan and the U.S. that was at the center of Japan's experience of the Cold War. The gangster in *The Rambling Guitarist* wants to dispossess his brother-in-law in order to build an amusement center; the similar figure in *The Rambler in the Sunset* (*Akai yuhi no wataridori*, 1960) wants to build a tourist hotel on a family ranch; while in *The Rambler Rides Again* (aka *Wanderer of the Great Plains*) (*Daisogen no wataridori*, 1960), he wants to obliterate an Ainu village that sits on the land of a sulfur mine owner in order to build an airport for tourists. The films often revolve around such contests between a deterritorialized, criminal capitalism and deeply rooted small businesses, though the allegorical positions sometimes come unglued. As Hiroshi Kitamura (2012) points out in his excellent analysis of *The Rambler Rides Again*, Taki's defense of the Ainu, the original inhabitants of Hokkaido who were colonized by the Japanese, is exoticizing and paternalistic (41). The film also never questions the colonial history of the sympathetic Japanese who owns the land on which the Ainu village is built, nor the role of his daughter, Taki's love interest, in selling Ainu art. But the interest of these films as a Cold War cultural infrastructure lies not so much in confused allegory as in a kind of ambivalent fantasy enabled by the intertextuality of film style. Like several other films in the series, *The Rambler Rides Again* plays like a Hollywood Western in which its narrative of violence and victimization is presented through an absurdist mélange of desirable Americana.

The *Wataridori* series is remembered as perhaps the most representative series of Nikkatsu's "action films without nationality" (*mukokuseki akkushon*) subgenre. As Kitamura (2012) points out, Kobayashi, the main antagonist Shishido Jo, and director Saito Buichi were all fans of the Hollywood Western, which was often referenced in publicity for the films (35). The *Wataridori* films draw explicitly on films such as George

Stevens' *Shane* (1953) and Howard Hawks' *Rio Bravo* (1959), as well as more generally on the significance of land. The "grass plain" (*daisogen*) in the Japanese title of *The Rambler Returns* cites a thematic that was common to many Westerns, such as Elia Kazan's striking *Sea of Grass* (1947; titled *Daisogen* in Japan and released in 1949). Westerns had always been popular in Japan, from the early 1920s (when foreign, mostly Hollywood, films made up about 75% of the Japanese box office) to 1960 (when Japanese cinema was dominant). According to Kitamura (2012), the figure of William S. Hart as the "good bad man" was the foundation of the "wandering yakuza" or *matatabi mono* subgenre of period fiction established first in literature by Hasegawa Shin in the 1920s and then adapted into period films (*jidaigeki*). Citing Sato Tadao and pointing out the connection to Taki's character, Kitamura describes the protagonist of those films as a "rootless hero who cares for the weak (i.e., women and children), gambles and eliminates the villains, but can never settle down because of his stigmatized social status" (35). Westerns were banned during the war, but one of the last to be shown in Japan, John Ford's *Stagecoach* (1939), was rereleased in 1951 and was the fourth most successful foreign film that year. There were five other Westerns in the top ten for 1951, all but one distributed by the Central Motion Picture Exchange (CMPE), which distributed Hollywood films in Occupied Japan and benefited from SCAP's refusal to admit "Soviet propaganda."[4] Three Westerns made the top ten in 1952, and *Shane* was the second biggest foreign film of 1953. After a lull, the genre came back strongly at the end of the decade, taking the top three spots in 1959 (with *Rio Bravo* at number one) and placing three more films in the 1960 top ten. Even though Hollywood's overall market share was in decline at the end of the 1950s, Westerns were surging.

A major reason for the renewed popularity of the genre in the cinema was the proliferation of Westerns as television series. Promoted as a medium for anti-communist propaganda, the American-appointed Radio Regulatory Commission (RRC) fast-tracked the spread of television in Japan by directing that the broadcast signal be identical to the U.S. NTSC standard (Partner 1999, 78–87). Ownership grew from 2.3% of households in 1956 to 44.7% in 1960, the fourth highest in the world (247). The common standard allowed Japanese companies to import American technology and know-how, but it also meant that in addition to the sports and variety shows that played into the burgeoning celebrity culture, many of the early drama shows on Japanese television were bought cheaply from the U.S. The pioneers were *Cowboy G-men* on NTV in 1956 and *The Lone Ranger* on TBS in 1958, followed by *Rawhide* (NET), *Gunsmoke*, and *Wanted Dead or Alive* (both Fuji TV) in 1959, with *Laramie* (NET) and *Bonanza* (NTV) in 1960. Those TV shows formed the semiotic background to the *Wataridori* series, along with singing cowboys such as Roy Rogers, whose family-friendly image was surely foundational to Taki's appeal.[5]

How can we reconcile protests against the America-Japan Security Treaty with the popularity of American culture in Japan? It is important to recognize that although many Japanese resented the "occupation mentality" of many of the 100,000 American military and dependents in Japan, who drove big foreign cars and lived in big houses with exclusive access to luxury hotels, golf courses, and resorts, the *Anpo* protests expressed anxieties about corruption, militarism, and war rather than straightforward anti-Americanism (Packard 2010, 157; Reischauer 1960, 23). In Nikkatsu films, there was a strain of "hard-boiled" anti-Americanism that appealed to the studio's young male audience by highlighting what Yoshimi (2003) calls the "violence" of the U.S. But there was also a broader project of emulation that appealed to what Yoshimi calls the "desire" for American culture. Although Ishihara Yujiro's first starring role, in Nakahira Ko's *Crazed Fruit* (*Kurutta kajitsu*, 1956), gave voice to the resentment young Japanese felt toward rich Americans (Yujiro cuckolds an American businessman), his later films emulate, rather than resist, that businessman's (male) privilege. The first Nikkatsu films shot abroad showed Yujiro traveling in northern Europe, Spain, and Egypt, speaking English and standing tall among foreigners.[6] In his films set in Japan after *Anpo*, he often echoes the "hard boiled" stance by standing up to foreigners, though the main narrative line shows him as an idealist fighting against Japanese criminality and corruption.[7] Rather than reject the West, Yujiro's early 1960s films featured a plethora of gratuitous foreigners in the background and staged scenarios in which, as with the "Kennedy-Reischauer Line" introduced in 1961, Japan and the United States stood in an "equal partnership" (Schaller 1997, 162; Packard 2010, 154). Two of Yujiro's films were in the domestic box office top ten in 1957, four in 1958, five in 1959, and by 1960, his films were dominant: four of the top six were star vehicles for Yujiro. When he appeared in Ken Annakin's *Those Magnificent Men in the Their Flying Machines* (Twentieth Century-Fox, 1965), he represented Japan as part of the "cinematic free world."

The films without nationality are more complicated. They are not imitations but adaptations: they value playing at being American but never forget the geopolitical incline that gave the lie to the "equal partnership" between Japan and the United States. At the same time, they don't take that hierarchy seriously. Unlike most Westerns, the *Wataridori* films are set in modern Japan and Taki sometimes wears a suit (though he typically wears a leather jacket and scarf, or a leather waistcoat and bandana) and rides a horse. His appearance is something like a cross between Elvis Presley and a singing cowboy, signifiers that were already confused in Japan because rockabilly and rock 'n' roll was introduced through a series of "Western Carnival" concerts at the biggest theater in Tokyo, starting in 1958. But *The Rambler under the Southern Cross*, whose foreign locations gave it the biggest box office take of the series (second place in 1960), is not a Western at all: Taki is an abandoned war orphan (*zanryu koji*) who discovers that his lost brother is the honorable bandit the "Tiger of Laos." The stolen treasure in the film puts Japan on the side of the exploiters, not victims, and the "inscrutable" Chinese villain (played by a Japanese series regular) and Taki's jet-setting role are reminiscent of contemporary "runaway productions" in Asia such as Richard Quine's *The World of Suzie Wong* (World Productions, 1960). In fact, the only ubiquitous elements in the *Wataridori* series in addition to the exotic locations are Kobayashi's gun and guitar (named "Diana" after the song by Paul Anka, whose "Lonely Boy" was also big in Japan and gave a hint to Kobayashi's characterization of Taki). That pop intertext is also confused: Kobayashi's high reverb tenor and the mix of pop and folk songs are similar to Ricky Nelson in *Rio Bravo*, but in addition to his rendition of Japanese folk songs, Kobayashi's "The Rambling Guitarist" theme song that is repeated in at least seven of the nine films in the series also has the traditional 7-5 rhythm. As some critics at the time noted, the tension between "American" and "Japanese" elements in these films is not resolved, as in Yujiro's films, but rendered absurd.

Critical Readings of the Cold War Cultural Infrastructure

Critics who turned their attention to popular cinema in the 1950s and 1960s looked at the *Wataridori* films from the side of the audience. Uryu Tadao thought the depictions of rural Japan offered a nostalgic appeal to workers from provincial towns who had come to the major cities during the period of high economic growth (Nishiwaki 1971b, 51). In contrast, the writer who has done most to establish the importance of Nikkatsu action films, Watanabe Takenobu, insisted on the artificiality of the world represented in the films. He pointed out the stereotyped nature of the plots and characters, which are essentially the same from film to film: where Yuriko Furuhata focuses on a "cinema of actuality," Watanabe takes pleasure in an absurd pastiche, a cinema of non-actuality (Watanabe 2004, 121). He argued that even a local would see these images as "worn out compositions, like tourist postcards" and mocked the way that it is always the day of the festival when Taki leaves town, like something in the 1970s "Discover Japan," Japan Railways' advertising campaign (127). It is typical of the conflicted positions of identification in the *Wataridori* films that they exemplify the touristic vision that the hero defends against and the villain aims to exploit. Aaron Gerow (2005) develops those ideas, recognizing with Watanabe that the films present a utopian image of autonomous agency in historical conditions that made that agency very difficult, but at the same time commodify provincial Japan in a touristic discourse (411). In a similar vein, Hiroshi Kitamura (2012) identifies the danger of this kind of domestication: not only are the Japanese provinces dominated by the metropolitan center but the borrowing of popular tropes from Western cinema works to secure Japanese films' dominance of the box office—what Kitamura regards as the "paradox of transnationalism" (32).

Kitamura calls Watanabe's writing on the *Wataridori* films "overly celebratory," but I think we would do well to consider what Iwasaki, Watanabe, and Nishiwaki were looking for in popular cinema. They were not simply writing as film fans but trying to understand how audiences engaged with texts. Of course they were not alone: the field of cultural studies grew out of a similar attempt to rethink the impasse between claims for the autonomy of art and orthodox base-superstructure models in Marxism. One such attempt was Raymond Williams' idea of "structure of feeling," which he introduced in a short book called *Preface to Film* (1954) aimed at adult education before developing the idea in his more well-known works (Williams 1961, 1977). Williams used the phrase to refer to unarticulated, untheorized patterns of everyday life during times of historical change. It emerges, he argued, in the disjunction between received modes of thought and the next generation's new experience. For Williams, artists do affective work in a social context, which can only be understood as a non-analytic "*structure of feeling* of a period… only realizable through experience of the work of art itself, as a whole" (Williams 1954, 22). Those works were not necessarily successful: we can see signs of a structure of feeling in what cannot be properly articulated in a work, or what remains unsaid. In that sense, the concept of "structure of feeling" itself reveals the structure of feeling of this period in the history of the New Left, dissatisfied with established parties and disaffiliated from both sides of the Cold War, a period in which Williams struggled to describe the affective dimension of an emergent culture at a point when that culture did not have the language or the concepts to articulate it clearly.[8] In 1961, Williams used the concept of "structure of feeling" to analyze the affective state of contemporary Britain; some Japanese critics were engaged in a similar project, studying popular films as a means of coming to terms with the Japanese experience of the Cold War.

Iwasaki's idea that the films are "tied to history" sees them as expressive, even when they are confused, of the pressures felt by their Cold War audiences. Watanabe does not simply celebrate Kobayashi Akira as a superlative romantic hero who rights all wrongs. Recognizing the importance of the discourse on land, in the films and more broadly, he argues,

> It is the essence of the charm of the *Wataridori* series to mix the landscape of the Hollywood western into the "Japanese, everyday landscape" [*Nihon-teki, nichijo-teki na fukei*].
>
> In other words, the "non-nationality" of the *Wataridori* series is not something autonomous but is supported by the antagonistic tension between national indigeneity [*nashonaru na dochakusei*] and a vagrancy [*horosei*] that attempts to lightly ignore it.
>
> (Watanabe 2004, 143)

Watanabe reads that charm ironically: "It is the very absurdity [*koto mukei*] of the series that tips romanticism into nihilism, such that even the most comical scenes have an intellectual refraction" (167). Thought splits in the face of the absurdity of the *Wataridori* films, but it is precisely their unserious representations that enable ways of thinking Japan's Cold War situation in the mode of play. Writing in the New Left film journal *Eiga hihyo* in the early 1970s, Nishiwaki Hideo (1971a) contrasted 1960s Toei yakuza films with the Nikkatsu films without nationality. Whereas the former, in which old-fashioned yakuza fought with Westernized and capitalist usurpers, challenge the audience with the question, "Are you even Japanese?" the Nikkatsu films respond "dialectically": "Yes, we're Japanese but were also stateless (*mukokuseki-mono*)" (96). Many on the left despised those films without nationality, but Nishiwaki argues that they can be understood symptomatically, as a response to the failure of the Japanese left to undo the Cold War bargain that tied Japan to the United States:

> When the great failure [*dai zasetsu*] of the *Anpo* struggle in 1960 revealed the peace, stability, and development of postwar Japan to be no more than a dream, no wonder youth felt boundless doubt toward their land [*tochi*] and could only understand the situation as a nihilistic parody.
>
> (Nishiwaki 1971b, 52)

Conclusion

I have argued that the Cold War was the determining environment of Japanese cinema in the 1950s and 1960s. Although there were interventions from both right and left to propagandize audiences during this period, the majority of films (and audiences) paid no overt attention to the Cold War dispensation that made Japan subordinate to the United States. But if we understand cinema as part of a cultural infrastructure that includes television, popular music, and publication culture, we can discover a complex enfolding of feelings of both desire and violence toward the United States in popular films such as the *Wataridori* series. Employing a strategy common throughout the history of Japanese cinema that I have elsewhere called "transcultural mimesis" (Raine 2014), the *Wataridori* films drew on the entwined history of Japanese and American cinema, imitating and parodying Hollywood film while also performing an implicit critique of the geopolitical incline between Japan and the U.S. by asserting a post-*Anpo* sympathy for the occupied, and the exploited. The ironic and absurd structure of feeling of the films diverged from the victim consciousness (*higaisha ishiki*) of mainstream leftist films on the Cold War such as *The Japanese Archipelago* (*Nihon retto*, Nikkatsu, 1965), directed by Kumai Kei, who had joined Nikkatsu from the Independent Production sector in the 1950s. It also anticipated new wave films such as Imamura Shohei's *The Insect Woman* (*Nippon konchuki*, Nikkatsu, 1963) by foregrounding but also questioning the nostalgia for indigeneity (*dochakusei*) that accompanied 1960s economic growth.[9] Combining all three aspects of transcultural mimesis, the *Wataridori* films try to have it all: they express resistance to the Cold War geopolitical incline by having Taki beat up English-speaking bullies and defeat the exploitative, Western-coded gangsters; they also indulge in an irresponsible and unserious identification with the unencumbered Western hero; and they simultaneously foreground the absurdity of that identification through their contradictory narratives and the disparity between Kobayashi's skinny body, marked by war and deprivation, and the robust heroes he impersonates.

That ironic understanding of hybrid culture came under attack during the 1960s, as Japanese economic growth gave rise to a revanchist cultural nationalism. Ishihara Yujiro's brother, the left-wing novelist in the process of becoming right-wing politician Ishihara Shintaro, for example, argued:

> A critic once claimed that, in an age when man is exploring the rest of the universe, the world is moving towards the creation of an internationally oriented civilization, based on the whole globe as a single entity. The very cultural confusion of today's Japan, he suggested, presents itself as a prototype of the new world civilization to come.
>
> I cannot accept such a facile theory of civilization. Confusion is confusion. The argument that a better child will be born of a sluttish woman who sleeps with anybody than from a chaste woman is a strange perversion of the law of probabilities.
>
> (Ishihara 1964, 78)

Against Ishihara's indigenous absolutism, the *Wataridori* films without nationality offered Nikkatsu's predominantly young, male, and working-class audiences a more pleasurable (and less misogynistic) opportunity to layer their situatedness in the Cold War security arrangement with both the desire *and* the violence of America in postwar Japan. They reduced the tension raised by the Cold War political and military dispensations that underlay the presence of American culture in Japan by treating that culture with irony and absurdity.

Notes

1 The project was encouraged by David W. Conde of the CIE, who was later banned from Japan for his communist activities. Conde (1970) went on to write exposes of the CIA's role in corrupting Japanese politics.

2 Distribution revenue for *Mito Komon* was 353,335,000 yen (*Eiga nenkan* 1959: 46), which made up just over 50% of the gross (*Besuto obu Kinema junpo* 1950–66: 768) at an average ticket price in 1957 of 62 yen (data from Motion Picture Producers of Japan, www.eiren.org/toukei/data.html).

3 For an expansion of this argument, see Michael Raine (2020).
4 All box office figures are from https://ja.wikipedia.org/wiki/年度別映画興行成績, originally compiled from *Kinema junpo besuto ten 85kai zenshi* (2012). The lists do not represent actual calendar years; the year usually runs from March to March. For an account of how SCAP obstructed Soviet film and allowed CMPE to double the box office share of Hollywood film while it propagandized "America" in early cold war Japan, see Kitamura (2007).
5 According to Zavatsky (1975), Roy Rogers was popular in Japan, and his films were still revived in art houses. I cannot establish whether Rogers' 1950s TV show was ever broadcast in Japan.
6 For example, Takizawa Eisuke's *Love and Death* (*Sekai o kakeru koi*, 1959) and the accompanying documentary *Yujiro's European Diary* (*Yujiro no oshu o kakearu ki*, 1959), Masuda Toshio's *Man at the Bullfight* (*Togyu ni kakeru otoko*, 1960), Nakahira Ko's *Tempest in Arabia* (*Arabu no arashi*, 1960).
7 For example, Yujiro takes on an arrogant university French teacher in Masuda Toshio's *Tree of Youth* (*Seinen no ki*, 1960).
8 Kapur (2018) describes the Japanese New Left in similar terms.
9 See Raine (2019) for a development of this argument.

Works Cited

Baskett, Michael. 2014. "Japan's Film Festival Diplomacy in Cold War Asia." *The Velvet Light Trap* 73: 4–18.

Besuto obu Kinema junpo 1950–1966. 1994. Tokyo: Kinema junposha.

Bronson, Adam. 2016. *One Hundred Million Philosophers: Science of Thought and the Culture of Democracy in Postwar Japan*. Honolulu, HI: University of Hawai'i Press.

Christy, Alan. 2012. *A Discipline on Foot: Inventing Japanese Native Ethnography, 1910–1945*. Lanham, MD: Rowman & Littlefield.

Conde, David W. 1970. *CIA: Core of the Cancer*. New Delhi: Entente.

Dower, John. 1999. *Embracing Defeat: Japan in the wake of World War II*. New York: W.W. Norton & Co.

Eiga nenkan 1959. 1960. Tokyo: Jiji eiga tsushinsha.

Furuhata, Yuriko. 2013. *Cinema of Actuality: Japanese Avant-Garde Filmmaking in the Season of Image Politics*. Durham, NC: Duke University Press.

Gerow, Aaron. 2014. "Critical Reception: Historical Conceptions of Japanese Film Criticism." In *The Oxford Handbook of Japanese Cinema*, edited by Daisuke Miyao, 61–78. Oxford: Oxford University Press.

Gerow, Aaron. 2005. "Nation, Citizenship, and Cinema." In *A Companion to the Anthropology of Japan*, edited by Jennifer Robertson, 400–14. Malden, MA: Blackwell.

Hirano Kyoko. 1994. *Mr. Smith Goes to Tokyo: Japanese Cinema under the American Occupation, 1945–1952*. Washington, DC: Smithsonian Inst Press.

Howard, Christopher. 2016. "Re-Orienting Japanese Cinema: Cold War Criticism of 'Anti-American' Films." *Historical Journal of Film, Radio and Television* 36 (4): 529–47.

Imamura Shohei. (2004). *Eiga wa kyōki no tabi de aru*. Tokyo: Nihon keizai shinbunsha.

Inui Takashi and Minami Hiroshi. "Eiga kankyakuso no kiban: Mi-ha- shinri no kenkyu." In *Besuto obu Kinema junpo 1950–1966*. Tokyo: Kinema junposha.

Ishihara, Shintaro. 1964. "Lament for the Samisen." *This is Japan* 12: 77–79.
Iwasaki, Akira. 1958a. *Gendai Nihon no eiga: sono shiso to fuzoku*. Tokyo: Chuo koron sha.
Iwasaki, Akira. 1958b. "Makkasa kara Yujiro made." *Eiga hyoron* 15 (8): 20–1.
Jesty, Justin. 2012. "Tokyo 1960: Days of Rage & Grief: Hamaya Hiroshi's Photos of the Anti-Security-Treaty Protests." *MIT Visualizing Cultures*. https://visualizingcultures.mit.edu/tokyo_1960/anp2_essay01.html.
Kapur, Nick. 2018. *Japan at the Crossroads: Conflict and compromise after Anpo*. Cambridge, MA: Harvard University Press.
Kitamura, Hiroshi. 2012. "Shoot-Out in Hokkaido: The 'Wanderer' (*Wataridori*) Series and the Politics of Transnationality." In *Transnational Asian Identities in Pan-Pacific Cinemas*, edited by Philippa Gates and Lisa Funnell, 31–45. New York: Routledge.
Kitamura, Hiroshi. 2009. "Hollywood's New Orientalism: The Case of *Tokyo File 212* (1951)." *Historical Journal of Radio, Film, and Television* 29 (4): 505–22.
Kitamura, Hiroshi. 2007. "Exhibition and Entertainment: Hollywood and the American Reconstruction of Defeated Japan." In *Local Consequences of the Global Cold War*, edited by Jeffrey A. Engel, 33–56. Stanford, CA: Stanford University Press.
Lee, Sangjoon. 2017. "The Asia Foundation's Motion Picture Project and the Cultural Cold War in Asia." *Film History* 29 (2): 108–37.
Lee, Sangjoon. 2014. "The Emergence of the Asian Film Festival: Cold War Asia and Japan's Reentrance to the Regional Film Industry." In *The Oxford Handbook of Japanese Cinema*, edited by Daisuke Miyao, 226–45. Oxford: Oxford University Press.
Minami, Hiroshi. 1954. *Nihon no eiga: Shakai shinri teki ni mita*. Tokyo: Iwanami shashin bunko.
Morse, Ronald. 1990. *Yanagita Kunio and the Folklore Movement: The Search for Japan's National Character and Distinctiveness*. New York: Garland.
Naoe, Hiroji. 1953. "Post-War Folklore Research Work in Japan." *Midwest Folklore* 3 (4): 213–22.
Nishiwaki, Hideo. 1971a. "Autoro- no kodoku na fukkatsu: Toei yakuza rosen no suitai to Nikkatsu boryokudan rosen no taito." *Eiga hihyo* (February): 94–104.
Nishiwaki, Hideo. 1971b. "'Shinigai' no jidai e no iko: Autoro- no kodoku na kobo sono ni: 1959–63." *Eiga hihyo* (December): 50–9.
Ogi, Hiromichi, Sato Tadao, and Okada Susumu. 1994. "Atarashii eiga to atarashii eiga hihyo." In *Besuto obu kinema junpo 1950–1966*, 814–9. Tokyo: Kinema junposha.
Osgood, Kenneth. 2006. *Total Cold War: Eisenhower's Secret Propaganda Battle at Home and Abroad*. Lawrence, KS: University Press of Kansas.
Packard, George III. 2010. *Edwin O. Reischauer and the American Discovery of Japan*. New York: Columbia University Press.
Packard, George III. 1966. *Protest in Tokyo: The Security Treaty Crisis of 1960*. Princeton, NJ: Princeton University Press.
Partner, Simon. 1999. *Assembled in Japan: Electrical Goods and the Making of the Japanese Consumer*. Berkeley, CA: University of California Press.
Peters, John Durham. 2015. *The Marvelous Clouds: Toward a Philosophy of Elemental Media*. Chicago, IL: University of Chicago Press.

Prados, John. 2009. *Safe for Democracy: The Secret Wars of the CIA*. Chicago: Ivan R. Dee.

Raine, Michael. 2020. "The Japanese Musical: *Heibon* and the Popular Song Film." In *The Japanese Cinema Book*, edited by Hideaki Fujiki and Alastair Phillips. London: Bloomsbury/BFI.

Raine, Michael. 2019. "*The Insect Woman*, or: The Female Art of Failure." In *Killers, Clients and Kindred Spirits: The Taboo Cinema of Shohei Imamura*, edited by David Desser and Lindsay Coleman. Edinburgh: Edinburgh University Press.

Raine, Michael. 2014. "Adaptation as 'Transcultural Mimesis'." In *The Oxford History of Japanese Cinema*, edited by Daisuke Miyao, 101–23. Oxford: Oxford University Press.

Reischauer, Edwin O. 1960. "The Broken Dialogue with Japan." *Foreign Affairs* 39 (1): 11–26.

Samuels, Richard. 2001. "Kishi and Corruption: An Anatomy of the 1955 System." Japan Policy Research Institute Working Paper 83. http://www.jpri.org/publications/workingpapers/wp83.html.

Schaller, Michael. 1997. *Altered States: The United States and Japan Since the Occupation*. Oxford: Oxford University Press.

"Suta ni kiku: Miki Ayuro no gaito rokuon. Yu-chan ga senshi shite mo ii ka, Kishi-san! Watashi-tachi no iken mo kite!" 1960. *Heibon* 2 (23): 46.

Togawa, Naoki. 1960. "Taishu no kuno to warai no hakkutsu: medatsu sakka no shinchintaisha." *Eiga geijutsu* (June): 42–6.

Toshio, Matsumoto. 2012. "Zen'ei kiroku eiga ron." *Cinema Journal* 51 (4): 148–154.

Tsumura, Hideo. 1943. *Eiga seisakuron*. Tokyo: Chuo koronsha.

Tsurumi, Shunsuke. 2005. *Shiso no kagaku gojunen: Genryu kara mirai e*. Tokyo: Shiso no kagakusha.

Tsurumi, Shunsuke. 1959. *Gokai suru kenri: Nihon eiga o miru*. Tokyo: Chikuma shobo.

Watanabe, Takenobu. 2004. *Nikkatsu akushon no karei na sekai (gappon)*. Tokyo: Miraisha.

Williams, Raymond. 1977. *Marxism and Literature*. Oxford: Oxford University Press.

Williams, Raymond. 1961. *The Long Revolution*. New York: Columbia University Press.

Williams, Raymond. 1954. "Film and the Dramatic Tradition." In *Preface to Film*, edited by Raymond Williams and Michael Orrom, 1–56. London: Film Drama.

Yamada, Kazuo. 1970. *Nihon Eiga no gendaishi*. Tokyo: Shin Nihon shuppansha.

Yamamoto, Kajiro. 1998. *Katsudoya jitaden*. Tokyo: Shobunsha.

Yoshimi Shun'ya. 2003. "'America' as Desire and Violence: Americanization in Postwar Japan and Asia during the Cold War." *Inter-Asia Cultural Studies* 4 (3): 433–50.

Zavatsky, Bill. 1975. "Some Japanese Poems about Roy Rogers." *New York Times*, September 21. www.nytimes.com/1975/09/21/archives/some-japanese-poems-about-roy-rogers-the-guest-word.html.

7 Vehicles of Modernity

Gender, Mobility and Music in Evan Yang's MP&GI films

Jessica Tan

MP&GI, Vernacular Modernism, and the Cold War

In the entry dated "1958" in Shanghai émigré film director Evan Yang's (Yi Wen, also known as Yang Yanqi, 1920–78) autobiography, Yang writes about the purchase of his first automobile:

> Purchased a German Opel in early February. Lüyun drove the car initially. Received my driver's license at the end of March and started driving on my own.
>
> (Yi 2009, 82)

This was the first, but definitely not the last, mention of his automobile purchases in his autobiography; subsequently, Yang writes of buying a new Opel in June 1962, a new Ford Escort in June 1969, and a Japanese Honda in 1970. Besides recording his automobile purchases, Yang frequently notes the airlines that he took, the hotels that he stayed at while travelling, and even the purchase of his family's first television set in 1963. Belonging to a generation of Shanghai émigré filmmakers caught in the intricate web of Cold War politics in Hong Kong, Yang's autobiography is surprisingly devoid of political ruminations. Rather, amid the recollections of his social engagements, literary endeavors, and film career, his autobiography is peppered with details of a middle-class Shanghai émigré's material lifestyle and his travels as a cosmopolitan filmmaker throughout "Free Asia" during the Cold War.

The vignettes of Yang's middle-class lifestyle are, in fact, similar to the lives of urbanites in a cosmopolitan and modernizing Asia, that were often featured in his Motion Pictures and General Investment (MP&GI in short) films such as *Air Hostess* (*Kongzhong xiaojie*, 1959), *Our Dream Car* (*Xiangche meiren*, 1959), and *It's Always Spring* (*Tao li zheng chun*, 1962)—a corpus of works that he eventually became well known for.[1] The transnational film company that he was working for, MP&GI, was arguably established among political and commercial negotiations made by Hong Kong film studios during the Cold War.[2] In 1956, the Singapore-based Cathay Organization absorbed Yung Hwa

Motion Pictures Studio's facilities and reorganized its distribution arm, International Films Distribution Agency, into MP&GI, to produce films to support its growing exhibition networks in Southeast Asia.[3] This reorganization reflects the company's adoption of Hollywood's modern studio system that vertically integrates production, distribution, and exhibition, while also retaining characteristics of an Asian family business. Modeled after Hollywood, MP&GI's star system led to the meteoric rise of actresses such as Grace Chang (Ge Lan) and Linda Lin (Lin Dai); the company also established an impressive scriptwriting team that comprised renowned southbound literati who fled communist China, such as playwright Yao Ke and writers Eileen Chang and Evan Yang (Law 2009, 34–9; Shu 2009, 40–50). Notably, a bulk of MP&GI's productions were influenced by Hollywood genre films such as the musical, and these films constituted a space for Asian audiences to encounter modernity through music and fashion (Needham 2008, 41–56). By focusing on producing romantic comedies, urban melodramas, and glamorous Hollywood-influenced musicals, MP&GI successfully distinguished itself from its competitors such as the Shaw Brothers, and rose to become one of the dominant Mandarin film companies in Hong Kong during the late 1950s.

The influences of Hollywood on MP&GI's films, both as an aesthetic and a method of industrial organization, can be understood within the context of what Miriam Hansen (1999) terms as "vernacular modernism." Hansen argues that Hollywood films had a global appeal as they provided a collective sensorium to negotiate the shocking effects of modernity, helped to constitute new subjectivities, and provided models of identification for being modern (68). Although Hansen is referring to early classical Hollywood cinema in the wake of urban and industrial modernity during the early twentieth century, this chapter proposes that a parallel can be drawn in the context of Cold War Asia, in which films served as a platform for audiences to negotiate emerging mass commodity cultures and changing gender dynamics of an urban middle-class in a modern "Free" Asia, amid strong ideological contentions.

Poshek Fu (2009) argues that the influence of Hollywood on MP&GI's films is not unexpected, as Hollywood films epitomized the culture of modernity and showcased the power of the capitalist system during the Cold War, thereby inspiring those in developing countries who sought to modernize their lives (28). Yet, it is also critical for us to consider the ways in which Hollywood cinema was reconfigured in local contexts of reception, especially in a volatile political period such as the Cold War. Zhen Zhang (2005), who builds on Hansen's theory in the Chinese context, reminds us of the polemical and participatory dimensions of vernacular modernism in early Shanghai cinema, and argues that films are often open to and dependent on a mass-mediated authorship and spectatorship.[4] I derive my understanding of vernacular modernism from both scholars, but focus particularly on the aspects of authorship, spectatorship, and the participatory potential of vernacular modernism as a form of cultural practice.

In the context of this chapter, I investigate vernacular modernism as an open-ended and self-reflexive cinematic practice that creates a liminal space for audiences to buffer the hyperstimulus of capitalist modernity, and for filmmakers to negotiate the creative tensions that arise from contesting cultures and traditions during the Cold War. In other words, while acknowledging the Hollywood modern sensibilities in MP&GI films that have been discussed compellingly by other scholars, this chapter seeks to highlight the complexities of Cold War Hong Kong film production that are entwined with negotiations of aesthetic traditions and the diasporic routes of filmmakers. Specifically, it examines Evan Yang's MP&GI's articulations of vernacular modernism from another perspective—Shanghai's literary modernism of the 1930s. As a close associate of Shanghai modernist writers such as Liu Na'ou and Mu Shiying during his undergraduate days, I argue that the case study of Yang and his films will help us historicize and contextualize the aesthetic choices of Shanghai filmmakers who were working in Cold War Hong Kong's film industry, adding a productive perspective to what Poshek Fu (2003) calls the Shanghai-Hong Kong nexus (xii), while also unpacking the ambiguities of Cold War vernacular modernism in Hong Kong film history. Building on the premise that the relationship between the modern woman and vehicles was one of the critical ways in which modernity was construed in 1930s Shanghai modernist literature, this paper examines three of Yang's films—*Air Hostess*, *Our Dream Car,* and *It's Always Spring*—and argues that Yang's filmic spectacles of capitalist modernity, which are often complemented by the bodies of modern women and vehicles, constitute a rewriting of the 1930s Shanghai literary tropes of women and transportation into the 1950 and 1960s Cold War Hong Kong films. This chapter proposes that Yang's representations of gendered mobility and modernity are not only linked to ideas of speed, transnational movement, capitalism, and cosmopolitanism within the Cold War context, but should also be contextualized as a transcultural aesthetic that gained a new life through the diasporic routes of Shanghai émigrés in Cold War Hong Kong.

Shanghai Neo-sensationalism: From Soft Films to Modern Women

Born in Beijing in 1920, Evan Yang moved to Shanghai with his parents when he was five. He grew up in Shanghai and studied at Shanghai's St. John's University—the U.S. Anglican missionary-founded Western liberal arts college. Yang was bilingual and culturally steeped in both Eastern and Western cultures. When he was an undergraduate, Yang became acquainted with Shanghai filmmakers Huang Jiamo and neo-sensationalist writers Mu Shiying and Liu Na'ou, a group of literati whose modernist works and film theories would later become contentious subjects in China's leftist-dominated film and literary historiographies. In his autobiography, Yang recalls visiting Shanghai's dance halls and forging close friendships with Liu and Mu, who were also frequent patrons of these places. Yang had also provided the voice-over for Liu's documentary *China's Railway*. The fact that Yang fled to Hong Kong after the assassination of Mu and Liu in 1940 for fear of implication best suggests their close relationship (Yi 2009, 54). Yang eventually settled down in Hong Kong permanently after 1949. While based in Hong Kong, his social network spanned different groups of left-wing and pro-Taiwan politicians, literati, and filmmakers, which suggests the complexities in Cold War Hong Kong cultural production, and on a broader level, the liminal site of Hong Kong at the forefront of ideological struggles.[5]

Yang was originally working at Xinhua Film Company with Zhang Shankun when he was first introduced to Albert Odell from Cathay's International Films Distribution Agency; he signed a three-year contract with International Films in 1955 to make four films each year beginning 1956 (Yi 2009, 79). Demonstrating a keen acumen in capturing modern sensibilities, many of Yang's MP&GI films are Hollywood-influenced musicals or romantic comedies that feature female protagonists who embody modern lifestyles and liberal values in a modernizing Free Asia. Yang's use of the fair sex to symbolize an epoch's character can arguably be understood as a continuation of an aesthetic tradition that stems from Shanghai's neo-sensationalist writers (a term derived from the Japanese neo-sensationalist school *shinkankakuha*) such as Mu Shiying and Liu Na'ou, who marked the first wave of Chinese modernism. These writers are known for using textual montages of intense sensations and fragmented images to provoke their readers' sensibilities, in a way mirroring the alienating effects modernity had on people in 1930s semicolonial Shanghai. More often than not, the figure of the cosmopolitan modern girl is imbued with ideas of modernity and speed, and foregrounded as a central trope in their literary experimentation and film theoretical discussions.

One of the key controversies pertaining to this group was a theoretical debate regarding "soft" and "hard" films in Shanghai between 1933 and 1935.[6] The terms "soft" and "hard" films first appeared in a 1933 article by Huang Jiamo in *Modern Screen*; Huang argues that cinema should be soft like its medium—the celluloid film—and likens it to "ice-cream for the eyes and sofa for the heart and mind." To Huang, films are meant for pleasure, yet left-wing filmmakers have "hardened" the medium by overloading it with ideologies that discount its entertainment value. He argues that modern audiences enter theaters to gain a temporary release from their daily burdens and not to be bombarded by didactic teachings (3). Huang's comments, which emphasize aesthetics over ideology and foreground film-going as a form of bourgeoisie leisure, naturally drew the ire of left-wing filmmakers who were keen to use film to mobilize the masses in times of national crisis.

While Liu Na'ou does not explicitly use the term "soft film," his extensive writings on film aesthetics have placed him within the same school of "soft film" advocates. Liu is concerned about film aesthetics, paying attention to the ways in which cinematic techniques such as montage, lighting, and mise-en-scène convey meaning and influence the film's effect on viewers. In his short essay "Cinema and the Beauty of Women," Liu writes that the silver screen enables the discovery of the female body and the dissection of female beauty; he describes the delicate female body in parts and praises the medium for showcasing moving women from different parts of the world—"Parisian women speaking elegantly, Spanish women dancing the Tango, America's modern girls dancing on the pavements" (Ge 2001, 248–9). Liu's essay reveals his fascination with the film camera not only for enabling new visual expressions of female physiognomy and movement, but also for its ability to take audiences on an international tour through the parading of modern, cosmopolitan female bodies within the short span of reel time. The female body thus becomes a key sight and site that signifies the hallmarks of modernity—transnational mobility, cosmopolitanism, and speed.

This fascination with the female body as emblematic of modernity is also reflected in their writings. The modern girl and her body is often used as a metaphor for the city, while the emotions that she evokes in male protagonists mirror the feelings of seduction, fascination, and alienation that one feels toward rapid modernization. Notably, automobiles, as an integral component of the Shanghai neo-sensationalist's representation of a fast-paced city landscape and an emerging consumerist culture, are often juxtaposed with the modern girl. These vehicles are used as material symbols of capitalist modernity to allegorize the speed of urban life and the transient nature of romantic escapades. For instance, the male protagonist H in Liu Na'ou's "Two People Impervious to Time" scores a date with a modern girl. While walking along the busy commercial street, H is temporarily seduced by an automobile Fontegnac 1929, but prides himself for not neglecting the "fair sex" beside him and keeps up with her walking speed. However, the modern girl, who boasts of never spending more than three hours with a single guy and argues that lovemaking should be done in a racing car in the wind, eventually dumps H for another date (Liu 1929, 25). In the story, both the modern girl and automobiles are seductive lures of the urban landscape, setting not only the momentum of the new lifestyle, but also threatening to abandon those who cannot catch up with their new pace. The woman's love for speed and vehicles even becomes a dangerously illicit affair, such as in Mu Shiying's "Shanghai Foxtrot" that features an "incestuous" relationship between a stepmother and her son; Mu satirically parallels the speed of the couple's new vehicle with their avant-garde attitude toward love—"driving a new 1932 Baker, but their minds set on a dating style of 1980" (Mu 1932, 114). Ye Lingfeng (1933) brings the woman-vehicle relationship to another extreme by fusing the description of a femme fatale's corporeal body with the material body of an automobile in "Influenza." Likening the woman's breasts to the car's headlights, Ye augments the feelings of defamiliarization, together with nuances of corporeal seduction, and challenges one to come to terms with foreign capitalist materialism and the speed of modern life:

> She, like a new 1933 car, in the orange-tinted air of May, on the asphalt pavement, glides through the crowd like an eel... The gear shifts from fourth to fifth. Heading into the wind, a sculpted handsome beauty of 1933: V-shaped radiator, two half-moon lights, Isadora Duncan–styled short, flying hair.
>
> (As quoted in Shih 2001, 268)

The sleek female body, which was used to signify a modern lifestyle that seduced and threatened male protagonists in the 1930s, continued to be a key site for negotiations of a capitalist modernity in Cold War Hong Kong film culture. The relationship between the modern woman and her vehicle remains strong in Yang's MP&GI films, as suggested by the Chinese titles of his films *Air Hostess* (*kongzhong xiaojie*, which literally means "lady in the air") and *Our Dream Car* (*xiangche meiren*, which means "fragrant car and beautiful woman"). These titles indicate the continued relationship between female and vehicular bodies, as well as the notions of gendered modernity and transnational mobility. Nonetheless, unlike the threatening aura of women in Shanghai's neo-sensationalist fiction, the modern woman in Yang's films is configured as a conservative body for the articulation of fantasies, uncertainties, and anxieties within the Cold War context. She becomes an ambivalent site in which the hyperstimulus of capitalist modernity is domesticated through her moving body and voice, and explicates the contradictory promises of capitalism and gender politics.

The Cult of Speed: Vehicles as Spectacles of Capitalist Modernity

Vehicles in Yang's films, like in Shanghai's neo-sensationalist fiction, are employed as spectacles of capitalist modernity and representations of a newfound speed. Yang often utilizes scenes of modern transportation such as automobiles, cruise ships, and airplanes in his films to showcase the vibrant cityscapes, as well as the feasibility of traveling to and within these prosperous Asian cities. Similar to the ways in which the automobile was an American symbol of individuality and freedom in the 1950s, automobile ownership in Hong Kong symbolized self-regulated mobility, high speed, and elevated social status. Likely inspired by his first automobile purchase and the acquisition of his driver's licence, Yang began the production of *Our Dream Car*, a light-hearted film that showcases a developing capitalist and consumerist culture that revolves around the automobile as a symbol of physical and social mobility in 1958 (Yi 2009, 82). *Our Dream Car* opens with Grace Chang's song "Car Beauty" while featuring actual footages of an automobile exhibition and beauty pageant in Hong Kong. In the film, the couple Zhang Daming (Chang Yang) and Li Jiaying (Grace Chang) travels daily between Hong Kong Island and Kowloon by ferry for work. Running into his wife's former lover who works as an automobile dealer, Zhang decides to purchase an automobile from him to prove that Li did not make the wrong choice of marrying him; here, the automobile is depicted as a symbol not only of physical mobility, but also one of social class mobility. The automobile does not only enthral Zhang; Li is equally enticed by this new expression of speed and self-determined mobility. The film shows a confident modern Li who admires different models of automobiles, participates in an automobile pageant, and daydreams about driving around speedily in her own automobile: "I can drive at 50 miles per hour, yet still think that this is too slow!" Unlike the American automobile culture that is usually highly masculine in nature, the automobiles in Yang's films offer modern females an alternative, liberating mode of self-expression.[7]

The empowerment of the free individual through a liberating experience of speed in one's car is critical in Yang's portrayal of a rapidly modernizing Free Asia. If the automobile provided one with "genuinely modern pleasure" during the early twentieth century, the rise of air travel during the mid-twentieth century condensed spatial distances, allowed faster transnational connections between countries, and forged a cosmopolitan ideal that is possible only through flying (Huxley 2001, 263). For instance, *Air Hostess* is the story of a modern woman Lin Keping (Grace Chang) who rejects marriage to pursue a modern career as an air hostess. The modern experience of flying is emphasized during an announcement on board a flight to Taiwan: the plane is flying at a height of 15,000 feet and at a speed of 300 miles per hour. These statistics of speed and height, while likely unfathomable to audiences who have never flown before, resonate well with Lin's air hostess dream of "flying into the green skies" and being "as carefree as a god," as expressed in her opening musical sequence.

As MP&GI's first color production, *Air Hostess* is noted for its lengthy travelogue footages of spacious airports, broad highways, bustling city traffic, and exotic tourist attractions that were filmed on-site in Hong Kong, Taiwan, Thailand, and Singapore. Yang's cinematic representations of Asia's urban cities, which are connected by modern transportation, deliver the cinematic illusions of increasing transnational connections that facilitate healthy capitalist economic development, as well as the ease of untrammeled travel within a cosmopolitan "free" Asia. As suggested by Christian Klein (2017), Cold War cosmopolitanism is often less about an embrace of universality, but rather a highly restrictive discourse that pertains to transnational connections within the "Free World"; it emphasizes the forging of ties between non-communist countries and pursues ideals of individualism, personal freedom, capitalist exchange, and a commitment to social and technological modernization along Western lines (283). Modernity, in the context of Yang's films, is signified through the discourse of self-determined mobility and speed achieved by means of transnational commercial air travel or personal automobiles within a "Free World" geopolitical imaginary. The fascination with self-determined mobility, in other words, is also the celebration of individualism and autonomous subjectivity—a key concept that was prized as the alternative to discourses of Soviet collectivism. Hence, the free and speedy travel evinced in Yang's films can also be read in implicit contrast with the highly regulated timetabling of locomotive travel that underscores collective movement and discipline to avoid falling behind schedules in socialist countries.

More critically, this cult of speed is not only limited to the speed of traveling, but is also implied by the speed in which these spectacles of capitalist modernity are reproduced and distributed for consumption by mass media technology. During a self-reflexive moment in *Our Dream Car*, a party crowd gathers around the television to watch scenes from the automobile exhibition and beauty pageant that was held earlier on in the same day. A medium shot of the crowd cuts to a close-up shot of the television set that is replaying footage of car models and the pageant's contestants that were seen earlier in the film (Figures 7.1 and 7.2). The film self-reflexively showcases the ability of the television, as a form of mass media, in disseminating footages quickly to audiences beyond the

Figure 7.1 A medium shot of a model participating in the automobile beauty pageant in *Our Dream Car*.

Figure 7.2 The television at the party replaying footage from the automobile beauty pageant screened earlier in *Our Dream Car.*

original crowd present at the morning's exhibition. In the television's mechanical reproduction of automobiles and beautiful women, one is reminded of the powerful visual dimension that lies beneath the logic of consumption and the ways in which commodity fetishism is often triggered by vision. In this regard, the film exhibits the emergence not only of a material culture, but also of a visual culture that meditates consumerism behavior and facilitates commodity desire.

While capitalism celebrates individual subjectivity though concepts such as self-determined mobility and personal consumer choices, this self-reflexive moment in *Our Dream Car* nonetheless exposes the inherent contradictions of an individualistic consumerist culture. When an advertised commodity is conflated with gendered qualities, as when the speedy automobile is juxtaposed alongside the modern woman as desirable capitalist objects of modernity in *Our Dream Car*, we see the internalization of a problematic gaze by Li Jiaying and Zhang Daming; the couple believes that Li needs fashionable clothes and accessories for the beauty pageant, and this eventually causes them to end up in debt due to their purchases. Thus, despite the fact that the speed and mobility associated with the automobile has presumably allowed Li a form of liberating self-expression, she is still subjected to control by a form of commodity logic. Even with its promises of the subversion of gender hierarchies and the formation of autonomous subjectivity through the adoption of a modern capitalist lifestyle, the discourse of gendered mobility is arguably fraught with ambivalence.

Embodying Mobility: Women as Vehicles of Modernity

In the context of Cold War gender politics, the status of women was often used as a measure of social and national progress. Communist

China, for example, has sought to promote the equality of women and men, which is ironically often achieved through de-emphasizing sexual differences and suppressing feminine corporeal traits. This is evident in the portrayal of prototypical masculinized "iron girls" engaged in revolution or physical labor in the revolutionary arts and propaganda posters, which suggests women's liberation from both class and gender hierarchies. Conversely, the sensuous female body is often the site where consumerism, mobility, and commodification are exhibited in capitalist societies. The female body is a key visual component of Yang's films; in particular, Yang often directs the audiences' gaze to the movements of women's legs through the use of close-up shots. These shots dissect the female body into visual fragments reminiscent of the women depicted in Shanghai's neo-sensationalist works—women who never have a full body as an object for visual inspection, but exist merely as a phantom image and as an "embodiment of an exotic ideal with all the accoutrements from foreign sources" (Lee 1999, 198). While acknowledging the erotic appeal of these women's bare legs, the close-up shots of legs in Yang's films should not only be regarded as phantasmagorical images of sexuality, but also as visuals that foreground the films' thematic concern of women embodying modernity through her mobility.

Social mobility and physical mobility are implied in the woman's relationship with modern vehicles, such as women relocating for career advancement, the transnational dimensions of an air hostess' work, and the possibility of an upward social movement as suggested by the couple's possession of a car. The film, *It's Always Spring*, opens with Li Ailian (Julie Yeh), a popular Nanyang singer, relocating from Singapore to Hong Kong in search of better career prospects, and *Air Hostess* highlights the transnational mobility of air hostesses by celebrating them as people who "shorten the distance between people and facilitate the transnational movement of people and capital" ("Ge Lan" 1957). The handbill of *Air Hostess* includes promotional slogans such as "the successful career of an air hostess" and "a reflection of the life of an airhostess" that depict the job as a gendered modern occupation and as a critical component of the flight experience. As argued by Fu (2018), this film represents modernity by showcasing an emerging Asian airline business as an incubator of a transnational capitalist corporate culture, and, more importantly, foregrounds an "American Fordist-Taylorist value system, which demands total dedication and emotional identification of workers to the mass production regime" (35–42). In other words, the modern life embodied by the mobility of Lin as an air hostess entails not just glamor and luxury, but also professionalism and strict discipline required by the capitalist corporate culture.

The tension between the stringent capitalist corporate culture and the air hostesses' freedom to fly is best exemplified in the domestication of the female body. The corporeal domestication is implied by the long and almost voyeuristic footages of pre-employment body check-ups and industrial training, in which Yang's camerawork focuses on the moving bare legs of women as they are being examined physically or serving passengers in the plane. As stressed in a publicity article on *Air Hostess*, the film "realistically goes through the training of air hostess stressing that *service is more important than glamour*" (italics mine) ("Air Hostess" 1957). Through emphasizing the specific mannerisms that air hostesses have to adhere to, these scenes are suggestive of how female bodies are integrated into a Fordist-Taylorist assembly production line setup through corporeal disciplining. The disciplining of the moving female body is not only limited to the scenes of industrial training in *Air Hostess*, but is also suggested in *Our Dream Car*'s beauty pageant, as well as in the dancing scenes of *It's Always Spring*. Donning fashionable outfits and airline uniforms while parading in specific formations, modern females are not presented as autonomous individuals, but rather as part of a larger performative body that is subjected to visual commodification, consumerist desires, and industrial requirements. Thus, despite demonstrating new models of femininity, the rigid disciplining and synchronizing of female corporeal movements in these films, as a kind of capitalist spectacle, paradoxically expose the contradictions within the modern notions of freedom, mobility, and speed that the female body is supposed to embody.

As such, Yang's characterization of women as vehicles of modernity is more conservative compared with Shanghai's modernist writers' depictions of sexually liberated modern women or seductive femme fatales. In Yang's films, the sexually promiscuous femme fatales of Shanghai's neo-sensationalist fiction are transformed into modern women who are fiercely loyal to their husbands, boyfriends, or careers, despite being proponents of modern liberal values. In *Our Dream Car*, Li Jiaying insists on participating in the beauty pageant as "Mrs. Zhang" instead of "Miss Li Jiaying" and on having her husband chauffer her in their new car—a wedding anniversary present—at the competition. Despite the conflicts that arose over car ownership, the film ends on a happy note when Li uses another "car"—a baby pram—to announce her pregnancy to her husband. In *It's Always Spring*, Tao Haiyin (Lee Mei), a career-driven singer who is initially averse to marriage, eventually accepts her boyfriend Xu Zhaofeng's (Roy Chiao) proposal. Marriage is also deemed a viable alternative to an unsuccessful career, as in the case of Chen Huan (Dolly Soo) in *Air Hostess*, who ends up marrying a pilot Li Wenbin (Kelly Lai) after she fails as an air hostess due to her introverted personality.

Most intriguingly, the Westernized and modern weddings in Yang's films often take place on board moving modern vehicles. In *Air Hostess*, Chen Huan and Li Wenbin's marriage occurs in a commercial passenger-filled airplane and is officiated by none other than the manager of the airline crew, Miss Kang (Tang Zhen). In *It's Always Spring*, the engagement party between Tao Haiyin and Xu Zhaofeng takes place on a sailing boat that is a wedding proposal gift from Xu to Tao named after her. While it is possible to read these happy marriages on board moving vehicles in light of Yang's personal history as a Shanghai émigré's successful "marriage" into Hong Kong's society, these scenes could also be understood in the larger socioeconomic context of Cold War Asia. If we regard these moving vehicles as microcosms of the Free Asian societies that have embarked on a journey toward modernity through rapid social development and economic changes, the notion of being in transit becomes ambivalent considering the ways in which capitalist modernity has unsettled or even reinforced gender hierarchies.

The instability of this transitional period and the reworking of gender hierarchies are signified by the eruptions of queerness in these marriage scenes. In *Air Hostess,* it is the airline manager Miss Kang, rather than Chen Huan's husband, who puts on the wedding ring for Chen. Additionally, we do not see any visual unions of Xu Zhaofeng or Tao Haiyin in the scenes of the engagement party in *It's Always Spring.* Instead, we see the "union" between Tao Haiyin and Li Ailian, the latter cross-dressed as a male and assuming the role of Tao's dance partner during the performance of a love song, "Peach Blossom River." As Tao breaks out into a sexy dance and the camera focuses on her bare dancing legs, the film cuts to a close-up shot of Li smiling in astonishment at her partner's moves. Interestingly, Li's cross-dressing in a white tuxedo and her low sultry singing voice present a sensual androgynous female image—a female ideal that had once fascinated Shanghai modernists during the 1930s (Zhang 2005, 288). Female androgyny then was read as a sign of cosmopolitanism and the transgressive nature of modernity allegorically. Likewise, Li's cross-dressing in *It's Always Spring* epitomizes her status as a chameleon-like modern girl. She is able to transgress not only geographical boundaries by crossing the seas from Singapore to carve a successful career for herself in Hong Kong, but also gender boundaries through her performance and gaze. The homoerotic tension in this scene, marked by Li's intent gaze of her dance partner, is intriguing insofar as it seems to challenge Laura Mulvey's (1999) notion of the male gaze (833–44). This is a keen demonstration of how modern women in Yang's films are gazed upon not only by men, but also by other women who deem them as desirable modern subjects and role models. This triangulate network of visual desire implies a pedagogical dimension that teaches one to relate to these modern women in Yang's films. Extending Hansen's argument of vernacular modernism as providing "models of identification for being modern" to the discussion of Yang's films, I contend that there is a similar pedagogical impulse to educate the audiences on what it means to be modern by leveraging on the figure of the modern songstress—whose lineage can be traced to early Chinese cinema.[8]

The Modern Songstress: Music as a Pedagogical Vehicle

If the Shanghai neo-sensationalists were concerned with new visuals of female corporeality and speed in the 1930s, Yang was evidently aware of the soft power of the female lyrical voice and its ability to circulate as independent audiovisual commodities even more widely than visuals. Yang was attuned to the demands of musical films and was probably one of the few directors who wrote lyrics for most of the songs featured in his films. Yang particularly favors the use of musical sequences and the affective power of singing women as pedagogical tools to facilitate the audience's encounter with modernity. A case in point is Li Jiaying in *Our Dream Car,* who sings to teach one how to drive a car. The sequence begins with Li holding a toy car and singing about her newly purchased car. During the interlude after the first stanza, the screen is divided into two triangles, and a car cruising in Hong Kong's New Territories emerges in the upper screen. The scene of this moving car then cuts to a close-up shot of a future Li driving and singing enthusiastically about "travelling independently on a good sunny day to places, such as the Peak and waterfronts, and admiring the sceneries along the way," while the gaze of Li and her husband in the lower screen is directed upward toward the future Li in the upper screen. The editing creates an interesting visual connection between the two spaces of temporality, which implies an orientation toward the future and the desire for upward social mobility.

While the musical sequence becomes a utopian moment for Li Jiaying to daydream about her social and physical mobility, audiences are drawn into the musical sequence through Li's demonstrations of how to drive a car, such as holding the steering wheel and releasing the clutch pedal. Li, as a female mediator of modernity, makes these modern technologies accessible through singing songs with catchy lyrics, written by none other than Yang himself:

> Be careful when the road isn't smooth
> Always pay attention while driving
> Always watch your direction
> Step steady on the gas clutch
> Do not worry, do not rush
> I'm so skillful that I can drive 50 miles per hour
> And I still think that it is too slow

Musical sequences in Yang's films function not only as a momentary suspension of the film's diegesis, but also as a discursive space mediated by the voices and bodies of singing women to convey knowledge regarding modern technologies. Yang complements the lyrics with pedagogical visuals to maximize the sequence's affectivity and educational value, and hence audiences are invited to participate in this emerging modern middle-class lifestyle by emulating the protagonist's ways.[9]

More importantly, the suspension of the diegesis also provides a space for audiences to connect directly with the modern songstress. The musical sequences in Yang's films often break down the fourth wall and enable the singer to communicate with her audiences, thus exemplifying the participatory nature of vernacular modernism as audiences relate to the singing woman directly. For example, in the opening sequence of *Our Dream Car*, Grace Chang sings to her audiences in her personal capacity and invites them to join her on this couple's journey:

> (In this film) I play the role of a car beauty
> This is a story that can possibly happen anywhere
> It is hard to tell if this is a happy or sad story
> So please join me and watch *Our Dream Car*

The idea of performance is made clear self-reflexively, while Chang's invitation and her emphasis that "this is a story that can possibly happen anywhere" immediately shorten the distance between the audiences and herself.

There is a cultural specificity to the figure of the modern songstress giving voice to an epoch's structure of feeling. This lineage can be traced to early Shanghai actresses such as Zhou Xuan, who embodies national victimization and sings in the teahouse in Yuan Muzhi's *Street Angel* (*Malu tianshi*, 1937), and also to the literary tropes of dance hall or nightclub singers who reflect the vicissitudes of modernity in early Shanghai modernist literature. However, unlike the victimized songstress in teahouses or seductive dance hall singers who are restricted to claustrophobic spaces of performance, these singing women in Yang's films walk out of the teahouses or dance halls to assume their place in other urban locales. For example, the female protagonist Li Kailing (Grace Chang) in *Mambo Girl* (*Manbo nülang*, 1957) sings and teaches mambo moves in her cozy middle-class Hong Kong abode; Tao Haiyin and Li Ailian in *It's Always Spring* perform on a sailing boat in Hong Kong, while Lin Keping sings of the progress of Free China in Taipei's Yuanshan Grand Hotel and of her desire for love along the banks of Bangkok's Chao Phraya River in *Air Hostess*. Literally taking the Free World as her singing stage, the figure of the modern songstress represents an updated cosmopolitan feminine ideal from the 1930s, embodying transnational mobility not only through her physical travels within the film's narrative, but also through the transnational circulation of her lyrical voice in the form of soundtracks beyond the film's diegesis.

In the most compelling example, MP&GI's star system successfully created a cosmopolitan, feminine, and border-crossing star persona for Grace Chang, and Chang's cosmopolitan image is best epitomized by the trans-Pacific crossings of her voice. Chang's dynamic vocal performances fostered a modern, Chinese feminine imaginary that circulated among postwar Sinophone communities in Hong Kong, Taiwan, and Southeast Asia, reaching even as far as the United States at the height of her popularity. Wearing a cheongsam, Chang appeared on the Dinah Shore Chevy Show on America's NBC-TV under an episode titled "Pacific Festival" in October 1959, which featured talents from Hong Kong, Tokyo, Manila, and Korea, and was said to have attracted an audience of 60 million Americans ("Television Review" 1959, 26; "Zai liu qian wan" 1959). The opening sequence of her segment is reminiscent of the palace classroom scene in Walter Lang's *The King and I* (1956); assuming the role of Anna Leonowens in the opening, Shore introduces Chang as "China's lovely motion picture star" to the group of Asian children surrounding her. The camera then cuts to Chang, who appears from behind a screen of beaded curtains, singing a Chinese ballad "The Autumn Song." She interacts with Shore in fluent English and performs a multilingual version of *The King and I*'s theme song "Getting to Know You" alongside Shore and the Japanese actress Asaoka Yukiji ("Zai liu qian wan" 1959). The harmonious, multiracial interaction between the three women of different nationalities, dancing, and singing about friendship in different tongues, is itself a spectacle of Cold War cosmopolitanism; it not only demonstrates the soft power of the feminine lyrical voice, but can also be read allegorically as the symbolic friendship between the United States and the non-communist parts of Asia, with Grace Chang representing "China." After this successful performance in the United States, Chang would go on to release, in 1961, an American LP with Capital Records titled "Hong Kong's Grace Chang: The Nightingale of the Orient—Singing Popular Songs in Chinese," which includes tracks such as "I Love Calypso" and "Flying Up In The Sky" from *Air Hostess* ("Ge Lan" 1961). The circulation of Chang's voice as a pedagogical tool of modernity sought not only to educate audiences within Asia itself, but also to inform American audiences of another cosmopolitan reality in Asia that existed beyond the shores of the United States. The close geopolitical connections during the Cold War and cosmopolitan worldliness exemplified by the singing and reception of Chang's performances thus suggest the formation of a transnational Free World community—an imagined community bound together by the voice of the modern cosmopolitan Chinese songstress—while also reminding us of the gendered dimensions of popular culture during the Cold War era.

Conclusion

Grace Chang's performances constitute an important audiovisual memory of the postwar era that would continue to circulate well beyond the golden age of 1950s and 1960s Hong Kong Mandarin musicals. Her songs "I Love Calypso" and "Flying Up in the Sky" from *Air Hostess*, for example, are featured in contemporary films such as Tsai Ming-liang's *The*

Hole (*Dong*, 1998) and, more recently, Jon Chu's Hollywood romantic comedy *Crazy Rich Asians* (2018), serving as a vehicle that transports audiences on a nostalgic journey back to a cosmopolitan postwar past. If Chang's performances in Evan Yang's musical films during the 1950s can be understood as an amalgamation of early Shanghai and Hollywood influences, we witness the poignant circulation of Chang's "Flying up in the Sky" from *Air Hostess* back onto the Hollywood screen of *Crazy Rich Asians*. Screened nearly 70 years apart, Lin Keping's desire for a modern career as an air hostess and resistance against traditional patriarchal values, articulated through Chang's voice, find an unlikely resonance with *Crazy Rich Asians'* Asian-American protagonist Rachel Chu (Constance Wu), who finds herself caught between traditional Asian values and her liberal Western ideas after arriving in Singapore from the United States.

The contemporary cinematic recuperations of a bygone cosmopolitan era through the voice of the modern songstress highlight the significance of MP&GI's films in postwar Hong Kong film history. Yet, the nostalgic effect from the consumption of these songs through these contemporary films potentially obscures readings of Yang's MP&GI works within the Cold War context. By reading Yang's MP&GI films both textually and historically, this chapter positions them in the lineage of Shanghai's neo-sensationalism, while seeking to contextualize questions of gender, travel, and mobility within the historical context of the Cold War Hong Kong. While the issue of gendered mobility can serve as symbolic entry points into understanding vernacular and cultural modernity during the Cold War, this chapter demonstrates how the body and voice of the modern woman in Yang's films are configured with much ambivalence and that his stylized tropes of modernity—women and vehicles—often expose its inherent contradictions.

The main motive of situating Yang's MP&GI works in this lineage is to foreground the issues of diasporic routes, aesthetic traditions, and individual agency that tend to be obscured in scholarship pertaining to filmmaking in volatile political milieus such as the Cold War. Yang's works, in particular, demonstrate the translation of aesthetic ideas from 1930s Shanghai into Cold War Hong Kong that is made possible through the diasporic routes of Shanghai émigrés. Furthermore, this chapter is premised on the belief that the "hard" and "soft" films debate of the 1930s regarding the role of films in light of political turbulences can also inform our understanding of Cold War Hong Kong's film industry. Grappling with restrictions such as censorship and the market accessibility, the dichotomy between soft and hard films became increasingly blurred during the Cold War, as both right- and left-wing filmmakers sought to diffuse overt, contentious, political ideologies by making films more accessible to audiences in the form of "entertainment." In the same vein, it becomes critical for us to consider the stakes of "vernacular modernism" in Yang's MP&GI films within the context of Cold War Asia. Vernacular modernism has often taken on a relatively apolitical dimension, despite its association with Hollywood hegemony and soft power as a form of capitalist modernity. Yet, if we focus on aspects of spectatorship and the participatory nature of vernacular modernism, to what extent can these films, which disseminate knowledge regarding modern values, occupations, technologies, and lifestyles through the lyrical voice and corporeal bodies of modern women, be considered as propaganda? How should we distinguish between pedagogy, entertainment, and propaganda in Cold War filmmaking? Perhaps the difficulties of discerning these discursive boundaries best suggest the fluidity and volatility of filmmaking entwined with gender politics in Cold War Hong Kong.

Notes

1 After joining MP&GI in 1956, Yang directed approximately 40 films over the following two decades and wrote nearly 200 lyrics for film songs. For the complete list of films and song titles, see Yi (2009, 134–43).

2 For more information regarding the background of Cathay Organization and its leading figure Loke Wan Tho, see Fu (2018, 30–4), Wong (2009), as well as Lim and Yiu (1991).

3 Despite the fact that Loke Wan Tho had provided loans to Yung Hwa Motion Pictures Studio at the request of Taiwan's Nationalist government, it could not cope financially after the closure of China's film market and had to close down (Chung 2009, 10–19).

4 Zhen Zhang (2005) gives "vernacular modernism" in the Chinese context more political and historical depth by examining it in relation to the vernacular movement propagated by the Chinese intellectuals during the May Fourth Movement (1–40).

5 Evan Yang's autobiography sheds light on his involvement in Nationalist newspapers such as *Hong Kong Times*, Hong Kong right-wing film studios such as Asia Pictures, and even pro-Beijing film studios such as Great Wall Movie Enterprise. Despite his family background and connections with Nationalist officials, Yang's multifaceted career arguably complicates our understanding of him as an outright Nationalist supporter. See Yi (2009, 54–71).

6 Zhen Zhang (2005) argues that the debate over "hard" and "soft" films first started off as an issue of aesthetics, but quickly escalated into an ideological battle between left-wing filmmakers and modernists; the site of contention is the body of the modern girl and the meaning of what it means to be cosmopolitan (244–97).

7 Cotton Seiler (2008) discusses the relationship between gender, automobility, and national culture during the Cold War in the United States. He argues that its automobile culture is gendered, which is reflected in mainstream media's reinforcement of the idea that automotive mastery was a matter of gender; the act of driving thus can be considered as a form of "palliative ideological exercise" that reverses the post-war decline of the individual and the deterioration of the American character of a heroic and expansionist past (85–8).

8 For a comprehensive study of the lineage of the songstress in Chinese cinema through the case studies of Zhou Xuan, Chung Ching, and Grace Chang, see Ma (2015).

9 The close relationship between MP&GI's films as "models of identification for being modern" and their public outreach is also suggested by the fact that Grace Chang and Chang Yang were invited as special guests to Hong Kong's Sixth Annual Traffic Safety Exhibition as part of their promotional activities of *Our Dream Car*. The posters and car models used in the Exhibition to educate the public on road safety were designed and constructed by Rex Fay, an art consultant of MP&GI ("Grace Chang" 1958).

Works Cited

"Air Hostess: A Spectacular Picture in Eastman Color." 1957. *International Screen*, no. 22 (August).

Chung, Po-yin Stephanie. 2009. "A Southeast Asian Tycoon and His Movie Dream: Loke Wan Tho and MP&GI." In *The Cathay Story*, rev. ed., edited by Wong Ain-ling, 10–19. Hong Kong: Hong Kong Film Archive.

Fu, Poshek. 2018. "More than Just Entertaining: Cinematic Containment and Asia's Cold War in Hong Kong, 1949–1959." *Modern Chinese Literature and Culture* 30 (2): 1–55.

Fu, Poshek. 2009. "Modernity, Cold War and the Hong Kong Mandarin Cinema." In *The Cathay Story*, rev. ed., edited by Wong Ain-ling, 24–33. Hong Kong: Hong Kong Film Archive.

Fu, Poshek. 2003. *Between Shanghai and Hong Kong: The Politics of Chinese Cinema*. Stanford, CA: Stanford University Press.

"Ge Lan: bei cheng wei quanneng yishujia" (Grace Chang: an all-rounded artist). 1961. *International Screen*, no. 66 (April).

"Ge Lan, Ye Feng, Su Feng: fang kongzhong xiaojie" (Grace Chang, Yeh Feng, and Soo Fung: interviews with air hostesses). 1957. *International Screen*, no. 20 (June).

Ge Momei (Liu Na'ou). 2001. "Dianyiing yu nvxing mei" (Cinema and female beauty). In *Liu Naou quanji: dianying ji* (Complete Works of Liu Na'ou: Film Series), edited by Kang Lai-shin, 248–49. Tainan: Tainan xian wenhua ju.

"Grace Chang and Chang Yang Attend Traffic Exhibition." 1958. *International Screen*, no. 30 (Apr): 20–1.

Hansen, Miriam B. 1999. "The Mass Production of the Senses: Classical Cinema as Vernacular Modernism." *Modernism/modernity* 6 (2): 59–77.

Huang, Jiamo. 1933. "Yingxing yingpian yu ruanxing yingpian" (Hard films and soft films). *Modern Screen* (December): 3.

Huxley, Aldous. 2001. *Aldous Huxley: Complete Essays, 1920–1925*. Edited by Robert S. Baker and James Sexton. Chicago: Ivan R. Dee.

Klein, Christina. 2017. "Cold War Cosmopolitanism: The Asia Foundation and 1950s Korean Cinema." *Journal of Korean Studies* 22 (2): 281–316.

Law, Kar. 2009. "A Glimpse of MP&GI's Creative/Production Situation: Some Speculations, Some Doubts." In *The Cathay Story*, rev. ed., edited by Wong Ain-ling, 34–9. Hong Kong: Hong Kong Film Archive.

Lee, Leo Ou-fan. 1999. *Shanghai Modern: the Flowering of a New Urban Culture in China 1930–1945*. Cambridge, MA: Harvard University Press.

Lim, Kay Tong, and Yiu Tiong Chai. 1991. *Cathay: 55 Years of Cinema*. Singapore: Landmark Books.

Liu, Na'ou. 1929. "Liangge shijian de buganzhengzhe" (Two People Impervious to Time). *The Modern Lady* 7 (11): 21–25.

Ma, Jean. 2015. *Sounding the Modern Woman: The Songstress in Chinese Cinema*. Durham, NC: Duke University Press.

Mu, Shiying. 1932. "Shanghai de hubuwu" (Shanghai Foxtrot). *Les Contemporaines* 2 (1): 112–120.

Mulvey, Laura. 1999. "Visual Pleasure and Narrative Cinema." In *Film Theory and Criticism: Introductory Readings*, edited by Leo Braudy and Marshall Cohen, 833–44. New York: Oxford University Press.

Needham, Gary. 2008. "Fashioning Modernity: Hollywood and the Hong Kong Musical 1957–64". In *East Asian Cinemas: Exploring Transnational Connections on Film*, edited by Leon Hunt and Leung Wing-fai, 41–56. London: I.B Tauris.

Seiler, Cotton. 2008. *Republic of Drivers: A Cultural History of Automobility in America*. Chicago: The University of Chicago Press.

Shih, Shu-mei. 2001. *The Lure of the Modern: Writing Modernism in Semicolonial China 1917–1937*. Berkeley and Los Angeles: University of California Press.

Shu, Kei. 2009. "Notes on MP&GI." In *The Cathay Story*, rev. ed., edited by Wong Ain-ling, 40–50. Hong Kong: Hong Kong Film Archive.

"Television Review: Tele Follow-up Comment—Dinah Shore Chevy Show." 1959. *Variety*, October 28, 1959: 26.

Wong, Ain-ling, ed. 2009. *The Cathay Story*, rev. ed. Hong Kong: Hong Kong Film Archive.

Ye, Lingfeng. 1933. "Liuxingxing ganmao" (Influenza). *Les Contemporaines* 3 (5): 643–54.

Yi, Wen. 2009. *Yousheng zhi nian: Yi Wen nianji* (Evan Yang's autobiography). Edited by Lan Tianyun. Hong Kong: Hong Kong Film Archive.

"Zai liu qian wan meiguo guanzhong zhiqian yanchu" (Grace Chang captivates 60 million American TV audiences). 1959. *International Screen*, no. 49 (November).

Zhang, Zhen. 2005. *An Amorous History of the Silver Screen: Shanghai Cinema 1896–1937*. Chicago: The University of Chicago Press.

8 Socks and Revolution

The Politics of Consumption in *Sentinels under the Neon Lights* (1964)

Calvin Hui

I begin by telling a story concerning the trials of Wang Guangmei, the wife of Liu Shaoqi, the second president of the People's Republic of China (PRC), in 1967. During the most turbulent times of the Great Proletariat Cultural Revolution, Liu was labeled as "China's Khrushchev" and considered as the "capitalist roader" (*zouzipai*) within the Chinese Communist Party (CCP). His wife was also radically critiqued. On April 10, 1967, three trials of Wang were held. These sessions partly focused on her fashion and feminine presentations while she was traveling outside of China. According to the red guards, when Wang visited Indonesia with Liu in 1963, she appeared in a Shanghai designer dress and a hat. Similarly, when she revisited Indonesia in 1966, she wore a qipao made in Hong Kong; she also brought her hairdresser with her. In addition, she wore a brooch/necklace that Jiang Qing, the wife of Mao Zedong, did not endorse (Hinton 1980, 1705). The red guards also accused Wang of not having spent sufficient time with Indonesian Communist Party leader Aidit. According to them, the specific ways in which Wang engaged with the anti-communist leader Sukarno were problematic. For example, she helped Sukarno light his cigarettes and allegedly flirted with him (Hinton 1980, 1701–2). These behaviors led the red guards to criticize Wang for helping her husband engage in "wife's diplomacy" (*furen waijiao*). They accused her of permitting Liu to use her feminine charms to flirt with the political reactionaries. In these trials, the red guards also asked Wang to take a political position on specific persons, publications, and incidents. They thoroughly interrogated her political ideologies.

In her recent work, historian Tani Barlow creatively appropriates Alain Badiou's theory of the event to conceptualize and historicize the event of women in the context of modern China. In her research concerning Maoism and gender, Barlow considers the Cultural Revolution as a politicized event amid the backdrop of the depoliticized Cold War era. According to her analysis, what the red guards opposed was the fact that Wang had depoliticized the subject of woman while she was traveling overseas. They criticized her for being apolitical or anti-political; they maintained that she was not qualified to be a woman (a political category) in those specific situations.[1] Following Barlow's logic, the difference between Jiang's uniform (and its association with proletarian and revolutionary femininity) and Wang's qipao (and its conceivable connection to bourgeois and commodified femininity) can be intellectualized, respectively, as the tension between the politicization and depoliticization of womanhood. These pieces of clothing quietly disclose the contradiction between the politicized event, namely, the Cultural Revolution, and the depoliticized era, that is, the Cold War. Ultimately, these debates regarding fashion and gender turn out to be serious contestations about culture and hegemony.

Similar to Barlow, I am interested in clothes, history, class, and politics in the context of Chinese socialism in the mid-1960s. However, deviating from her examination of historical narratives, I delve into Chinese socialist cinema. Whereas she places the red guards' trials of Wang alongside Badiou's theory of the event, I juxtapose Chinese socialist cinema with Fredric Jameson's (1981) concept of the "political unconscious." Jameson's groundbreaking work empowers me to examine the complexly mediated relationships among fashionable clothes, political history, social class, and geopolitical economy in the context of socialist China. It enables me to argue that the representation of clothes in Chinese socialist cinema, in a symptomatic way, unravels the political nuance and complexity of the Cold War.

This essay grows out of my book manuscript regarding fashion, media, and consumer culture in contemporary China. Specifically, my focus here is on nylon socks (*nilong wazi*), class struggles, and socialist revolutions in Wang Ping and Ge Xin's film *Sentinels under the Neon Lights* (*Nihong dengxia de shaobing*, 1964), which was adapted from Shen Ximeng's play of the same title (1963). Some of the questions I want to explore in this essay are as follows: what does this story about nylon socks reveal about politics? Does fashion reflect class ideologies—for example, are nylon socks bourgeois? In this essay, I argue that the consumption of nylon socks in *Sentinels* can be considered as a productive site to decipher the historical, social, and political-economic contradictions—that is, the "political unconscious"—of the film. Borrowing from Jameson's research on first-world literature from Europe, I work with second-world films from the PRC. I suggest that the depiction of nylon socks in *Sentinels* is a privileged locale to glimpse the otherwise invisible contradictions with which Chinese socialism was confronted in the mid-1960s. This story about socks surprisingly reveals the contradictions of revolutionary China against the backdrop of the struggle between socialism and capitalism in the Cold War period. It releases secret codes about the Sino-Soviet split (due to Soviet revisionism) and the battle between PRC-led socialism and U.S.-led capitalism. Furthermore, this narrative about socks can be interpreted as a socialist attempt to foreclose the possibility of what former U.S. Secretary of State John

Foster Dulles called the "peaceful evolution" (*heping yanbian*) of socialist countries into capitalist countries within a few generations. In short, the fictional narrative of *Sentinels* offers us a strategic position to confront some stark truths of the Cold War.

In terms of organization, this chapter is divided into three parts. In the first part, I engage with Zhuoyi Wang's 2014 book *Revolutionary Cycles in Chinese Cinema, 1951–1979* and provide a brief overview of Chinese cinema during the socialist period. In the second part, I demonstrate that *Sentinels* is a cautionary tale of the danger of fashion and consumption in the everyday life of socialist China. I emphasize how the young proletarian characters' desires for consumption and leisure ultimately lead to serious political consequences. In the third part, I argue that this negative portrayal of consumption and leisure is not a mirror reflection of the Chinese socialist reality; instead, it is a symptomatic expression of the profound contradictions with which Chinese socialism was confronted at the dawn of the Cultural Revolution. In this section, I converse with cultural critic Tang Xiaobing, who, in his analysis of Cong Shen's 1963 play *Never Forget*, coins the term "anxiety of the everyday life" (Tang 1993). I borrow Tang's idea and explain how the narrative of *Sentinels* similarly discloses the socialist anxiety of the everyday life. The story of *Sentinels* allegorizes the tensions between production and consumption, between work and leisure, between political revolution and economic construction, and between socialism and capitalism. This essay shows that the nylon socks in *Sentinels* store secret information about historical issues, social anxieties, and political-economic concerns against the backdrop of the Cold War.

Periodizing Chinese Socialist Film History

In his book entitled *Chinese Cinema: Culture and Politics since 1949*, Paul Clark (1986) offers an early overview of Chinese cinema during the socialist period.[2] He distinguishes between the Yan'an and Shanghai traditions and explains how these traditions influenced socialist filmmaking. Clark's effort has recently been updated by Zhuoyi Wang (2014), who provides a nuanced, meticulous, and complex picture of the conflicts and balances of power in the Maoist revolutionary campaigns and cinematic productions.[3] Specifically, Zhuoyi Wang examines how scriptwriters, directors, party authorities and bureaucrats, cultural critics, audiences, and other social actors contested and negotiated the meanings of films produced during the socialist period. Diverging from the conventional periodization that divides the socialist period into the "seventeen-year" period (1949–66) and the "Cultural Revolution" period (1966–76), he breaks up the socialist era into five distinctive phases as a new way to historicize Chinese socialist cinema. The first phase (1951–55) is called the "Nationalization" period because the film industry and studios were nationalized soon after the PRC had been founded. Zhuoyi Wang analyzes how film artists, such as Sun Yu and Zheng Junli, and the CCP authorities took part in the production and reception of the politically contentious films *The Life of Wu Xun* (*Wuxun chuan*, 1951) and *Song Jingshi* (*Song Jingshi*, 1957). The second phase, called the "First Hundred Flowers" period, was short-lived. It began with the "Hundred Flowers Campaign" in 1956 and ended with the "Anti-Rightist Campaign" in 1957 and the "Campaign to Wrench Out White Flags" in 1958. Zhuoyi Wang engages with Guo Wei's film *Blooming Flowers and the Full Moon* (*Huahao yueyuan*, 1958), an adaptation of Zhao Shuli's novel *Sanlian Village* (*Sanliwan*, 1955), and explains how this film epitomizes the uneasy tension between political agenda and commercial appeal. He also explores Lü Ban's satirical comedies (*fengcixing xiju*), particularly *The Unfinished Comedies* (*Meiyou wancheng de xiju*, 1957), that ridicule bureaucratic corruption and party-line didacticism. For this film, the author tells us, the director was labeled a rightist and got into trouble. The third phase took place during the "Great Leap Forward" period (1958–61). Zhuoyi Wang engages with Zheng Junli's film *Nie Er* (*Nie'er*, 1959), a biography of the composer of the PRC's national anthem, to illustrate the flourishing of the combination of revolutionary realism and revolutionary romanticism (as opposed to the Soviet-style socialist realism). For the fourth phase, which is called the "Second Hundred Flowers" period (1961–64), the author explores the revival of star cultures and a particular kind of comedy called "praising comedies" (*gesongxing xiju*).[4] The fifth phase, which lasted from 1964 to the Cultural Revolution, witnessed the intense politicization of cultural productions and everyday life. Zhuoyi Wang calls the pendulum swings from propaganda/education to entertainment and back the "revolutionary cycles in Chinese cinema." Zhuoyi Wang's work is instrumental in helping me locate the filmic representations of fashion and consumption in the "First Hundred Flowers" and "Second Hundred Flowers" periods. In this essay, I focus on the latter period.

In the mid-1960s, Chinese socialist films were peppered with stories concerning the dangers of fashion and consumption. This can be observed in Xie Tieli's film *Never Forget* (*Qianwan buyao wangji*, 1964), an adaptation of Cong Shen's play originally entitled *Wish You Good Health* (*Zhuni jiankang*, 1963) and later reworked and renamed as *Never Forget* (*Qianwan buyao wangji*, 1964). In this film, a young factory worker called Ding Shaochun purchases a high-quality suit (*liaozifu*), shoots wild birds, and becomes irresponsible with his factory duties. Because he has forgotten about class struggle, his father has to educate him. Similarly, in Zhao Ming's film *The Young Generation* (*Nianqing de yidai*, 1965), an adaption of Chen Yun's play of the same title (1964), recent college graduate Lin Yusheng buys a dress (*lianyiqun*) for his girlfriend and enjoys urban life. In his spare time, he indulges in petty-bourgeois trivialities, such as listening to music, reading novels and poetry, and watching movies after work. Preferring to stay in Shanghai, he is reluctant to return to the faraway and barren land of Qinghai to continue contributing to socialist constructions. Similarly, his father has to give him a lesson.[5]

The intriguing connection between fashion consumption and political regression can also be noticed in Fu Chaowu's film *Family Problems* (*Jiating wenti*, 1964), an adaptation of Hu Wanchun's short story of the same title (1963). The narrative concerns worker Du Fumin, who has just completed professional training in college. Feeling that the hat (*maozi*) his father has bought for him is too old-fashioned and does not match with his newly cut and stylish "airplane hairstyle" (*feijitou*), Du desires to have a more fashionable hat. Moreover, he is dissatisfied with the fact that his elder brother has spoiled his shirt. According to Du, "the workers' hands are too coarse." He looks down on the factory workers and loathes manual labor. Similar to the previous examples, his father has to school him. As we are about to see, the relationship between fashion consumption (specifically nylon socks) and ideological deterioration is expressed in *Sentinels* as well. From the high-quality suit in *Never Forget* to the dress in *The Young Generation*, and from the hat in *Family Problems* to the nylon socks in *Sentinels*, the filmic narratives concerning fashion and consumption in the mid-1960s are indeed a crucial site of intense political debates and ideological contestations. Part of the socialist education movement (1962–65), these stories propagate Mao's idea of continuous class struggle even after the initial success of socialist revolutions.

To Desire or Not to Desire

Sentinels tells the story of the People Liberation Army's (PLA) entrance into Shanghai in 1949, and how the junior soldiers are allured to materialistic temptations in this cosmopolitan and Westernized city. The narrative centers on the young, innocent, politically confused, and ideologically immature PLA soldiers named Chen Xi and Tong Anan. Chen, the third platoon commander, is older and has more experience in the battlefield than the new fighter Tong. In the film, these "middle characters" (*zhongjian renwu*)[6] are subjected to two different kinds of influence: the positive and the negative. On the one hand, the positive side is embodied by the proletariat who, under the direction of the CCP, represents socialism. The proletarian characters comprise PLA senior soldiers, namely, instructor Lu Hua and old monitor Hong Mantang. Below them are the good and slightly flawed characters, including commander Lu Dacheng, who has an overbearing and dominating personality, and Eighth Monitor Zhao Dada, who has an impulsive and impatient character. Although Lu Dacheng and Zhao are slightly better than Chen and Tong in the sense that they do not consume, they are not as politically established and ideologically robust as Lu Hua and Hong. On the other hand, the negative side, namely capitalism, is denoted by the bourgeoisie complicit with the American imperialists. The bourgeois characters consist of Old K (*Lao K*) (K probably stands for the Kuomintang or Guomindang, that is, the Nationalist Party) and his female spy Qu Manli. The other bourgeois characters, including Lin Naixian, the mother of female student Lin Yuanyuan, and Luo Kewen, the cousin of Lin Yuanyuan and a dandy who only cares about music but not politics, are slightly more preferable than Old K and Qu. However, they are still not politically trustworthy or reliable.

Upon their arrival, Chen and Tong are immediately fascinated with the formerly capitalistic and semicolonial Shanghai. For instance, enthralled with Shanghai's cosmopolitan and urban cultures, Tong voluntarily takes off his military uniform and unarms his weapons. After requesting permission from Chen, his senior commander, Tong leaves his work duties early in order to attend a garden party. Accompanied by his female classmate Lin Yuanyuan, a politically progressive student born and bred in a national bourgeois family, they go to have dinner at the International Hotel. According to Tong, everyone is equal after the communist liberation, therefore he can also dine at this restaurant.

Meanwhile, Chen is completely absorbed by Shanghai's commercial cultures. He is so enchanted with them that he exclaims, "Even the wind [in this city] smells fragrant!" On Nanjing Road, he falls victim to materialistic temptations and becomes unguarded toward bourgeois revisionism. This is demonstrated in how he is fascinated with the fashionable nylon socks sold in Shanghai. In an early scene in the film, the audience is presented with the views of modern department stores and neon lights in Shanghai. Then one sees, from Chen's perspective, the shop window and the different styles of nylon socks on display. According to the advertisement, these nylon socks are "the king of socks" (*wazhong zhiwang*). These colorful socks look modern. In addition to presenting the perspective of Chen, who looks at these fashionable commodities, the film also features the "point of view" of the nylon socks, thus giving the viewer an impression that these commodities are actively looking at Chen as much as Chen is looking at them. In fact, one can go further to propose that Chen has always already been looked at by these fashionable nylon socks, to such an extent that he is the object whereas the nylon socks are the subject. Moreover, Chen looks at the gaze of the commodities and feels powerless by the allure of these beautiful socks. Such intense exchanges of gazes, including how Chen looks at himself being looked at by the commodities, are eventually interrupted by the arrival of his peasant wife Chun Ni from the rural area.

Chen's downfall is shown most prominently in his attitude toward his socks. The film implies that he has purchased the nylon socks before attending the garden party. He may want to impress Qu and her fellow students with his new socks. Chen also attempts to abandon his old socks made of cloth. This is vividly dramatized in the film (and in the play). In one scene in the film, Chen is in a good mood and cheerfully sings in his dormitory. He admires his new and colorful nylon socks. Disgusted with his old and coarse socks, he throws them out of his room toward the corridor. (In the play, he throws them out of the window.) In both cases, the old monitor Hong picks them up and tosses them back into Chen's room without saying a word. This scene is significant insofar as it symbolizes the fact that Chen has abandoned proletarian frugality and begun to succumb to bourgeois materialism. In other words, he has been hit by what the socialist authority calls the "sugar-coated bullets" (*tangyi paodan*).

In fact, Chen's desire for the nylon socks in *Sentinels* can be contrasted with Lei Feng's refusal to buy new socks in Dong Zhaoqi's film *Lei Feng* (1965). In the latter film, Lei is also a PLA soldier. However, unlike Chen, Lei grew up as an orphan. His father was killed by the Japanese and his mother committed suicide due to the harassment of the landlords. In other words, he is a victim of imperialism and feudalism. Raised by members of the CCP, Lei later joins the PLA. He diligently studies Chairman Mao's works and aspires to become a screw in the socialist machine. This socialist new person is fully dedicated to revolutions and constructions. During his spare time, Lei volunteers to serve his community. For example, he does manual labor at a construction site but does not claim credit for his contribution. He also helps a woman by carrying her sick son on his back even though it is raining heavily. Moreover, when he is informed that the hometown of Wang Dali, his fellow soldier, has been badly flooded, he volunteers to go there to help. He also sends Wang Dali's mother 20 yuan without telling anyone about it. Although Lei's own income is very modest, he also donates 100 yuan to a local village. Significantly, Lei refuses to consume. While washing Lei's clothes at a river, Wang Dali discovers that Lei's socks are old, rough, and have holes. Because of this, Wang Dali buys new socks for Lei. However, Lei politely turns them down and instead donates these new socks to the villagers. Indeed, Lei is a socialist "workaholic": he labors all the time and does not take time off. He works even when he is not supposed to. It seems that this socialist new person is uninterested in consumption and leisure.[7]

In *Sentinels*, Chen's downfall is disclosed not only in his attitude toward his socks, but also in how he interacts with his class enemy, his coworker, and his wife. To begin with, Chen enjoys the admiration of the young and feminine Qu, who, unbeknown to him, turns out to be Old K's spy. In addition to persuading Chen to permit Tong to leave his work duty early so that Tong can attend the garden party, Qu constantly flatters and compliments Chen. For instance, she praises him for his military achievements, asks him for an autograph, and invites him to tell revolutionary stories to her fellow students. In fact, Qu's influence on Chen is gradual and subtle. At one point in the film, after she has said goodbye to Chen in the park, she waves to him in a particular manner. Chen unconsciously imitates her gesture and waves back to her in exactly the same way. Later, when Chen is about to return to his work duty, he says goodbye to his wife and waves to her in exactly the same way that Qu has waved to him before. It shows that Chen has been influenced by this spy without realizing it. Moreover, after he has settled down in Shanghai, Chen becomes slightly arrogant. He starts to look down on his fellow soldier Zhao, who comes from a poor and uneducated background. Chen comments on his dark skin and asks him to stand aside on Nanjing Road. Even worse, when Chen's wife comes to visit him in Shanghai, he is cold and unkind toward her. He ignores her and asks to be left alone. Not only does he not want the eggs that his wife has prepared for him, he also blames her for making his military uniform dirty. (Here, the smell of the eggs can be contrasted with what Chen calls the "fragrant" wind in the city). Moreover, Chen has lost the sewing kit (*zhenxianbao*) that his wife meticulously prepared for him for their wedding. It is obvious that Chen, alongside Tong, has fallen victim to bourgeois influences and materialistic temptations on Nanjing Road.

While Chen desires to have new nylon socks, the socialist authority figures interpret this yearning as an expression of not being vigilant toward bourgeois revival. They regard this longing as a symptom of having forgotten about class struggle. In the film version, Lu Dacheng strongly urges Chen to take off his new nylon socks and wear his old cloth socks instead. Lu Dacheng says:

> I have already discussed this problem with the instructor [Lu Hua]. As a member of the Communist Party, we need to remember Chairman Mao's words and cannot abandon our tradition of being simple, tough, and frugal. [Then, he takes out Chen's old socks, which have already been washed and sewn for him.] Do take off your colorful socks and wear this pair of cloth socks instead. This old pair remains strong and durable. You can stand steadily. In the past, by wearing these socks, you could overcome the three big mountains [imperialism, feudalism, and bureaucratic capitalism]. Today, you can wear them and transform Nanjing Road! I hope your reflection will begin with these socks. From them, you can look for the origin of your thinking.

In the original play, the senior instructor Lu Hua explains to Chen the seriousness of Chen's behavior. Lu Hua says: "Your thoughts have started to mold. They have begun to show rotten spots. If I don't draw your attention to this problem immediately, they will appear all over your body!" He then goes on to lecture on the danger of bourgeois revisionism and on the importance of continuing revolutions in the socialist everyday life. Lu Hua says:

> Don't think everything is fine after the enemy in arms has been defeated. To revolutionaries like us, this is just the first step of the Long March. You think Shanghai is peaceful and a safe haven? No! This is a battlefield; it's a different kind of battlefield. Our enemies have not slept! The ghosts of American imperialism are still haunting. Appearing like wind and fog, they will surround and attack us from all different directions. Old K is just one of them. While our enemies have not forgotten to plot against us, you have already abandoned your weapons and surrendered! [...]
>
> The important question lies on understanding the meaning of this battle: it is either that we fall on Nanjing Road, or that we, under the leadership of the Party, and with the help of the working class in Shanghai, transform Nanjing Road. This is a life-and-death struggle. (Shen 1963, 30; my translation)

The political message of the film and the play is obvious: never forget class struggle even after the success of socialist revolutions!

In terms of reception, *Sentinels* was enthusiastically received in China in 1963 (when the play came out) and in 1965 (when the film was released). More critics commented on the play than on the film. According to Shen Shoufu (1963) and Cheng Pulin (1963), there are three major types of PLA characters in the narrative. They include (1) Lu Hua and Hong, (2) Lu Dacheng and Zhao, and (3) Chen and Tong. Furthermore, these characters refer to three different political approaches toward Shanghai's Nanjing Road. Lu Hua and Hong are calm, solid, intelligent, and analytical. They realize that the appearance of Old K and Qu hints at the possibility of capitalist recuperation in the socialist context. Meanwhile, Lu Dacheng and Zhao, as well as Chen and Tong, are not the most politically mature and robust. For example, contrary to Chen and Tong, who embrace the materialistic temptations of Shanghai, Zhao is impatient with the jazz music, neon lights, fashionable commodities, and bourgeois lifestyles. Rather than staying in Shanghai, he would prefer to go back to the battlefield. Inspired by Mao's 1957 essay entitled "On the Correct Handling of Contradictions among the People" (*Guanyu zhengque chuli renmin neibu maodun de wenti*), Cheng further adds that the tension between Lu Dacheng and Zhao on the one hand, and Chen and Tong on the other hand, should be considered as "the contradictions among the people" (*renmin neibu maodun*) (24–6). In fact, Mo Yan, who directed the first theatrical performances of *Sentinels* back in 1963, also emphasizes the difference between the contradictions between the people and the enemy (*diwo maodun*) and those among the people themselves. According to him, the primary source of contradictions should center on the struggle between the PLA soldiers and their bourgeois enemy Old K, rather than on the tension among the PLA soldiers themselves (Mo 1963, 15–21). In the language of Mao, the performance should prioritize the contradictions between the people and their political enemy.

Repression and Displacement

In my analysis, *Sentinels* concerns the problem of time management in the context of Chinese socialist modernity. There are 24 hours in a day. If one-third of the time is devoted to sleep, another one-third is devoted to production and labor (e.g., military work in the PLA), then the remaining one-third can be devoted to leisure and consumption. However, how should these eight hours of leisure and consumption be organized in the socialist modernity? What should socialist everyday life look like? What can socialist leisure and consumption be like?

In the film, the primary source of conflict has to do with fashion, consumption, and leisure. For instance, Tong leaves work early in order to attend the garden party. He also has dinner with his classmate at the International Hotel. Meanwhile, Chen desires the modern and fashionable nylon socks displayed in the department store's window. He also plans to get rid of the old and coarse socks made of cloth. These consumerist activities take place outside of the time and space of PLA's military work. They also happen outside of the parameters of socialist power and governmentality. In this sense, this film expresses the socialist regime's anxiety toward the unsettling, even disruptive, potentials of fashion, consumption, and leisure. It reveals the socialist administration's unease and discomfort toward industrialized modernity and urban life.

If cultural critic Tang Xiaobing watched *Sentinels*, he would probably agree that this film expresses the socialist government's "anxiety of the everyday life." In a 1993 essay entitled "The Historical Meaning of *Never Forget*—The Anxiety of the Everyday Life and Modernity," Tang examines Cong Shen's play *Never Forget*. This play concerns the growing up experience of the proletarian "middle character" Ding Shaochun, who is shown purchasing a high-quality suit, shooting wild birds, and forgetting about class struggle. According to Tang's analysis, the construction of the character Ding Shaochun exposes the distinctions between production and consumption, between work and leisure, between the factory and the home, between the public and the private, and between the collective and the individual. However, from the characterizations of socialist authority figure Ding Haikuan and of the socialist new person Ji Youliang, one can observe the suppression of these separations (228–9). In fact, this logic can also be applied to *Sentinels*.

In this film, the proletarian "middle characters" Tong and Chen are fascinated with the cultures of Shanghai's colonial modernity. These problematic characters similarly uncover the differentiations between work and leisure, between the collective and the individual, and between revolution and consumption. In contrast, the positive proletarian characters Lu Hua and Hong are completely devoted to socialist revolution; they are simply indifferent to leisure, play, consumption, and urban life. The division between production and consumption is repressed in these senior PLA characters. (In fact, the same is also true for the socialist new persons Lei Feng in *Lei Feng* and Ma Tianming in *Today Is My Day Off*. They work all the time and never consume.)

In his essay, Tang suggests that *Never Forget* symptomatically expresses the contradictions with which the Chinese socialist regime is confronted concerning industrialized modernity. According to him:

> The play has fully captured the contradictory imaginations of an age toward industrialized modernity. It has expressed a strong desire for modernity, but at the same time it refuses and resists it.
> (229; my translation)

In my interpretation, the contradiction is as follows: on the one hand, the socialist government desires and embraces the productivity of industrialized modernity. On the other hand, it is also worried about the problems brought about by industrialization. Thinking with Tang, I suggest that the arrival of industrialized modernity contributes to the breaking up of traditional organization of time and space, resulting in the separations between work time and leisure time, and between work place (e.g., the factory) and home. To overcome this crisis of temporal fragmentation and spatial dislocation, the socialist regime attempts to cancel and erase the divisions between production and consumption, and between labor and leisure. According to Tang, in *Never Forget*, this solution can be detected in the construction of the positive characters Ding Haikuan and Ji, who work all the time and do not take time off. This desire is also evidenced in Ding Haikuan's condemnation of Ding Shaochun for purchasing a high-quality suit, shooting wild birds, and forgetting about class struggle. In fact, this same logic also operates in *Sentinels*. The positive characters Lu Hua and Hong, who are fully committed to socialist revolutions, also blame Tong and Chen for falling victim to bourgeois materialism.

In my analysis, the socialist leadership responds to this concern by obliterating the spatial and temporal divisions of work and leisure. However, rather than considering modernity as a site of intense political contestation, or, more precisely, instead of arguing that socialism can be as modern as, or perhaps more modern than, capitalism, the socialist regime manages its own "anxiety of the everyday life" by repressing and displacing its fear to its external enemy, that is, the bourgeoisie. Tang (1993) explains:

> The historical meaning of *Never Forget* is that it has displaced and repressed the root of the problem, and because of this, it has recorded the collective anxiety of its historical period. If *Wish You Healthy* [the earlier title of the play] expresses the desire of overcoming modernity, *Never Forget* [the final title of the play and of the film] symptomatically expresses the avoidance of answering the question. It has externalized its internal anxiety onto the other – "bourgeois quagmire/slime-pit", "disease/virus", and "class enemy" etc.
>
> (233; my translation)

Tang briefly mentions that repression and displacement are at work. Adding to his insight, I engage with Freudian psychoanalysis to explain how repression and displacement function in *Sentinels*.

In fact, the formal structure of *Sentinels* resembles what Sigmund Freud (2008), in *The Interpretation of Dreams*, calls dream-work. According to Freud, dreams comprise of two layers, namely, dream-contents (manifest content) and dream-thoughts (latent content). Similar to two languages that are unintelligible to each other, dreams require translation, interpretation, and analysis. To protect sleep, the dream-thoughts unacceptable to the conscious mind will be censored and filtered. They will be distorted and transformed into acceptable dream-contents. This way, one can acknowledge their existence and will not be troubled by them. This process is called dream-work, which consists of transformative mechanisms such as condensation and displacement.

According to Freud, when dream-thoughts are transformed into dream-contents, repression and displacement are at work. In fact, similar processes can be observed in *Sentinels*, which can be compared to a dream. In the first scenario, the characterizations of Lu Hua and Hong reveal the repression of the divisions between production and consumption, between work time and leisure time, and between factory and home. In the second scenario, the socialist regime's "anxiety of the everyday life" produced by the industrialized and urbanized modernity is displaced to an external other. In this film, this class enemy is personified by Old K, who is associated with the American imperialists and his spy Qu. The national bourgeoise is also embodied in Lin Naixian and Luo, and, to a lesser extent, in Lin Yuanyuan.[8]

In *Sentinels*, although the important issue of socialist consumption is brought up, it is insufficiently addressed and prematurely foreclosed. This question is repressed, and the blame is shifted, rechanneled, and displaced to bourgeois revival and capitalistic revisionism. What is equally problematic is that socialist consumption is irreversibly entangled with moral and ethical judgments. For instance, the fact that Tong attends the garden party and has dinner with his classmate at the International Hotel is unfairly intertwined with his political ignorance and immaturity. He does not realize the cruel fact that his class enemy Old K has killed his father in a labor uprising until the senior solider Hong tells him so. Similarly, Tong does not know that Old K's gang has badly threatened and injured his elder sister A Xiang by throwing her into the river. Correspondingly, Chen's consumption of the nylon socks is unfortunately entangled with his poor behaviors toward his coworker and his wife. While stationing on Shanghai's Nanjing Road, Chen becomes vain (e.g., he desires the nylon socks), arrogant (e.g., he mocks Zhao for having dark skin and asks him to stand aside), ungrateful (e.g., he is cold toward his wife and ignores her), and careless (e.g., he loses the sewing kit that his wife has meticulously prepared for him). Because these incidents are not causally or logically related, it is not possible to have an honest and productive discussion about the possibility of consumption and leisure in Chinese socialist modernity.[9]

In the discussion, I have presented two scenarios: the first focuses on the socialist authority figures Lu Hua and Hong. Fully dedicated to socialist revolutions, these positive characters do not consume or have any hobbies outside of the revolutionary setting. Because they do not consume, they do not make any mistakes. The second scenario concerns the young PLA officers Chen and Tong. They consume, engage in leisure activities, and make mistakes. However, in my analysis, there is no simple causal and logical connection between the desire to consume and the consequence of forgetting about class struggle and socialist revolution. The fact that Tong desires to go to the garden party and have dinner at the International Hotel does not inevitably mean that he will definitely become less committed to class struggle, nation building, or world revolution. In fact, he can enjoy the garden party and the restaurant while being politically committed. Likewise, Chen's desire for new nylon socks should not necessarily be seen as being detrimental to his work performance. In fact, it is possible for him to wear the nylon socks while responsibly performing his duties. Nevertheless, this "work hard and play hard" attitude is not offered as an option in *Sentinels*.

Ultimately, the problem with *Sentinels* is that it is not daring enough to imagine a third option, one that can simultaneously accommodate revolution/production and consumption/leisure against the backdrop of the Cold War. The film does not attempt to envision what socialist everyday life can look like. It is not bold enough to picture how socialist consumption and leisure can be different from, or even better than, its capitalist counterpart. Moreover, the film oversimplifies and underanalyzes capitalism and its ideology. Rather than presenting the complexity of bourgeois hegemony, *Sentinels* simply represses the root of the problem (i.e., socialist consumption), displaces it to an external source (i.e., the bourgeoise and capitalism), and condemns it with a moralistic judgment. Indeed, as Cai Xiang (2016) explains in his book *Revolution and Its Narratives*, Chinese socialism, in the first half of the 1960s, is strong in terms of politics but weak in terms of culture (see Chapter 7).[10] Responding to this cultural crisis, the subsequent Cultural Revolution in the second half of the 1960s can be understood as a radical attempt, by the Chinese socialist authority, to regain and reconstruct ideological hegemony in the realm of the everyday life. The Cultural Revolution is not only a revolution of politics but also a revolution of culture.[11]

Notes

1 I thank Professor Tani Barlow for generously sharing her work-in-progress with me. In addition, see Barlow (2017, 2009) for related discussions.

2 For a summary of Paul Clark's book on socialist cinema, see his essay entitled "Artists, Cadres, and Audiences" (2012).

3 For more discussion on Chinese socialist cinema, see Braester and Chen (2011) and Ward (2011).

4 According to Paul Clark (1986), Chinese films produced in the mid- and late 1950s and early 1960s vary in genres. They include filmic adaptations of literary works (e.g., Sang Hu's *New Year's Sacrifice* [*Zhufu*] [1956], Shui Hua's *The Shop of the Lin Family* [*Linjia puzi*] [1959], Xie Tieli's *Early Spring in February* [*Zaochun eryue*] [1963]), opera films (e.g., Xie Jin's *Two Stage Sisters* [*Wutai jiemei*] [1965]), war films (e.g., Guo Wei's *Dong Cunrui* [*Dong Cunrui*] [1955] and Shui Hua's *Living Forever in Burning Flames* [*Liehuo zhong yongsheng*] [1965]), films about ethnic minorities (e.g., Wang Jiayi's *Five Golden Flowers* [*Wuduo jinhua*] [1959], Liu Qiong's *Ashima* [*Ashima*] [1964], and Li Jun's *Serfs* [*Nongnu*] [1963]), and films about contemporary life in socialism (e.g., Su Li's *The Young People in Our Village* [*Women cunli de nianqingren*] [1959], Xie Jin's *Big Li, Little Li, and Old Li* [*Dali xiaoli he laoli*] [1962], and Lu Ren's *Li Shuangshuang* [*Li Shuangshuang*] [1962]).

5 A remake of this film, also called *The Young Generation* and directed by Ling Zhihao and Zhang Huijun, was released in 1976.

6 The middle character is a character type that appeared in early 1960s China. Later, it was replaced by the positive and heroic character marked by the "three prominences" (*san tuchu*) during the Cultural Revolution. The aesthetic theory of the "Three Prominences" is as follows: among the characters, the positives ones should be prominent; among the positive ones, the heroes; and among the heroes, the main hero should be the most prominent. For discussions on the "three prominences," see Gu (2010).

7 A socialist new person, Lei Feng can be compared to the policeman Ma Tianming in Lu Ren's film *Today is My Day Off* (*Jintian woxiuxi*, 1959). In this "praising comedy" film, Ma, played by Zhong Xinghuo, volunteers to help his fellow comrades and citizens during his day off. Similar to Lei, Ma works all the time and does not take time off. He does not consume or engage in leisure. For a summary of this film, see Krista Van Fleit Hang (2013).

8 From Qu's influence on Chen to Lin Yuanyuan's impact on Tong, I argue that in the socialist context, gender is imagined as a medium through which the bourgeoisie may counterattack and weaken the socialist body. The downfall of the masculinized proletarian characters is portrayed as a gendered affair.

9 The reason I bring this up is that I observe a pattern of moral judgments in my research regarding the narratives of fashion and consumption in Chinese socialist plays and films produced in the mid-1960s. For example, in *The*

Young Generation, the proletarian "middle character" Lin Yusheng desires to stay in the city and engage in leisure activities, such as listening to music, reading novels and poetry, watching movies, going to the park, and spending time with friends. He also organizes a birthday party and buys two bottles of wine, some candy, and a dress for his girlfriend. However, these consumerist activities should not necessarily lead to the conclusion that he must have forgotten about socialist revolutions. Rather than discussing socialist consumption on its own terms, Lin Yusheng's problem is linked to the fact that he has forged a medical note and has exaggerated his illness, which is later discovered by socialist new person Xiao Jiye. Lin Yusheng's "problem" is also connected to the fact that his father Lin Jian and his mother Xia Shujuan are not his biological parents. In fact, 24 years ago, Lin Yusheng's biological parents, due to their involvements in the labor movements, were captured, imprisoned, and eventually executed by Guomindang (KMT) officers. Before she was killed, Lin Yusheng's biological mother had left him a note, reminding her son: "You [Lin Yusheng] must never forget the world that still harbors our class enemies! You must struggle for the sacred ideals of communism!" The fundamental issue, namely, whether there can be a place for individual happiness, amid the background of collective struggle in the socialist context, is repressed and displaced. It is labeled as a moral and ethical concern.

10 Cai (2016) is the English translation. For the original in Chinese, see Cai (2010).

11 For a different interpretation of *Sentinels*, see Braester (2010).

Works Cited

Barlow, Tani. 2017. "Jiang Qing, Seriously." *The PRC History Review* 2 (4): 1–3.

Barlow, Tani. 2009. "Wang Guangmei: The Great Proletarian Cultural Revolution and the Event of Women." Duke University's Feminist Theory Workshop, March 21, 2009. www.youtube.com/watch?v=XKzpWk4OWfQ.

Braester, Yomi. 2010. "A Big Dyeing Vat: The Rise of Proletarian Shanghai and the Fall of Nanjing Road." Chap. 2 in *Painting the City Red: Chinese Cinema and the Urban Contract*. Durham, NC: Duke University Press.

Braester, Yomi and Tina Mai Chen. 2011. "Film in the People's Republic of China, 1949–1979: The Missing Years?" *Journal of Chinese Cinemas* 5 (1): 5–12.

Cai, Xiang. 2016. *Revolution and Its Narratives: China's Socialist Literary and Cultural Imaginaries, 1949–1966*, edited by Rebecca Karl and Xueping Zhong. Durham, NC: Duke University Press.

Cai, Xiang. 2010. *Gemin Xushu: Zhongguo shehui zhuyi wenxue—wenhua xiangxiang, 1949–1966* (Revolution and its Narratives: China's Socialist Literary and Cultural Imaginaries, 1949–1966). Beijing: Beijing daxue chubanshe (Peking University Press).

Cheng, Pulin. 1963. "*Nihongdeng xia de shaobing de chengjiu yu tese*" (The achievements and characteristics of *Sentinels under the Neon Lights*). *Shanghai Xiju* (Shanghai Theater), no. 5: 24–6.

Clark, Paul. 2012. "Artists, Cadres, Audiences." In *A Companion to Chinese Cinema*, edited by Yingjin Zhang, 42–56. Malden, MA: Wiley-Blackwell.

Clark, Paul. 1986. *Chinese Cinema: Culture and Politics since 1949*. Cambridge: Cambridge University Press.

Freud, Sigmund. 2008. *The Interpretation of Dreams*. Oxford: Oxford University Press.

Gu, Yizhong. 2010. "The Three Prominences." In *Words and their Stories: Essays on the Language of the Chinese Revolution*, edited by Ban Wang, 283–304. Leiden and Boston, MA: Brill.

Hinton, Harold C., ed. 1980. *The People's Republic of China 1949–1979: A Documentary Survey. Volume 3: 1965–1967 The Cultural Revolution Part I.* Wilmington, Del.: Scholarly Resources.

Jameson, Fredric. 1981. *The Political Unconscious: Narrative as a Socially Symbolic Act.* Ithaca, NY: Cornell University Press.

Mao, Zedong. 2007. "On the Correct Handling of Contradictions among the People." In *On Practice and Contradiction*, edited by Slavoj Zizek, 130–166. London: Verso.

Mo, Yan. 1963. "*Nihongdeng xia de shaobing de daoyan gousi*" (The director's conceptualization of *Sentinels under the Neon Lights*). *Xiju bao* (Theater Journal), no. 4: 15–21.

Shen, Shoufu. 1963. "*Laogu shuli jieji douzheng de guandian—huajiu nihongdeng xia de shaobing geiwo de qifa jiaoyu*" (Secure and establish the view of class struggle—the Play *Sentinels under the Neon Lights*' inspiration to me). *Shanghai Xiju* (Shanghai Theater), no. 5: 22–3.

Shen, Ximeng, Mo Yan, and Lü Xingchen. 1963. *Nihong dengxia de shaobing (Nanjinglu jinxingqu zhi yi)* (*Sentinels under the Neon Lights* [The March of Nanjing Road I]). *Juben* (Script), no. 2: 2–41.

Tang, Xiaobing. 1993. "*Qianwan buyao wangji de lishi yiyi – guanyu richang shenghuo de jiaolü jiqi xiandaixing*" (The historical meaning of *Never Forget*—the anxiety of the everyday life and modernity). In *Zai jiedu* (Reinterpretations), edited by Tang Xiaobing. Hong Kong: Oxford University Press.

Van Fleit Hang, Krista. 2013. *Literature the People Love: Reading Chinese Texts from the Early Maoist Period (1949–1966).* New York: Palgrave Macmillan.

Wang, Zhuoyi. 2014. *Revolutionary Cycles in Chinese Cinema, 1951–1979.* New York: Palgrave Macmillan.

Ward, Julian. 2011. "The Remodeling of a National Cinema: Chinese Films of the Seventeen Years (1949–66)." In *The Chinese Cinema Book*, edited by Song Hwee Lim and Julian Ward. 87–94. New York and London: Palgrave Macmillan and British Film Institute.

9 Archive Revisionisms

Reevaluating South Korea's State Film Censorship of the Cold War Era

Hye Seung Chung

Not long after arriving in the United States in 1997, when I took up film studies as a graduate student at a university on the East Coast, I met with my advisor, an American cinema specialist. One of the first questions he asked me concerned the issue of film censorship in my home country. To paraphrase his initial inquiry: "Isn't censorship in South Korea strict and severe because of the country's long history of military dictatorships?" To be sure, as a cultural outsider, he had little direct knowledge of Korean cinema—its canonical texts, authors, and industrial history. But he had a vague, impressionistic idea of it being harshly censored and therefore non-conducive to the freedom of artistic expression that has long been prized in the West. This college professor's instinctual understanding of film censorship as the anthesis to creative independence and, more broadly, constitutional democracy is, in fact, a widespread phenomenon throughout both the United States and South Korea, shared by many others within academia. In the eyes of many, censorship is an inherently negative word that not only connotes a violation of First Amendment rights (in the U.S. context) but also gestures toward fundamentally contrary political systems around the world, such as Fascism and Communism. Similarly, for South Koreans, censorship is synecdochically tied to a non-democratic past, a period stretching back to the early history of Japanese colonialism (1910–45) through the Cold War-era authoritarian regimes of Park Chung Hee (1961–79) and Chun Doo Hwan (1980–88), all of which have been viewed by contemporary critics through an ever-darkening lens of accumulated resentment.

However, as with the other types of power-based relationships theorized by Michel Foucault (1990), censorship is not simply a "mode of subjugation" or "a general system of dominance," as one might presume (92). Rather, in a way that is indicative of the French philosopher's notion of discursively constructed power, film censorship can be understood as "the multiplicity of force relations immanent in the sphere in which they operate," or, in other words, "the process which, through ceaseless struggles and confrontations, transforms, strengthens, or reverses them." As Foucault explains, "Where there is power, there is resistance." The existence of power relationships "depends on a multiplicity of points of resistance" (95). When applied to censorship studies, this idea can assist in theorizing filmmakers' creative circumvention of prohibitions and rules through textual ambiguity, visual symbols, distant framings, use of offscreen space, and narrative strategies steeped in allegory and displacement.

In the United States, Joseph I. Breen, a former journalist and devout Irish Catholic, headed the Production Code Administration (PCA) from 1934 to 1954, and was in charge of ensuring that Hollywood productions met certain industrial standards in order to ready them for external censorship review by seven state boards, 31 municipal boards, and 200–250 ad hoc local boards, not to mention mostly government-controlled foreign censorship boards (Doherty 2007, 115).[1] Members of the Motion Picture Producers and Distributors Association (MPPDA, now MPAA) had made a pact among themselves not to distribute or exhibit any films lacking the PCA's seal of approval.[2] This conditional release practice gave enforcing power to the in-house regulator, who was entrusted with the task of interpreting and implementing the Production Code, a detailed self-regulatory treatise catering to various external censorship demands, from suppression of sex, violence, and profanity to respectful representations of religion, law enforcement, and foreign nationals. Breen and his staff processed approximately 3,500 story materials per year, supervised script development at every step of the process, demanded rewrites and changes for any Code violations, and reviewed final prints before issuing their certificates (Doherty 2007, 84). However, the internal censors did not have unilateral power over producers, who often negotiated with Breen and even benefited from creative suggestions from PCA staff. Film historian Thomas Doherty (2007) argues that formal restrictions imposed by PCA censorship were "preconditions for the creative act," just as the 14-line (stanza, quatrain, and couplet) rule was an inspirational, rather than limiting, structural form for Shakespearean sonnet poets (98). In a sense, the give-and-take negotiation process between studios/filmmakers and censors can be likened to Foucault's (1990) description of the mutually reinforcing pleasure of exercising and evading power:

> The pleasure that comes of exercising a power that questions, monitors, watches, spies, searches out, palpates, brings to light; and on the other hand, the pleasure it kindles at having to evade this power, flee from it, fool it, or travesty it.
>
> (45)

Drawing upon archival evidence, this chapter will demonstrate similar Foucauldian dynamics of productive power manifest in state censorship of the South Korean film industry during the harshest period of Chun Doo Hwan's military dictatorship in the 1980s. Moreover, by evaluating

Korean case studies in relation to the MPPDA Production Code's regulatory standards for Hollywood cinema, it aims to promote a more nuanced understanding of film regulation (concerning such sensitive content as sex, crimes, and law) in a transnational, comparative context.

The KOFA Digital Archive and a New Historiography of Korean Film Censorship

Film censorship studies in U.S. academia have flourished since the Motion Picture Association of America (MPAA) opened its PCA files to the public at the Margaret Herrick Library in Los Angeles (beginning in 1983). Subsequent research and scholarship drawn from the archive (including Jacobs [1991], Vasey [1997], Doherty [1999, 2007], and Scott [2015]), as Daniel Biltereyst and Roel Vande Winkel (2013) argue, enabled a "more sophisticated view on film censorship [as a] key mediating factor in discourses that govern American film industry and film culture" (2). These studies prove that the U.S. film industry's self-regulation was not simply prohibitive but also productive in generating more nuanced representations of sex, violence, race, ethnicity, and nationality. The availability of censorship documents was crucial in reevaluating the role of the Production Code and its enforcement agency, the PCA (which was replaced by the MPAA rating board in 1968). In the 1981 book *A History of Narrative Film* (printed prior to the opening of PCA files to researchers), David A. Cook grumbled, "The Code as a whole was obviously restrictive and repressive...and in a very real sense, kept [American films] from becoming as serious as they might have been, and perhaps should have been" (267). After public access to the PCA archive enabled empirical research on censorship documents of individual films (detailing the internal censor's day-to-day operations and extensive communications with studio personnel, external censors, foreign diplomats, civic pressure groups, and other concerned parties), academic discourse began to shift and become more nuanced, highlighting how censorship might contribute to greater, rather than less, *productivity*. This revisionist recalibration of critical discourse is epitomized by Doherty's (2007) archive-based evaluation:

> Far from being an impediment, the in-house censorship regime facilitated the artistic creativity and industrial efficiency of the vaunted Golden Age of Hollywood. The Breen Office maintained the gold standard by helping the major studios refine the substance, polish the surface, and corner the market.
>
> (77)

Korean film historians and researchers had to wait another three decades from the point of MPPA's opening of its PCA archive to access censorship documents of their national cinema and initiate a reevaluation of state regulation as a productive contributor to filmmaking. Primary documents of the government agency that administered film censorship between the 1960s and the 1980s—the Ministry of Public Information (Kongbobu), or the Ministry of Culture and Public Information (Mungongbu) since 1968—were unavailable to the public until 2010. Prior to that point, researchers tended to base their arguments on secondary evidence including oral histories of filmmakers (particularly directors) or newspaper articles, contributing to the circulation of rumors, myths, and legends, some of which have been debunked by recent revisionist studies in the Korean language. Spearheaded by a small group of Seoul-based film historians, this new scholarship owes its existence to the state-subsidized Korean Film Archive (KOFA), which made available its fully digitalized database of government censorship documents for 4,000 Korean films to visitors in 2016.[3] In that same year, KOFA published an edited collection entitled *The Censorship System inside Korean Film History* (*Han'guk yŏnghwa sok kŏmyŏl chedo*) with scholarly essays that cite excerpts of censorship documents from the archive. As KOFA chief researcher Cho Jun-hyoung (2018) notes, previous scholarship has erected a false binary between the oppressive state/censor and film artists who, much like sacrificial lambs, saw their work and vision cut up and undermined by a hegemonic apparatus imposing anti-communism, nationalism, and other official ideologies of Cold War military regimes (52–3). This abstract construction of film censorship as a propaganda tool of the authoritarian state, as Cho points out, neglects the micro-level, procedural process of "complicity, collaboration, bargaining, and negotiation" between censors and the censored that universally applies regardless of macro-level political systems (democracy, socialism, military dictatorship, etc.) under which motion pictures are regulated (74).

Beyond Cold War Oppression: Productive Censoring of Corruption and Sexual Violence in *The Last Witness*

The earlier methodology of mobilizing directors' interviews and testimonies as evidence of censorship (in lieu of archival documents) was flawed and biased, as it often generated "inaccurate information, [distortion] of the entire censorship system, or [exaggeration] of damage" (Cho 2018, 83). Unlike the case of PCA regulation in the United States, Korean directors were not participants in day-to-day censorship administration as communications with government censors were exclusively handled by production companies. As such, the reliability of secondhand accounts by directors (who often had artistic or political agendas of their own, hence their antagonistic stance vis-à-vis the censors) is compromised and questionable. Cho (2018) singles out the case of Yi

Tu-yong's *The Last Witness* (*Ch'oeju ŭi chŭngin*, 1980) to demonstrate the fallacy of reconstructing censorship history based on directors' recollections (54–60). Adapted from Kim Sŏng-jong's 1974 murder mystery of the same title, *The Last Witness* follows the investigative road trip of Detective O Pyŏng-ho (Ha Myŏng-jung), who is in search of clues that might help him solve the murder case of Yang Tal-su (Yi Tae-gŭn). A full synopsis of the film is beyond the scope of this chapter. It suffices to note that Yang, a rich local brewer who lived with a young mistress named Sŏn Chi-hye (Chŏng Yun-hŭi), had been a leader of the anti-communist youth association during the Korean War. After the war, he was involved in a plot that, with the help of corrupt prosecutor Kim Chung-hyŏp (Han Chi-il), framed Sŏn's husband for murder. Sending the innocent man to jail allowed Yang to take advantage of his heartbroken wife and build a brewery with her family fortune (inherited from Sŏn's deceased father who was the commander of North Korean guerrillas during the war).

Rediscovered as a "lost classic" when its restored 154-minute director's cut was screened in the Korean Cinema Retrospective of the 2002 Jeonju International Film Festival, Yi's film has frequently been cited as Exhibit A of the Chun Doo Hwan regime's draconian censorship measures. Legend tells us that the authoritarian government ordered several cuts (totaling anywhere from 40 minutes to one hour of screen time) due to sensitive themes and images, including representations of North Korean partisans, corruption of the judicial system, and victimization of the socially weak. In the post-screening question-and-answer session at the Cinematheque Friends Film Festival in January 2008 (where the restored director's cut of *The Last Witness* was screened), director Yi Tu-yong stated,

> The film was made from May 1979 to April 1980 when the democratic movement was forming in the city of Kwangju.... I was told that '[my] ideology was suspicious' because of this movie. Without consulting me, the censors cut 50 minutes. Later, when the movie opened at Myŏngbo Theater, the time table showed it was 90 minutes long. There were too many deleted scenes and I ended up leaving the screening. That was a dark age for filmmaking.
>
> ("Yi Tu-yong's" 2019)

Voice actor Yang T'aek-jo, Yi's longtime collaborator who was also present at the question-and-answer session, corroborated the director's statement with his own recollection:

> I worked with director Yi on postproduction dubbing for most of his films. Perhaps because it was the longest project, I was most attached to *The Last Witness* out of all those films and regard it as the highest artistic achievement. I saw it at Myŏngbo Theater too and

> one hour [of footage] was cut out. "Don't ridicule law enforcement." Cut. "A prosecutor shouldn't be lustful toward Chŏng Yun-hŭi [the actress who plays Sŏn Chi-hye]." Cut. Cutting here and there ruined the whole film and it really angered me. Among the victims of censorship, director Yi Tu-yong's *The Last Witness* and director Yi Man-hŭi's *The Wild Flowers in the Battle Field* (*Tŭlgukhwa nŭn p'iŏtnŭndae*, 1974) were the most wasteful to me and I am so happy to see the former revived [in its original form].
>
> ("Yi Tu-yong's" 2019)

In a 2016 interview with the *Korea Times* (*Han'guk Ilbo*), Yi Tu-yong reaffirms his account, stating,

> After an industry preview, someone reported to the government. Called it a "communist film." I was called to the prosecutor's office many times. Later I saw [the 90-minute cut] at a theater and it was in a wretched form. It made me consider quitting filmmaking. "This is not my film," I thought, and I never looked back [until the restoration of the director's cut].
>
> (Kim 2016)

Any cursory look at the Internet search results (in both English and Korean) on *The Last Witness* reveals uniform references to censorship that allegedly eliminated 30–40% of the film's original running time. Moreover, both Yi's and Yang's oral histories implicitly link this notorious case of Korean film censorship with political oppression during the Chun Doo Hwan regime via allusions to Kwangju—where the massacre of estimated 2,000 citizen protestors by Chun's paratroopers took place in May 1980, six months prior to the film's release—and inferred political motivations behind the censoring of scenes. It is also alleged that dictatorial strong-arm tactics not only butchered Yi's masterpiece (noted for its self-conscious use of nonlinear narration, *Citizen Kane*-like puzzle flashbacks, experimental sound bridges, expressionistic low-key lighting, tilted angles, whip pans, fast zooms, elliptical montage, subjective pansori/folk opera narration, etc.), but also nearly destroyed the director's will to continue honing his craft and pursuing future work in the industry.

The censorship file of the Ministry of Culture and Public Information on *The Last Witness*, however, tells a different story. According to documents in the file, a 158-minute preview print of the film (four minutes longer than the restored director's cut) was submitted on September 6, 1980, and it passed censorship review ten days later on the condition that four scenes be cut: Sŏn's gang rape by a group of North Korean guerillas during the Korean War, two scenes that depict Prosecutor Kim's misconduct (taking a cash stack from Yang for the conviction of Sŏn's husband and sexually harassing Sŏn in his house, respectively), and a scene in which a court clerk openly demands a bribery in exchange for granting Detective O access to public documents. In the restored print (presumably with these four censored scenes eliminated or reedited, cutting four minutes from the 158-minute preview print), Sŏn's gang rape scene is gone, and the audience only sees a glimpse of the victim's brutalized face as an after-effect; the scene in which Yang drops a wad of cash on Prosecutor Kim's desk is eliminated altogether; the prosecutor's sexual harassment scene is still there but only partially and does not show the coerced sex act; and Detective O's brief interaction with the corrupt court clerk (who shows him court records) is present but there is no mention of bribery. Ultimately, the difference between the censorship review copy and the director's cut is minor. Caution against the gang-rape scene coincides with universal standards, and while the scene is abruptly halted with a cut, it is not difficult for mature viewers to conjecture what has transpired based on dialogue and a close-up of Sŏn's bloody and bruised face. The court clerk is such a minor character, appearing only fleetingly, that the depiction of his corruption would have been an irrelevant plot point distracting from the main investigation narrative. As for the scene that depicts Yang's bribery of Prosecutor Kim, one could argue that it would have made their criminal connection clearer, but suppression of that information can be also said to have strengthened the film's mystery as the linkage between them will only be revealed much later in the narrative.

The explanatory note found in the film's censorship file elaborates that the reason for eliminating the aforementioned three corruption scenes is not that portrayals of unethical behavior of government officials are disallowed. Rather, nine reviewers of the Public Performance Ethics Committee (PPEC; Kongyŏn yunri wiwŏnhoe), which conducted film censorship reviews under jurisdiction of the Ministry of Culture and Public Information (renamed as the Ministry of Culture in 1990) from 1979 to 1997, found such scenes dramatically implausible and contrived ("A Comprehensive Report," 1980b). The PPEC's objection to Prosecutor Kim's sexual misconduct scene on the grounds of narrative (im) plausibility is indeed not unfounded as it is puzzling why Yang takes the woman whom he himself is lusting after to another man's house at night. One can assume that he is either offering Sŏn to the prosecutor as a human bribe or pretending to be her advocate—someone who makes an effort to free her husband by introducing her to the big shot. (Later, after the conviction of Sŏn's husband in court, Yang feigns fury over Prosecutor Kim's deception to his mistress-to-be.) Regardless, the whole scene is gratuitous and contrived (Figure 9.1). A soft-focus, glamorous close-up of actress Chŏng Yun-hŭi, a screen goddess of the 1970s and 1980s, ostensibly framed by the perverted harasser's erotic gaze, verges on sexploitation and is out of place in this artistically rendered neo-noir (Figure 9.2).

Figure 9.1 Film censors of the Public Performance Ethics Committee opposed the corrupt behavior of Prosecutor Kim, who bargains a sexual favor from the defendant's wife in *The Last Witness* (1980).

Figure 9.2 A soft-focus, glamorous close-up of actress Chŏng Yun-hŭi, a screen goddess of the 1970s–80s, foregrounds her harasser's erotic gaze as if contained in a sexploitation flick.

Cynics might point out the disingenuousness of the PPEC/Ministry's excuse, seeing it as a mere thinly veiled cover-up for the Chun regime's more sinister intent of suppressing any expression of political dissent, including the aforementioned Kwangju Massacre. However, more objective investigations into archival evidence would lead to the conclusion that the PPEC's demand for the elimination of those corruption scenes was not inconsistent with similar regulatory acts in a more democratic context. For example, Hollywood's Motion Picture Production Code states, "The courts of the land should not be presented as unjust. This does not mean that a single court may not be represented as unjust, much less that a single court official must not be presented this way. But the court system of the country must not suffer as a result of this presentation" ("Appendix" 2001, 297). While the PPEC upheld a corresponding clause in South Korea's Motion Picture Law that prevents films from depicting "law-abiding citizenry or court of law in a slanderous way" (Motion Picture Producers Association of Korea 1968),[4] its explanatory comment goes further than simply forbidding the subject and opens up productive creative dialogue about the narrative logic and characterization of court officials.

If the minor cuts requested by censorship are inconsequential, why was *The Last Witness* shortened so dramatically in its final release print shown at Myŏngbo Theater in November 1980? According to documents available in the KOFA digital archive, the film's producer Kim Hwa-sik resubmitted a shortened, 120-minute print to the Ministry of Culture and Public Information on November 6, 1980, requesting censorship rereview. Forwarding this request to the PPEC, the Ministry explained that Sekyŏng Films, Corp. "requested re-censorship of a thirty-eight minute shorter version because the original running time [was] too long for the purpose of booking theaters" (The Minister of Culture and Public Information 1980). Censorship documents suggest that the production company voluntarily cut as many as 68 scenes in order to condense the film's length to 120 minutes, a standard "feature" length more likely to be favored by exhibitors whose profits would increase if turnovers were quicker and more screenings were scheduled per day ("A Comprehensive Report," 1980a). The Ministry approved the voluntarily cut version on November 13, 1980, two days prior to the film's release. Comparing this striking discrepancy between Yi Tu-yong's oral history and censorship documents, Cho (2018) considers different scenarios, including the fabrication of official documents to avoid a public scandal over excessive censorship. Ultimately, though, he settles with a more plausible explanation: the production company transferred blame to censorship so as to preempt the director's protest against cutting nearly 70 scenes for commercial reasons (59–60). As Cho concludes, the case study of *The Last Witness* exposes the risk of basing censorship scholarship on directors' testimonies without considering the perspectives of other players such as PPEC reviewers, bureaucrats within the Ministry of Culture and Public Information, producers, distributors, exhibitors, press representatives, and audiences, all of whom directly or indirectly participated in the complex process of film censorship (60).

From a Melodramatic Crime Film to an Experimental Social Satire: Uplifting *Declaration of Fools* through Film Regulation

Yi Chang-ho's experimental black comedy *Declaration of Fools* (*Pabu sŏnŭn*, 1983) is another oft-cited victim of censorship during the Chun era, with a legendary anecdote about the inception of its unusual title.

The film was originally planned as a sequel to the director's commercial breakthrough *People of Dark Streets* (*Ŏdum ŭi chasikdŭl*, 1980), and its initial title was *People of Dark Streets 2*. From the onset, Yi was determined to make a non sequitur film as rebellion against the foreign film quota system, which incentivized producers to make four domestic films a year in exchange for an import quota for one foreign film, thus resulting in hasty productions of "import quickies." Besides, the film was also meant to resist the government's double censorship of scenarios and film prints. In order to pass preproduction censorship, Yi wrote a placeholder treatment that paid lip service to mainstream morality. The Ministry of Culture and Public Information's censorship file on *Declaration of Fools* includes this treatment (submitted on March 17, 1983), which Yi (2000) later called a "scenario intended for the mentally challenged [i.e. duped censors]."

The story contained in the treatment has nothing to do with the completed film except that the protagonists in both versions have the same name: Tong-ch'ŏl. In the version submitted to the Ministry, he is a petty criminal who spent most of his adolescence and young adulthood in various correctional facilities. After being released from prison as an adult man, he continues to mix with bad friends in the underworld until encountering someone from his past: Kong Pyŏng-su, an ex-pickpocket who has been rehabilitated as a pastor. Tong-ch'ŏl's lost soul oscillates between Kong's moral mentoring and criminal girlfriend Kyŏng-ja's temptation. Kyŏng-ja persuades Tong-ch'ŏl to steal one last time in order to raise money for his seriously ill sister, but she runs away with the stolen jewels. After her betrayal, Tong-ch'ŏl surrenders himself to the police and serves three years in prison. Once regaining his freedom, he builds, with Kong's help, a private academy for juvenile delinquents in order to steer them away from the criminal path he took at their age. After reforming a group of street children, Tong-ch'ŏl releases them from his custody in order to accommodate other children in need. On the day when the children leave, a reformed Kyŏng-ja, now penniless and homeless, returns and Tong-ch'ŏl caresses her shoulders.

The censorship file contains a short reply that the Ministry sent to Hwach'ŏn Trading on April 4, 1983, advising the production company to rereview the whole project as it had the potential to "undermine law and social order" (The Minister of Culture and Public Information 1983a). On June 2, 1983, Hwach'ŏn submitted a revised script claimed to be completely different from the one that had been proposed earlier. Although it is unclear why the PPEC was not consulted (if it was, its review was not filed for some unknown reasons), the Ministry apparently requested the opinion of another government agency, the Korean Motion Picture Promotion Corporation (Yŏnghwa chinhŭng konga; now the Korean Film Council), which wrote the following after reviewing the revised script on June 8, 1983: "Before Tong-ch'ŏl's restoration of humanity, his wrong mentality and various criminal activities could harm social order. It is an exposé film that displays social ills, so it is advised to change the title and purify its content" (The Korean Motion Picture Promotion Corporation 1983). On June 13, 1983, the Ministry requested that the production company once again review the project for its potential harm to social order. Ten days later, Hwach'on submitted the second revision of the synopsis and screenplay to the Ministry. On June 29, 1983, the production company also submitted a request to change the film title from *People of Dark Streets 2* to *Declaration of Fools*, listing the rationale as a "satiric commentary on the protagonist Tong-ch'ŏl's foolish dream of becoming rich overnight" (Pak 1983). On July 2, the Ministry approved the title change. Four days later, it responded to the second revision with a warning against the following elements: a scene that might provoke a feeling of inferiority for disabled people, use of slang, and a sexually suggestive line that "undermines female college students' human rights" (The Minister of Culture and Public Information 1983b).[5] The Ministry urged the producer to use caution so as not to upset the sensibilities of adolescents and to uplift the quality of the film by heeding these elements. Hwach'on complied and deleted all objectionable scenes and dialogue before submitting the preview print on August 8, 1983. Based on the PPEC's recommendation to pass it with no deletions, the Ministry approved the film three days later.

Researchers who are familiar with the lengthy and detailed objections that were part of the Hollywood studios' negotiation process over classic gangster films (such as William A. Wellman's *The Public Enemy* [1931] and Howard Hawks' *Scarface* [1932]) might find the Ministry's handling of crime-related themes in the earlier scripts of *Declaration of Fools* to be unremarkable—especially so in the context of morality-based content regulation, prior to South Korea's late conversion to the rating system in 1997 (almost 30 years after its U.S. counterpart). What is most noteworthy is the government censor's advocacy for "political correctness" in portrayals of disability and college women. But this is also unsurprising and predictable if one is aware of similar tendencies in Hollywood's Production Code, as elaborated by Doherty (1999):

> [I]n the context of its day, the Code expressed a progressive and reformist impulse" which "evinced concern for the proper nurturing of the young and the protection of women, demanded due respect for indigenous ethnics and foreign peoples, and sought to uplift the lower orders and convert the criminal mentality.
>
> (6)

In the process of responding to the Ministry's concern and purifying the originally proposed criminal narrative, Yi Chang-ho turned the film into a surrealist, absurdist comedy about a crippled vagabond (an incarnation of Tong-ch'ŏl [Kim Myŏng-gon]) and a sex worker posing as a college student (Hye-yŏng [Yi Po-hŭi]), with whom the former falls in love at first sight and impulsively abducts (Figure 9.3). As the Ministry demanded, the completed film "uplifted" its status from a melodramatic crime film to an avant-garde social satire, allegorically indicting the capitalist class system that alienates social outcasts such as Tong-ch'ŏl and Hye-yŏng. The entire narrative unfolds in the form of a children's fable, intermittently narrated by director Yi's six-year-old son and bookended by a montage of enlarged children's drawings.

The first 37 minutes of the film are devoid of dialogue, resorting to slapstick action, pantomime, and experimental sound effects to comically frame Tong-ch'ŏl's trailing and abduction of Hye-yŏng. This extended section also foregrounds the dreams of the mismatched couple who, after a physical struggle in the back of the taxi, lose consciousness by inhaling chemicals on a handkerchief (a tool of the rookie kidnapper). Paired with another misfit, a plus-sized taxi driver named Yuk-dŭk (Yi Hŭi-sŭng), who accidentally becomes his accomplice in the abduction of Hye-yŏng, Tong-ch'ŏl is not a criminal as in the earlier scripts but a Don Quixote-like tramp who lives hand-to-mouth doing odd jobs such as food delivery. Reminiscent of Stan Laurel and Oliver Hardy, the famous comic duo of the silent era, Tong-ch'ŏl and Yuk-dŭk are childlike clowns who befriend their victim, a sassy woman who disciplines both men with beatings after waking up. After witnessing Hye-yŏng's abuse and death at the hands of a group of drunken rich men in a swimming pool party gone wrong and burying her in the mountains, life goes on for the wandering duo, who irreverently take off their shirts and break into an impromptu dance in front of the National Assembly

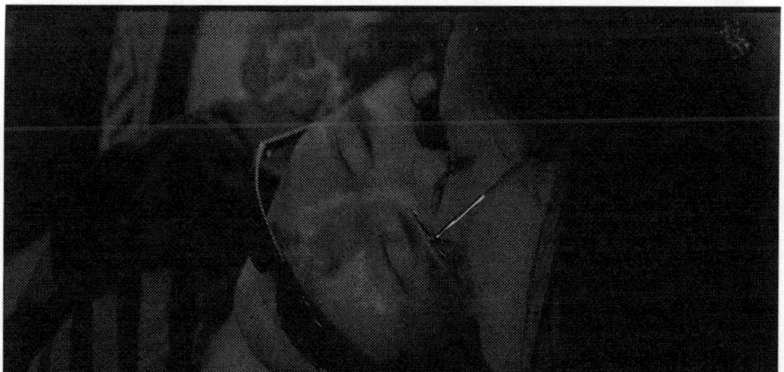

Figure 9.3 Tong-ch'ŏl, a cripple vagabond, and Hye-yŏng, a sex worker posing as a college student, are a mismatched slapstick couple whose mirrored marginalization allegorizes South Korea's oppressive class system in *Declaration of Fools* (1983).

Figure 9.4 The bare-chested clowns Tong-ch'ŏl and Yuk-dŭk dance uncontrollably in front of the National Assembly building in the closing scene of *Declaration of Fools* (1983).

building in the film's closing scene (Figure 9.4). For audiences expecting authoritarian censorship, it will come as a surprise that the PPEC passed this film's final print without demanding any alterations of a slow-motion, sensational scene detailing a repulsive, orgy-like swimming party of the social elite or a not-so-subtle affront to South Korea's legislative branch.

Yet the director's oral history tells a very different story. In Jang Sunwoo (Chang Sŏn-u)'s *Cinema on the Road* (1995), an English-language documentary about Korean cinema commissioned by the British Film Institute as a part of its "Century of Cinema" series, Yi Chang-ho is interviewed and recounts the trade legend of *Declaration of Fools*' censorship:

> When we sent the script of *People of Dark Streets 2* to the Ministry of Culture and Public Information for approval, they vetoed the use of that title. That was when the Chun Doo Hwan regime started to show its true face. I felt like quitting the movie business. So I decided to give up everything and make a nonsense movie. I wrote a ridiculous scenario for censorship approval from the Ministry. We came up with a string of nonsense titles… and one of them was *Declaration of Fools*. The producer took ten or more titles to the Ministry and told them we couldn't choose. We asked them to choose since we couldn't use *People of Dark Streets 2*. Government bureaucrats were dumbfounded, but they jokingly opted for *Declaration of Fools*. So we went with that. Armed with the title, I decided to go against everything I've done before.

There is no way to confirm whether or not the producer literally hand-delivered Yi's list of potential titles to the Ministry and the officials there half-jokingly chose *Declaration of Fools*. One can conjecture from evidence provided in archival documents that this was an unlikely scenario.

In 1979, four years prior to the production of *Declaration of Fools*, the Ministry of Culture and Public Information transferred film censorship operations of reviewing scripts and preview prints to the PPEC, a semiautonomous body consisting of 10–20 members appointed by the Minister (mostly civilians such as professors and journalists along with four officials from the Ministry). This transfer was partly in response to a bribery scandal involving Ministry officials and filmmakers four years earlier. In May 1975, the Prosecutor of Seoul arrested several Ministry managers and employees in charge of film censorship for taking cash bribes from famous film producers such as Shin Sang-ok (Sin Sang-ok) and Kim T'ae-su in exchange for expediting censorship reviews, extending exhibition permits, and nominating their films for state-sponsored "Good Film" (*Usu Yŏnghwa*) awards. The division chief was given a two-and-a-half year sentence and three of his underlings received suspended sentences. In his interview with KOFA researcher. Cho Junhyoung, Yi Nam-gi (who served as a film censor in the Ministry from 1974 to 1979) attests to government bureaucrats' fear of "strong-willed" (*tŭsaen*) civilians in the film industry and discusses his effort to transfer censorship power to a civil committee before quitting the Ministry in 1979. He explains,

> At that time, film censorship was mainly conducted by the Korean Central Intelligence Agency (KCIA: Chungangjŏngbobu), Security Bureau Headquarters (Ch'ianbonbu), and our Ministry. The KCIA was only interested in national security affairs and Security Bureau in matters related to children and adolescents.... Because there were only a handful of censorship reviewers in our Ministry, we were easy targets and shouldered the weight of responsibility. That's why we thought of transferring the duty to an independent committee and started to prepare for it.... Later, the PPEC took over film censorship and their committee members were private experts. The industry folks did not dare to touch them because there were fifteen of them. It was not possible to try to bribe all of them and that was the end of problems.
>
> (Cho 2018, 77)

This interview exposes rarely discussed dynamics between government censors and filmmakers during the Cold War era that support Foucault's theory of power, repression, and resistance alluded to earlier in this chapter. As Cho (2018) insightfully notes,

> From a layman's perspective, government bureaucrats in charge of censorship were transparent agents of the state.... They embodied the government's authority over the society/market. This leads to a perception that government censors had more power than filmmakers. Of course, this assumption is not entirely incorrect. However, in the process of specific contacts, the power relationship between censors and the censored could be ambiguous or capsized and the former was not necessarily on the side of power.
>
> (76)

In the above-quoted interview from *Cinema on the Road*, however, Yi Chang-ho automatically equates the Korean film censors with the Chun Doo Hwan regime and cites the censorship case of *Declaration of Fools* as evidence of political oppression in the early 1980s. He does this without acknowledging the censor's effort to improve images of disabled persons and female college students and to tone down foul language and criminal activities for underage viewers. Yi's testimony insinuates that the Ministry's request for title change was politically motivated. According to official documents, however, the title change was suggested by the Motion Picture Promotion Corp. for the purpose of conveying a clearer moral message. There is no document that indicates the Ministry's instructions to the production company to change the title. However, it can reasonably be inferred that such a request was made verbally over the phone or in a face-to-face meeting. Nevertheless, there is no reason to believe that Hwach'ŏn Trading submitted the paper-only change request with a made-up rationale after the Ministry had opted for *Declaration of Fools* as the new title. The most likely scenario is that the production company chose the title out of several alternatives that Yi Chang-ho came up with and filed the change with the Ministry shortly after submitting the second revision of the script. In his 2000 memoir, serialized in the weekly film magazine *Cine 21*, Yi concludes, "I don't call *Declaration of Fools* my film. I call it a film made by an age of dictatorship." This defiant statement inversely attests to the productive capacity of film censorship which, intentionally or not, contributed to transforming an unambitious contract job (which its production company greenlighted only to fulfill its production quota required for a foreign film import permit) into one of the most extraordinary creative expressions in the history of South Korean cinema.

Creating a "Cheerful" Cinema for Cold War Audiences

When General Park Chung Hee rose to power through the May 16 coup in 1961, one of the first things that his military junta did was to stop the public screenings of 35 domestic and 24 foreign films deemed "impure" (*pulsun*) prior to those motion pictures' re-censoring. Among those films were realist social problem dramas (e.g., *The Money* [*Ton*, 1958] and *The Stray Bullet* [*Obalt'an*, 1961]), crime dramas (e.g., *Hell's Flower* [*Chiokhwa*, 1958] and *Prisoner No. 72* [*72ho ŭi choesu*, 1959]), family dramas (e.g., *The Coachman* [*Mabu*, 1961] and *Third Rate Manager* [*Samdŭng kwajang*, 1961]), and cross-cultural literary adaptations (e.g., *Katusha* [1960] and *Jean Valjean* [1961]). After a six-month review, the new military government banned one Korean film (Yu Hyun-mok [Yu Hyŏn-mok]'s *The Stray Bullet*) along with six foreign ones. While foreign films (such as Claude Autant-Lara's *The Red and the Black* [*Le rouge et le noir*, 1954], Marc Allégret's *Lady Chatterley's Lover* [*L'Amant de lady Chatterley*, 1955], and Marcel Carné's *Young Sinners* [*Les tricheurs*, 1958]) were barred on moral grounds, Yu's masterpiece, touted by many critics as the best Korean film ever made, was singled out for political reasons due to its realistic portrayal of postwar poverty and social malaise (The Minister of the Interior 1961).

The censorship file for *The Stray Bullet* includes a report by the head of the Security Bureau of the Ministry of the Interior (Naemubu), defining the film as "pro-communist propaganda" that "denies any hope for Korean society, provokes rebellions and desperation of the unemployed and proletariats, and gives an impression that a communist revolution might be necessary" (The Security Bureau 1961). To contemporary readers, this evaluation might sound paranoid (recalling, to a certain extent, the Red Scare in McCarthy-era America), considering the fact that Yu's characters are ordinary apolitical citizens who simply struggle to survive under economic adversity rather than revolting against the social status quo. Notably, the family's black sheep younger son, an unemployed Korean War veteran, resorts to bank robbery out of desperation but is punished and eventually repents at the narrative's end. This case study alone might conjure up a sinister image of Korean film censorship under the successive military regimes of Park Chung Hee and Chun Doo Hwan during the Cold War era.[6] Along this line, Seung Hyun Park (2002) offers a predictable assessment of oppressive censorship during this period:

> Censorship has been the greatest barrier to the development of Korean cinema since its inception.... The military governments... further decreased the capacity for creative expression.... Until the end of 1986, it was possible for political authorities to control virtually every facet of a film through economic censorship of producers, whose primary concern was to ensure that no film got made that authorities presumed would be "offensive" or "detrimental" to the government.
>
> (120)

Fortunately, availability of government censorship documents of the period through the KOFA digital archive gives historians an opportunity to challenge this master narrative and to reevaluate the complex role of film censorship in Cold War Korea. As this chapter has indicated, while political suppression existed inside and outside the motion picture industry during this period, film censorship was not simply a tool for authoritarian dictatorship. Archival evidence makes it possible for scholars to resist the temptation to conflate the national (or macro) policies of oppressive regimes with the industry-specific (or micro) operations of film censorship, which, in fact, involved many different players (such as the Ministry of Public Information [later the Ministry of Culture and Public Information], the PPEC, the Security Bureau of the Ministry of the Interior, the Ministry of Education, the KCIA, the U.S. Central Intelligence Agency, film producers, and trade associations).[7] These players were involved in a multilayered process of regulating individual motion pictures with different agendas in mind—including, but not limited to, national security, public morality, suppression of obscenity, protection of children, and market demands—and repealing such decisions. One of the most noteworthy contributions that state censorship made during the Cold War era was to inject a relatively "cheerful" attitude or sensibility into Korean films, as exemplified by tacked-on optimistic endings to melodramas of the 1960s and a cycle of light comedies and youth films during the 1970s. A cultural war was thus being waged against pessimism and depression or social malaise onscreen.

This policy is, in essence, not far removed from World War II film policies in Great Britain and the United States. For example, Franklin D. Roosevelt's propaganda agency, the Office of War Information (OWI), discouraged the mass production of war films and urged Hollywood producers to provide more escapist entertainment to boost public morale. Nelson Poynter, the Chief of Hollywood Office of the OWI's Bureau of Motion Pictures, informed the *Hollywood Reporter* in 1943, "As life has become grimmer and more upset, there is greater need for pictures that offer the public escape from the realities of page one.... *More people than ever before will go to the movies*—to get away from the war. Hence war should not crowd escape pictures from the screen. The point cannot be emphasized more strongly that there should *not be too many war pictures*" (original emphasis). In the 1970s, Korean censorship reviewers were given a list of "encouraged directions of domestic productions" along with the Motion Picture Law as regulatory guidelines. In addition to content that deals with the nation's development, its economic and military self-reliance, anti-communism, modernization of national consciousness, traditional arts, and moral lessons for adolescents, wholesome entertainment that "cheers up everyday life" (*saenghwal ŭi myŏngranghwa*) was also encouraged ("Encouraged Directions," 1971). For directors such as Yi Tu-yong and Yi Chang-ho, the state-directed "tonal control" of cinema would be another example of repressive political censorship. However, for Korean film censorship studies to mature, it is imperative to avoid the auteurist trap and broaden critical perspectives on the role of government censors at a time of perpetual security crises stemming from regional and global Cold War conflicts.

Abbreviation

MCPRFCF Ministry of Culture and Public Relations Film Censorship Files. Korean Film Archive, Seoul, South Korea.

Notes

1 Seven states with motion picture censorship boards were Pennsylvania, Ohio, Kansas, Maryland, New York, Florida, and Virginia. The number of state censorship boards is sometimes counted as six because Florida did not have an autonomous board and followed the decisions made by the New York State.

2 Any violator of this agreement was required to pay a $25,000 fine. No major studios released their films without the Code certificate until United Artists temporarily withdrew from the MPAA to distribute Otto Preminger's racy romantic comedy *The Moon Is Blue* (1953), which had been denied the PCA's seal for its light treatment of illicit sex, seduction, and virginity.

3 The documents had been handed over to the KOFA in the late 1990s but were closed to public access until 2010, when the archive started to open them partially to selected researchers before transferring them to on-site digital open access in 2016.

4 Film censorship guidelines were introduced in the first Motion Picture Law of 1962, and revised in 1966, 1970, and 1974. See Chung and Diffrient (2015) for other provisions of objectionable film content (85–6).

5 The line can be roughly translated as "Don't forget that a female college student's mind and body are separate like beef bone soup with rice on the side [*ttarogukbap*]."

6 For more information about the censorship case of *The Stray Bullet*, see Yi S. (2013).

7 Although it was unusual for the Seoul branch of the U.S. Central Intelligence Agency to get involved in Korean film censorship, their opinion was sought in high-profile cases dealing with anti-communism and U.S. military presence such as Yi Man-hŭi's *Seven Female POWs* (*Ch'ilin ŭi yŏp'oro*, 1965).

Works Cited

"Appendix: The Motion Picture Production Code." 2001. In *The Dame in the Kimono: Hollywood, Censorship, and the Production Code*, rev. ed., edited by Leonard J. Leff and Jerold L. Simmons, 285–300. Lexington: University of Kentucky Press.

Biltereyst, Daniel, and Roel Vande Winkel, eds. 2013. *Silencing Cinema: Film Censorship around the World*. New York: Palgrave MacMillan.

Cho, Jun-hyoung. 2018. "An Exploratory Study of the History of Korean Film Censorship" (Han'guk yŏnghwakŏmyŏlsa ŭi myŏtgaji chuje e taehan sironjŏk yŏngu). *The Journal of Korean Drama and Theatre* (Han'guk kŭkyesul yŏngu), no. 59: 51–81.

Chung, Hye Seung, and David Scott Diffrient. 2015. *Movie Migrations: Transnational Genre Flows and South Korean Cinema*. New Brunswick: Rutgers University Press.

Cook, David A. 1981. *A History of Narrative Film*. 1st ed. New York: W.W. Norton.

"A Comprehensive Report on Film Censorship" (Yŏnghwa kŏmyŏl chonghap ŭigyŏnsŏ). 1980a. November 12, 1980. *The Last Witness* (*Ch'oeju ŭi chŭngin*), MCPRFCF.

"A Comprehensive Report on Film Censorship" (Yŏnghwa kŏmyŏl chonghap ŭigyŏnsŏ). 1980b. September 16, 1980. *The Last Witness* (*Ch'oeju ŭi chŭngin*), MCPRFCF.

Doherty, Thomas. 2007. *Hollywood's Censor: Joseph I. Breen and the Production Code Administration*. New York: Columbia University Press.

Doherty, Thomas. 1999. *Pre-Code Hollywood: Sex, Immorality, and Insurrection in American Cinema 1930–1934*. New York: Columbia University Press.

"Encouraged Directions of Domestic Productions" (Kuksan yŏnghwa kwŏnjang panghyang). 1971. *Voice* (*Moksori*), MCPRFCF.

Foucault, Michel. 1990. *The History of Sexuality, Vol. 1: An Introduction*. New York: Vintage Books.

Kim P'o-hyang. 2016. "Genre Problem Solver Yi Du-yong, 'I Want To Be a Lifelong Filmmaker'" (Changrŭ ŭi haegyŏlsa Yi Du-yong 'P'yŏngsaeng yŏnghwain ŭro salgo sipda'). *Korea Times* (*Han'guk Ilbo*), October 12, 2016. Accessed January 3, 2019. www.hankookilbo.com/v/3aa02f42d1b14231a7552ff4d9f640dd.

The Korean Film Archive. 2016. *The Censorship System in Korean Film History* (*Han'guk yŏnghwa sok kŏmyŏl chedo*). Seoul: The Korean Film Archive.

The Korean Motion Picture Promotion Corporation. 1983. Memorandum to the Minister of Culture and Public Information. June 30, 1983. *Declaration of Fools* (*Pabu sŏnŭn*), MCPRFCF.

The Minister of Culture and Public Information. 1980. "Re: A Request for Film Re-censorship" (Yŏnghwa kŏmyŏl chaeŭroe). Memorandum to the Chairman of the Performance Art Ethics Committee. November 6, 1980. *The Last Witness* (*Ch'oeju ŭi chŭngin*), MCPRFCF.

The Minister of Culture and Public Information. 1983a. "Re: A Reply for Feature Film Production Registration" (Kŭk yŏnghwa chejak singoe daehan hoesin). Memorandum to Pak Chong-ch'an. April 4, 1983. *Declaration of Fools* (*Pabu sŏnŭn*), MCPRFCF.

The Minister of Culture and Public Information. 1983b. Memorandum to Pak Chong-ch'an. July 6, 1983. *Declaration of Fools* (*Pabu sŏnŭn*), MCPRFCF.

The Minister of the Interior. 1961. "Report on Public Opinion Regarding Request for Impure Film Bans" (Pulsun yŏnghwa kŭmyŏng choch'i yomang e taehan yŏron pogo). Memorandum to the Minister of Education. May 23, 1961. *The Stray Bullet* (*Obalt'an*), MCPRFCF.

Motion Picture Producers Association of Korea. 1968. *Korean Cinema '68*. Seoul: Motion Picture Producers Association of Korea.

Pak, Chong-ch'an. 1983. Memorandum to the Minister of Culture and Public Information. June 29, 1983. *Declaration of Fools* (*Pabu sŏnŭn*), MCPRFCF.

Park, Seung Hyun. 2002. "Film Censorship and Political Legitimization in South Korea, 1987–1992." *Cinema Journal* 42 (1): 120–38.

Poynter, Nelson. 1943. "Hollywood Reporter." Nelson Poynter File, Box 1443, General Records of the Chief, Lowell Mellett, Records of the Bureau of Motion Pictures, Office of War Information Files, Record Group 208. National Archives and Records Administration, College Park, Maryland.

The Security Bureau. 1961. "Report on Public Opinion Regarding the Korean Film *The Stray Bullet*" (Han'guk yŏnghwa 'Obalt'an' egwanhan yŏron t'ongbo). Memorandum to the Minister of Education. May 26, 1961. *The Stray Bullet* (*Obalt'an*), MCPRFCF.

Yi, Chang-ho. 2000. "*Declaration of Fools*, A Film Made by an Age of Dictatorship" (Tokjae sidaega mandŭn yŏnghwa). *Cine21*, February 22, 2000. Accessed January 3, 2019. www.cine21.com/news/view/?mag_id=32064.

Yi, Sun-jin. 2013. "Cultural Logic of the Cold War System and Operation of South Korean Cinema: On Censorship Practices of *A Stray Bullet*" (Naengjŏn ch'eje ŭi munhwa nonriwa Han'guk yŏnghwa ŭi chonje pangsik). *Memory & Vision* (*Kiŏk kwa chŏnmang*) (Winter): 374–421.

"Yi Tu-yong's *Last Witness* Rediscovered by Director O Sŭng-uk" (O Sŭng-uk kamdok e chaebalgyŏnhan Yi Tu-yong ŭi *Ch'oeju ŭi chŭngin*). *Cinematheque de M. Hulot*. Accessed January 3, 2019. http://cinematheque.tistory.com/36.

10 Indian Cinema, Indian Democracy

An Unusual Cold War Saga, 1947–89

Rini Bhattacharya Mehta

The direct concordance between Indian cinema and the Cold War is somewhat intangible, due to India's position vis-à-vis the bipolar politics of the era. In the two World Wars, Indians as British imperial subjects were forced to supply natural, human, and economic resources, in varying degrees. In comparison, India's experience of the Cold War was far less immediate. India entered the Cold War era as a nation-state that was created in 1947 by the Partition of the British Indian Empire into India and Pakistan. Burdened with the effects of exploitation from its long colonial past, India, in 1947, faced a dual task: maintaining the hard-earned political independence and adopting accelerated methods for nation-building. Throughout the duration of the Cold War, India remained engaged in its postimperial, postcolonial project centered on the idea of a secular democratic nation-state. Its international policy was shaped by an allegiance to the Non-Aligned Movement, which kept the nation clear of any direct involvement in the core geopolitics of the Cold War.

Postcolonial Indian state had an ambiguous relationship with Indian Cinema. Cinema production in India—a multilingual and multilocal entity—grew from the third largest in the world in 1947 to occupy the first position from 1971 onward. At the core of this growth was popular cinema, made in an increasing number of regional languages. These popular film industries were funded privately, making Indian cinema the only private enterprise that grew at a steady space in India's quasi-socialist economy. The films were subject to censorship and taxation; the federal government based in New Delhi managed the process of certification and censorship through the Central Board of Film Certification (CBFC), while both federal and individual state governments imposed various taxes including entertainment tax. The popular film industry was not acknowledged as either an industry or a significant art form by the government, which saw cinema as a wild-grown cultural product that should be taxed and censored. On the other hand, the government actively encouraged arthouse films that eschewed the melodramatic overtones of Hindi cinema produced in Bombay (Mumbai since 1995).

It was also more sympathetic toward cinemas in regional languages, which were treated on equal footing with Hindi films in the annual national awards, instituted in 1954.

Global access to the multilingual and multilocal world of Indian cinema was clearly apportioned along the post-WWII geopolitical divide. While the metropolitan "First World" received access to the arthouse films that were encouraged and subsidized by the government and were appreciated by a minority elite Indian viewership, the socialist world and numerous other developing nations in Asia and Africa imported the predecessor of Bollywood films, that is, popular Hindi films produced in Bombay. As film production in postcolonial India grew during the Cold War, the differential ties between Indian cinemas and the national and global audience developed a complex dynamic with the content and style of films. This essay will scrutinize the evolution of popular Indian cinema between 1947 and 1989, with an eye on that dynamic. By situating the evolution of Indian cinema in the political climate of the Cold War, I will be engaging in a global history of a local popular cultural form, one that had developed in a democracy with a regulated quasi-socialist economy.

Indian Popular Cinema: From a Colonial Legacy to a Postcolonial Problem

The 1947 Partition left India with three major film-producing locales—Bombay, Calcutta (Kolkata), and Madras (Chennai)—within its boundaries. On the other hand, the coeval state of Pakistan had one center, Lahore, which had begun producing films only in the 1920s. At the time of the Partition, Lahore produced only 7% of all films exhibited in the regions marked as Pakistan. The Pakistani film industry would thus have to be constructed from the ground up after 1947, out of Lahore, which produced one film, Daud Chand's *Teri Yaad* (*Your Memory*, 1948) in the first year after independence. Through most of the Cold War period, India and Pakistan had a hostile relationship; they fought three major wars and continued to spar over the control over the territory of Kashmir. Import of Indian cinema into Pakistan, a logical necessity for both countries, became one of the contentious issues shortly after the Partition, due to the ongoing political conflicts between them. Indian Hindi cinema produced in Bombay and Bengali cinema produced in Calcutta were imported on a limited basis into West and East Pakistan except for the periods of total ban, such as during the war of 1965. In India, the 1947 Partition had a less direct yet more complex effect on cinema. While the immediate impact was in the form of the loss of majority population in the Punjab and Bengal regions to Pakistan, production went on unhampered, due to the economic forces that had transformed the Indian film industry during WWII.

The transformation of the Indian film industry from a studio-based model akin to Hollywood in the 1930s to a unique star-centric system of production by the late 1940s is integral to any understanding of the background of Indian cinema in the post-WWII era, and is crucial to the narrative of this essay that follows. Studios in the Indian colonial metropolises—Bombay and Calcutta—owned and operated by Indians grew in the 1910s, as many film distribution and exhibition companies invested in local production. Apart from Phalke & Co. that produced Dadasaheb Phalke's *Raja Harishchandra* (1913), Aurora Film Company and Madan Theatres of Calcutta and Imperial Studios and Kohinoor Film Co. of Bombay were among dozens of studios in those two colonial metropolises producing films. According to the records of the censor boards—established in 1920 following the Indian Cinematograph Act of 1918—1,286 silent films were made between 1920 and 1934. By the 1920s, the studios were endowed with enough infrastructure to begin shooting with live sound. The first sound films in 1931, produced in Bombay and Calcutta in five languages, inaugurated the unique Indian style of non-diegetic music that became the mainstay of all commercial cinemas in India. By the end of the 1930s, Bombay, Calcutta, and Madras produced around half of all films screened throughout India, a significant change from 1928, when less than 20% of films screened in India were locally produced. While none of the studios in Bombay or Calcutta had the kind of funding or clout that Hollywood studios had acquired during WWI, they loosely followed the Hollywood model of a vertically integrated company structure and a system of contracts for all employees, including stars. Like any other business, they faced an economic crisis at the onset of the WWII, when a shortage of resources led to the rise of a black-market economy across the subcontinent. However, the studios experienced a second and more serious fallout of the crisis when money procured from illegal gains found its way to the filmmaking business. The popularity of the film media in a diverse multilingual and largely non-literate demography of British India, along with the fact that cinema was a rare venture to which Indians had almost unlimited access, made filmmaking an attractive business proposition. The movie business looked easy and manageable from the outside; after all, most Indian filmmakers and technicians were self-taught, and the success of popular films seemed to hinge on the performance and marketability of film stars. The influx of illegal funding fueled the rise of independent producers, directors, and actors untethered to the studios. The studios with their permanent assets and financial structures could not compete with the solvent funding and had their operations terminated. The Indian government, which in 1947 inherited the system of taxation and censorship of cinema from its British predecessor, found itself facing a private entertainment industry with untraceable funding and uncontrollable qualities.

Despite the violence and chaos surrounding the partition of India, Indian film production, fueled by illegal funding, went on unhampered. The nascent nation-state of India was the third largest producer of films in 1947, with an output of 283 films. Tickets were taxed by the government on various levels from 1946 onward, and by 1949, the taxes amounted to 49% in some regions. Between 1948 and 1949, several government ordinances limited allocation of building material to only essential structures such as schools, hospitals, and factories to preserve resources. Movie theaters were deemed non-essential, and thus the number of theaters that existed in 1947 would continue to serve the burgeoning population until the 1960s, when new theaters were built. The remnants of the post-studio film industry, suffering from the influx of independent production and overburdened by taxes, felt the new government to be openly adversarial. Jawaharlal Nehru, the political successor of M. K. Gandhi, who was sworn in as the first Prime Minister of India on August 15, 1947, became not just the de facto administrative leader of the nation, but the architect of India's postcolonial political legacy as well. Under Nehru's stewardship, the Indian state was slated to emerge as a secular democracy with a new constitution, Soviet-style Five-Year plans, and patronage of India's multiple languages, literatures, and arts.

Popular cinema remained outside the purview of any form of outward support from the state. In the constitution that was completed in 1949, cinema was mentioned only with reference to its official business with the government, that is, certification and taxation. A documentary film facility that was initially created during WWII for wartime propaganda and discontinued in 1946, was rehabilitated by the government as Films Division in 1948. Documentaries on government programs and nationalistic themes were mandatory for exhibitors to screen before every instance of commercial screening, which contributed to their list of grievances against the government. In 1949, following a successful countrywide strike of film distributors to protest against excessive taxes, the government appointed a committee to study the state of the film industry and to provide recommendations to the government. Chaired by S. K. Patil, the Film Enquiry Committee Report was published in 1951, with a candid assessment of the studio system crumbling under pressure from illegal funding, and recommendation for the government to consolidate the censor system, relax the burden of taxation, provide impetus for the film industry to grow, and offer training and archives for the legacy of cinema to thrive. By the time the report was published, the censor boards were already integrated into a single national organization, which would be renamed as the Central Board of Certification (CBFC) in the 1960s. The other recommendations would not be implemented until the 1960s. The major official step that the government took was to pass the Indian Cinematograph Act in 1952, to replace the colonial-era act of the same name from 1918, retaining the two salient involvements of the state, censorship and taxation. But while the 1918 Cinematograph Act had articulated the racial anxieties of British administration about Indian masses getting lighthearted depictions about the "white race" from Hollywood, the 1952 Act reflected comparable anxieties of the nation-state. The Board appointed by the government had the right to refuse certification to a film or direct the applicant to excise or modify the film before it could be certified, which could easily channel the government's apprehensions toward the film industry in general. Moreover, the Board's right to censorship vis-à-vis the freedom of speech guaranteed under Article 9 of the Constitution was justified by that same Article's allowance of reasonable restrictions imposed in the interest of the greater common good. Since the definition of greater common good was unclear, state's power over cinema remained mostly unchallenged.

The consolidated censorship system and the Cinematograph Act of 1952 remained the official protocol on Indian cinema throughout the Cold War era, apart from an average of one amendment for each decade. However, beyond the mere officialities was an unofficial dynamic that played out in the most consequential and subtle way. The Indian state had control over the airwaves, and over all import and export of cinema and equipment as well. Moreover, the state's bureaucratic take on Indian cinemas, vis-à-vis the National Film Awards and the National Film Development Corporation, was contrapuntal to popular cinema's market and image. This dynamic, explored in the two sections that follow, had two important repercussions. First, it produced the bifurcation between parallel or art cinema on the one hand, and popular or commercial cinema on the other. Secondly, this dynamic fueled the enormous growth of multilingual and multilocal film industries without cinema being recognized as an industry. In 1956, India's federal government restructured the colonial-era administrative divisions within the nation by introducing a linguistic reorganization of states. Eschewing colonial divisions of religion, tribal origins, and caste, Nehru created the secular division of linguistic and cultural units, which also facilitated administration. Each state had a dominant language, which was the language of instruction in state-run public school and in state assemblies. Hindi and English were retained as the official languages on the national level: the business in the Indian Parliament is carried out in both English and Hindi, and all government documents such as passports and IDs have both Hindi and English versions. After the linguistic reorganization of the states, each state began offering incentives for cinema production and distribution within its boundaries. For example, the state of Karnataka began subsidies for films produced in the state, and the Kannada film industry became the primary beneficiary, with the output of Kannada films going up from 26 in 1967 to 88 in 1987 (Pendakur 1996, 166). The unusual burst of regional film production in the twentieth-first century—India produced 1,986 films in 43 languages between April 2016 and March

2017—can also be attributed to the cascading effects of the 1956 linguistic organization of states.

Whose Cinema? Industry vs. Nation-State

A possible reason behind the Indian state's apathy toward post-WWII cinema could be the illegality of its finances. The British exploitation of resources that had led to the growth of the black market in India during WWII was one of the many injustices Indians inherited from the colonial government. The long experience of colonialism that had arrived by way of trade by East India Company had made India's postcolonial government apprehensive about its resources, which helps explain the regulated, quasi-socialist economic system that India espoused from 1950 onward. In the case of cinema, however, there was no way of regulating production because of the absence of a grounded structure. The realization that there was no way of tracking and controlling the illegal funding that permeated the only medium that existed on a national scale set the government on a path of indirect control and normalization. Faced with limited choices, the government began a bureaucratic process of normalizing its relationship with the industry. The first effort of normalization came in the form of the annual National Film Awards (NFA), inaugurated in 1954 under the auspices of the Ministry of Information and Broadcasting. Dr. B. V. Keskar, India's longest serving Minister of Information and Broadcasting (1950–62), announced an "Award Scheme" in March 1954, to commence at the first NFA ceremony, consisting of the following items: (a) Regional Awards for the best feature films in the different linguistic groups; (b) an All India Award for the best feature film in the whole of India, (c) an All India Award for the best documentary film, and (d) an All India Award for the best children's film (MIB 1965, 72).

The structure and organization of the annual festival, especially in its first year, reflected more than anything else the categorically different worldview of the government on cinema. On the one hand, the government seemed sincere in its efforts to open up to cinema, by acknowledging the importance of the medium. However, in the absence of cinema's legal status, the Ministry of Information and Broadcasting took a paternalistic yet uninformed approach to legitimizing cinema as a new national art form. Representing the government's overall vision of regulation and supervision of cinema, the seven-member committee consisted of four bureaucrats, one renowned nationalist historian and a professor of history, and two poets. Of the two poets, one was also a professor, and Kamaladevi Chattopadhyay, the other poet, was the only woman member of the committee. The main content of the pamphlet has three parts: a five-page report entitled "The Film in India," a descriptive list of the award-winning films in the different categories, and a one-page statistical overview of the state of the industry in 1954. With a simple nationalist narration of Indian cinema's history, the pamphlet offered the basic official discourse, relentlessly drawing cinema, state, and the people into a state of happy union. In doing so, the pamphlet glosses over the lack of trust and cooperation that were also embedded in the relationship between the government and the film industry. During the time of the first NFA ceremony, the state-owned All India Radio—administered, like the Festival, by Ministry of Information and Broadcasting (MIB)—was engaged in a bitter battle with the industry over the broadcast of film songs, and indirect ban on construction of new movie theaters was still in place. Most histories of Indian cinema refer to the government's nonchalance at the S. K. Patil Committee Report (1949–51); the Film Finance Corporation and the Film Institute would be set up in 1960, almost a decade later. The festival pamphlet, however, co-opts the Committee Report within the government's own agenda:

> The various recommendations of the Committee have been considered and it is proposed to establish a National Film Board with a Film Production Bureau, a Film Institute and the Censorship Organisation as its constituent units. The Film Production Bureau is designed to give advice and guidance in regard to the selection of themes, treatment of the subject, the scenario, settings, costumes, music, etc. In the Film Institute, provision is to be made for training in the various technical departments and for research into problems of common concern and interest to the industry. It is also proposed to make suitable grants for educational films and children's films. It is considered that the best method of handling children's films would be to form a society under the Society's Registration Act for which steps have already been taken. Such a society can arrange to produce original films and prepare suitable children's versions of available films.
>
> (MIB 1954, 7)

The stylistically awkward use of the passive in this paragraph blunts the domineering attitude, which returns with a vengeance a few lines later, in the last paragraph:

> The Indian film has travelled a long way on the road to technical progress. There are signs that the industry is making efforts to realize its responsibilities towards new India after independence. It is hoped that with the co-operation of all concerned and by common endeavor the Indian film will increasingly fulfill its true role as one of the most powerful media for the expression of all that is best in India's tradition and culture.
>
> (MIB 1954, 8)

At best, there is condescension mixed in here with a forced optimism. The first instance of the government's honoring of Indian cinema, therefore, remained couched in the rhetoric of paternalism and dismissal. The year 1954 was crucial both nationally and internationally vis-à-vis Indian cinema's public image; the difference in the spirits of its reception by the authorities in the USSR and India could not be overemphasized. While the Indian Film Festival in the USSR (more on this later) celebrated the stars and directors from the Bombay film industry, the National event shifted the focus away from popular cinema. The only Hindi film that received certificate of merit is Bimal Roy's *Do Bigha Zamin* (*Two Acres of Land*, 1953), a "social realist" production with a cast and crew consisting of members of the leftist artists' group, Indian People's Theatre Association (IPTA). The best film and recipient of the President's Gold Medal was P. K. Atre's *Shyamchi Aai* (*Shyam's Mother*, 1953), a Marathi didactic social melodrama. The two other certificates of merit for feature films were awarded to Debaki Kumar Bose's *Bhagavan Sri Krishna Chaitanya* (*Lord Sri Krishna Chaitanya*, 1953) and *Khela Ghar* (*Toy House*, 1953), both in Bengali. *Khela Ghar* was chosen for the category of children's films, and it was deliberately refused the gold medal. The pamphlet had a full-page impression of the "Prime Minister's Gold Medal for the Best Children's Film," and an announcement following the list of awards claimed that "None of the entries in the Children's film section was felt by the Central Committee of Awards to be of a high enough standard for the award of the Prime Minister's Gold Medal." All three documentaries—*Mahabalipuram*, the winner of the President's Gold Medal and two other recipients of certificates of merit—were produced by Films Division, with its heavily bureaucratized system of production.

In 1955, NFA's Central Committee for Awards had three directors—V. Shantaram, S. S. Vasan, and Ardhendu Mukherjee—in addition to the bureaucrats and academics. The number of medals was increased to seven: two gold and five silver medals, and two Hindi films were among the recipients of medals. The overall tone of the event was less confrontational toward the industry than it was in the previous year. The program brochure had a balanced tone, its information mostly quantitative. It listed all 274 feature films that were approved for public exhibition in that calendar year and announced India as the third most prolific nation in the production of full-length feature films. It also listed all the documentaries made by various branches of the Films Division. A balanced tone was also evident in a comment on the quality of Indian cinema:

> In technical quality the Indian feature film has been considered to be as good as any produced elsewhere. As far as themes are concerned, there is a section of film producers who show awareness of the needs

> of a resurgent national and are trying to make the Indian film an artistic expression of human values.
>
> (MIB 1955, 4)

Over the years, the belligerent and the defensive tone of the first and second NFA had dampened, and the event became an annual civil exchange between the industry and the government in the late 1950s, the two planes connected like on a Möbius strip.

The nationalist framing of cinema in the 1954 NFA was very much in tune with the spirit of cultural revisionism. However, it was not representative of a consistent state policy toward cinema. Film songs, which were released on vinyl and played on the radio, determined a film's popularity and became part of popular cultural memory; they became the target of government's censure in the 1950s. The curious history of Hindi film music on the government-controlled All India Radio (AIR), was representative less of the Ministry of Information and Broadcasting in abstraction and more of the personal idiosyncrasies of the minister. Dr. B. V. Keskar, a political scientist by training and an enthusiast of Indian classical music, held the post from 1950 to 1962. He was responsible for an impasse that lasted for five years, from 1952 to 1957, between AIR and the Indian film industry. In the same year, his office paid officious tribute to the film industry by organizing the first national film festival; it failed to arrive at an amicable agreement with the Film Producers Guild of India over music rights. All historical accounts of the AIR impasse reflect on the contempt for film music that Keskar clearly expressed. By 1950s, it had become an established practice for film producers to send their discs to radio stations before the films were released. In 1952, however, Keskar's office issued instructions to radio stations "to screen both the text of the lyrics and the music and to approve for broadcast only such records which were in conformity with good taste" (Chatterji 1987, 49). Presented by Ameen Sayani, the film music program entitled *Binaca Geet Mala* began as a half-hour jackpot show, playing "winning" songs picked from a pool of letters. The first show received as many as 9,000 letters, posing an insurmountable amount of work on the scant team. The format of the show was changed in December of 1954 into an hour-long "hit parade" (Punathambekar 2010, 195). Ashwin Punathambekar describes how each week's show, recorded in Bombay, would be flown to Colombo and broadcast from 8:00–9:00 pm on Wednesday, and as Sayani reminisced, "the streets would be empty on Wednesday nights.... [I]n fact, Wednesday nights came to be known as *Geet Mala day*." By the mid-1950s, directors and stars from the film industry were participating in weekly sponsored shows on Radio Ceylon, and film publicity quickly became a central aspect of Radio Ceylon's programs (Punathambekar 2010, 192).

Binaca Geet Mala's popularity, spread through Radio Ceylon's powerful transmitters over all of Asia, eventually compelled AIR to resume the broadcast of film songs, albeit on a separate channel created for "light music" programming. Even in capitulating to the demands for film music, Keskar's office would not call out the name of the enemy. How do we even try to understand the cultural logic of Keskar's pathological view of culture? Since he was a self-proclaimed connoisseur of Indian classical music, the most reasonable place to start would be Keskar's lectures and articles on Indian music. Available in a slim volume entitled *Indian Music: Problems and Prospects*, his writings on the subject reveal an intense, somewhat irrational dedication to the subject. His conjectures on the origin and development of music are premised on a Hindu nationalist historiography. He uses the Indo-Aryan hypothesis (i.e., the belief of Indians and Europeans having a common, proto-Aryan ancestry) to establish a link between the roots of Western and Indian classical music, citing the heptatonic scale as evidence. In Keskar's view, Indian classical music reached its apex in ancient Hindu India, and declined during the Muslim rule; it was therefore a sacred duty of the government to educate itself and the public in the history and practice of an art that is worthy of national attention and priority. Keskar's policies were based on prejudices and stereotypes and lacked any coherent cultural logic: film music was a 'low' cultural form, unworthy of the state-run radio's support. Never one to mince his words and always eager to pass his personal preferences as educated opinion, Keskar had predicted in 1946 the disappearance of the game of cricket from India:

> Cricket can only thrive in the atmosphere of English culture, English language and English rule. It will never be able to survive the shock of disappearance of British rule from our country. With the fall of British power, it is bound to lose its place of honour and slowly grow out of date.
>
> (Brodbeck 2011)

In reality, cricket's popularity, instead of waning, rose steadily through the postcolonial decades, proving Keskar's hypothesis wrong. Notwithstanding his prejudices, Keskar had made a difference in the cultural experience of Radio listeners, beyond the realm of popular film music. In the same year film-music went off AIR, national programs of classical music—both vocal and instrumental, and Hindustani and Carnatic—began to be broadcast. Among the young artists recruited to conduct and play music were Ravi Shankar and the Carnatic Violinist T. K. Jairam (Kumar 2003, 2176). A lasting outcome of such programming was an archive of Indian classical music that became available to listeners in the 1990s when AIR began releasing compact discs of the recordings made in its studio. Though it is difficult to derive any coherent political line from his articulations, Keskar's policies have been understood as a conservative program, working toward "a new nationalist image, a countrywide broadcast of nationalist programmes and the promotion of Hindi as the national language" (Kumar 2003, 2176). Under Keskar's administration, AIR came to be known as Akashvani from 1957. In the absence of broadcast via television (television was officially launched in India in 1959, but daily service in select metros was available only from 1965 onward, with countrywide expansion from 1975 onward), Keskar used radio as the state's cultural arm, an antidote to morally decrepit medium of cinema, and acted upon that.

Parallel Lives of Indian Cinema

Indian commercial cinema received international exposure in the socialist world when the first major Indian film festival was hosted by USSR in Moscow and other cities, in 1954. The post-Stalin thaw in Soviet cultural policy had made song-infused Indian popular cinema, particularly Hindi films produced in Bombay, an attractive import. From 1955 to the end of the Cold War era, Indian cinema's international distribution remained divided into two broad categories. Parallel or art cinema in various languages was officially selected for film festivals and "panorama" events, mostly in Europe and North America. Popular Hindi films were exported to the USSR, parts of Asia, and Africa.

Sudha Rajagopalan's 2008 volume entitled *Indian Films in Soviet Cinemas: The Culture of Movie-Going after Stalin* offers considerable coverage on Indian cinema's travels in the USSR. Rajagopalan traces Indian cinema's ties with the USSR back to 1946, when Soveksportfil'm set up its office in Bombay. Representatives of Soveksportfil'm—which worked under the aegis of Goskino (State Committee for Cinematography)—scouted Indian film studios and theaters, followed news and trends in the Indian film industry, and summarized their findings in periodic reports to Moscow. The broad cultural logic of Cold War was aligned with an equal and efficient system of export and import between Soviet and Indian cinemas. However, this expectation remained unfulfilled as the flow of Indian films into the USSR was not remotely reciprocated, ever. Indo-Soviet film exchange began five years later, when Vesevolod Pudovkin, legendary director who served as the head of the Soviet Society for Cultural Relations (VOKS), and actor Nikolai Cherkasov visited India in early 1951. The visit was returned by a cultural delegation from India that visited studios in Kiev, Leningrad, and Moscow. "The Indian representatives lamented the lack of state help for cinema in India and praised the Soviet state's commitment to film-making. The delegation… returned to India with glowing accounts of Soviet cinematic accomplishments" (Rajagopalan 2008, 12).

The first Indian imports of Soveksportfil'm into the USSR were K. A. Abbas' *Dharti ke Lal* (*Children of the Soil,* 1946) and Nemai Ghosh's *Chinnamul* (*Rootless*, 1950) in 1949 and 1951, respectively. Both were productions of a radical leftist group of artists entitled Indian Peoples Theatre Association (IPTA) and received courteous treatment as progressive films by the Soviet critics, although the audience response was lukewarm at best. The significant breakthrough came in 1954 with the Indian Film Festival and the screening of Raj Kapoor's *Awaara* (*The Vagabond*, 1951), which became and remained the highest grossing film in the USSR for an entire decade. The 1954 Festival occurred in the shadow of de-Stalinization under Krushchev, and from that point onward, Indian cinema, especially popular Indian cinema—referred to frequently as *Indiiskie Melodramy* in the Soviet press—got embedded in the Soviet culture of the post-Stalin era. Dev Anand, Raj Kapoor, Nargis, Nirupa Roy, and K. A. Abbas were among the guests of the Festival, and the

> Soviet press was flooded with photographs of the visitors being warmly greeted by school students, film professionals, writers, and journalists. Indian actors spoke of the tremendous welcome they received and claimed that it outshone the reception they were accorded in other countries. They acknowledged the influence of Soviet cinematography on their work, and the Soviets talked of their new friends in India.
>
> (Rajagopalan 2008, 16)

Raj Kapoor, at the height of his popularity in the USSR in the 1950s, found little support and enthusiasm in the United States for his films. Despite his promotional tours in the U.S. (which he announced in a press conference), he felt that "American distributors continued to marginalize Indian cinema. This he contrasted with the Soviet Union, where he found expressions of friendship and respect to be 'genuine'" (Rajagopalan 2008, 16). For the greater part of the twentieth century, Indian cinema in the United States had little reach outside the circles of academics and critics and was represented mainly by the films of Satyajit Ray and other auteurs of Indian art cinema. On the other hand, popular stars such as Raj Kapoor, Dev Anand, Dilip Kumar, and even the early Amitabh Bachchan were known to huge numbers of fans not just in the Soviet Union but in the Middle Eastern and African nations as well, due to the various circuits of export for Indian commercial cinema.

If the song-infused Indian melodrama or Indiiskie Melodramy fit perfectly into post-Stalin cultural atmosphere of the Soviet Union, it failed to find a market in the U.S. A world of difference existed between India's dynamic with the U.S. and the USSR. Hollywood's organized marketing strategy placed India at the receiving end of an unfair export-import system. Motion Picture Export Association of America (MPEAA) was allowed to sell 100 titles every year to India (vs. the Soveksportfil'm's allowance of 20 per year) and it had the power to choose the titles to be sold. Owing to the MPEAA practice of block sales—a mixture of varying qualities of films packaged together—Indian viewers were exposed to a seemingly random repertoire of films. B films performed poorly in the U.S. and other locations in the global north. The problem that MPEAA could not solve was the Indian government's curb on the expatriation of foreign currency. This curb "meant a growing accumulation of Indian rupees in the control of MPEAA companies. Those monies, called 'blocked funds,' grew to $6.5 million by 1971; the MPEAA wanted them repatriated but the alarmed Indian government, being short of hard currency, could not allow it. This became the major bone of contention between the U.S. companies and the Indian government, leading to a trade embargo in 1971" (Pendakur 1985, 60–1). The relationship between Indian and the U.S. had soured over the Bangladesh War (1971) in which the Americans had turned a blind eye to the atrocities committed by their ally Pakistan on its own citizens. But there is no linear relationship between India-US relation on the one hand, and India's trade policies in effect regarding American cinema on the other hand. It is little more than a coincidence that during the fallout over the Bangladesh War, Indira Gandhi's government allowed India's agreement with MPEAA to expire. For the rest of the decade, India's NFDC would adopt policies to take control of all film imports into India.

Far apart from the worlds of American imports and Indian commercial films existed a different cinema that both the Indian government and the metropolitan West seemed to appreciate. The arthouse cinema movement in India had grown after 1955, following the recognition received by Satyajit Ray's debut film *Pather Panchali* (*Song of the Road*, 1955) at the Festival de Cannes. New Indian Cinema, as it was called in a manifesto published in 1960, came to be seen as an antidote to the overtly sentimental, melodramatic, and violent films produced by commercial filmmakers. The influx of films different from the commercial crop became instrumental in the government's creation of a media policy. In 1960, the Film Institute of India was set up by the Ministry of Information and Broadcasting in Pune on the premises of Prabhat Studios, which had ceased production in 1952. It was renamed Film and Television Institute of India (FTII) when it merged with the Television Training Centre, set up in 1971. FTII, offering courses in all aspects of filmmaking, was made into an autonomous body in 1974. Meanwhile, the Film Finance Corporation (later renamed the National Film Development Corporation) and the various State Film Development Corporations began facilitating New Cinema, thus allowing experimentation with techniques and application of the advanced training that students received at the Institute. With New Cinema came a favorable atmosphere for the making of low-budget films, and "growing emphasis on lighter equipment, outdoor shooting and smaller and more compact crews," which, in turn, influenced the subsequent training programs at the Institute as well (Murthy 1981, 82). Coeval with the FTII was the National Film Archive, which, in 1968, began a distribution service for film societies and study groups. It collaborated with organizations all over the country in conducting courses in film appreciation and played—and has continued to play—a key role in organizing retrospectives or panoramas of Indian cinema. The first "Panorama of Indian Cinema" in Paris in 1968 introduced the myriad world of Indian cinema—beyond the work of select auteurs such as Satyajit Ray, Mrinal Sen, Shyam Benegal—to Western viewers for the first time; according to Dharap, the compiler of Indian film records during the 1970s and the 1980s, 32 out of the 50 films exhibited were from the Archive (Ramachandran 1983, 535).

The rise of parallel cinema in India coincided with tumultuous political events of the 1970s that included the Bangladesh War between India and Pakistan, the quelling of various dissenting movements in India during the early years of the decade, the dissolution of the government and the declaration of the Emergency in 1975, and the rise and fall of Indira Gandhi (1971–77). The effect of each of these events was far-reaching and can be considered as a backdrop for many minor developments in Indian mainstream cinema. However, it was during the Emergency that the issue of media control and planning by the state took a crucial turn. According to Aruna Vasudev (1978), "The Emergency was to demonstrate more clearly than ever before the combination of scorn and suspicion with which the government has always tended to view the film industry" (150).

The dynamic between mainstream cinema and the state in India has always been complex and non-linear. The 1970s witnessed funding of alternate cinema by a proactive government, which led to the further meandering of commercial films from the state's idea of cinema. Writing on the government's largely positive though complicated engagement with Indian New Cinema, Ashish Rajadhyaksha (2009) argues that the link between "the state support of independent cinema and the vicious disciplining of the mainstream film industry" was indicative of "a national project around media control gone badly wrong" (233). The failure of Indian national projects around media control is not necessarily peculiar to this decade, and the biggest difficulty one encounters in discussing media control in India is the fact that it has always existed in a somewhat inconsistent manner. But this kind of inconsistency was more symptomatic of big government and an apathetic bureaucracy than of malicious and repressive control from above. Indian cinema as an unofficial industry has simply never been liked by the Indian government. But during the 19 months of the Emergency (1975–77), the industry came under direct attack on several different fronts and was in general constantly subjected to "a series of arbitrary orders which were issued with little or no warning, keeping producers, distributors, and exhibitors in a permanent state of suspense" (Vasudev 1978, 160). Censor boards were sent new instructions, members of the industry were temporarily made to broadcast their films on television before their release in the theaters, and film publicity material as well as journals and fanzines were subjected to strict censorship.

In 1975, while Indira Gandhi, India's prime minister, dissolved the parliament and declared an emergency, the image the "angry young man" who must bend the rules in his fight against injustice or an enemy became the mainstay of Hindi cinema. Amitabh Bachchan, the actor associated with the "angry young man" label, played the role for the first time in Prakash Mehra's *Zanjeer* (*Chains*, 1973). In 1975, his appearance in similar roles in Ramesh Sippy's *Sholay* (*Embers*, 1975) and in Yash Chopra's *Deewar* (*The Wall*, 1975) created a star-image that was unprecedented in Indian cinema. In the Cold War context, with India's regulated economy, governmental control of radio and the press, and censorship of cinema, Amitabh Bachchan's angry young male star-text was both political and cinematic in its significance. The influence of Hollywood was visible prominently in *Sholay*, which was a tableau Western shot in 35 mm and then blown up to 70 mm, as the producers wanted to create the kind of effect they had seen in J. Lee Thompson's *McKenna's Gold* (1969), which was widely popular in India. The plot of the film was drawn from John Sturges' *The Magnificent Seven* (1960), which was in turn based on Akira Kurosawa's *Seven Samurai* (1954). The film had a slow start, and there was discussion regarding modifying the ending and cutting the film to fit into the 3-hour slot, but sales picked up after the initial few weeks, and the film has become an all-time blockbuster in the history of Indian cinema. But besides the borrowing of action scenarios from Westerns, Amitabh Bachchan's screen presence seemed to echo Clint Eastwood in vigilante gritty roles such as in *Dirty Harry* (1971), which was popular in India. Apart from supporting the rise of Amitabh Bachchan as the action-hero, films such as *Zanjeer*, *Sholay*, and *Deewar* precipitated a new aesthetic of physical violence and suffering. Gashes, marks, and wounds on the body—especially the male body—became the new realistic norm that would persist and intensify in the following decade. While the political sphere in India imploded, and unemployment, forced migration, and suppression of civil liberties scarred public life, the physical action and struggle on the screen took a parallel path, with machismo triumphing over ahistorical evil or dying in the attempt to do so. At the end of the decade, action, violence, and sacrifice had all been rolled into a cathartic package that left the political questions simply unasked. This is the story of the Indian state and Indian cinema in the 1970s: both had severe moments of rupture during the middle years of the decade that changed their outlooks. An event such as the defeat of the Congress Party in the 1977 elections was unthinkable a decade earlier; things would never be the same in the parliamentary elections again. From 1977 onward, notwithstanding the rhetoric of the leaders, Indian democracy had ceased to be a tame idea imposed from above, clamoring from all directions instead to overturn any illusion of federalist control. How popular melodrama evolved through these tumultuous times is part of a complex narrative that unfolded over the next four decades, through the rise of Bollywood in the twentieth-first century. But one thing to remember is that the government, engaged in atrocities before and during the Emergency, continued to support—in the limited way it was used to—Indian art cinema.

Cinema, Liberalization, and the Decay of the Nehruvian State

Owing to its regulatory policies throughout the Cold War era, Indian government controlled most of the country's natural and human resources in the 1980s. A mixed economy with production in both public and private sectors, India had always striven to boost the public sector since the inception of the Five-Year Plans in 1951. In the early 1980s, while the Cold War and the bipolar global political balance were a seemingly permanent reality, Indian economy appeared to be reaping the results of its pro-public sector policies:

> While in 1951 there were only five [public sector] undertakings with an investment of 290 millions, by 1983 the number had shot up to 209 with an investment of over 300.4 thousand million rupees.
>
> So far the private sector is concerned, the government follows a licencing system to ensure that monopolies do not establish a disproportionate hold on industry.... In other areas the government gives preference to small and medium entrepreneurs.... Considerable attention has been paid to import substitution and the development of indigenous technology. This policy has been largely successful and today almost everything from a pin to giant machinery, excluding a few highly sophisticated types of defence equipment, is being manufactured in the country.
>
> (Chatterji 1987, 21–2)

The massive amount of state control as depicted in this description is significant in the context of the 1980s for an unusual reason; this was the picture of a system that was progressively incapable of sustaining itself. Defeated in the 1977 elections, Indira Gandhi was elected back to power in 1981, her dictatorial past seemingly forgotten by the electorate. In 1984, she was assassinated by her own bodyguards, who were Sikhs outraged by the Indian army's incursion into their holy shrine. India's state-controlled television and radio continued to heavily censor news coverage, as violence erupted against the Sikh community, especially in and around Indian's capital. Indira's son Rajiv Gandhi, chosen by the Congress to succeed her, won the election with an overwhelming number of "sympathy votes." Rajiv Gandhi's catchy and empty slogans for modernizing India, combined with his limited capability, education, and experience, did little more than create confusion. While a number of steps toward the economic liberalization of India were planned under Rajiv Gandhi's leadership, the 1980s remain in India's history as a decade of transition rather than of change.

In the aftermath of Indira Gandhi's assassination, India entered a period of economic and political transition, as the Nehruvian ideals of secularism and economic protectionism began to be challenged for the first time. However, the government's apathy toward popular cinema was as intense as ever. The 1980s was also the decade that Indian cinema entered the film studies curricula in universities, both in India and abroad. While histories of Indian cinema began to be written, the international focus of the Anglophone world was mainly on the art directors, such as Satyajit Ray, Shyam Benegal, Mrinal Sen, and Adoor Gopalkrishnan. It is as if once again, the "film industry"—yet to be recognized as such in the 1980s—was being treated as the rich vulgar aberration sidelined in serious discussion. But the government's control over the growth of cinema in any particular direction was as untenable as its control over the growth of the nation's economy. In the transitional decade of the 1980s, as Indian government unwittingly moved toward the decrepit financial status that would eventually lead to its embracing of global capitalism in 1991, the logic of the market led to a revival in the popular cinema. A plethora of young stars, including the three Khans of Bollywood—Aamir Khan, Shah Rukh Khan, and Salman Khan—replaced the older generation of stars, and there was a visible shift in popular films away from a nationalist ideology toward a more neoliberal individualist ethos. Mansoor Khan's *Qayamat Se Qayamat Tak* (*From Doom till Doom*, 1988), starring Aamir Khan, was the harbinger of the neoliberal discourse in Bombay-based Hindi cinema, the precursor of Bollywood.

The first significant change in the industry occurred in the production of film music. While in 1980 most of the playback music was recorded by HMV and sung by its less than half-dozen contracted singers, HMV was working hard for a share of the market by the end of the decade as a plethora of young artists had emerged, recording for emergent music production companies. The change was brought about by the introduction of audio-cassettes, a significantly cheaper option to vinyl records. As cassette players and recorders, manufactured in Japan, flooded the Indian market, the ownership and production of film songs became much more affordable. A few experimentations in recording and sales inaugurated a new line of entrepreneurship. The change did not affect just film music production but the music industry in its entirety. As Peter Manuel (1991) describes,

> By the mid-1980s, cassettes had come to account for 95 per cent of the recorded music market, with records being purchased only by wealthy audiophiles, radio stations and cassette pirates (who prefer using them as masters). The recording industry monopoly formerly enjoyed by HMV (now Gramophone Co. of India, or "GramCo") dwindled to less than 15 per cent of the market as over 300 competitors entered the recording field.
>
> (191)

Independent music production was a difficult task up until the 1980s, because competing with the gargantuan HMV meant both manufacturing vinyl records and cutting into a market where only a minority of the population owned record players. The enormous amount of control that the Indian government exercised on manufacturing industries, combined with the slow-moving and corrupt bureaucracy, made it almost impossible to initiate new enterprises. The result was the seemingly natural invincibility of a company such as HMV and the handful of artists it employed. The astonishing statistics associated with a handful of singers such as Lata Mangeshkar and Mohammad Rafi owe more to the closed loop that characterized the film music market. A handful of music directors were hired by film producers, who relied on HMV and its league of singers. Apart from the prohibitively expensive vinyl records, the only outlets for film songs were the state-controlled radio and television. With the limited field of exposure, the parent company of HMV was not making significant profit; it could continue as a powerful corporation only because it was catering to a captive and severely limited market. Once cassette players flooded the market, the possibility of selling music on cassettes and making substantial profit became a reality. Cassettes could be produced at a mere fraction of the cost of vinyl records, and even after keeping a profit margin unthinkable to vinyl producers, they could be sold at hugely affordable prices.

In the 1980s, the transition from vinyls to cassettes echoed the 1940s shift from studio-based production to the star-centric system. Both changes significantly reconfigured both the content and form of Indian popular cinema, and both were initiated by individual interventions that could not be controlled by the law. One individual who stands out in the list of entrepreneurs responsible for the revolutionary intervention into HMV's monopoly was Gulshan Kumar. He began selling cheap illegal copies of soundtracks on audio cassettes out of his fruit juice-selling stall in Delhi, and slowly began a low-cost recording company that produced cassettes under the "T-Series" label. His company, Super Cassette Industries, rose steadily through the mid-1980s; its position was made secure by the overwhelming success of the film *Qayamat Se Qayamat Tak*, featuring Udit Narayan and Alka Yagnik, who began their career as clones and would not have been able to showcase their talents without the intervention of Super Cassette Industries. The story of the rise of Gulshan Kumar invoked both admiration and disgust; he was the David who defeated HMV's Goliath, but he was also a common shopkeeper who verged on the criminal. The narrative is extraordinary, nonetheless, and the final twist in it was more unpredictable than its protagonist's achievements. Gulshan Kumar was shot dead in broad daylight in the city of Bombay in 1997; his murder was reported as related to Bombay industry's clandestine relationship with the underworld. Super Cassette Industries continue to dominate the film music market, having served as the platform for the rise of most of the leading playback singers since the late 1980s. Other companies which rose in the shadow of Super Cassette's success were Venus and Tips, and Sony Entertainment entered the market in 1998. HMV has since been able to absorb the initial shock, and remains one of the major producers, though most of its sales come from the recordings made in the pre-T-Series era. The government has since then closed the loophole in the copyright laws that enabled Gulshan Kumar and his peers to produce clone recordings, though piracy remains an issue for both the film and the music industries.

The end of the Cold War coincided with the India's embrace of capitalism. In 1991, India had to open its markets to foreign investment and capital. Seven years later, cinema was accepted by the government as a legal enterprise and, in 2001, Oxford English Dictionary inducted the word Bollywood into English language. In 2007, Sony/Columbia became the first Hollywood studio to make a Bollywood film, Sanjay Leela Bhansali's *Saawariya* (*My Love*). Bollywood, a sobriquet for Hindi film industry based in Bombay, has become a brand name, with 0.5 billion search results on Google, as opposed to less than 10 million search results for "Indian cinema." However, the long gone regulatory government's policy of nurturing non-Bombay films has rendered Indian cinema(s) an unparalleled diversity, as manifested in 1,986 films produced between April 2016 and March 2017, in 42 languages, in nine locations. Bollywood films, despite the name recognition and the influx of global capital, count for less than one-fifth of the total output of Indian cinema. The shadow of the Cold War, therefore, still hangs upon today's Bollywood and Indian cinema.

Works Cited

Brodbeck, Sam. 2011. *Sambordbeck.com*, October 29. Accessed March 15, 2013. http://sambrodbeck.com/2011/10/29/famous-last-words/.

Chatterji, P. C. 1987. *Broadcasting in India*. New Delhi: Sage Publications.

Keskar, B. V. 1967. *Indian Music: Problems and Prospects*. Bombay: Popular Prakashan.

Kumar, Kanchan. 2003. "Mixed Signals: Radio Broadcasting Policy in India." *Economic and Political Weekly* 38 (22): 2173–82.

Manuel, Peter. 1991. "The Cassette Industry and Popular Music in North India." *Popular Music* 10 (2): 189–204.

MIB (Ministry of Information and Broadcasting). 1965. *Indian Cinema.* New Delhi: Ministry of Information and Broadcasting, Government of India Publications Division.

MIB (Ministry of Information and Broadcasting). 1955. *State Awards, 1955.* New Delhi: Government of India Publications Division.

MIB (Ministry of Information and Broadcasting). 1954. *State Awards, 1954.* New Delhi: Government of India Publications Division.

Murthy, N. K. 1981. "Training for Cinema." In *Fifty Years of Indian Talkies: 1931–1981*, edited by B. K. Karanjia, 81–2. Bombay: Indian Motion Picture Academy of Arts and Sciences.

Pendakur, Manjunath. 1996. "India's National Film Policy: Shifting Currents in the 1990s." In *Film Policy: International, National, and Regional Perspectives*, edited by Albert Moran, 148–71. London: Routledge.

Pendakur, Manjunath. 1985. "Dynamics of Cultural Policy Making: The U.S. Film Industry in India." *Journal of Communication* (Autumn): 52–72.

Punathambekar, Aswin. 2010. "Ameen Sayani and Radio Ceylon: Notes towards a History of Broadcasting and Bombay Cinema." *BioScope: South Asian Screen Studies* 1 (2): 189–97.

Rajadhyaksha, Ashish. 2009. *Indian Cinema in the Time of Celluloid: From Bollywood to the Emergency.* Bloomington: Indiana University Press.

Rajagopalan, Sudha. 2008. *Indian Films in Soviet Cinemas: The Culture of Movie-going after Stalin.* Bloomington and Indianapolis: Indiana University Press.

Ramachandran, T. M., ed. 1983. *70 Years of Indian Cinema (1913–1983).* Bombay: CINEMA India-International.

Vasudev, Aruna. 1978. *Liberty and Licence in the Indian Cinema.* New Delhi: Vikas Publishing House.

Part III

Struggle for Hearts and Minds

11 Tropical Cold War Horror

Penumpasan Pengkhianatan G30S/PKI and the Traumatized Culture of Suharto's New Order

Michael G. Vann

This chapter situates an analysis of the Indonesia film *Penumpasan Pengkhianatan G30S/PKI* in the context of Cold War Southeast Asia. We can loosely translate the full title as "Crushing the Treachery of the Indonesian Communist Party and the September 30 Movement." My clumsy English rendering does not capture the snappiness of the original Indonesian with its hints at the country's love for an alphabet soup of acronyms and initials. Indeed, released as a 271-minute feature film in 1984 and later available in a shorter 217-minute home video, Indonesians often refer it to as simply *G30S/PKI*. That this shorthand is also the widely accepted term for the failed September 30, 1965 coup d'état, which was used as a pretext for the destruction of the Indonesian Community Party (PKI) and a wide range of progressive groups and individuals labeled "communist," underlines the significance of the film. Repeatedly seen by almost everyone in Indonesia for some 15 years, *G30S/PKI* was central to a state-directed campaign that created the current conventional knowledge of these historical events (Surono 2017). I argue that the film's impact was so profound that it became Indonesia's collective memory, making it one of the most successful propaganda films of all time. Furthermore, *G30S/PKI*'s lurid violence and sexuality and disturbing messages further traumatized the nation during President Suharto's genocidal New Order (*Orde Baru*, 1966–98). As it was forced upon a generation of children, the legacy of the film continues into the era of democratic reform (*Reformasi* or "Reformation," 1998–present; although some wags now call the period starting in 2018 "*Regrasi*" or "Regression"). Recently, a new generation of Indonesian historians have coined the term "Lubang Buaya Narrative" for this state-imposed historical memory (Djakababa 2009; Sullivan 2019). Named for the site of the most disturbing and unforgettable scene from *Penumpasan Pengkhianatan G30S/PKI*, their terminology recognizes the film's importance in Indonesia decades after the Cold War.

I hold that *Penumpasan Pengkhianatan G30S/PKI* should be considered as one of the most successful propaganda films of the twentieth century. Its success is due to the mandatory television screenings every September 30, the anniversary of the failed coup, until the fall of Suharto. Furthermore, teachers would march their students to local theaters where the film was being screened. Because it was so widely viewed and because the regime violently repressed counternarratives, the film shaped Indonesian mass culture during the Cold War. Unlike other Cold War era films that we can read as the product of a dominant cultural attitude, *G30S/PKI* actually created that attitude or perspective. The film created the nation's collective memory. In 2000, *Tempo* magazine published a survey of students in Indonesia's largest cities. In all, 97% of the respondents had seen the film, the vast majority many times. Nine out of ten credited *G30S/PKI* as a major source of information about the events of 1965 (Heryanto 2006). Feminist novelist Intan Paramadhita, whose work often engages the macabre, wrote that "[f]or some of us, watching the film *Pengkhianatan G30S/PKI* was an initiation to adulthood. We suddenly learned that we had a history built upon eye-gouging women and decomposed, tortured bodies" (Paramadhita 2011). Elsewhere, Leila S. Chudori (2012) and Laksmi Pamuntjak (2013) reference the film in novels that wrestle with the violent legacies and lingering traumas of 1965. Despite its ubiquitous presence in the minds and lives of many Indonesians, the film is not widely known outside of the world's fourth largest nation-state. While scholars such as cultural theorist Ariel Heryanto (2006), historian Katharine McGregor (2007), and film studies expert Katinka van Herren (2012) have examined *G30S/PKI*, few scholars have situated the film in the larger history of Cold War Indonesia.

A Star is Born

Before discussing what *G30S/PKI* tells us about Cold War cinema from the outside of the American, Soviet, and European perspectives, let us look at a figure from a more recent film about Indonesia in and after the Cold War. In 2012, a star was born. This star arrived unexpectedly and belatedly from the Southeast Asian hot battles of the Cold War. Anwar Congo suddenly achieved a certain degree of global fame, at least in cinema circles, thanks to his starring role in Joshua Oppenheimer's Oscar-nominated documentary *The Act of Killing* (2012). However, Anwar thought he was starring in another film, a surreal memoir of his time in a death squad in the Cold War's largest anti-communist massacre.

Hailing from the hot, humid, and notoriously corrupt North Sumatran city of Medan, the septuagenarian self-described gangster (*preman* in Indonesian) who never made it past the fourth grade might seem to be an unlikely celebrity. However, as Anwar explains in the film, which explores his role in the mass murder of between 500,000 and 2,000,000 members, alleged members, and associates of the PKI and its affiliated organizations, he has a background in show business and knows what makes for a good movie. He tells us that between stints as a mass murderer and an extortionist, his real job, which he loved, was as a projectionist in a Medan theater. He also ran a crew of street hustlers who sold stolen tickets in front of his workplace.

In *The Act of Killing*, after he watches the dailies of himself explaining how he strangled his victims to death and desecrated their bodies in 1965 and 1966, Anwar protests that the story should be presented in a more cinematic style. Citing his expertise from years of watching the films he projected, the murderer starts to direct a film within the film. Perhaps mentally unstable, Anwar throws together a surreal combination of scenes. His film includes costumes inspired by Francis Ford Coppola's *The Godfather* (1972) and American Westerns, obese gangsters singing in drag, and a reenactment of his death squad's attack on a village of planation laborers, casting friends and family members as victims. The recreation of the assault on the plantation workers is so brutal that many of the children working as extras on the set are deeply traumatized by the violence. For reasons that are difficult to explain, Anwar's nightmarish passion project culminates with his own decapitation. The cross-dressing *preman* Herman eats Anwar's liver as his still cognizant severed head watches. Throughout the process, he insists on showmanship and reiterates his commitment to proving how cruel he and his fellow killers were. At one point, he is reunited with an old buddy from the days of bloodshed, and they say that their film will finally get them the recognition that they deserve as merciless killers. They bitterly claim that *Penumpasan Pengkhianatan G30S/PKI* convinced too many people that the PKI were the real savages. Equating violence with power and savagery with strength, they are furious that anyone would think their victims were more violent than their death squad. Anwar holds that if only Indonesians knew how ruthless they were, they would be recognized as national heroes, not forgotten in obscurity. Throughout *The Act of Killing*, most of the cast show signs of profound posttraumatic stress disorder.

Western viewers come away from *The Act of Killing* stunned by Anwar and the other murderers' frank and open discussions of brutal violence. Many are perplexed by the culture that could produce such monsters. This chapter considers the fundamental role of *Penumpasan Pengkhianatan G30S/PKI* in shaping Indonesia's Cold War culture. If *The Act of Killing* shows the profound legacies of the Cold War in contemporary Indonesia, where the state-enforced silence regarding the mass murder of roughly a million unarmed civilians continues to fester in the collective subconscious, Suharto's annual screenings of *G30S/PKI* served as a tropical horror show that retraumatized the national culture.

Cold War Chaos as Context

Penumpasan Pengkhianatan G30S/PKI can only be understood in the context of Indonesia's chaotic Cold War experience (Chamberlain 2018).

Suharto's seizure of power marked one of the Cold War's most dramatic political reversals. The Javanese general redirected the course of the world's fifth (now the fourth) largest nation. Not only did he oust the charismatic President Sukarno, Suharto launched a systematic attack on a variety of progressive forces. This involved not just the elimination of the PKI and a realignment of Indonesia's international alliances, but also the destruction of organized labor, the end of a land reform campaign, the repression of a significant women's rights movement, and the silencing of a generation of intellectuals and artists. Under the name of anti-communism, the New Order held hundreds of thousands of political prisoners for over a decade and imposed strict censorship laws. Geoffrey Robinson (2018) characterizes Suharto's 32-year regime as a Foucauldian surveillance project with the state governing via discipline and punishment.[1]

Prior to September 30, 1965, Indonesia was on a leftward trajectory. President Sukarno dominated the nation's politics. A veteran of the nationalist cause since the 1920s, Sukarno was a brilliant orator. Jailed by the Dutch, the Japanese released him during WWII to work for the cause of "Asia for Asians." Faced with the empire's collapse and unwilling to see a return to European colonial rule in Asia, Japanese officers encouraged Sukarno and a group of nationalists to declare independence on August 17, 1945 (Anderson 1972). After four years of intermittent war against the Netherlands, Sukarno became independent Indonesia's first president from 1949 to 1967. Sukarno espoused an egalitarian populism that he called "Marhaenism" (named after a poor peasant he met) to heal the wounds of centuries of colonial rule. Wishing to be called "Bung Karno" ("*bung*" literally means "brother," but we could translate it as "comrade" or even "dude"), he wanted Indonesia to lead other nations out of colonialism and toward an independent socialist future, while avoiding the Cold War's bipolar traps. In 1955, he hosted the Asia-Africa Conference in Bandung, which became the basis for the Non-Aligned Movement. In dramatic speeches, Sukarno decried the Cold War as a new form of imperialism. If he was willing to work with the United States, he reserved the right to have friendly relations with Moscow and Beijing. Following the Cold War's Manichaeism, the Eisenhower, Kennedy, and Johnson administrations deemed Sukarno a threat to American interests and tried to destabilize Indonesia (Kahin and Kahin 1995; Simpson 2008). From supporting Islamist regional rebellions in the late 1950s to a range of covert operations, which included leaking a fake sex tape with an actor playing the Indonesian leader (admittedly, the Bung was a notorious playboy), in the 1960s, American interference infuriated Sukarno. He coined acronyms such as NEKOLIM, "Neo-Colonial Imperialist," and declared Indonesia would lead the newly independent nations of the world, what he called the NEFOS or "Newly Emerging Forces," against the OLDEFOS, "Old Established Forces."

By the mid-1960s, Sukarno was mistrustful of the United States, bored by the Soviet Union's new bureaucratic conservatism, and increasingly friendly with the Chinese leadership. Indonesia's nationalization of foreign firms angered American strategists and scared Western investors. When he spoke of a Jakarta-Phnom Penh-Hanoi-Beijing-Pyongyang Axis, Sukarno personified radical Third Worldism.

Cold War Southeast Asia saw Indonesian communism's unique path to success. The first communist party to be founded in Asia and one of several anti-colonial movements, the PKI grew quickly in the 1920s, only to be crushed by Dutch authorities after a failed revolt in 1926 (Shiraishi 1990). Arrested, imprisoned, or driven underground, the party members who survived the Japanese occupation joined a variety of resistance groups during the war against the Dutch. The party was closely tied to the labor movement, especially the railway workers' union (Suryomenggolo 2013). In 1948, disaster struck again when a regional branch of the PKI in East Java got into a dispute with the central republican government. Fighting erupted near the city of Madiun, leaving several thousand party members dead and ruining the already tense relations between the party and the recently founded Indonesian army. Faced with two military catastrophes in 22 years, a new generation of PKI leadership, including D. N. Aidit, decided to pursue a peaceful path to power. Aidit's electoral strategy stood in sharp contrast to contemporary armed Marxist insurgencies in Vietnam, Malaya, and the Philippines. Choosing the ballot box over the Kalashnikov, the party mobilized for the 1955 national elections. It received 6,000,000 votes (16% of the electorate), earning a respectable and surprising fourth-place finish. In the 1957 district elections, the PKI won 7,000,000 votes and came in first in many of the races on Java. However, Sukarno grew frustrated with a chaotic parliament, suspended elections in 1959, and declared "Guided Democracy" for Indonesia. Had electoral contests continued, even greater PKI successes seemed likely (Roosa 2017).

In the early 1960s, the PKI grew to an estimated 3,500,000 million members, making it the largest communist party outside of the Soviet Union and the People's Republic of China (Mortimer 1974). The party forged alliances with mass organizations such as the progressive Indonesian Women's Movement (Gerakan Wanita Indonesia or Gerwani), the left-wing artists of the People's Cultural Institute (Lembaga Kebudayaan Rakya or Lekra), and the All-Indonesia Trade Union Centre (Sentra Organisasi Buruh Seluruh Indonesia or SOBSI), bringing another 20,000,000 activists under its umbrella. In addition to appealing to the urban working class and plantation workers, the PKI won over many peasants in central and east Java through concerted efforts to respond to their issues in a language they could understand. Party cadres visited villages to explain their program. The PKI's Indonesian Peasants Union (Barisan Tani Indonesia or BTI), a rural mass organization that advocated for farmer's issues, brought the party into the countryside. The party also organized festive rallies in which local singers and dancers performed regional folk culture favorites.[2] Songs such as "Genjer Genjer" became PKI anthems, with wide populist appeal. Local branches of the PKI won further support by sponsoring a series of direct actions to force the implementation of ignored land reform laws. As PKI and BTI mobilization won over poor peasants, it angered and frightened large landowners, many of whom had close ties to conservative Muslim parties and the officer corps. PKI educational campaigns drew others to the party. Following Lenin's quip that communism equaled literacy plus electricity, the PKI created schools where illiterate workers and peasants could get an education that rivaled cash-strapped state schools and private Islamic boarding schools (McVey 1990). More than a political party with an economic agenda, the PKI called for a social and cultural revolution.

Under Guided Democracy (1959–65), Sukarno had to satisfy both the army and the PKI. This balancing act has often been likened to a *dalang wayang kulit* (a shadow puppeteer), a tiresome but still apt cliché.[3] A gifted orator who knew how to win over his Indonesian audiences, Sukarno promoted an inclusive ideology he called NASAKOM. Coining an acronym drawn from "*Nasionalisme, Agama, dan Kommunisme*," he argued that nationalism, religion, and communism could work together for a stronger, united Indonesia. Despite the president's support of the assault on the PKI in the 1948 Madiun Affair, Sukarno and the party leader Aidit forged an alliance in 1959. The party threw its weight behind Sukarno, who, in turn, would shield it from anti-communist generals. When the charismatic Sukarno gave speeches in his massive eponymous sports stadium, tens of thousands of PKI cadres would dutifully march in to cheer Bung Karno's radical proclamations. Meanwhile, Sukarno's regionally aggressive foreign policy would benefit the military. The 1962 occupation of Irian Jaya, the Western half of the island shared with Papua New Guinea and the Netherlands' last colonial possession in the archipelago, created opportunities for career advancement among the officer corp. Admittedly, the army's response to the quixotic "Crush Malaysia!" campaign was tepid and ambiguous.[4] More importantly, the nationalization of foreign-owned petroleum fields and plantations could lead to lucrative army administration of such infrastructure (Redfern 2010). Nonetheless, Sukarno had a difficult task. PKI efforts at labor organization challenged military control in these sectors, and the BTI's land reform campaign threatened property-owners with links to the officer corps. Wealthy landowners were often prominent figures in local Islamic institutions, combining their spiritual and material opposition to the allegedly godless PKI. Furthermore, many officers had received anti-communist ideological training first from the Japanese during the

Occupation and more recently from American cold warriors. It was the United States' strategy to cultivate generals and colonels friendly to Uncle Sam's interests (Crouch 1978). In a tactic that prefigured Reagan-era policies, the CIA funded Islamist groups hostile to the PKI. By blending culture, economics, and politics, the PKI and its enemies further polarized Indonesia.

By the middle of 1965, NASAKOM's inherent contradictions made both the left and the right increasingly paranoid. The military feared the growing power of PKI and worried that it might establish an armed wing with Chinese assistance, and the PKI heard rumors of a "council of generals" ready to seize power. When Sukarno collapsed and vomited at a public event, there was palpable anxiety in the streets of Jakarta. On the night of September 30, 1965, a rebellious faction of middle-level officers, claiming loyalty to Sukarno, tried to kidnap the army's top leadership (Roosa 2006). In the poorly planned and quickly botched operation, six generals and a lieutenant were either shot in their homes or killed at a remote rubber grove known by the sinister sounding name Lubang Buaya ("Crocodile Hole") on the Halim airbase in South Jakarta. All of their bodies were dumped in an abandoned well. In the chaos of the kidnapping, General Nasution escaped by jumping over a wall, but his five-year-old daughter Ade bled to death in her mother's arms. The coup remains shrouded in mystery, but the presence of Sukarno and Aidit at the Halim airbase indicates some element of collusion. Regardless, the coup was a small affair produced by conflicts within the armed forces. And it could have remained an internal military affair had it not been skillfully exploited by the dictator-to-be. Within hours, General Suharto (who was curiously not on the list of targets) rallied his elite commando unit and took control of the national radio station. He then launched an assault on the airbase, dispersing the remaining rebels. Usurping the chain of command and engaging in insubordination, Suharto pressed Sukarno to give him unprecedented authority to restore order. One of his first orders was to close scores of independent or left-leaning newspapers.

Previously little-known outside of military circles, Suharto adopted a public persona in sharp contrast to Sukarno. Reserved, quiet, and dispassionate, the general offered maturity and seriousness in place of Bung Karno's emotional populism. Wishing to be known as "Pak Harto" ("*pak*" is short for "*bapak*" or father, a term of respect in Indonesian), this general was no bung. As the dust settled, Suharto assembled a media team to record his horror at the exhumation of the generals. He gave a powerful speech calling for revenge against the rebels, whom he condemned as "counter-revolutionaries." Held on the armed forces day with full radio and television coverage, the generals' funerals were turned into a national event. A ceremony for little Ade deepened the emotional impact. Within days, the army and the right-wing press published articles claiming that the PKI had masterminded the coup. By branding the plot as GESTAPU, shorthand drawn from the Indonesia term "September 30 Movement," the military purposely evoked the image of the sinister Nazi secret police. The acronym was expanded to GESTAPU-PKI to directly smear the communists. Such linguistic moves indicate an effort to blend ideological confusion with moral clarity. Sukarno, realizing that power was slipping through his fingers, tried to stop the violence by rebranding the coup as the less threatening sounding GESTOK or "October 1 Movement." But Pak Harto quickly outmaneuvered Bung Karno and GESTAPU-PKI stuck. Later, it would be modified to the terse G30S/PKI.

As Suharto's propaganda incited popular opinion against the PKI, military units moved on the party throughout Java and Sumatra. Jess Melvin's (2017, 2018) research reveals substantial preparation and coordination, indicating that elements of the officer corps were waiting for their operations to receive a green light. In a pattern repeated throughout the vast country, the army mobilized anti-communist mass organizations including Muslim, Catholic, and Hindu groups as well as nationalists and organized criminals known as *preman*, giving them training, weapons, and lists of targeted victims (Robinson 2018). The killing started in northern Sumatra and central Java in October 1965. Over the following weeks, army units moved eastward through Java, inciting violence along the way. There are truly horrifying accounts of the slaughter of entire villages, rivers choked with rotting and bloated corpses, and severed heads on public display. The most gruesome rituals indicate that killing was intended to terrorize survivors (Dwyer and Santikarma 2007). When the army arrived in Bali, it set in motion a fearsome bloodletting that saw 80,000 deaths in a few weeks (Robinson 1995). According to Robinson's research, areas such as Jakarta and West Java, which had fewer murders in 1965–66, nevertheless saw the mass incarceration of hundreds of thousands.

Beyond blaming the PKI leadership for the kidnappings and murders, the army press and reactionary newspapers such as the newly opened *Api* spread false rumors that the generals were brutally tortured (Anderson 1987). In what Siskia Wieringa (2011) terms "sexual slander," the propaganda machine promoted lurid tales of sexually licentious Gerwani members singing and dancing as they sliced the generals' faces and genitals with razor blades. In revenge, the army forced female prisoners to strip naked and dance in a recreation of the alleged orgiastic frenzy of Lubang Buaya. In Bali, the newspapers reported that Gerwani women were posing as prostitutes in order to castrate men. Rhetorical misogyny incited brutal patterns of violence against women in the coming months and years. Rape and sexual mutilation were common tactics in the subsequent mass murders. The thousands of women detained in the New Order's prisons suffered through further violations from casual daily humiliations to sexual slavery (Budiardjo 1996; Pohlman 2015). Rachmi Diyah Larasati (2013), herself from a Javanese family of performers deemed "politically unclean" during the New Order, has shown how female folk dancers were particularly vulnerable to state violence, incarceration, and surveillance. *G30S/PKI* played a central role in institutionalizing violence against women under the New Order.

While this gendercide and gendered violence occurred in the specific context of the New Order's assault on Gerwani as a PKI-allied organization, it should also be understood as part of the larger cultural reaction against Guided Democracy's promises of liberation (Sullivan 2019). Even after Suharto's fall from power, political rehabilitation of former Gerwani members has been difficult (McGregor and Hearman 2007). In addition to Gerwani members, peasants associated with the BTI, artists who worked with Lekra, and union activists on plantations and the railways faced death, imprisonment, or decades of state harassment. Suharto even banned the singing of "Genjer Genjer." As Larasati (2013) discusses in her memoir, popular folk dances, some of which were ribald, were suppressed in favor of refined elite dances from the feudal courts of central Java. The New Order curtailed female agency and promoted a vision of patriarchal social order.

Suharto radically realigned Indonesia's global positioning. Publicly, he broke relations with the People's Republic of China and reestablished close ties with the United States of America. Soon American capital and later weapons would flow into New Order Indonesia. Behind the scenes, the CIA and other Western intelligence agencies assisted with the crushing of the PKI (Scott 1985; Easter 2005). In the space of a year, the fifth most populous nation went from being home to the world's largest non-governing communist party to one of the most staunchly anti-Marxist regimes on the planet. Once the birthplace of the Non-Aligned Movement, Indonesia was now firmly in the American camp, just as the war in Vietnam was reaching a new level of violence.

The combined overthrow of Sukarno and destruction of the PKI served as a model for future anti-communist Cold War operations. In Cambodia, both right and left paid attention to Suharto's actions. As early as 1967, enemies of Khmer Rouge applauded Prince Sihanouk's 1967 threat: "We do not lack our Suhartos and Nasutions in Cambodia." A decade later, a Khmer Rouge document invoked Indonesia's mass violence as a justification for its own brutality (Kiernan 1985, 235; 252). In Chile, the 1973 coup against Salvador Allende was code-named "Operation Jakarta." Echoing Suharto's violence against Gerwani, SOBSI, the BTI, and Lekra, Pinochet's soldiers rounded up party members, union leaders, student activists, and even folk singers such as Víctor Jara, killing the idealists and dreamers in the name of anti-communism and authoritarian capitalist development.

Art Becoming Reality

The New Order is an excellent example of a propaganda state. While Peter Kenez (1985, 1992) developed this term to refer to mass mobilization in the early Soviet Union, it is useful to describe the multifaceted state campaign to shape public memory in Cold War Indonesia. To promote the official narrative of 1965, the Suharto regime wrote school curriculum, funded studies of *Pancasila* (the official state ideology), monitored civil servants for political hygiene, built statues and monuments, renamed streets, held ceremonies, and produced films (Cohen 1991; Djakababa 2009; Pusat Sejarah TNI 2013; Sullivan 2019). *Penumpasan Pengkhianatan G30S/PKI* was one of the most important pieces of the campaign to vilify the PKI and justify Suharto's initial seizure of power and subsequent decades of authoritarian rule. The New Order's propaganda greatly exceeded that of its contemporary right-wing authoritarian neighbors in the Philippines, Taiwan, and South Korea (Greitens 2016). Indeed, Suharto's political longevity was due to the combination of state violence, neoliberal economic development, and a concerted effort to manufacture consent (Lippmann 1922; Herman and Chomsky 1988).

Penumpasan Pengkhianatan G30S/PKI premiered in 1984. Several years in the making, the Center for State Film Production (Pusat Produksi Film Negara; PPFN) commissioned the film as a docudrama in 1981. Brigadier General Gufran Dwipayana, who ran the PPFN, made sure that there was clear state oversight of the production and carefully vetted the filmmakers. The script was drawn from a 1968 report by Brigadier General Nugroho Notosusanto and Lieutenant General Ismail Saleh (1971), two army officers tasked with writing the Suharto regime's official version of the events. A New Order loyalist, Saleh served as Attorney General (1981–83) and Minster of Justice (1983–93). Notosusanto, head of the army's department of history, was the main author of the source material. McGregor (2007) has detailed the ways in which Notosusanto played an essential role in crafting the New Order's Lubang Buaya narrative (earlier he had written the official history of the 1948 Madiun Affair). By the time the film went into production, Notosusanto was rector of the University of Indonesia and Minister of Education and Culture. PPFN chose Arifin C. Noer to direct the propaganda piece. As powerful members of the New Order's inner circle wrote the history that was the basis of *G30S/PKI*, the film was closely tied to Suharto's political agenda and goals (Heryanto 2006).

A native of Cirebon, Noer was a student in Yogyakarta during the tumultuous years of the mid-1960s. Located in Central Java, the city was home to both Suharto and many of the troops who participated in the September 30 movement. Indeed, the only violence outside of Jakarta during the coup d'état was the murder of two officers in Yogyakarta.

However, the wave of anti-PKI violence, including right-wing and religious student protests, rocked the city in the following months. Noer would have witnessed these events. During the 1970s, he traveled to the United States to participate in the Writer's Workshop at the University of Iowa, began to write and direct stage plays and films, and published books of poetry. In the early 1980s, he began his collaboration with Dwipayana. In 1982, they released *Serangan Fajar* (*The Dawn Attack*), which is about the March 1, 1949 attack on the Dutch in Yogyakarta. The film, like the 1980 *Janur Kuning* (*Yellow Coconut Leaves*), overemphasizes the role of Suharto, then a young lieutenant colonel. At the Indonesian Film Festival, *Serangan Fajar* won a number of awards including Best Picture, Best Director, and Best Original Story. In the Suharto era, such awards can be read as the president's approval. Thus, Noer was a natural choice to direct *G30S/PKI*.[5]

G30S/PKI is a key document to understanding the cultural history of Cold War Indonesia. The four-and-a-half-hour-long film dramatizes events leading up to and following the failed coup d'état on the night of September 30/October 1, 1965. The film opens with a bewilderingly quick series of scenes in a variety of cinematic styles. The opening scene starts with several static shots of the 1969 monument of the slain generals and the bas-relief that decorates the base of the statue. As a narrator explains the importance of the monument, the camera lingers over images of Sukarno holding a book marked "NASAKOM" and depictions of the generals being beaten and killed as women perform a provocative dance. Next, there is a scene of PKI members attacking a mosque during prayers. They desecrate the holy Koran and assault *kyai*, traditional Javanese Islamic scholars. The narration returns as we see a montage of newspaper articles about PKI actions. The film then cuts to still photos of the Madiun Affair, including images of rotting corpses before another montage of PKI demonstrations in the streets of Jakarta. More newspaper articles and narration inform the viewer that Sukarno angered anti-communist army officers by meeting Zhou Enlai, thus situating the narrative in classic Cold War tension. An abrupt transition leads to close-ups of someone receiving acupuncture on their torso, an allusion to the rumors of Sukarno's kidney disease. Before we actually see the president, there are shots of a herd of deer running about on the grounds of the neoclassical presidential palace in the hills of Bogor and a team of Chinese doctors slinking about the luxurious palace interior. Sukarno finally appears alone in his room. Dressed in pajamas, he broods and stares out the window as mysterious organ music plays. With these gothic scenes, Noer establishes Sukarno's poor physical and mental health. The Bung is a far cry from the man who recently had thrilled tens of thousands with his brilliant oratory skills. Another abrupt edit takes us to scenes of village poverty as women line up for water, debt collectors harass desperate men, and listless starving children mill about. The camera lingers on a man's leg with some sort of festering wound before panning about his shack, where the only decoration is a photograph of Sukarno. The message is that the average people do not live in a palace with an army of servants and a team of foreign doctors. This is followed by images of a PKI militia training camp. Soldiers march, shoot, and scream before the film takes us back to Bogor Palace where Sukarno continues to mope about in front of a framed photograph of Nehru. From a large collection of books in various languages, the Bung selects *Politics Has No Morals* by Norman Beasley. The title, in English, is visible, but one wonders if an Indonesian viewer could read it. The 1949 book is a curious choice for the film as it was actually an anti-communist and anti-FDR diatribe, and the incongruence is especially evident as the camera pans over to a volume by Mao Zedong.

The film then spends half an hour depicting a series of conspiratorial meetings of the PKI leadership. In these meetings, the ailing President Sukarno is implicated in the plot to eliminate the army's leadership, as is Air Marshall Omar Dani. As the film moves closer to the action, that is, the kidnapping and murder of the generals, there are a series of scenes of the victims in their homes with their wives and children. While the army generals are all family men, religious (Muslim and Catholic), and display the refined good manners known as *halus* in Indonesian, the PKI members are unkempt, rude, and sloppy. The PKI meetings are full of smoke and loud voices. One individual sips spilled coffee from a saucer, embodying the emotional vulgarity known as *kasar*. Piety and family values are an important theme in the film. *G30S/PKI* depicts Marxism as an assault on morality, religious belief, and the home. Intermixed with the scenes of the PKI's conspiratorial activity are a few minutes in Ade Naustion's kindergarten. Peaceful and clean children sing for their adoring teacher, and little Ade shines with purity and youthful innocence.

The turning point in *G30S/PKI*'s plot happens roughly 90 minutes into the film. The next 45 minutes recreate the events of the night of September 30. After watching the unsuspecting officers retire for the evening in their spacious villas in the calm Menteng neighborhood, the camera cuts to wild activity at the Halim air force base. Gerwani women chat and cheer as troops mobilize for the coup. As *kasar* leaders harangue them, the rank and file rebels tie red scarves around their necks. Back in the calm of the home of a general, he awakes from a dream and hears a mysterious bird-like sound. His wife assures him that it is just a dream. Later, during the kidnapping, the haunting sound will return. With this scene, *G30S/PKI* flirts with the supernatural, and the next section of the film has elements of the horror genre. Under the cover of darkness, PKI-controlled units attempt to kidnap seven generals from their homes. Noer uses a variety of camera angles and styles to build excitement and tension. Tight shots of boots running on concrete are reminiscent of Gillo Pontecorvo's *The Battle of Algiers* (1966). At one point, the rebel troops jump from their truck in slow motion; at another, the camera moves through the bushes outside of a home, offering the kidnappers' visual point-of-view. The crass and vulgar rebel troops behave as beasts, "outside the realm of the human" (Vickers 2012). As with many of the cultures of Southeast Asia, the supernatural figures prominently in Indonesia. As spirits, ghosts, and the undead can appear in political discourses, *G30S/PKI*'s adoption of the horror film motifs was a shrewd directorial decision (Kwon 2006, 2012; Vann 2013; Vickers 2010).

In a series of predawn raids, Lieutenant Colonel Untung commanded seven units from the Tjakrabirawa presidential guard to seize the generals. Faced with resistance, the kidnappers killed Commander of the Army Lieutenant General Ahmad Yani, Major General Haryono, and Brigadier General Pandjaitan in their homes. Major General Soeprapto, Major General Parman, and Brigadier General Sutoyo were taken alive and driven to Lubang Buaya on the Halim air force base. The highest-ranking target, Coordinating Minister for Defense and Security and Armed Forces Chief of Staff General Abdul Haris Nasution, escaped by climbing over a wall into the neighboring Iraqi Embassy. In the confusion of the attack, his personal aide, First Lieutenant Pierre Tendean, claimed to be Nasution and was taken away by the kidnappers. In an emotional scene, Nasution's daughter, Ade, is shot. Her mother picks her up and bravely confronts the kidnappers as Ade stoically bleeds in her mother's arms. In one of the most important scenes, Ahmad Yani berates the kidnappers and slams a door in their face, only to be shot in the back in front of his son. He then dies on the floor in front of his well-stocked bar (Vann 2019). The rebels drag his body to a truck, leaving a trail of smeared blood.[6] Noer includes a lingering shot of blood dripping down the dead general's face. In Sutoyo's home, the rebels smash various objects out of contempt, spite, and class-envy as children cower in fear and the general behaves with dignity and grace. The rebel soldiers terrorize General Pandjaitan's domestic servants, killing one. Albert Naiborhu, the general's nephew, is also shot and later dies of his wounds. As General Haryono tries to resist, the kidnappers smash furniture, set a fire, and unleash volleys from their automatic weapons. We see his children screaming in fear before he is finally shot in the back. His traumatized children scream as blood spills out across Haryono's body, clad only in white undergarments. The emotional impact reaches a peak when Pandjaitan, who has agreed to go with the kidnappers but insists on dressing in his formal uniform, slowly walks past his wife and daughters and out of his home. When the general, a Christian, stops to pray, the rebels grow impatient and shoot him in front of his family. As they drive off with Pandjaitan's body in the back of their truck, one of his daughters rushes outside and falls to her knees in a puddle of his blood. As she wails in grief, she rubs her hands in his blood and then smears it across her face. In the background, the Western-sounding organ music that started when Pandjaitan was praying competes with her screams. In the dénouement of the kidnapping sequences, we see the now widowed Ibu Haryono mop up her husband's blood from their bedroom floor.

After almost two and a half hours, an intermission follows these images of murder. Taken as a whole, the kidnapping sequences combine Cold War politics with elements of a horror film. First, the communists are beasts or demons. Their inhuman violence is seemingly without bounds. Their manners are crass, *kasar* in the face of the *halus* dignity of the officers. The Gerwani women are witch-like and capable of the utmost cruelty. Second, communism poses a threat to bourgeois domesticity. The conspirators violate the home, destroy property, and threaten women, children, and servants. The collateral damage includes a beaten maid, a dead nephew, and the martyred Ade. Third, the PKI represents a threat to religion. While Indonesia is a majority Muslim nation-state, *G30S/PKI* includes Christians as potential targets of Marxist violence. When the anti-PKI backlash came, much of the killing was done by religious organizations who loathed the alleged atheism of their PKI victims. Fourth, the PKI's conspiratorial behavior—secret meetings, hidden bases, and actions taken under the cover of dark—has a sinister, even gothic air. Finally, Noer drenches these scenes in blood. This is not a film for the squeamish, even though a generation of school children were forced to watch it every September 30.

After the intermission, the film resumes with shots of troops setting up defensive positions in front of Monas, the national monument, and other strategic sites around Merdeka (Freedom) Square in the center of Jakarta. Haunting organ music accompanies these scenes. Meanwhile, General Suharto, seated before traditional Javanese imagery, receives word that something is amiss. For almost 30 minutes the film cuts back and forth between the orgy of violence at Lubang Buaya and Suharto calmly assessing the situation and taking control of loyal troops. As the trucks arrive at the PKI camp with either blindfolded or dead generals, rebel soldiers chant and shout PKI slogans and run about in a state of chaos. The camp is lit by smoky torches, giving it a frightening air. As a corpse is dragged past, a woman throws her shoe at the dead general. The bloody bodies are discarded on the dirty floor of an empty room as kidnappers viciously push and yell at the blindfolded generals. When the latter are brought into a room for interrogation, they are tied up and threatened with knives if they do not sign a confession that they are part of a secret "Council of Generals" who were conspiring against Sukarno and the PKI. As a kidnapper unties a red blindfold, he sneers "The color of blood is red, General, like anger!" In an infamous sequence, a witch-like woman, assumed to be a Gerwani member, pulls a razor blade from a hiding place in a wall and slashes the face of General Soeprapto. While the scene is graphic, the details are unclear. The implication is that she cut out the man's eyes. Later, he is beaten with bamboo poles and thrown to the floor. In another scene, a male interrogator threatens to cut out a general's eyes with a sickle unless he signs the statement. Lieutenant Pierre Tendean is tied to a post and beaten before his hands are burned with a cigarette. General Sutoyo is stabbed, thrown to the floor, and kicked. Outside, the crowd sings festive folk songs, dance in a ribald fashion, and chant PKI propaganda in a brainwashed state. The torturers finally finish off all four victims with close-range blasts of machine gun fire and then allow the mob, now in an ecstatic frenzy of bloodlust, to further insult the bodies with kicks to the head. Some of the bodies have blood around the groin, implying sexual mutilation. All seven are dragged through the dirt and leaves and dumped in an abandoned well. The conspirators shoot into the impromptu grave and then carefully cover it up with a replanted banana tree. Then rebel units take over a radio station and broadcast that the September 30 Movement has taken over.

The action of the kidnapping, torture, and murder of the generals stands in sharp contrast to the first and final thirds of the film, which are dominated by meetings, telephone conversations, and other political maneuvering. Interestingly, the most vicious torture images are cut out of the shorter three-and-a-half-hour edit released for home viewing.

The final hour of *G30S/PKI* depicts General Suharto's rise to power over the next few days. He secures the support of anti-PKI officers, such as Colonel Sarwo Edhie, who led the assault on rebel-occupied buildings in Jakarta and then the subsequent mass murder of 1965–66. We see Suharto methodically discover the coup plot and his allegedly reluctant seizure of control of the military from PKI-allied Air Marshall Omar Dani. He then takes political control from President Sukarno, depicted in a tropical gothic seclusion in his old colonial palace. The calm and cool Suharto exposes a PKI's secret stockpile of arms, leads an attack on the Halim Airbase, and supervises the discovery of the bodies. The low-action assault on Halim is intercut with scenes from a hospital where Ade Naustion slowly dies of her wounds. As the troops find the grave, images of the generals' suffering are replayed as flashbacks to remind the audience of the horror buried in the well, forcing the viewers to relive the trauma yet again. Indeed, the ritual repetition of trauma is central to the entire film project. As the bodies are exhumed, the film plays a recording of Suharto's speech (given on October 4, 1965) blaming the murders on the PKI and Gerwani. Subtitles scroll across the screen to make sure that the audience understands these important words. The final emotional scenes recreate the events of October 5, 1965. On the national Armed Forces Day, the country mourns the death of the generals as their bodies are transported on a Panzer tank through the streets of Jakarta. To establish its authority as the true record of the events, the end of the film adopts a newsreel style, similar to the final scenes of *The*

Battle of Algiers, and finishes with a voiceover from one of Suharto's speeches calling for vengeance for the martyred generals. The film ends with Suharto's words as we see Ade shut her eyes for the last time. A sheet is pulled over her face. A mournful choir replaces Suharto's voice, and a montage of newspaper articles about the coup and PKI's guilt plays behind the credits.

Telling the New Order Narrative

Importantly, *Penumpasan Pengkhianatan G30S/PKI* stops at October 5, 1965. The film does not even begin to discuss the massive campaign of violence unleashed against the PKI and its allies. While the film has the feel of a low-budget 1970s slasher film, it was intended as a serious propaganda tool to promote Suharto's dictatorial rule and to justify the murder of PKI members as well as their families, union leaders, and other activists. The American press and policy makers famously cheered the mass killings. *Time* magazine infamously called it "the West's best news from Asia in years" (Kwok 2016). Instead of scenes of the military, Muslim and Catholic youth groups, and criminal gangs systematically executing at least half a million unarmed civilians in Java, Bali, and Sumatra, and the mass arrests, torture, and deportation of hundreds of thousands to brutal prison camps such as Buru Island, we see communists plotting and murdering less than a dozen individuals. Suharto's narrative thus silences the real crime of anti-communist mass politicide by overemphasizing the PKI's alleged brutality toward a handful of people. Furthermore, *G30S/PKI* implies that whatever violence was to come was the righteous vengeance of a wronged nation. The message is that the PKI deserved mass murder for its alleged betrayal, treason, and treachery.

The annual ritual of forcing students to view the film in theaters and broadcasting it on state television ensured that *Penumpasan Pengkhianatan G30S/PKI* played an important role in establishing New Order ideology. The film worked in unison with Suharto's other anti-communist propaganda such as the rituals of Sacred National Ideology Day (Hari Kesaktian Pancasila or HAPSAK) on October 1, and Armed Forces Day on October 5, when memorials were held at Crocodile Hole on the Halim Airforce Base (van Herren 2012). The site was also turned into the Museum of the Treachery of the Indonesian Communist Party, with both miniature and life-size dioramas depicting the murder of the generals and little Ade, complete with a "Veranda of Torture," a statue of the slain generals demanding revenge, and the well that served as the general's grave reinforced in concrete and painted blood red. The museum even contains displays with still photos from the film presented as evidence, blurring the lines between art and reality (Vann 2019). With very bold and obvious moves, the Suharto regime sought to mobilize all of Indonesia against the forces of communism.

We should also read *Penumpasan Pengkhianatan G30S/PKI* with an eye to gender. The film and New Order propaganda deployed strong misogynistic themes that linked communism to alleged threats to the nation's values. Scenes of Gerwani members torturing the generals and dancing with delight at Crocodile Hole appear not just in the film but also on official monuments. Government agents placed rumors of sexual savagery and sadism in the anti-communist press, leading many to believe the myth of PKI women sexually mutilating the generals. This film was part of a coordinated rewriting of history that turned the figure of the communist woman into a witch-like beast capable of unspeakable cruelty. Instead of the PKI image of strong and liberated women engaged in transforming Indonesia, Suharto's New Order endorsed an anti-communist *ibuisme* ("motherism") in which good women were mothers who stayed at home to rear children. The *Dharma Wanita* program of charity work for upper-middle-class wives offered an institution for social activism within the controls of the authoritarian state. *G30S/PKI* laid the groundwork for this male supremacist reaction by reminding Indonesia of the dangers of liberated women.

If the generals' deaths shocked some, the subsequent year of mass murder definitely traumatized Indonesia's collective consciousness. Suharto's use of the memory of these murders only served to intensify the culture of trauma. The rabidly anti-communist dictator's silencing of the real horrors of perhaps nearly a million butchered men, women, and children and the subsequent decades of political repression and political stigmatization, together with the emphasis on the myth of the grisly killing of six generals and one little girl, kept images of violence in the national psyche without allowing an avenue for coming to terms with the mass deaths of 1965–66. As Larasati (2013) recalls, the annual ritual of the forced screening of *Penumpasan Pengkhianatan G30S/PKI* served Suharto's anti-communist goals as it reminded the nation of the unresolved trauma. As a Fulbright scholar in 2012–13 and in 2018–19, I interviewed several dozen adult Indonesians who bitterly recalled being forced to watch the film as young school children. Frequently, they asked the angry rhetorical question: "Who would make children watch such a thing?"

Returning to the star at the beginning of this piece, *G30S/PKI* weighs heavy on the mind of Anwar Congo. Joshua Oppenheimer, director of *The Act of Killing* and its companion piece *The Look of Silence* (2014), reflected on the importance of *G30S/PKI* in contemporary Indonesia:

> We see this with Anwar in *The Act of Killing*, when he and Adi [a fellow 1965 executioner] are watching the *Penghianatan G30S/PKI* (*Treachery of the PKI/G30S*) government propaganda film. Adi says to Anwar "it's a lie", and Anwar replies, "I know it's a lie, but it's the one thing that makes me feel better", which means he knows

> and doesn't know. He believes but he doesn't believe. It's cognitive dissonance. It's self–deception. So of course there may be some parts of the younger generation who simply don't know the history, but the problem that the film exposes is what people know but refuse to believe because it's too painful.
>
> (Melvin 2015)

For historians of Cold War cinema, *Penumpasan Pengkhianatan G30S/ PKI* is significant for looking at non-super power representations of the Cold War but also for showing the lingering impact of the Cold War in today's world. Suharto's anti-communist culture, political rhetoric, and rituals would outlast the PKI (which was exterminated by 1966), the Cold War (which ended in 1989 or 1991), and even Suharto himself (who was overthrown in 1998, and died in 2008). Anwar Congo's 2012 appearance in *The Act of Killing* showed the world how Indonesia has yet to overcome the horrifying legacy of what a 1983 Western film romanticized as a year of living dangerously.

Notes

1 While Robinson (2018) is the definitive synthesis of the existing scholarship, Melvin (2018) contains the most damning documentation of Suharto and other generals' direction of the slaughter.
2 Ahmad Tohari's beautifully written trilogy of novels published together in English as *The Dancer* (2012) fictionalizes the heart-breaking fate of a young Javanese ronggeng dancer who naively performs at PKI rallies and suffers the New Order's wrath.
3 See the satirical anonymous piece "How to Write about Indonesia" (2012).
4 After Sukarno's successful acquisition of Western New Guinea (Papua) in 1962, the last Dutch colonial possession in Asia, he turned his attention to Malaysia. Arguing that the new nation was a colonial construct and a likely tool of British neocolonialism, Sukarno threatened to invade Malaysia. While the "Crush Malaysia' campaign (1963–66) did see small skirmishes in Borneo (Kalimantan) and British bombers flying over Indonesian territory, this undeclared war quickly wound down as Suharto came to power.
5 Interestingly, it was *Janur Kuning* and not *Serangan Fajar* that the regime screened every March 1 until the fall of Suharto. Most informed viewers would agree that while *Serangan Fajar* exaggerates Suharto's importance in 1949, *Janur Kuning* is true hagiography. Noer directed a third film, *Djakarta 1966*, about Suharto's seizure of the reins of government from Sukarno in the infamous March 11 SUPERSEMAR edict. Alternating between tedious meetings, conversations between an ailing and out-of-touch Bung Karno and a determined and somber Pak Harto, and chaotic street demonstrations by a bewildering collection of student groups, *Djakarta 1966* was never a crowd pleaser. Completed in 1982, it was not released until 1988. Of course, *Djakarta 1966* won awards at the Bandung Film Festival.
6 Yani's home was turned into a museum to the martyred general in 1966. Visitors may still visit the site where he was murdered. While the bullet holes in the door are there, in an effort to pander current Islamist sensibilities, the museum directors have tried to cover up his bar.

Works Cited

Anderson, Benedict. 1987. "How Did the Generals Die?" *Indonesia*, no. 43: 109–34.

Anderson, Benedict. 1972. *Java in a Time of Revolution: Occupation and Resistance, 1944–1946*. Ithaca, N.Y.: Cornell University Press.

Budiardjo, Carmel. 1996. *Surviving Indonesia's Gulag: A Western Woman Tells Her Story*. London: Cassell.

Chamberlin, Paul Thomas. 2018. *The Cold War's Killing Fields: Rethinking the Long Peace*. New York: Harper.

Chudori, Leila S. 2012. *Pulang*. Jakarta: Kepustakaan Populer Gramedia.

Cohen, Margot. 1991. "Red Menace Alive and Well in Java Museums." *Wall Street Journal*, November 14.

Crouch, Harold. 1978. *The Army and Politics in Indonesia*. Ithaca, NY: Cornell University Press, 1978.

Djakababa, Yosef M. 2009. "The Construction of History under Indonesia's New Order: The Making of the Lubang Buaya Official Narrative." PhD thesis, University of Wisconsin, Madison.

Dwyer, Leslie, and Degung Santikarma. 2007. "Speaking from the Shadows: Memory and Mass Violence in Bali." In *After Mass Crime: Rebuilding States and Communities*, edited by Beatrice Pouligny, Simon Chesterman, and Albrecht Schnabel. 190–214. Tokyo: United Nations University Press.

Easter, David. 2005. "'Keep the Indonesian Pot Boiling': Western Covert Intervention in Indonesia, October 1965–March 1966." *Cold War History* 5 (1): 55–73.

Greitens, Sheena Chestnut. 2016. *Dictators and Their Secret Police: Coercive Institutions and State Violence*. Cambridge: Cambridge University Press.

Herman, Edward S., and Noam Chomsky. 1988. *Manufacturing Consent*. New York: Pantheon Books.

Heryanto, Ariel. 2006. *State Terrorism and Political Identity in Indonesia: Fatally Belonging*. London and New York: Routledge.

"How to Write about Indonesia." 2012. *New Mandala*, December 14, 2012. Accessed February 25, 2018. https://newmatilda.com/2012/12/14/how-write-about-indonesia/.

Kahin, Audrey, and George Kahin. 1995. *Subversion as Foreign Policy: The Secret Eisenhower and Dulles Debacle in Indonesia*. New York: New Press.

Kenez, Peter. 1992. *Cinema and Soviet Society, 1917–1953*. Cambridge: Cambridge University Press.

Kenez, Peter. 1985. *The Birth of the Propaganda State: Soviet Methods of Mass Mobilization, 1917–1929*. Cambridge: Cambridge University Press.

Kiernan, Ben. 1985. *How Pol Pot Came to Power: Colonialism, Nationalism, and Communism in Cambodia, 1930–1975*. New Haven, CN: Yale University Press.

Kristanto, J. B. 2005. *Katalog film Indonesia, 1926–2005*. Jakarta: Grafiasri Mukti.

Kwok, Yenni. 2016. "*The Look of Silence* and Indonesia's Quest for Truth and Reconciliation." *Time*, June 27.

Kwon, Heonik. 2012. *Ghosts of War in Vietnam*. Cambridge: Cambridge University Press.

Kwon, Heonik. 2006. *After the Massacre: Commemoration and Consolation in Ha My and My Lai*. Berkeley: University of California Press.

Larasati, Rachmi Diyah. 2013. *The Dance that Makes You Vanish: Cultural Reconstruction in Post-Genocide Indonesia*. Minneapolis: University of Minnesota Press.

Lippmann, Walter. 1922. *Public Opinion*. New York: Harcourt, Brace and Company.

McGregor, Katharine. 2007. *History in Uniform: Military Ideology and the Construction of Indonesia's Past*. Honolulu: University of Hawaii Press.

McGregor, Katharine E., and Vannessa Hearman. 2007. "Challenges of Political Rehabilitation in Post-New Order Indonesia: The Case of Gerwani (the Indonesian Women's Movement)." *South East Asia Research* 15 (3): 355–384.

McVey, Ruth T. 1990. "Teaching Modernity: The PKI as an Educational Institution," *Indonesia*, no. 50.

Melvin, Jess. 2018. *The Army and the Indonesian Genocide: The Mechanics of Mass Murder*. London and New York: Routledge.

Melvin, Jess. 2017. "Mechanics of Mass Murder: A Case for Understanding the Indonesian Killings as Genocide." *Journal of Genocide Research* 19 (4): 487–511.

Melvin, Jess. 2015. "Interview: Joshua Oppenheimer on the Look of Silence." *Inside Indonesia*, no. 119 (January–March). Accessed August 4, 2018. www.insideindonesia.org/interview-oppenheimer-on-the-look-of-silence?highlight=WyJnMzBzIiwicGtpIiwicGtpJyIsInBraSdzIiwiJ3BraSIsIidwa2knIiwicGtpJy4iLCJwa2knLCIsImczMHMgcGtpIl0%3D.

Mortimer, Rex. 1974. *Indonesian Communism under Sukarno: Ideology and Politics, 1959–1965*. Ithaca, NY: Cornell University Press.

Notosusanto, Nugroho, and Ismail Saleh. 1971. *The Coup Attempt of the September 30 Movement in Indonesia*. Jakarta: Pembimbing Masa.

Pamuntjak, Laksmi. 2013. *Amba*. Jakarta: Gramedia Pustaka Utama.

Paramadhita, Intan. 2011. "Questions on witnessing violence." *The Jakarta Post*, April 4, 2011. Accessed September 1, 2018. www.thejakartapost.com/news/2011/04/04/questions-witnessing-violence.html.

Pohlman, Annie. 2015. *Women, Sexual Violence and the Indonesian Killings of 1965–66*. Abingdon and New York, Routledge.

Pusat Sejarah TNI. 2013. *Buku Panduan: Monumen Pancasila Sakti*. Jakarta: Pusat Sejarah TNI.

Redfern, William. 2010. "Sukarno's Guided Democracy and the Takeovers of Foreign Companies in Indonesia in the 1960s." PhD diss., University of Michigan.

Robinson, Geoffrey B. 2018. *The Killing Season: A History of the Indonesian Massacres, 1965–1966*. Princeton, NJ: Princeton University Press.

Robinson, Geoffrey. 1995. *The Dark Side of Paradise: Political Violence in Bali*. Ithaca, NY: Cornell University Press.

Roosa, John. 2017. "Indonesian Communism: The Perils of the Parliamentary Path." In *The Cambridge History of Communism, Volume 2: The Socialist Camp and World Power 1941–1960s*, edited by Norman Naimark, Silvio Pons, and Sophie Quinn-Judge. 467–90. Cambridge: Cambridge University Press.

Roosa, John. 2006. *Pretext for Mass Murder: The September 30th Movement and Suharto's Coup d'État in Indonesia.* Madison: University of Wisconsin Press.

Scott, Peter Dale. 1985. "The United States and the Overthrow of Sukarno, 1965–67." *Pacific Affairs* 58 (2): 239–64.

Shiraishi, Takashi. 1990. *An Age in Motion: Popular Radicalism in Java, 1912–1926*. Ithaca, NY: Cornell University Press.

Simpson, Brad. 2008. *Economists with Guns: Authoritarian Development and US–Indonesian Relations, 1960–1968*. Stanford: Stanford University Press.

Sullivan, Charles. 2019. "Years of Dressing Dangerously: Women, Modernity, National Identity and Moral Crisis in Sukarno's Indonesia, 1945–1967." PhD thesis, University of Michigan.

Surono, Agus. 2017. "Film 'Pengkhianatan G30S/PKI' dan Tahun 1965 Yang Tak Pernah Berakhir." *Intisari Online*, September 20, 2017. Accessed September 30, 2018. http://intisari.grid.id/read/03100048/film-pengkhianatan-g30spki-dan-tahun-1965-yang-tak-pernah-berakhir?page=all.

Suryomenggolo, Jafar. 2013. *Organising Under the Revolution: Unions and the State in Java, 1945–1948*. Singapore: NUS Press.

Tohari, Ahmad. 2012. *The Dancer*. Lontar: Jakarta.

van Herren, Katinka. 2012. *Contemporary Indonesian Film: Spirits of Reform and Ghosts from the Past*. Leiden: KITLV Press.

Vann, Michael G. 2019. "Suharto's Shadow Still Lingers in Indonesian Museums." *The Diplomat*, February 6, 2019. Accessed February 25, 2019. https://thediplomat.com/2019/02/suhartos-shadow-still-lingers-in-indonesian-museums/.

Vann, Michel G. 2013. "Haunted house, haunted history." *Inside Indonesia*, no. 112 (Apr-Jun). Accessed August 17, 2018. www.insideindonesia.org/haunted-house-haunted-history.

Vickers, Adrian. 2012. "Sakti Reconsidered: Power and the Disenchantment of the World." In *Southeast Asian Perspectives on Power*, edited by Liana Chua, Joanna Cook, Joanna, Nicholas Long, Nicholas, and Lee Wilson, 51–66. New York: Routledge.

Vickers, Adrian. 2010. "Where Are the Bodies: The Haunting of Indonesia." *The Public Historian* 32 (1): 45–58.

Wieringa, Siskia. 2011. "Sexual Slander and the 1965/66 Mass Killings in Indonesia: Political and Methodological Considerations." *Journal of Contemporary Asia* 41 (4): 544–65.

12 Entertainment and Propaganda

Hong Kong Cinema and Asia's Cold War

Poshek Fu

The Cold War was as much a bipolarized international order dominated by the U.S.-Soviet conflicts as a struggle between two contrasting ideologies and social systems (Westad 2017). In the past two decades, with unprecedented access to archives, new generations of scholars have produced a rich array of scholarship that bring forth important East and Southeast Asian perspectives to the global conflicts. They focus largely on the diplomatic or military history and state-level power politics. My chapter supplements these works by bringing attention to the dynamic role of popular culture in Asia's Cold War. It explores the covert political mobilization and propaganda warfare of Hong Kong Mandarin cinema from around 1946 to 1960, a period characterized by the struggles of the United States and its ally—Nationalist Taiwan—to contain the expanding cultural influences of Chinese Communism in the region. Hong Kong was an imperial outpost on the South China coast that the British recolonized immediately following the end of WWII. The victory of Mao's revolution greatly changed the course of Hong Kong's history. Dubbed by the press as the "Berlin of the East" or "Tangier of Asia," Hong Kong had become China's "window" to the West and the Free World's "watchtower" to counter Chinese Communism. It was also a major battleground of the unfinished civil war between the Communist and the Nationalist regimes. This intermingling of superpower rivalry with cross–Taiwan Strait conflicts made the colony one of the world's capitals of rumor-mongering, secret services, and covert propaganda. Hence, although peripheral to global geopolitics, the colony was nevertheless a central battlefield of Asia's cultural Cold War.

Hong Kong cinema was on the front line of the cultural Cold War. Particularly involved in the conflicts were exiles and émigrés from the mainland who continued to make films in what they regarded the language of Chinese nationhood, Mandarin. Their works and careers crisscrossed with the fierce competition among China, Taiwan, and the U.S. to win the hearts and minds of ethnic Chinese across the region that divided the film industry into a Manichean conflict between pro-Communist "patriotic" studios and "Free China" studios. The extant literature on the role of Hong Kong Cinema in the Cold War focuses mostly on the pro-Beijing side (e.g., Xu L. 2017). This chapter joins it with what I call "cinematic containment," the efforts of U.S. and Taiwan propaganda agents and "Free China" studios to produce films that were more than just entertaining and could draw audiences away from Communist influence. It also discusses in depth the cultural and political context of the popular song-and-dance film *Air Hostess* (*Kongzhong xiaojie*, 1959), especially how it got made and what messages lay beneath its highly entertaining surface, to illustrate the complex politics of cinematic containment in mid-twentieth-century Hong Kong.

From Shanghai to Hong Kong

Immediately after WWII, the British took advantage of China's weakness by retaking the city after losing it to Japan in 1941. Life was a misery under Japanese rule. However, in contrast to the mainland, where one war followed another, Hong Kong recovered in a remarkably short time. By 1948, the colony's trading business revived spectacularly, and as in prewar times, once again it became the world's gateway to the China market. The revived trade economy led to stability, which attracted a continuous exodus of refugees from the mainland, especially after the Communist victory in 1949, and the Nationalists fled in exile to Taiwan. The colony's population grew dramatically: from 600,000 in 1945 to 1.86 million in 1950 and over 2.8 million in 1956, and by 1960, it reached 3.128 million (Government of Hong Kong 1954, 27).

The majority of the refugees were peasants and poor laborers from neighboring Guangdong, but there were also some economic and cultural elites from Shanghai and its environs. Some of the Shanghai émigrés were old hands in the film business. A number of them moved to the British colony to take advantage of its financial stability to make movies in Mandarin for the mainland market. Some left-wing filmmakers and writers, who had fled the Nationalist reign of terror, endeavored to help rebuild the China Communist Party (CCP)'s cultural apparatus (that had been destroyed during the Japanese occupation) in the colony, which included several small film studios and film publications, to mobilize popular support for the Communist efforts.

Bearing the brunt of the Communist attacks was Yung Hwa (Yonghua), undoubtedly the largest film studio in the Chinese-speaking world, which was founded in 1947 by Li Zuyong, scion of a Shanghai business magnate closely affiliated with the Nationalist regime. Its debut *National Spirit* (*Guo hun,* 1948, d. Pu Wancang), which tells the story of a thirteenth-century loyalist refusing to surrender to the Mongol conquerors, was a lavish historical epic imbued with unprecedented production value. Chiang Kai-shek allegedly sent several copies of it to the frontline to boost his armies' morale. Widely popular, the film was blasted by leftists for allegorizing the Communist army as the alien Mongols.

The conflicts and vitriol were soon to take on new levels of politicization and ideological intensity after the CCP swept to power. As we shall see, with its large concentration of émigré filmmakers of divergent backgrounds and its state-of-the-art facilities, the studio became the first battlefield in the colony's cinematic Cold War.

Managing the Cold War City

The "loss of China" sent shock waves to Washington. Shortly after the founding of the People's Republic of China (PRC), Mao made his first overseas trip to visit Moscow, where he signed the Sino-Soviet Treaty of Friendship, Alliance, and Mutual Assistance, cementing China's formal entry to the Soviet Bloc. In June 1950, Kim Il-sung's forces pushed into South Korea. The Truman administration responded by ordering the U.S. Seventh Fleet to neutralize the Taiwan Strait, thus breathing new life into Chiang's rump regime. Stalled in his plan to take over Taiwan and with the advent of U.S. containment efforts, China intervened, in October, in the Korean conflict. The Cold War moved to Asia.

Less well known than these events is what happened across China's southern border. Hong Kong was in the grip of fear and uncertainty. Back in late 1949, the Communist forces could have seized the colony as they were sweeping through the South and taking Guangdong, but it did not happen. The consensus among scholars is that CCP leaders were likely worried about the possibility of provoking the U.S. military intervention at a time when it needed to concentrate on finishing off Chiang's remnant forces. As the Cold War rivalry heightened, this political expediency had the additional benefits of driving a wedge in the Anglo-American special relationship and shaping Beijing's policy of pragmatic accommodation that was to last until the 1980s. Indeed, the British colony benefited China in many important ways. For instance, under siege by the U.S.-led global blockade, it served as a "window" from which to gather information about Taiwan and Western capitalism, and a "ventilation shaft" through which to smuggle in Western-made strategic material and to obtain foreign currency through trade and remittance from overseas Chinese. "To make full use of Hong Kong," as Premier Zhou Enlai articulated it into a guiding principle, "in the interest of long-term planning." But they also allegedly warned that the colony could be tolerated only to the extent that it would not serve as a "bastion of anticommunism" that allowed the Nationalists, among others, to endanger New China's territorial security. However, it is far from clear when the policy was officially adopted and how many party members in Hong Kong learned about it and when (Jin 2005; Walton 2013, 332–6; Jiang 2012, v.1).

China's accommodation created a fundamental challenge to the colonial government. Just as Hong Kong was Beijing's "window" to the Western world, it was also what the CIA's Board of National Estimates officer Jack Smith called a "watchtower on China," thanks to its various connections with the mainland and the massive number of Chinese refugees who were an invaluable source of information about life on the mainland. It was at the same time "a crossroads" for ethnic Chinese from around the globe and, especially, a battlefield of the extended Chinese civil war where the Nationalists and Communists maintained huge intelligence and smuggling networks. They also vied for control and domination of trade unions, educational institutions, businesses, and the mass media. Several violent riots broke out as a result of this rivalry. All this happened even as Taiwan did not have official representatives in Hong Kong because the British government had granted de jure recognition of the PRC in January 1951. In addition to these political troubles, the colony's economy went downhill as a result of the trade embargo against China imposed in 1951 by the U.S. and the United Nations, which worsened long-standing problems of housing shortages, unemployment, poverty, racism, and social inequality. These mounting problems gave fuel to increasing anti-Americanism and anticolonialism, especially among the poor and socially vulnerable, sentiments ready to be exploited by local Communists or Nationalist activists. Social unrest was on the rise (Kennedy 2001; Zhou 2002, 49–153).

To bolster its claim for legitimacy amidst this complexity of superpower conflicts and maneuverings and to avoid provoking Beijing's intervention, the colonial authority tried to act, to use a familiar metaphor, like an umpire on the battlefield: claiming in the name of law to be neutral and impartial in dealing with all the Cold Warriors. As Governor Alexander Grantham, who ruled the colony from 1947 to 1957, told his readers: "One of the most important things for which the free world stands is freedom of expression and liberty of the press. We preferred to rely on the judicial process" (Grantham 1965, 148), In an effort to create such a legal framework for maintaining order and security, the government pushed through a series of laws and ordinances that included the Emergency Regulations Ordinance (re-enacted 1949), Societies Ordinance (1949), Sedition Ordinance (amended 1950), Deportation of Aliens Ordinance (1950), and Representation of Foreign Powers Ordinance (1949), which required all organizations (of more than ten people) affiliated with any foreign country (including Taiwan) to register as means to prevent covert foreign intervention. Throughout the Cold War period, the colonial administration came down hard on any "subversive" activities that it found threatening to its legitimacy, jailing or deporting "trouble-making" Nationalist and Communist activists alike, kept pro-Communist schools and trade unions of various political backgrounds under constant surveillance, and checked American espionage and, mostly coordinated with Nationalist agents, paramilitary activities against China. (Jiang 2012, 1: 25–119; Mark 2004, 15–8; Snow 2003, 312–31).

The Hong Kong government was vigilant against political advocacy of all kinds or anything that openly promoted ideological agendas for fear of compromising its claim of "neutrality." It would also not tolerate any challenge to the white race. Mass media, especially newspapers, magazines, and film, were subjected to constant and intense monitoring and suppression on political grounds (Kennedy 2001; Lilley 2004, 83–95; Rand 1952, 3–46). In cinema, which was popular with young and old, literate and illiterate, the government feared increasing Communist influence immediately after the regime change. Similarly, some film studios had difficulty in the early 1950s in getting film stock from Europe or Japan because the government feared they would resell it to Beijing, which was in dire need of film materials (Mccfadyen 1951). The draconian Film Censorship Regulations were promulgated in 1953 to uphold the racial and political prerogative of the colonial authority. Films of all national origins had to be sent to the Censors Board for screening permission. The Board forbade nudity, violence, and political and racial "bias," which notably involved "anything which is liable to provoke feelings of racial or national hostility, for example, anti-foreign slogans, misleading comparisons between different political systems" and "anything which incites any section of the community to attempt to overthrow by force the rule of law and order or the established government" (Ng 2008, 26). Although the pro-Beijing film community has to this day complained bitterly about the anti-Communist prejudices of film censorship, which, for one thing, did not allow images of Mao's face or the PRC flag to be on display, some Western observers had a different view of it. It was a "ticklish situation" for Hong Kong film censorship, as an American journalist commented:

> There are hundreds and thousands of Communists there and many a Western pictures get clipped if it stresses too strongly the more advantages [*sic*] of life according to the Capitalism and free enterprise system or smears Red nations. This is done to avoid possible trouble and picketing.
>
> ("Censorship" 1960–61, 8)

Indeed, no side could possibly have been in accord with the Censor Board's standards because its mission was precisely to uphold colonial authority and legitimacy by keeping in check the cinematic war among China, Taiwan, and the U.S. to win over Chinese audiences in the region.

Telling China's Stories to the World: "Patriotic" Cinema

The Communists were in a strong strategic position to win the cinematic war. With the founding of the PRC, which vowed to usher in a new era of national strength and sovereignty, many émigré filmmakers were swept by an enthusiasm for the new regime. Indeed, at least in the 1950s and early 1960s, members of the pro-Communist film community called themselves "patriotic" filmmakers, not "leftists," a term with negative connotations that became common after the Cultural Revolution–inspired 1967 riots. They identified with the Communists as the only legitimate government in building a new, modernized China. This sense of nationalism was certainly conjoined with a deepening concern for personal survival. Because the mainland market was the "lifeline" of émigré Mandarin cinema, it would be important to show allegiance to the new rulers. In the late 1940s, many film artists and technicians had joined underground Communist study groups, and in mid-1951, many of them formed a delegation to visit and entertain troops in Guangzhou (Chu 2001, 148–50; Wang 2006, 111–7).

Some filmmakers established connections and found work in China shortly after the trip, but others were advised to stay behind to help galvanize overseas Chinese support for the Revolution. One of the chief Communist aims was to take over Yung Hwa. At the time, there was fierce competition between the Nationalists and the Communists (for allegiance and control of the colony's key Guomindang (GMD) organizations such as the Bank of China and China Civic Aviation Corporation. Although never owned by the Nationalists, Yung Hwa was a prime target because of its top-of-the-line production facilities and its internal problems. It had been in financial trouble since the Communists swept to power, which brought down Li's family business empire, and he was unable to pay salaries, surviving principally on loans from its Southeast Asian distributor, the Cathay Organization (more later). Leftist employees tried to take advantage of the situation to produce films with pro-Communist messages. Li refused to give ground. The conflicts led to a strike in late 1951. It coincided with the rising tide of labor activism, especially from the pro-Beijing trade unions, which saw the Communist triumph as a call for anti-imperialist, anticolonial struggle. The colonial authority was adamant in suppressing the strikes in an effort to asset its legitimacy. It intervened in the Yung Hwa strikes, deporting 12 accused ringleaders, all key members of the leftist film circle, to the PRC.

Yung Hwa came out a loser too. Although Li won praise from pro–Free World press as a hero of "anti-Communist loyalty" and received a loan from the Chiang regime to resume production, the Colonial authority took back the studio's crown land. Burdened with added relocation costs, Yung Hwa folded in 1956, and ownership of its studio facilities passed to its major creditor, the Cathay Organization, which went on to reorganize it into Motion Pictures and General Investment (MP&GI). In retrospect, the fight for control of Li's studio started the cinematic Cold War in Hong Kong.

One reason the colonial government came down hard on the Yung Hwa strike was that the Communists had a strategic position in the film industry, thanks to the strong apparatus it had created before 1949. Despite the failed coup, pro-Beijing filmmakers made headway in building an interlocking network of production and distribution facilities in 1950–53 that aimed to take advantage of the "window" the colony afforded to bring the story of New China to overseas Chinese audiences in the region. They included, most prominently, Great Wall (Changcheng) Movie Enterprise and Phoenix (Fenghuang) Film Corporation, both focused on Mandarin film, Cantonese studio Sun Luan (Xinlian or United Film Corporation), and Southern (Nanfang) Film Corp., a covert PRC-owned company that distributed China-made films to the world and brought pictures from Hong Kong to the mainland. All camouflaging as private enterprises with overseas Chinese investment to neutralize their political stance, the pro-Beijing studios were what historians call a state-private network.

Some untapped sources regarding Great Wall bring to light the workings of the so-called "Chang-Feng-Xin" group. The prehistory of Great Wall was fraught with controversy, but suffice for us to start with the takeover of the studio in 1950 by Yuan Yangan, a former Shanghai lawyer and relative of Fei Yimin, publisher of Hong Kong's Communist organ *Dagong bao*. Because the studio was deeply in the red, Yuan brought in Lu Jiankang, a shipping tycoon with Beijing connections, and shifted the business strategy to make films for the mainland market. He let a few superstars go, and in their place recruited new talent from among young émigrés. Carefully groomed, three of them, Moon Hsia (Xia Mang), Fu Qi, and Shi Hui, steadily rose to the top of the pro-Communist screen, and their star power helped push Great Wall products to market. According to a U.S. document, Great Wall got a HK$50,000 loan in 1957 from a Communist bank for each of the films it made, "against the profit from the mainland screening" (Dawson 1953). Another 1954 source, however, revealed that the studio received preproduction fees every year for four pictures to sell to China, ranging from HK$200,000 (A-class) to HK$120,000 (C-class) (Hsu 1954). Although they cite different figures, both claims could be true: either the amounts and forms of the subsidies changed over time (given Beijing's periodic political turmoil) or, more likely, the studio needed both to survive, because the average cost of a black-and-white Mandarin film in the 1950s was around HK$200,000. It was not clear, however, whether the subsidy agreement included sales to the Southeast Asian markets, which, along with Hong Kong, were the targeted markets for all pro-Communist companies, or whether Great Wall could keep at least part of the box-office receipts from overseas markets. Indeed, boasting that it covered "all overseas Chinese areas," the studio aimed to reach ethnic Chinese audiences in practically all major Southeast Asian countries.

Although the subsidies were small, they were a stable source of revenue. Stability was of paramount importance to the Mandarin filmmaking industry in the 1950s, a period characterized by a horrendous business environment thanks to the geopolitical turmoil, economic uncertainty, and volatile market conditions in the region. "Patriotic" studios managed to keep their overhead costs low, which helped keep them afloat. If we can trust recent Chinese sources, their staff had the lowest pay in the industry; what inspired them appeared to be a mix of idealism and a sense of community. Equally important was the sense of community the studio administration carefully orchestrated to emphasize a collective life, both morally and politically superior to the decadent and egotistic lifestyle of the majority of Hong Kong filmmakers. Instead of partying and hobnobbing with the riches, for example, they organized "wholesome, collective" activities such as picnics, hiking, basketball games, and various trips to China. Most important for the rank-and-file workers was the South China Film Industry Workers Union, which, after 1952, devoted principally to providing support and welfare for the poor and destitute among its members ("Extract" 1960). Again, although this financial assistance was small, it meant a lot to those on the lower rung of the film industry. In fact, American and Taiwan intelligence agents always blamed the Union as the prime reason for the frequent defection of pro-Nationalist studio employees to pro-Communist studios. All these arrangements contributed to making the "patriotic" studios far less dependent than other private studios on box-office performance.

The "patriotic" studios, like other local Communist media organizations, reported through the CCP Hong Kong and Macao Work Committee to the State Council Foreign Affairs Staff Office in Beijing. Probably in coordination with the Ministries of Culture and Propaganda, Liao Chengzhi, Premier Zhou Enlai's lieutenant responsible for overseas Chinese and united front affairs, was charged with supervising the Hong Kong Communist media work. According to various sources, despite all the ideological twists and turns on the mainland up throughout the first decade of Mao's rule, Liao emphasized a moderate policy that emphasized telling New China's stories to the 12 million overseas Chinese, especially in Southeast Asia, in order to sway them against American imperialism and the "reactionary" Chiang regime. Liao counseled visiting Hong Kong filmmakers to, unlike their Socialist counterparts on the mainland, make "patriotic films" that emphasized China's beauty and rich history, which, at the same time, avoided provoking the censors in the region and increased box-office receipts (Liao 1990, 215–9, 275–9, 323–5).

Indeed, except for a brief period following the Communist victory, most of the films Great Wall or Phoenix produced became what American cultural warfare officers sarcastically called "pinkies" ("Survey" 1956). In the name of making "healthy, uplifting entertainment," emphasis was increasingly put on star appeal and popular genres, including light comedy, social satire, and opera film. Shot mostly in black and white, with carefully drawn characters and a humanistic touch, the films gently poked fun at the hypocrisies of capitalist society or the intricacies of human relationships, or brought to the screen an ancient China, drawn from folk culture, that offered justice to the weak and the disadvantaged. Throughout the 1950s, pro-Beijing cinema enjoyed a strong fan base in the region, especially among well-educated audiences (Mandarin-speaking or not).

This trend coincided with the strategy of distributor Southern Motion Picture Corporation to bring China-made opera films to the overseas market; even if they passed the censors, Communist propaganda movies drew few spectators to the theater. After many missteps and flops, in 1954, Southern launched Sang Hu's Shanghai-produced *The Butterflies* (*Liang Shanbo yu Zhu Yingtai*), a lavishly made, culturally rich, romantically themed Shaoxing opera film shot in color. It was an instant sensation, shattering all box-office records in Hong Kong. It then moved to Singapore, Malaya, as well as the Philippines and Thailand, which otherwise prohibited China-made movies, again with big success. The great success of *The Butterflies* "opened the Communist eyes to a new approach," as a *Wall Street Journal* critic put it, and demonstrated the importance of Hong Kong as "Asian film buyers watched [its] box office returns before ordering them." He went on to warn his readers: "Red China's soft-peddling of propaganda" would make their influences far and wide among overseas Chinese in the region (Searls 1957). Indeed, two blockbuster films followed suit: Shi Hui's Huangmei opera film *Marriage of a Heavenly Princess* (*Tian xian pei*) in 1956, and Xu Tao's Cantonese opera film *Searching a School* (*Sou shuyuan*) in 1957. They brought the opera film sensation in Chinese communities across the region to a "climax" (Xu D. 2005, 35–9; Xu L. 2017). This "unprecedented movie sensation" and the popularity of "patriotic" films, again, raised deep concern from their enemies. All this was "a new Chinese Communist offensive on the propaganda-cinematic front," wrote two Hong Kong field officers of the Asia Foundation (TAF), a CIA-front cultural warfare group (more details later), to their headquarters. They went on to compare the sensational popularity of opera film to the low turnouts both to a performance by U.S. State Department-sponsored singer Marian Anderson and to Free Chinese cinema. Their message was all too clear: how can we contain the Communist cinematic influence in Asia? To bring home the sense of urgency of the memorandum, the headquarters forwarded it to all field officers working in Southeast Asia as well as to Taiwan ("An Intra-Office Memo" 1957). And it is to the cinematic containment that we now turn.

Taiwan, the United States, and Cinematic Containment

After fleeing to Taiwan, the Nationalist regime legitimatized itself as the sole representative of China by claiming to be the custodian of Chinese civilization and demonizing the CCP as "traitors" selling out to the Soviets. It launched a series of policy changes and political and military reforms with the aim of strengthening its authoritarian rule with the goal of "fighting back to the mainland." In its effort to appeal to overseas Chinese, whose support was deemed instrumental in building a global anti-Communist crusade under Nationalist leadership, Chiang Kai-shek's son, Chiang Ching-kuo, in charge of national intelligence, placed strong emphasis on psychological warfare, beyond the overt, "black" propaganda tools, such as radio broadcasts, loudspeaker broadcasts from the offshore islands, or air dropping of leaflets. He started new initiatives to fashion cinema into a vehicle of political mobilization (Liu 1985, 10–36; Rawnsley 2000).

The Taiwan film industry, however, was small and underdeveloped in both technology and Mandarin-speaking artists. Hong Kong had a large concentration of refugee film workers and an established entertainment infrastructure, which made it a natural site for the Nationalists to launch their propaganda warfare. Because the Communists had the upper hand in the cinematic warfare, the main strategy was to contain its increasing influence in the region. The Nationalists initiated secret efforts to enlist support of the leaders of the émigré film community in the propaganda war. The timing was right: after the PRC closed its film market, as mentioned earlier, the few studios that did not turn left, such as Great Wall, were in a state of turmoil. Demand for Mandarin films in Southeast Asia—especially Vietnam, Indonesia, and the Philippines—had been in decline since 1952–53 because of political violence, currency fluctuation, or increased censorship in the context of decolonization and superpower rivalries. Additionally, production costs greatly increased, thanks to the high salaries of big stars who were key to sales in overseas markets ("Survey" 1956). Struggling to stay afloat without the institutional support enjoyed by "patriotic" studios, and not sure what the future held, the more enterprising studio heads began to turn their attention to Taiwan, while others yearned nostalgically to return to the mainland.

In 1953, a few anti-Communist studio chiefs took a goodwill tour of Taiwan; they returned to Hong Kong a week later allegedly to organize another delegation to celebrate the presidential inauguration of Chiang Kai-shek. Thus started Taiwan's involvement in Hong Kong's cinematic Cold War. In May 1954, as the Nationalists were trying to sign a mutual defense treaty with Washington, a well-publicized delegation of 64 top Chinese-language cinema celebrities from Hong Kong visited the island, and their ten-day visit included meeting with Chiang and entertaining the troops on the offshore islands of Matsu and Quemoy. The stars drew enormous crowds everywhere they went on the entertainment-deprived island, and their various activities became a media sensation in Chinese diaspora communities across the world. The purpose of the visit was made all too clear by superstar Li Lihua when she told the solders in Quemoy: "We come with our warm hearts to link with yours as one," and (pointing a rifle across to the mainland) "Let's fight back to our homeland!" (Gong 1954; Yi 1954). Chiang Kai-shek was reportedly deeply impressed by the delegation's success and by the subsequent meetings with some of its key members about the cinematic war with the Communists. As he wrote in his diary on June 16, 1954, motion pictures were "indeed an important instrument of propaganda" and concurred with his son's plan to "quickly put into effect" political warfare (Chiang, n.d.).

According to Taiwan historian Huang Ren (2009, 72–5), the 1953 and 1954 delegations were masterminded by Chiang Ching-kuo, whose propaganda initiatives dispatched agents and gave loans, tax breaks, and various kinds of financial assistance to struggling independent producers that vowed to support "Free China." In 1957, after several years of squabbling with the colonial government, which was aware of its political intent, the quasi-Nationalist Hong Kong and Kowloon Free Filmmakers General Association (Gangjiu dianying xiju shiye ziyou zonghui, hereafter HKFFGA) was formed to covertly coordinate what it called "stem the Communist Bandits Cold War offense," which formally buttressed the binary division in Hong Kong film culture that lasted at least until the 1970s: "free" cinema versus "patriotic" cinema, freedom versus Communism. Among its major activities was scrutinizing all movies destined for the Taiwan market for their ideological content as well as the political backgrounds of their casts and crew members. It also kept surveillance on the film industry to inform Taiwan about its developments—under the cover of studio networks, Nationalist intelligence and propaganda agents came to the colony to infiltrate and spy on the refugee filmmakers. Also important was its annual competition with the pro-Communist film community over National Day commemorations: October 1 (PRC) and October 10 (Taiwan). The competition in numbers of participants marching and prominence of flags displayed became a ritual in buttressing the Manichean boundaries in the cinematic Cold War ("Xianggang" 1959; Huang 2009, 75–7).

A key indicator of political victory was getting filmmakers to cross borders, so to speak; studios on the two sides launched raids against each to try to encourage defections. Since 1953, with support from the U.S. cultural warfare agents, the Nationalists in particular engineered a series of high-profile defection campaigns to undercut the Communist influence. The biggest catch of all was the leading lady Li Lihua, who, in many ways, embodied the struggle of refugee film artists to survive the vagaries of Cold War politics. She broke into the film world in Japanese-ruled Shanghai. After the war, with a giant shadow of "traitor" looming over her career and recently divorced, she fled to Hong Kong with her mother and daughter. She worked for some left-wing studios to make ends meet and quickly rose to the top of Hong Kong's film world. She also began to get involved in Communist-sponsored activities.

However, she was not welcomed back to postrevolutionary Shanghai, and her contract with the reorganized Great Wall expired. This made her a prime target for the Nationalist recruitment efforts. As far as we can reconstruct, Li signed up with the pro-Taiwan Shaw studio in 1953 and, according to her close friend Chia LeeNi, supposedly received the promise of an American green card so she "could leave the political turmoil behind" (Chia 2016). This marked her double-border crossing that was to become prevalent later in Hong Kong's cinematic containments: switching political allegiance and working in collaboration with overseas film studios friendly with Taiwan as a way to show unity with the Free World.

In what would become a Nationalist political ritual in the cinematic Cold War, Li Lihua published what was in effect a penitence in *World Today,* a "grey propaganda" weapon camouflaged as a glossy enrichment magazine launched by the United States Information Service (USIS) that reached a large audience in the region. At the heart of it was a binary Cold War narrative highlighting her regret for involvement in Communist filmmaking and her new life: to "make the best pictures for the benefits of the audiences among overseas Chinese and in Free China" (Li 1954; Chang 2014). Li's defection sparked a round of Nationalist media frenzy, which declared 1953 as the "year of Red fading" (*tui hong nian*) that marked the beginning of the "decline of Communist influences" in the battle for the hearts and minds of the overseas Chinese. It was no surprise that with her prominent role in the well-orchestrated cinematic containment efforts, Li's career throughout the 1950s was beset by rumors of all kinds and of political controversies. She allegedly received physical threats, for example, and was frequently booed and subjected to all sorts of verbal abuse by Beijing sympathizers for her "political betrayal" on her tours on behalf of Free China to the U.S. and to Southeast Asia. Similarly, she was received by pro-Taiwan with suspicion and occasional contempt for her lingering loyalty to the Communists (Ma 1954; Shao 1954).

The Nationalist containment strategy against pro-Communist cinema went in tandem with the American anti-Communist crusade in Asia. As the principal listening post for China and a regional propaganda hub, the colony's U.S. Consulate General was "one of the very largest American posts in the world at that time, larger than most embassies," and central to the contest for ideological supremacy was USIS, which used it as a production and distribution base for Chinese-language propaganda warfare in the region (Dizard 1961; Mark 2004: 193–202; Schmidt 1988). As Mao's revolutionary stature rose steadily in the Third World from the Korean War onward, Washington was obsessed with combating the domino effect of Communism in resource-rich, politically volatile Southeast Asia. And USIS (along with the CIA) saw overseas Chinese as one of its primary targets of covert Cold War mobilization, and thereby collaborated with the Nationalist agencies in trying to win their loyalty for Chiang (Lilley 2004, 66–152; Osgood 2006, 210–6). As the USIS "Country Plan" of June 1953 revealed, its chief goals were to contain Communist influence among Hong Kong's refugees and ethnic Chinese across Southeast Asia. And this strategic emphasis on Chinese outside the mainland in part shaped U.S. policymakers' perception of "China": the plan defined China not in terms of geography but of culture, especially of the "common language" that was Mandarin. This perception of a culturally defined "Chinese" national community went hand in hand with the claim of the rival regimes across the Taiwan Strait of citizenship for ethnic Chinese in foreign lands and implementing a hegemonic language of Chineseness as a way to impose national unity and cultural cohesion. To speak Mandarin was to speak "Chinese." It was thus no surprise that Mandarin, not Cantonese or other regional dialects, became the American (and Nationalist) official language in the contest with the Communists for Chinese audiences (Harrington 1953; Lombardo 2000). Washington changed its position regarding overseas Chinese in relation to citizenship, language, and ethnic origins in the 1950s, and yet, up until 1960, for example, at a National Security Council meeting about whether the U.S. should send military forces in the event of Communist-inspired civil disturbances in the colony, CIA Chief Allen Dulles described the colony as "a key base for information programs with respect to Communist China and the Far East in general. Hong Kong was particularly useful as a listening post and as a publishing center for anti-communist [propaganda]" ("Memorandum of Discussion" 1960, 2). Motion pictures constituted a major instrument of propaganda. As USIS Information Officer Richard McCartney, who had close ties to the "white Chinese" cultural circle, particularly with literary and film personalities, remembered: "We did a fair amount of work supporting filmmakers who were producing anti-communist pictures in Hong Kong and Chinese- language pictures in Southeast Asia. So we were very much involved in the Chinese motion picture industry" (O'Brien 1988). Indeed, endeavoring to promote the American Way and "reduce the circulation of Communist publications and motion pictures," as the Country Plan instructed, USIS was involved notably in the Nationalist celebrity defection campaigns, for example, and it provided marketing support to pro-Taiwan studios; to highlight Free World unity, it organized tours of Hollywood celebrities (e.g., Clark Gable, Frank Sinatra, and Alfred Hitchcock) to the region and of Hong Kong stars to the U.S., Japan, and Southeast Asia ("Dongnanya" 1956). Surely, national interests were also at stake in this border-crossing flow of people and ideas: to maintain and extend Hollywood domination on Asian screens, the mid-twentieth century witnessed huge efforts to globalize American movie business, and some critics raised the specter (exaggeratedly) over the business threats of mainland-made opera films.

Along with USIS, the Asia Foundation (TAF) was also deeply involved in the cultural warfare in Hong Kong. Part of what author Frances Saunders (2000) provocatively calls the "CIA's designated Cold War venture capitalists" (108), TAF was originally called the Committee for a Free Asia along the same lines as the Committee for a Free Europe, aiming to penetrate the "Bamboo Curtain" through propaganda without "bearing [a] US label." ("Committee for a Free Asia" 1951). In Hong Kong, its major propaganda hub, one of TAF's major goals was the use of moving images to contain Communist influence in overseas Chinese communities. TAF responded to what it considered the "danger" of "Communists trying to squeeze out all non-Communist pictures in Hong Kong," by, in the pungent words of officer Charles Tanner: "[helping Hong Kong studios] make their films more entertaining thereby bigger at the box office, and…entertaining enough and big enough in the theater to drive out the Commie products" ("Mr. Guard" 1953). It collaborated with the USIS in bringing American technical and managerial consultants to Hong Kong and facilitated the organization of the Asia Film Festival, with the aim of creating an "inter-connected" Free Asian film industries both technologically modern and modeled along the lines of Hollywood system. It also secretly funded the high-profile Asia Pictures studio (along with its publishing enterprise, Asia Press), which, between 1953 and 1960, produced a few technically strong refugee-focused dramas, such as Pu Wancang's *Long Lane* (*Chang xiang*, 1956) and the now forgotten anti-Communist thriller *The 11th Commandment* (1960) directed by Zhang Cengze.

Air Hostess: Political Warfare as Popular Entertainment

Despite the official show of appreciation and promise of support, Mandarin-language film studios' hopes of gaining full access to the Taiwan market were frustrated by draconian censorship, fluctuating exchange rates, tariffs on imported film equipment, a confusing and predatory distribution network, exorbitant entertainment taxes, and the market domination of Japanese, American, and Taiwanese-language movies on the island. They also complained about the preferential treatment of the big companies—Shaw Brothers and MP&GI—which enjoyed all kinds of privileges, such as lower taxes, while also making distribution and exhibition deals with the pro-Communist studios. At the same time, critics and propaganda officials in Taiwan blasted Hong Kong films for their lack of commitment against Communism, as expressed notably in their failure to set films in Taiwan or celebrate Nationalist achievements; instead, they were filmed in Japan or even in Thailand. So why give them subsidies and special privileges, these critics asked? (e.g., Yan 1956; "Film Producer" 1956).

This controversy prompted a newspaper editor to remind the Nationalist leadership of the significant role of Hong Kong filmmakers in the anti-Communist crusade. He urged the Nationalist leadership to provide more financial and organizational support to Hong Kong's émigré cinema because of its significant role in the anti-Communist cause:

> In our anti-Communist war, military warfare happens only intermittently, but political warfare is fought with ferocity almost every single day. And the battlefront of political warfare is over- seas, in the overseas Chinese areas. In the past few years Taiwan has always enjoyed a clear edge [over the Communists] in the political warfare, especially successful in this was the Hong Kong cinema ... Although most of the films that [promoted "Free China"] were not produced in Taiwan, but were in Hong Kong, all who were involved in this endeavor were Free filmmakers all the same. They touched the hearts of overseas Chinese around the world, who were [as a result] yearning for Freedom.
>
> (Chen 1959)

Like the U.S. propaganda agents just cited, he went on to point out the hostile environment in Hong Kong—the dominance of pro-Communist cinema in the region and the colonial film censorship; hence, the battle for supremacy became fiercer than ever. And he identified MP&GI in particular, the largest and best-equipped film studio at the time, as making the greatest contribution to the containment war.

Founded in 1956 through the takeover of Yung Hwa's studio facilities, MP&GI was the production subsidiary of Cathay Organization, a Singapore-based business conglomerate composed of mining, plantations, hotels, real estate, and more. By 1959, Cathay also controlled a chain of around 260 theaters, stretching from Singapore and Malaya to Sarawak, Borneo, and Thailand. At the helm of the empire after World War II was the Cambridge-educated Dato Loke Wan Tho, whose enormous wealth, cosmopolitan lifestyle, elegant appearance, and artistic accomplishments made him something of a celebrity, with extensive networks of friends in business and cultural circles around the globe. His status and economic power allowed him to build strong ties with, particularly, the Singapore and Malayan governments, for whom his well-equipped Malay outfits—Cathay Film Services and Cathay-Keris Film Studio—regularly produced publicity shorts with an anti-Communist slant. He was also on friendly terms with officials of the British empire in the region.

With this background, it is not surprising that newly available research material shows that MP&GI had close ties with the U.S.-Nationalist propaganda campaigns. A global business tycoon passionate about gentlemanly pursuits, Loke was averse to extremism and, further, he apparently identified with the Nationalist regime in exile, which claimed to be the guardian of Chinese civilization and the sole representative of the Chinese people across the Free World. In a widely publicized press conference in Hong Kong, for instance, he was reportedly upset when a pro-Communist reporter challenged his claim of proudly "being a Chinese" by blasting his Western education, Westernized dress, and failure to speak more than a few basic words of Chinese. The tycoon regretted his poor Chinese, but he stressed that this made him "no less a Chinese, and he loved China" and that his aspiration was to help modernize Chinese cinema. The "China" he referred to, of course, was the cultural China represented by Taiwan ("Lu" 1959).

The production strategy of MP&GI films also had to do with the top staffers Loke hired to run his studio's production business. They were mostly "white Chinese" artists and intellectuals, like Loke himself, with strong backgrounds in Western cultures. The two best examples were producer-translator Stephen Soong (Song Qi) and writer-director Evan Yang (Yi Wen), both of whom came from prominent Shanghai literati families and were much-revered figures in the émigré cultural scene. Soong was a liberal- minded English literature scholar before fleeing the Communist takeover; to survive, he took a translation job at USIS under Richard McCarthy. He then got hired to take charge of MP&GI's production. He was also close to the Asia Foundation, which had considered supporting the publication of his translation magazine.

Evan Yang was an urbane, romantic literary man who graduated from Shanghai's American-run St John's University. Yang was a rising star in Shanghai's literary scene before he escaped with his young family to the colony after the Communist takeover. To feed his family, he worked for a Nationalist-owned newspaper, while pursuing his creative dream of writing scripts for studios, including Great Wall. This showed his personal connections across the political divide, not unusual given the colony's small refugee cultural circle, and also the political fluidity of the film industry before 1953–54. Indeed, increasingly known for his knack for Hollywood narrative techniques, after his return from the 1954 celebrity delegation to Taiwan, he started working full-time for a small pro-Nationalist studio, the Xinhua. In 1956, he joined MP&GI and quickly became one of its most productive leading directors, best known to audiences for his polished, sensitive portrayals of romantic entanglements and family relationships.

The corporate culture of MP&GI meshed with Cold War cultural politics. Between 1957 and 1960, a period widely recognized as the heyday of its influence in the region, the studio released a string of sleekly made comedies and urban romances, mostly filled with North American pop music and dance numbers such as jazz, cha-cha, and mambo, and apparently targeting the émigré community: Tang Huang's sensitively drawn refugee family drama *Her Tender Heart* (*Yunü siqing*, 1959), Evan Yang's *Mambo Girl* (*Manbo nülang*, 1957), and Wang Tianlin's noir-inspired *Wild, Wild Rose* (*Ye meigui zhi lian*, 1960). Along with obvious melodramatic elements and atmospheric settings reminiscent of 1940s Shanghai filmmaking, the indelible Hollywood influences in plot structure, generic conventions, lighting, and editing styles in most MP&GI products exhibited a strong ethos of American middle-class values and aspirations and a capitalist consumerist lifestyle.

Recent studies reveal that MP&GI executives and directors took frequent trips to Taiwan to meet with film and propaganda officials about production plans, talent recruitment strategies, and, especially, better access to the Taiwan market. One major question repeatedly raised in these meetings was the long-standing need to project the scenic beauty of the "treasure island" (*bao dao*, a.k.a. Taiwan) and the Nationalist government's economic achievements onto the screen, even if MP&GI could not openly promote anti-Communism because of censorship back in Hong Kong (Huang 2009, 73–6). The studio took up the challenge in 1959 and launched Evan Yang's *Air Hostess*, which was produced by Stephen Soong and starred the great singer-dancer Grace Chang (Ge Lan), a member of the 1954 celebrity visit to Taiwan who had migrated to Hong Kong with her Nationalist official parents. Long in the making and massively publicized across the region, *Air Hostess* was a big budget, Eastman-color film that involved varied location shootings in Hong Kong, Taiwan, Thailand, and Singapore. These high-cost, high-tech, star-studded transnational production strategies made the film one of the most significant Hong Kong Cold War movies. Indeed, the strategies clearly served to highlight two of its main themes: what it means to be modern and how to become modern in a rapidly changing Asia. This modernity is best represented by the emergent Asian airline business, which functions as both an incubator of a new mobile and professional lifestyle for both men and women and an embodiment of a new transnational capitalist corporate culture in Free Asia.

Air Hostess is a musical that tells the story of the search of a young woman, Lin Keping (Grace Chang), for a meaningful career that can give her freedom and independence and of her evolving romance with pilot Lei Daying (Roy Chiao). The film opens with a masquerade ball scene in which Keping sings of her dreams in "Flying to the Sky" (Wo yao fei shang qing tian) to an admiring crowd. She yearns for independence, a life of glamour, and, above all, the thrills and freedom of jet-setting around the globe. When the camera cuts to her home, we see Keping explain to her mother that she couldn't fulfill her wish and marry a wealthy but boring man whose only desire would be to keep her in the role of a traditional housewife. "I don't want to be a bird in a gilded cage," she proclaims. Rather, she wants to be a modern, professional woman, to pursue her dream of becoming an air hostess.

In mid-twentieth century, few people in Hong Kong traveled outside of the city and even fewer traveled by plane. Because it was a new, novel profession, the choice of flight attendant as a subject of the film captured the audience's imagination. In fact, as abundantly demonstrated in other films of the day (e.g., Wang Tianlin's *The Greatest Civil War on Earth* [*Nan bei he*, 1961]), the smart-looking air hostess invariably conjured up in the public imagination the lure of modernity in contrast with the banality of traditional life. Further, in *Air Hostess*, such modernity was associated with a blatantly American lifestyle. After Keping passes the interview testing her skills in English, French, and Mandarin, the film shifts to a series of long sequences in which she has to go through several drills and training sessions with the other applicants. Dressed in Western-style tight-fitting uniforms, they learn how to move, walk, and say "coffee or tea" in ways comparable to what one would see on the Hollywood screen. They were Americanized objects of fantasy displayed for the voyeuristic pleasure of the audience.

Focusing on flight attendants also allowed the loosely linked narrative to develop in various urban locations in East and Southeast Asia. As an MP&GI advertisement put it:

> The airline business marks the progress of human civilization... Working up in the sky, serving the people, the air hostess is a new profession, a most modern profession... They help shorten the distances among people and help facilitate movement among nations.
> (*Guoji dianying* [International Screen], June 1957, 27)

In fact, the film is mostly not set inside airplanes; instead, it follows Keping and other hostesses as they cross borders and tour big Asian cities, inviting the audience to view Asia as a modern, flourishing region of interconnected urban centers of capitalist growth and cultural richness. The film showcases, for instance, the affluence and vernacular modernity of Singapore through montages of the Raffles' Landing Site and Cathay-owned movie palaces, as well as the majestic beauty of Bangkok's Buddhist temples. Nowhere in the film, however, could audiences find the poverty and rampant injustice and racial strife that sparked the escalating anti-colonial and revolutionary insurgency in the areas. In the film's attention to the movement of the hostesses across borders, pro-U.S. nations are linked together into an anti-Communist bloc of an integrated and flourishing Free Asia.

At the heart of this narrative of Free Asia modernity is a long scene celebrating the capitalist prosperity and natural beauty of Nationalist-ruled Taiwan: a postcard-like mise-en-scène of the luxurious Grand Hotel, the President's Office, Taipei's orderly traffic, and several spectacular tourist attractions. The camera follows Keping as she tours the Grand

Hotel and moves to a medium close-up of her singing at a reception in the lobby to a crowd of her colleagues. She sings a Westernized folk tune, "Song of Taiwan" (Taiwan xiaodiao), with lyrics written by the director, to express her love and pride for the "treasure island." The song includes these lines:

> I love my fellow Taiwan compatriots
> All the harbors are so strategic
> The most forward outpost in the Pacific Ocean
> Taiwan is called a Treasure Island
> Laughter and happiness everywhere in the countryside
> Every family is well fed
> What makes us so proud is that People stick together like glue
> We are all of the same mind

Pro-Communist critics were quick to point out that the film was not only boring and lacking drama but also unabashedly promoted the Chiang regime in Taiwan and extolled its U.S.-supported capitalist industrial modernity and agricultural reforms. And, in particular, the lines "Laughter and happiness everywhere in the countryside. Every family is well fed" were clearly meant to bring to audiences' attention the political turmoil, massive poverty, and starvation in the mainland as a result of Mao's disastrous Great Leap Forward, information about which was widely publicized in the region's press and contributed to the Cold War anti-Communist propaganda (Gao 1959). Pro-Nationalist critics, not surprisingly, were uniformly enthusiastic about *Air Hostess*. For example, He Guan (better known later as film director Chang Chieh) praised the film for its polished camera work and awesome images of Free China, but he also pointed out a contradictory characterization of Keping, which reveals something about the Cold War ideology of *Air Hostess*. On the one hand, she is portrayed as a "modern woman" who pursues freedom and independence and refuses to obey her mother's wishes for her to become a traditional housewife; on the other hand, she comes to accept, although with childish tantrums, all the seemingly unreasonable rules and the rigid masculine culture of the airline, including suppressing individuality for the sake of "the customer is always right." Further, she falls in love with the macho pilot Lei Daying, a taciturn company man, a male chauvinist who is a workaholic, apparently oblivious to her feelings and desires (He 1959).

Indeed, Keping seems, on the surface, crafted in the mold of the "new woman" (*xin nüxing*) in Shanghai cinema since the 1930s: a young, educated woman fighting vainly (more often than not they fail in melodramatic fashion) against patriarchal injustice in the quest for independence. Now, in the Cold War context, will Keping gain independence as she "flies up to the sky" with her dream job and falls in love with the pilot, whose name, Daying, or Big Eagle, clearly alludes to the American way? Indeed, I would argue that in *Air Hostess* the airline as a transnational capitalist enterprise expresses an American Fordist-Taylorist value system, which demands total dedication and emotional identification of workers to the mass production regime, with its hierarchy, rationality, efficiency, and discipline for the sake of maximum profit. According to its proponents, if the system was harsh and impersonal, it was only because of its need to create a disciplined, efficient workforce dedicated to serving the corporate mission; in fact, it was a fair, mostly scientific system of organization that rewarded the most hardworking and dedicated of its workers. Daying represents precisely the Fordist-Taylorist capitalist values of efficiency and discipline.

As *Air Hostess* develops, we see Keping become so frustrated with her job that she thinks of quitting. But the matriarchal airline manager (Tang Zhen) advises her: the company is a family to all its employees, and in spite of its stringent demands, it cares deeply for their well-being, especially her. However, after another quarrel about her work, Keping becomes even angrier and more frustrated when one of her flights is canceled because of bad weather and she misses her mother's birthday dinner. She decides to quit. Everything changes in the next sequence, however, when the experienced Daying discovers a transnational smuggling scheme masterminded by one of his passengers and, in the manner of a white knight, dramatically rescues her from being caught up in it.

Again, Keping changes her mind about quitting. Standing tall in his crisp pilot uniform outside a majestic Bangkok temple, Daying apologizes to Keping for his rudeness and insensitivity to her feelings, explaining that when he is at work he feels as if he is "part of a machine." The camera pans slowly to a medium close-up of Keping, smiling appreciatively: "I know that you are only devoted to your work… I'd do the same if I were you." This time, Keping appreciates even more how much she has to learn and that, like Daying, she needs dedicate herself to her professional duty. She stays on—the manager hands back her resignation letter with a nod of understanding—and their romance blossoms. Modern life, *Air Hostess* seems to suggest, entails not just glamour, independence, and novelty, but more importantly the hard work, discipline, respect for rule and order, and professionalism required for the rapid development of a modern and global capitalist economy.

Air Hostess concludes with two airline employees' American-style wedding ceremony of Keping's colleagues inside the cabin. Hosted by the manager, the passengers relish the merriment of the ceremony made possible by the new technology and the company's benevolence. This narrative structure, upon closer examination, reveals a deep analogy to a key theme of the Cold War American containment ideology. In response to the Soviet propaganda that portrayed American capitalism as inhuman, unjust, racist, and imperialistic, the Eisenhower administration launched a global propaganda campaign to advertise its economic system as a "people's capitalism." As the president's Advertising Council pamphlet "People's Capitalism in the USA" proudly proclaimed: "American capitalism at Mid-Twentieth Century is not the capitalism of colonialism, it is not the capitalism of Karl Marx, it is not even our own capitalism of 50 years ago. It is, instead, a capitalism so widely invested in by so many people, with the benefits in goods and wages shared in by so many people, that it is truly People's Capitalism." The USIS magazine *Today's World*, which claimed its readership among MP&GI executives and actors, and carried ads for its products, had published many versions of this idea of "Renmin ziben zhuyi." Barely contained in this loosely linked narrative of urban romance and air travel is, thus, a celebration of the Cold War ideologies of "people's capitalism" and "Free China"; work ethic and the American capitalist corporate system, private property and economic freedom, not class struggle and Maoist revolution, would increase productivity and lead to a higher standard of living, technological progress, and more consumer choice for everyone in East and Southeast Asia. Most of the *Air Hostess* crew members and MP&GI executives, as previously mentioned, were refugees fleeing Communism. Yet it is wrong to read the film as an unequivocal advocacy of the American way; lurking within this anti-Communist narrative is a dissenting voice raising questions about the contradiction of Cold War cultural politics.

For example, the film draws attention to the disjuncture between the liberal democratic values of freedom and self-realization and the capitalist corporate values demanding organization, discipline, and order. In a well-choreographed sequence after Daying scolds her for not following the company motto, "the customer is always right," Keping is stranded in a Singapore hotel because of bad weather. She goes to a party, where she dances to a tune of calypso music. Calypso was known among Asian music lovers for its anti-establishment, anti-hierarchy ethos. In fact, Keping sings "I Love Calypso" (Wo ai Kalisu) to an excited crowd to express her discontent against the airline management's rigid norms and Daying's chauvinistic, disciplinarian attitude, which leave no room for individual freedom and self-fulfillment. Although the "calypso" incident stops short of articulating a critique of capitalist corporate culture, it brings attention to a comment by Daying at a marriage ceremony in response to someone who asks him when they would marry: as Keping looks away, he half-jokingly replies that it might take place after he gets promoted to chief pilot and, most likely, after Keping retires. So, just like Daying, her life is now totally interwoven with what the manager likes to call the "family" of the airline. This open ending raises an uneasy question: is Keping doomed to fail in her struggle for independence as she escapes one "gilded cage" only to enter another cage of American capitalist values? All this made *Air Hostess* a thoroughly entertaining anti-Communist film that contained certain ambivalence to the American Way.

Most important for the cinematic containment efforts in the region, however, the film was big, colorful, and visually impressive with its spectacular scenery, passionate performances, entertaining songs and dance numbers, and eye-opening scenes of air travel, and it made some headway in drawing large audiences into the theater to watch the modern, capitalist "Free World" and its projection on the big screen of the global anti-Communist crusade in Asia.

Epilogue

Hong Kong was at the center of a global war of intelligence and propaganda even as it was located at the periphery of Big Power diplomacy and military contests. It was in many ways a Cold War frontier city that created a haven for the Chinese refugees whose struggle for a better life was enmeshed with the cultural contestation between Mao's China and its enemies. But until very recently, the growing scholarship on the cultural Cold War has focused mainly on areas outside Asia. The Mandarin film industry in Hong Kong was, in fact, analogous to major cultural industries in other parts of the world with regard to its role and function in ideological mobilization. It was also different: the colonial imperative to stay neutral in the Chinese civil war and a brutally volatile regional market caused the cinematic Cold War to appear deceptively commercialized even as it became politicized.

And the cinematic Cold war was, by definition, border-crossing because of the commercial and political imperatives to connect with overseas Chinese communities in Southeast Asia. I have argued that, contrary to popular belief, it was the pro-Communist cinema that had a strategic edge in the propaganda warfare of the 1950s. The concept of cinematic containment is thus useful in helping us map out the "Free" Chinese cinema's role, strategy, and mission to dull that edge. Even as a Manichean division emerged, especially after the celebrity delegation to Taiwan in 1954, the boundary was porous and imbued with ambivalence. Thus, although pro-Nationalist distributors sold pro-Communist dramas and China-made opera films to overseas markets, for example, pro-Communist theaters also showed Hollywood pictures. And film artists often switched political affiliations for reasons of ideology, financial need, lifestyle preference, personal connections, or a combination of some of these.

I suggest, by way of an epilogue, that there are many questions about the complexity of the cinematic Cold War in Asia that only further archival research can tell us. At this point, it seems that although China, Taiwan, and the U.S. fought with each other on the cinematic front to become the savior and leader of the pan-Chinese world, their approaches were strikingly similar, namely, politicization of popular culture as weapons of ideological persuasion, clandestine use of private enterprises for political propaganda, and instrumentalization of overseas Chinese communities. The interwoven histories of Yung Hwa, Great Wall, Phoenix, and Cathay-MP&GI, along with the many refugee filmmakers who tried to survive the political turmoil, add important dimensions to a more nuanced understanding of the global Cold War from the edges of the conflicts in Asia.

Acknowledgments

This chapter is an abridged version of "More than Just Entertainment: Cinematic Containment and Asia's Cold War in Hong Kong, 1949–1959" in *Modern Chinese Literature and Culture* 30 (2) (Fall 2018): 1–55. Many thanks to MCLC for the reprint permission.

Bibliography

"Censorship Becoming Big Problems." 1960–61. *Far Eastern Film News*, Special Supplement.

Chia, LeeNi. 2016. Personal Interview. March 22, 2016. New York.

Chang, Jing Jing. 2014. "China Doll in Flight: Li Lihua, World Today, and the Free China-US Relationship." *Film History* 26 (3):1–28.

Chen, She. 1959. "Zhengfu yao zhuyi de" (The government should pay attention). *Lianhe bao*, July 23, 1959.

Chiang, Kai-shek. n.d. *Chiang Kai-shek Diaries, 1917–1972*. Stanford, CA: Hoover Institution Archives, Stanford University.

Chu, Donna. 2001. "Hu Siao-fung." Oral interview. In *Lixiang niandai: Changcheng yu Fenghuang de rizi rizi* (Age of Idealism: The Days of Great Wall and Fenghuang), edited by Huang Ailing et al. Hong Kong: Hong Kong Film Archive, 143–71.

Committee for a Free Asia. 1951. "December 13, 1951, Declassified and Released by Central Intelligence Agency Sources Methods Exemptions 302B Nazi War Crimes Disclosure Act Date 2007." Accessed August 23, 2018. www.cia.gov/library/readingroom/docs/DTPILLAR%20%20%20 VOL.%201_0085.pdf.

Dawson, Sue. 1953. "But Where Are the Love Scenes." *China Mail*, May 6, 1953.

Dizard, Wilson. 1961. *The Strategy of Truth: The Story of the United States Information Services*. Washington, DC: Public Affairs Press.

"Dongnanya yingyi jiaoliu" (Film arts cooperation in Southeast Asia). 1956. *Xinwen shijie*, no. 113 (December 1): 2–3.

"Extract of the Ta Kung Pao." 1960. Box TU/260/6, Hong Kong Public Records Office, Hong Kong.

"Film Producer Urges Hong Kong Producers to Collaborate with Taiwan." 1956. Newspaper Excerpts, March 29, 1956. Box-P58, Asia Foundation Collection, Hoover Institution Archive, Stanford University, CA.

Gao, Shanyue. 1959. "*Kongzhong xiaojie* bieyou yongxin" (The secret motive of *Air Hostess*). *Dagong bao*, June 10, 1959.

Gong, Deyuan. 1954. "Yinse huiguang changzhao Baodao" (Treasure Island under the silver lights). *Xinwen tiandi*, no. 329 (June 5): 10–12.

Government of Hong Kong. 1954. *Hong Kong Annual Report* 1953. London.

Grantham, Alexander. 1965. *Via Ports: From Hong Kong to Hong Kong*. Hong Kong: University of Hong Kong Press.

Harrington, Julian F. 1953. "Julian F. Harrington to Dept. of State, Subject: Draft Country Plan for USIS Hong Kong." June 9, 1953. #2526, 511.46G 6-953, RG59, United States National Archives, College Park, MD.

He, Guan. 1959. "*Kongzhong xiaozhe*" (*Air Hostess*). *Xinsheng wanbao*, June 14, 1959.

Hsu, Raymond. 1954. "New Schemes of the Great Wall Motion Picture Enterprise." Box P-58, Asia Foundation Collection, Hoover Institution Archive, Stanford University, CA.

Huang, Ren. 2009. "Gangjiu dianying xiju shiye ziyou zonghui de jiaose he yingxiang" (The role and influences of HKFFGA). In *Lengzhan yu Xianggang dianying* (The Cold War and Hong Kong Cinema), edited by Huang Ailing and Li Peide, 70–80. Hong Kong: Hong Kong Film Archive.

"An Intra-Office Memo from the Representatives, Hong Kong to the President, Asia Foundation." 1957. October 4, 1957. Box P-58, Asia Foundation Collection, Hoover Institution Archive, Stanford University, CA.

Jiang, Guansheng. 2012. *Zhonggong zai Xianggang* (Chinese Communists in Hong Kong). 2 vols. Hong Kong: Cosmos Books.

Jin, Yaoru. 2005. *Xianggang wushi nian yiwang* (Remembering Hong Kong in the past fifty years). Hong Kong: Jin Rouru jinian jijin.

Kennedy, Charles Stuart. 2001. "Charles Cross." *Association for Diplomatic Studies and Training*. Accessed August 25, 2018. www.adst.org/OH%20TOCs/Cross,%20Charles%20T.toc.pdf.

Li, Lihua. 1954. "Wo de zizhuan" (My autobiography). *Jinri* shijie, no. 46 (February 1): 8–9.

Liao, Chengzhi. 1990. *Liao Chengzhi wenji* (Collected essays of Liao Chengzhi). 2 vols. Hong Kong: Sanlian shudian.

Lilley, James. 2004. *China Hands: Nine Decades of Adventure, Espionage, and Diplomacy in Asia*. Washington, DC: Public Affairs.

Liu, Yongxi. 1985. *Jiang Jingguo zai Tai sanshi nian* (Thirty Years of Mr. Jiang in Taiwan). Hong Kong: Dalian.

Lombardo, Johannes. 2000. "A Mission of Espionage, Intelligence and Psychological Operations: The American Consulate in Hong Kong." In *The Clandestine Cold War in Asia, 1945–1965: Western Intelligence, Propaganda and Special Operations*, edited by Richard Aldrich et al., 69–70. London: Frank Cass.

Ma, Xingkong. 1954. "Xianggang yingcheng tuihong nian" (The year of red fading in Hong Kong cinema). *Xinwen tiandi* no. 309 (January 16): 9–11.

Mark, Chi-kwan. 2004. *Hong Kong and the Cold War: Anglo-American Relations, 1949–1957*. Oxford: Clarendon Press.

Mccfadyen, Q. A. A. 1951. "On Interview of 19-6-1951, to Hon C.L. [Commissioner of Police]." Box TU/260/2, Hong Kong Public Records Office, Hong Kong.

"Memorandum of Discussion at the 447th Meeting of the National Security Council." 1960. *Foreign Relations of the United States*. Accessed August 25, 2018. https://history.state.gov/historicaldocuments/frus1958-60v06/d528.

"Mr. Guard to C. M. Tanner, sub: Motion Picture Projects—Comments." 1953. July 28, 1953. Box-57, Asian Foundation Collection, Hoover Institution Archive, Stanford University, CA.

Ng, Kenny. 2008. "Inhibition vs. Exhibition: Political Censorship of Chinese and Foreign Cinemas in Postwar Hong Kong." *Journal of Chinese Cinemas* 2 (1): 23–33.

O'Brien, Jack. 1988. "Richard McCarthy." *Association for Diplomatic Studies and Training.* Accessed August 26, 2018. www.adst.org/OH%20TOCs/McCarthy,%20Richard%20M.toc.pdf.

Osgood, Kenneth. 2006. *Total Cold War: Eisenhower's Secret Propaganda Battle at Home and Abroad.* Fayetteville: University Press of Arkansas.

Rand, Christopher. 1952. *Hong Kong: The Island Between.* New York: Alfred A. Knopf.

Rawnsley, Gary. 2000. "Taiwan's Propaganda Cold War: The Offshore Islands Crisis of 1954 and 1958." In *The Clandestine Cold War in Asia Western Intelligence, Propaganda and Special Operations*, edited by Richard J. Aldrich et al., 82–104. London: Frank Cass.

Saunders, Frances. 2000. *The Cultural Cold War: The CIA and the World of Arts and Letters.* New York: The New Press.

Schmidt, G. Lewis. 1988. "Earl Wilson." *Association for Diplomatic Studies and Training.* Accessed August 26, 2018. http://adst.org/wp-adst.org/content/uploads/2012/09/Hong-Kong.pdf

Searls, Guy. 1957. "Red China Switch to Love, Soft Pedal Marx to Sell Movies." *The Wall Street Journal*, September 26, 1957.

Shao, Mingchun. 1954. "Xianggang yingtan tuihong nian" (Year of red fading). *Xinwen tiandi*, no. 309 (January 16): 9–10.

Snow, Philip. 2003. *The Fall of Hong Kong: Britain, China, and the Japanese Occupation.* New Haven, CT: Yale University Press.

"Survey of and Statistics in the Mandarin Motion Picture Industry in Hong Kong." 1956. Box P-58, Asian Foundation Collection, Hoover Institution Archive, Stanford University, CA.

Walton, Calder. 2013. *Empire of Secrets: British Intelligence, the Cold War, and the Twilight of Empire.* London: Harper Books.

Wang, Weiyi. 2006. *Nanwang de suiyue* (My Memories). Beijing: Zhongguo dianying.

Westad, Odd Arne. 2017. *The Global Cold War: A World History.* New York: Basic Books.

"Xianggang ziyou zonghui tongguo fanji Gongfei lengzhan tian" (Free Association proposal to combat the Communist bandits). 1959. *Lianhe bao*, May 29, 1959.

Xu, Dunle. 2005. *Kenguang tuoying* (Developing Cinema). Hong Kong: MCCM.

Xu, Lanjun. 2017. "The Southern Film Corporation, Opera Films, and Cultural Diplomacy in Cold War Asia." *Modern Chinese Literature and Culture* 29 (1): 239–82.

Yan, Pei. 1956. "Xianggang yingren zuohe zunbei" (Hong Kong filmmakers should be prepared). *Guoji* dianying, no. 6 (June): 38.

Yi, Yan. 1954. "Ying Xianggang ziyou yingjuren lai Tai" (Welcome "free" makers of film and drama to Taiwan). *Lianhe bao*, May 19, 1954.

Zhou, Yi. 2002. *Xianggang zuopai douzheng shi* (A History of the Leftist Struggle in Hong Kong). Hong Kong: Liwen.

13 The End of an Era

The Cultural Revolution, Modernization, and the Demise of Hong Kong Leftist Cinema

Man-Fung Yip

The aim of this chapter is to look into the decline and demise of Hong Kong leftist cinema in the late 1960s and 1970s. This is a subject that has received very little, if any, critical attention, despite the recent interest in Hong Kong's leftist filmmaking (Ho 2011a; Zhang 2010) and in the Cold War's connections to and impact on Hong Kong cinema (Du 2017; Fu 2013, 2018; Wong & Lee 2009). In most studies, including an earlier article of mine that explores the extensive surveillance on leftist film workers and film companies in Hong Kong (Yip 2017a), it is presumed that Chang Cheng (Great Wall), Feng Huang (literally "phoenix"), and Sun Luen—the three major leftist studios in Hong Kong—went into a sharp decline after the Cultural Revolution broke out in China in 1966. Meddling and interference from the extreme left, according to this line of argument, posed a serious impediment to creative freedom and turned the leftist films of the period into overt political propaganda that chased viewers away. At the same time, the Cultural Revolution-inspired strikes, demonstrations, and riots that beset Hong Kong during much of 1967 are also said to have made many local people disillusioned and alienated from the communist cause, thus further pushing the leftist films into oblivion.

Such an argument, widespread as it may be, has never been tested or substantiated. It is not even clear if leftist films of the late 1960s and 1970s were as politicized as is usually believed, for little analysis has been given to them. More importantly, even if we admit that political factors did play a role in the waning of Hong Kong leftist cinema, an exclusive focus on them is too narrow and fails to address other forces at work. There is little doubt that Hong Kong leftist film companies, backed financially by the Chinese communist government and watched over by political operatives sent from Beijing, were subject to the influence from the north. Indeed, it is reasonable to assume that political and ideological control had intensified following the radical left turn ushered in by the Cultural Revolution. Yet it is also clear that Hong Kong leftist cinema existed in a broader context, shaped and controlled by a confluence of forces comprising not only the political maneuver from the Chinese communist regime, but also an array of social and film-industrial processes such as the rapid expansion of Hong Kong into a modern industrial society, the coming-of-age of the baby boomers and thus the changing demographics of the film-going population, and a local cinema that was moving increasingly toward an entertainment-based ethos. In the rest of this chapter, I will take a closer look at these multiple forces and try to give a more nuanced picture of what brought Hong Kong leftist cinema to its downfall.

The Rise of Hong Kong Leftist Cinema

But before I do this, a quick review of the rise of leftist filmmaking in Hong Kong is in order. As a result of the civil war between the communists and the nationalists after WWII, which ended in the communist victory and takeover of mainland China in 1949, many film producers, directors, scriptwriters, and stars relocated from Shanghai to Hong Kong and began making Mandarin films in a primarily Cantonese-speaking territory. While a lot of these émigré film workers were politically unaligned and only wanted to work in a place with a relatively stable political climate, there were also quite a few, including Cai Chusheng, Ouyang Yuqian, Zhang Min, Ke Ling, Bai Yang, and Wang Weiyi, who were dedicated communists trying to escape the persecution of the nationalists. Despite being in exile, they sought to accomplish the agenda of the Chinese Communist Party (CCP) to set up a base in Hong Kong cinema and founded Da Guangming, Nanqun, Nanguo, and other "progressive" studios in the then British colony. Some of them also joined Yung Hwa—a studio founded by Shanghai tycoon Li Zuyong (with the aid of veteran producer Zhang Shankun) in 1947—and were responsible for making some of the company's most left-wing productions, notably *Virtue in the Dust* (*Chuncheng hua luo*, 1949) and *A Fisherman's Honour* (*Hai shi*, 1949), both scripted by Ke Ling and directed under the helm of Cheng Bugao, and Wu Zuguang's *A Peasant's Tragedy* (*Shanhe lei*, 1949). To foster a spirit of comradeship and promote the communist cause among staff members, leftist activists in Yung Hwa also organized a host of different activities, from picnics and dance parties to lectures and "study groups" (*dushu hui*) focused on Marxist-Leninist doctrine (Law and Bren 2004, 148–9).

Yung Hwa, however, was not the only Hong Kong film company that saw some kind of "infiltration" by pro-communist filmmakers at the time. Great Wall Pictures Corporation, which Zhang Shankun cofounded with Yuan Yang'on shortly after the former fell out with Li Zuyong and left Yung Hwa in 1949, also saw a palpable left turn following a reshuffle in the company that led to Zhang's ousting in 1950. Tong Yuejuan, the wife of Zhang, recalled the incident in this way:

> [W]e were approached by members of the Communist Party who asked us to join the Chinese People's Political Consultative Conference. We refused and refrained from stepping foot on the Mainland.

> So we made some enemies there. Later, we left on a trip with Nancy Chan, on the pretext of promotion, and went to countries like Singapore [and] Thailand. We didn't come back until two months later, and we found that Great Wall had been turned into a kind of leftist study center. We were booted out. That year should be around 1950.
> (As quoted in Wong 2000, 41)

For Tong, then, Zhang Shankun was forced out of Great Wall on political grounds. But George Shen (Shen Jianzhi), the eldest son-in-law of Yuan Yang'an, told a rather different story. According to him, Zhang left due to a dispute with Yuen over the dire financial situation of Great Wall, which was in severe debt because Zhang had been borrowing money to fund new productions (Shen 2001, 295–6). What actually happened is beyond the scope of this essay, but it is evident that after Zhang's departure, the restructured Great Wall, renamed as Great Wall Movie Enterprise, turned left noticeably by forging stronger links with the communist regime in Beijing and would become the leading leftist film company in Hong Kong in the following two decades.

Further boosting the influence of leftist cinema in Hong Kong were two film companies that emerged soon after the restructuring of Great Wall. Feng Huang, established in 1953, drew its members primarily from two studios—Wushi Niandai ("The Fifties") and Loon-Ma ("Dragon-Horse")—that operated briefly in the early 1950s. Zhu Shilin, whose *Festival Moon* (*Zhongqiu yue*, 1953) was Feng Huang's inaugural production, played an essential role in steering the direction of the company and would remain its major creative figure until his death in 1967. The third major leftist film company in the period was Sun Luen: founded in February 1952, the studio differed from Great Wall and Feng Huang in devoting itself exclusively to the making of Cantonese-language films. As such, it represented an attempt of Hong Kong leftist cinema to extend its influence to Cantonese-speaking viewers. Underlying this attempt was the recognition that Cantonese was spoken by the majority of people in Hong Kong, and that only Cantonese films would take root in the territory from a long-term perspective (Zhou 2011, 56).

Considering that Hong Kong cinema—the Mandarin film industry in particular—had, by the early 1950s, become a kind of Cold War cultural battleground where the interests of communist China and the capitalist "free world" coexisted and contested with one another, the increasing leftist presence did not go unnoticed and was met with hostility and obstruction from various forces. For instance, the British and the colonial authorities in Hong Kong, despite their efforts to maintain a semblance of neutrality so as not to provoke the communist leaders in Beijing, sought to restrain local leftist filmmaking through a variety of measures, including monitoring and tracking of film workers, deportation of individuals deemed "deviant" and "subversive," and censorship. The exiled nationalist government in Taiwan, on the other hand, tried to counter the leftist tide in Hong Kong cinema by mobilizing anti-communist filmmakers in the territory, sending political agents to infiltrate and work inside the leftist studios, and offering financial and market incentives to politically unaligned film companies and filmmakers in exchange for their support (Lee 2013, 186). Even the United States government, as part of its global battle against communism, was (covertly) involved, most notably in providing funding, through the Asia Foundation, to a "right-wing" or pro-Taiwan studio in Hong Kong known as Asia Pictures. But even with all the surveillance, blockade, and isolation, leftist film companies still found a way to survive; in fact, their films can be said to be thriving throughout the 1950s and early 1960s, drawing praises from viewers and performing well in both local and regional markets.

The Cultural Revolution and Its Impact

The 1950s and early 1960s were the heyday of leftist filmmaking in Hong Kong. During the early to mid-1950s, before Motion Picture and General Investment (MP&GI) and Shaw Brothers fully established their dominance in Hong Kong cinema, the productions of Great Wall and Feng Huang did very well at the local box office for Mandarin-language films.[1] Even in the late 1950s, when the urban romances and musicals of MP&GI and Shaws' costume pictures became popular and provided stiff competition, the leftist companies were still able to hold their own. In fact, the number of Great Wall and Feng Huang productions reached a peak precisely around this period: 17 films in 1957, 18 films in 1958, and 17 films again in 1959. The production pace slowed down in the 1960s, but was still kept at an average of 10 to 11 films per year throughout the decade. Meanwhile, in the Cantonese-language cinema, Sun Luen was also quickly establishing itself as a force to reckon with. At the outset, the company was only able to make one to two films each year due to lack of its own contract directors and stars, but its emphasis on quality productions with positive, healthy contents attracted many established names (such as Ng Wui, Lee Sun-fung, Cheung Ying, Ng Chor-fan, and Pak Yin) to work on its films. And a strategy shift in 1956 saw the studio making a concerted effort to increase output and to develop its own roster of stars by seeking young new talent. Production started to pick up as a result, the films became more diverse in genre and content, and Sun Luen would quickly grow and establish itself as one of Hong Kong's four major Cantonese film companies (Chung 2011, 44–7, 35).

Despite growing competition from rival companies and what I call the "surveillance ethos" arising from the Cold War politics in postwar Hong Kong cinema (Yip 2017a, 33), then, Great Wall, Feng Huang, and Sun Luen were all able to find a firm footing in the local industry and turned out films at a steady rate throughout the second half of the 1950s and 1960s.

The early to mid-1970s, however, saw a sharp decline in the studios' production output: a mere two films were released in 1971, five (including two documentaries) in 1972, six in 1973, seven in 1974, and four (of which two were documentaries) in 1975.[2] This decline has usually been attributed to the Cultural Revolution, which is said to have brought lasting damage to Hong Kong leftist cinema. Zhang Yin (2010), for instance, argues that ultra-leftist thought spread to the communist leadership in Hong Kong—including that within the leftist film companies—during the Cultural Revolution, which, in turn, resulted in an exodus of film talent, a decline in creative energies, and ultimately, a drastic reduction in the number of films produced (172–80). Likewise, Sam Ho (2011b) sees the Cultural Revolution as the main reason for the downturn of Sun Luen, whose films are said to become "politicized" (*zhengzhi gua shuai*) and "distorted" (*niuqu*), turning away from their admirable tradition of depicting "the lives of ordinary citizens" (*xiao shimin shenghuo*) (29).

Such views, I should add, are not just shared by critics but have been voiced by those who were working in the leftist film companies at the time. Bao Fong, a major actor and later director at Feng Huang and Great Wall, described the situation thus:

> Good things never last. Then came the Cultural Revolution. The finances of Great Wall, Feng Huang and Sun Luen were connected to the Mainland. Our direction was also influenced by its cultural policies. We made good period pictures, but later we were not allowed to make any costume romances or imperial court dramas. It got worse when we had to make movies about workers, peasants and soldiers. It was painful for everyone. Hong Kong had workers, but all the peasants had gone to England to run restaurants and soldiers were all Gurkhas.
>
> ("Bao Fong" 2001, 115)

A similar point was made by Hu Xiaofeng, another actor-turned-director at Great Wall:

> Before the Cultural Revolution, we were democratic. We could write on any issues. But [after the Cultural Revolution broke out] we were having too many worries and they were giving people too many labels. Things went too far left and everything was criticized. Concerns for people's problems were replaced by lip service to patriotism. In the end, the work suffered. We had devoted ourselves to motivating the people but with all those labels, anything we did could be attacked. We were worried and our interests waned. Afraid to make mistakes, we couldn't get emotionally involved. That's why we made so few films during the Cultural Revolution.
>
> ("Hu Xiaofeng" 2001, 168)

The main criticisms, then, have to do with political interference and the imposition of an explicit and rigid ideological agenda. These charges are not totally unfounded, given that the films made by the leftist companies in this period did show an increasing adherence to the party line by focusing on workers [e.g., Zhu Feng's *The Sisters* (*Jiemei tong xin*, 1973)], peasants [primarily in martial arts films such as Huang Yu's *The Village of Crouching Tiger* (*Wohu cun*, 1969) and Zhang Xinyan's *The Red Tasseled Sword* (*Hong ying dao*, 1975], and soldiers [mostly in the form of anti-Japanese resistance fighters, as in Chen Jingbo's *Pull Out the Tiger's Teeth* (*Hukou ba ya*, 1969)]. Many of these films, especially those after 1970, were also more politicized and would touch on a sensitive issue such as strike.[3] A case in point is Huang Yu's *The Younger Generation* (*Xiao dangjia*, 1971): exploring issues of wealth inequality and labor exploitation (including illegal child labor), the film focuses on two young characters, A Lan and her teenage brother A Niu, who are forced to find full-time work in order to support their younger siblings after their widowed mother dies in an accident. After taking a job as a maid and subsequently quitting it because of the ill-treatment from her employers, A Lan ends up working in an electronics factory. The exploitation, however, does not stop there: in the name of boosting efficiency, the factory management introduces an automatic assembly line and has it run at such a speed that puts significant burden on the workers. One of the workers collapses due to exhaustion and is fired. Infuriated, the workers organize a strike and succeed in forcing the factory manager to reverse the firing and to reduce the speed of the assembly line. Meanwhile, A Niu is able to find work at another factory, but after he and a few other child laborers are caught in a government inspection, the boss withholds much of their salary to "compensate" for his loss—the fines he has to pay to the government. As with the female workers, the child laborers band together and demand successfully full pay from the boss.

Made just a few years after the 1967 riots triggered by a series of workers' walkouts and protests, the use of a strike as a key plot point in *The Younger Generation* reflected to a large extent an ideologically more "hardline" stance in Hong Kong leftist cinema—especially considering, as we will see later, its earlier strategic emphasis on a more "depoliticized" approach. No less revealing in this regard is the film's espousal of a "collectivist" ideology, as can be seen in the emphasis on worker unity or solidarity as a way to defend against capitalist greed and exploitation. In fact, this focus on the collective was a more general trend and can be observed in other leftist productions of the period. Consider, for instance, Hu Xiaofeng's *The Hut on Hilltop* (*Wu*, 1970): focusing again on the difficult lives of the working class as in *The Younger Generation*, the film tells the story of a construction worker who builds homes for others, but who himself is unable to provide a decent place for his own family. An opportunity finally comes, and the worker's family is allocated a piece of hillside land on which to build a hut, only to discover later that since the area is agricultural land, it has to be turned into a vegetable field if the family is to stay in its newly built home. With less than a week before government inspection, the family appears destined to be evicted until the son's class teacher, upon knowing what is happening, mobilizes her colleagues and an army of students to help the family cultivate the land.

What follows is a sequence that epitomizes the collectivist ideology of the film. With the recurrent images of teachers and students turning the soil, the sense of collective effort is palpable in the scene. But no less revealing are the alternating shots between the laboring teachers and students and the worker protagonist, who is often depicted alone (Figure 13.1). This is significant because the film has, up to this point, portrayed the protagonist as a poor but individualistic worker who stresses self-reliance and does not accept or want help from others. In an earlier scene, for instance, the worker reproaches his son for accepting food from a friend working in a restaurant and demands the food to be taken away. And he is also shown to be a loner at work, distancing

Figure 13.1 Individualism vs. collectivism in *The Hut on Hilltop* (1970).

himself from his co-workers and refusing to get involved in the negotiations about delayed salary payments between his co-workers and the management. In many ways, the sequence mentioned earlier in which the teachers and students help to turn the hillside into a cultivated field marks a key turning point in the film—a moment when the worker finally realizes the failings of his individualist stance and begins embracing a more collectivist mindset. This change in outlook is clearly manifested toward the end of the scene, when the worker stops being a mere observer and actively joins the group in their labor (Figure 13.2). In a later sequence, after the worker protagonist witnesses his son's reluctant but candid criticisms, in a class assembly, of his self-centeredness and lack of concern for an injured co-worker, he pays a visit to the co-worker and goes back later with a handmade crutch and some urgently needed financial relief. And he also resolves to give his son's fellowship away to those more in need, thus putting in action what the class teacher has said earlier in the film: "We can only unite together. Only then can we master our fate." As if all this does not make the primacy of collective solidarity over individualistic self-reliance—and by extension, communism over capitalism—evident enough, the film ends with one last display of the collectivist ideology by showing the united effort—by the co-workers, the class teacher, and scores of students—in helping the worker's family rebuild their home after it has been destroyed by a powerful storm.

This emphasis on collectivist values can also be observed in *Red Azalea* (*Ying shan hong*), a 1970 film jointly directed by Huang Yu and Chang Tseng. The story of the film is very simple; it is about Red Azalea, a Robin Hood figure who steals from the rich and gives to the poor. But what is immediately intriguing is the way in which the film plays with the question of who Red Azalea is: unlike most martial arts films, where one can predictably find an individual protagonist, the eponymous figure in

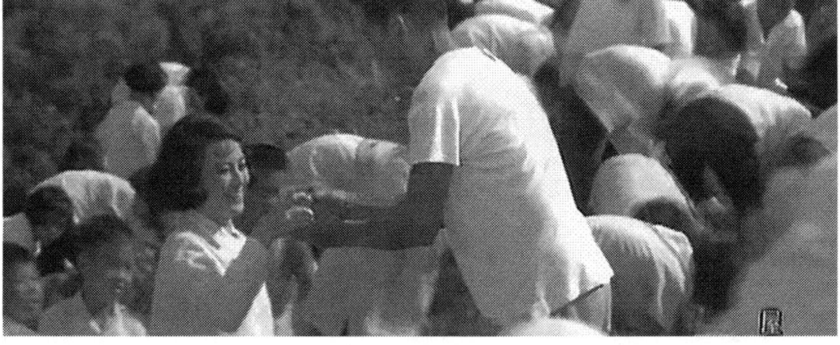

Figure 13.2 The worker protagonist joins the group in *The Hut on Hilltop* (1970).

Red Azalea turns out to be not a single person, but rather a group comprising a wide range of people—male and female, old and young, strong and frail. In this way, then, the collectivist ideology of the film is already evident at the narrative level.

No less illuminating is a scene featuring the song "Wolf Grandmother" (*lang waipo*). With pressure mounting for the arrest of Red Azalea after several failed attempts, an imperial envoy is dispatched to investigate the case. Using what is called a "psychological tactic" (*gongxinji*) in which "pacification" (*anfu*) goes hand in hand with "suppression" (*qingjiao*), the head of the local prefecture is ordered to open up the granary for the villagers, in an attempt to co-opt the latter (and thus to isolate Red Azalea from them). The song in question, using montage to jump between diverse groups of people—people of all ages and walks of life—and thus to highlight the involvement of the entire village, shows the failure of such a tactic and satirizes the government's sly show of benevolence:

> Grandma, grandma, jackal and wolf in disguise
> Sweets and cakes in hands to lure the little child
> Grandma, grandma, jackal and wolf in disguise
> Amicable look but atrocious heart
> Ravaging people relentlessly
>
> Wolf grandma, however you make up
> However you disguise, you're still a wolf
> Wolf grandma, wolf grandma
> You eat people flesh and bone
> Keep your eyes wide open
> Expose its plot

The sense of collective solidarity among the villagers is unmistakable in the sequence, but what is also worth noting here is the thinly veiled critique to Hong Kong's colonial administration. In the aftermath of the 1967 riots, the Hong Kong government invested a huge amount of energy and material resources in organizing the Hong Kong Week—a seven-day program comprising a range of cultural and recreational activities, including concerts, sporting events, parades, and special exhibitions and displays. A similar celebration, renamed as the Festival of Hong Kong, would be held in 1969, 1971, and 1973. While mainstream opinions applauded the government's efforts in bringing fun and amusement to the Hong Kong people and in fostering a sense of community in them, the leftist press, according to a government report, was highly critical, condemning the organization of such festivities as "nothing but a waste of money, a fascist plot in disguise and an attempt to give a false air of 'stability and prosperity'" to divert attention away from "the appalling crime rate, the rent increases and the treacherous colonial rule" (Government Information Services 1969; also see Yi 1973). Seen in this light, it is evident that the satire against the opening of the granary in *Red Azalea* was ultimately directed at the Hong Kong colonial government and its alleged attempts to buy popular support.

As with *The Hut on Hilltop*, *Red Azalea* ends with a strong collectivist note, showing an enlarged group of Red Azaleas celebrating their victory over government oppression. In fact, such collectivist endings, where images of mass celebration, mass marching, and so forth evince not just a feeling of closure but a strong sense of hope and purpose, can be found in many other Hong Kong leftist films of the period (Figure 13.3). The problem, however, is that these images of collectivity and class solidarity were far removed from the realities of Hong Kong at the time. Embarking on an accelerated process of industrialization and modernization, Hong Kong was emerging as one of the fastest growing economies in the region and was thus more attuned to the rational and utilitarian individualism of capitalism than to the group-based mentality of collectivism. The contradictions between the two ideological positions are well illustrated by the following incident recalled by Bao Fong:

> Zhu Feng made a film [*The Sisters*] about women workers standing up to exploitation. We made it with passion. One day in a bus, some

Figure 13.3 Images of collectivity in *The Village of Crouching Tiger* (1969; above) and *The Patriotic Knights* (1971; below).

> women workers recognized me. I asked them what they thought about the film. At first they didn't want to speak, then one said: "(The goal of) you film is difficult to realise. If we strike because of 20 cents, how could we making a living?" Well said. We were fighting for the people but we lost touch of the people. She also said: "We know you mean well, but you're nor practical." It made me cry. The Cultural Revolution went too far left.
>
> ("Bao Fong" 2001, 115–6)

At the same time, even with the ideological shifts, Hong Kong leftist films were still attacked for their alleged reactionary tendencies by Chinese communist officials. A good case in point is, again, *The Hut on Hilltop*, which was criticized for "blackening the image of workers" because the working-class protagonist is depicted as having some "dubious" traits such as smoking, drinking, and buying a lottery ticket. Hu Xiaofeng, the director of the film, was censured "for being poisoned by American imperialist films" ("Hu Xiaofeng" 2001, 170). Another example is Bao Fong's *Chu Yuan*—a biopic about Qu Yuan, a poet and minister during the Warring States period of ancient China, the film was deemed a "safe" project because Mao Zedong had reportedly given a copy of *The Songs of Chu* (*Chu Ci*), an anthology of poetry of which Qu Yuan is historically attributed as the co-author, to Japanese Prime Minister Tanaka Kakuei when the latter visited China in 1972. But subsequent political fights in China spread to historiographic debates about the achievements of Qu Yuan and other figures during the Warring Sates era, which, in turn, prompted repeated revisions of the script. And when the film was finally completed in 1974, James Wong, an influential writer and media figure, saw a preview of it and wrote an article suggesting that the film was an implicit critique of the political situation of China at the time. Apprehensive of the reaction from Beijing, the studio management pulled the film just before its release, and it was not shown in theaters until 1977, after the end of the Cultural Revolution (Bao 1999, 118–24).

Negotiating Modernity and Youth Culture in a Cold War Context

As can be seen from above, there is some truth to the argument that the radical left turn associated with the Cultural Revolution led to the downturn of Hong Kong leftist cinema. Yet such a stance is arguably too restricted and places too much emphasis on the effects of heightened political and ideological control at the expense of other important factors. One such overlooked aspect, for instance, pertains to the complex dynamics between leftist films and the market-oriented film industry of Hong Kong. Unlike its state-run counterpart in China, Hong Kong cinema has always been a capitalist enterprise where the law of the market reigns supreme.

Granted, the leftist film companies in Hong Kong received financial backing from the communist government in Beijing—up to HK$100,000 per film in the 1950s (Fu 2018, 14–5)—but they still needed to keep abreast of and adapt to market trends in order to survive. In fact, Yuan Yang'on, the general manager of the restructured Great Wall until his departure in 1957, made this point clear in an article appearing in the inaugural issue of *The Great Wall Pictorial*, the official publication of the studio:

> I do not reject the concerns of producers about 'market value' (the so-called 'business eye'). I think that a narcissistic attitude, one that only aims to create audiences and refuses to adjust to them, is too high-sounding. Making concessions to audiences under certain conditions is not just not bad, but necessary.
>
> (Yuan 1950)

Almost a decade later, George Shen (1959) raised a very similar idea in the same magazine:

> What kind of films should we produce? This question is often raised among film producers. There is no denying that a film, however good, is still a failure without an audience, because film as a form of art is the medium through which we hope to exercise some good influence upon the public, and you can hardly achieve this goal when not many people have seen it. This of course does not mean that we should lower our standards unconditionally to suit the tastes of the public. Rather, we should get our audience by producing better and better films, which are entertaining yet provided with a clear conscience on the part of producers.
>
> (4)

There is no question that the leftist studios of Hong Kong, in an attempt to remain competitive in the Hong Kong film market, gave ample attention to the entertainment values of their films. The significance of this is thrown into even sharper relief if we consider the unique strategic position of Hong Kong leftist cinema, which, from the very beginning, was given a specific role—not so much to undermine British colonial rule or propagate communist ideologies, but rather to build a tactical presence in the Hong Kong film industry and maintain a point of contact with the world. In particular, Hong Kong's leftist films were viewed as a means of influencing and winning over the overseas Chinese in Southeast Asia and around the world (Liao 2011). For this reason, leftist companies eschewed explicit political propaganda in their films in order to avoid head-on conflicts with the colonial authorities that would jeopardize their crucial strategic role. This explains why very few of the films produced by Great Wall, Feng Huang, or Sun Luen—at least those made prior to the shift to radical leftism in the late 1960s and early 1970s—were overtly subversive from a political or ideological perspective. Rather, the films embraced a softer approach and sought to be both educational and entertaining at the same time, following the basic premise of "guiding the audiences to be good" (*dao ren xiang shan*) ("1950" 2009, 259).

However, this goal of maintaining a balance between educational aspirations and entertainment values was not always easy, and the tension became especially evident from the late 1950s and early 1960s onward, when rapid economic growth and demographic changes brought about a radical reorientation of mass culture (of which cinema was an integral part) in Hong Kong. There is a general consensus that the 1960s and 1970s constituted a key transitional period in Hong Kong society and culture. The United Nations embargo on trade with China during the Korean War (1950–53) threatened to derail the local economy by undermining its all-important entrepôt trade. Thanks in part to the capital, entrepreneurship, and labor of postwar Chinese refugees, Hong Kong was able to avert the crisis by shifting its economic base to export-based manufacturing, transforming itself in the process into a modern industrial city. Indeed, due to this economic restructuring, Hong Kong experienced rapid and tremendous growth during the 1960s and 1970s, which, in turn, served as the catalyst for a burgeoning mass culture—what Yung Sai-shing (2006) calls a "dazzling audiovisual sensory world" that delineated "the imagined modernity of post-war Hong Kong" (36). With a mélange of entertainment and leisure options from pulp fiction, comics, radio, cinema, and (since 1967) broadcast television to cafés, dance halls, department stores, and shopping malls, the cultural landscape of Hong Kong had not just become more diverse, dynamic, and modern; it had grown to be increasingly capitalistic and market-oriented, with the different mass cultural outlets "locked in heated competition for audiences" (Yung 2006, 26).

Furthermore, this changing cultural scene emerged out of a specific demographic context, one marked by a rapidly expanding young population as the postwar baby boomers came of age. In 1961, the number of Hong Kong people aged between 15 and 29 was 0.62 million. The figure rocketed to 0.95 million in 1971 and to 1.3 million in 1976, which constituted about 25 and 30% of the total population, respectively.[4] This surge of teens and young adults, who were constantly looking for entertainment options and showed greater receptivity to modern trends and styles and to thrilling sensations, further pushed the local mass culture into a path of modernization and sensationalism.

The film industry responded to these developments by changing to a mode of mass production and turning out more youth- and entertainment-oriented films. This was especially clear from the mid-1950s onward, as Motion Pictures and General Investment Co. (MP&GI), and later Shaw Brothers, moved their production operations to Hong Kong and fundamentally changed the industrial practices and production trends of Hong Kong Mandarin cinema. While MP&GI was best known for its comedies, melodramas, and musicals that drew on Hollywood and American culture and celebrated modern urban lifestyles, Shaw Brothers, at least in its initial phase, focused on opulent costume pictures that evoked a strong sense of nostalgia and cultural nationalism. Yet this seeming traditionalism is misleading and masks the *modern* quality of the films as mass commodities. Even more than MP&GI, Shaw Brothers built itself as a modern industrial organization with a massive studio facility (i.e., the Movietown) and hundreds of employees under long-term contract. This allowed the company to adopt an assembly-line model of production for maximum efficiency and profit. At the same time, Shaw Brothers sought to make its films more glamorous and stimulating by appropriating a range of new technologies (e.g., color and widescreen cinematography) and techniques (handheld camera; rapid editing), thus setting a new standard for Hong Kong cinema. Even the hitherto conservative Cantonese cinema made a concerted attempt to modernize itself in the face of mounting rivalries and challenges. In doing so, Cantonese films not only became more diverse and sensational in terms of subject matter and style; they brought to prominence a new generation of stars—notably Tse Yin, Wu Fung, Chan Po-chu, and Siao Fong-fong—who appealed to an increasingly young audience.

Against these contexts of growing competition and changing social circumstances, left-wing film companies also followed a more entertainment-oriented ethos, capitalizing on the glamor of youthful stars and turning out diverting genre films. Many of these films, such as Hu Xiaofeng's *Those Bewitching Eyes* (*Yaner mei*, 1958) and Zhu Shilin's *Sweet as Honey* (*Tiantian mimi*, 1959), were modeled on MP&GI's highly popular romantic comedies and teenage musicals, and reflected to a large extent the concerns and sentiments of the petit-bourgeoisie (Sek 1983). At about the same time, after a number of mainland Chinese opera films and Shaw Brothers' *huangmeidiao* musicals became box-office sensations in Hong Kong and Southeast Asia, Great Wall put into production several Shaoxing opera films, including Hu Xiaofeng's *Bride Hunter* (*Wang laohu qiang qin*, 1961) and Li Pingqian's *The Princess Falls in Love* (*San kan yumei Liu Jinding*, 1962).[5] And following the success of Shaws' "new school" (*xinpai*) martial arts films in the mid- to late 1960s, leftist companies, again, sought to capitalize on the trend and turned out their own swordplay movies (e.g., *The Jade Bow* [*Yunhai yugong yuan*, 1966], Hu Xiaofeng's *Flying Dragon Heroes* [*Feilong yingxiong zhuan*, 1967], Chen Jingbo and Xu Xian's *The River Dragon* [*Guo jiang long*, 1971], and Zhang Xinyan's *The Patriotic Knights* [*Xiagu danxin*, 1971]).

As is evident from above, the attempt to go along with market demands and follow box-office trends continued even after the Cultural Revolution had started. Indeed, it is worth noting that not all Hong Kong leftist films that came out during the Cultural Revolution, especially in the first few years, were propaganda movies about workers, peasants, or soldiers. Huang Yu's *Love Songs of the Twins* (*Shuangnü qingge*, 1968), for instance, is a musical based on the folk songs of ethnic minority groups in Yunnan. *Destiny of Love* (*Yinyuan dao shang*, 1969), directed by Bao Fong, is a romantic comedy about an author trying to put an end to his bachelorhood, while Zhang Zheng and Wu Jingping's *Enchanting Whirlpools* (*Miren xuanwo*, 1969), a loose remake of Inoue Umetsugu's Shaw Brothers production *Hong Kong Nocturne* (*Xianggang hua yue ye*, 1967), tells about the story of three teenage girls embarking on separate careers and journeys of life after graduating high school. All these films, I hasten to add, retained the goal of disseminating progressive content, which generally meant exposing social problems and inequalities, or simply motivating one to embrace a positive attitude toward life. Yet none of them can be said to be overtly politicized, let alone espousing a radical anti-colonial or anti-capitalist ideology, and they all sought to balance their "hard" didactic messages with "soft" entertainment values, drawing on various popular genres to attract viewers. As such, they were not far different from previous leftist films, which, as noted earlier, were also not conceived as a political or ideological weapon but as a tool to establish contact with the world. But in spite of the similarities in their approach, those earlier films were much more successful at the box office and thus did a better job in achieving the strategic goal of Hong Kong leftist cinema. The differences in reception can in many ways be explained by changes in Hong Kong society and in the demographics of its population. For in continuing the progressive tradition of 1930s Shanghai cinema and striking a balance between didacticism and entertainment, leftist films were highly popular in the first half of the 1950s, a period of recovery when ordinary people, in Hong Kong as in many other Chinese communities, were still living a life of scarcity and hardship and thus more receptive to questions of social justice and equity. This situation, however, had changed rapidly since the mid-1950s, as the advent of capitalist modernization and the surge of postwar baby boomers turned Hong Kong cinema, in the words of Poshek Fu (2000), into "a ferocious world of economic rivalries, sensationalism, and commercialism" (81). The leftist film companies thus found themselves in a constant catch-up game with fast-changing market trends, volatile audience tastes, and a growing propensity for big-budget productions (especially from Shaw Brothers) with which their underfunded films had an increasingly hard time to compete.

The needs and vicissitudes of catching up with box-office trends have been noted by Hu Xiaofeng:

> Making films in Hong Kong is not determined by the artist but by the box-office. Trends and audience tastes are constantly changing.

> We are forced to follow the best-selling trends... But as soon as you follow, audience tastes have already changed. You're always falling behind and you never develop your own style.
>
> ("Hu Xiaofeng" 2001, 169)

While Hu went on to say that the Cultural Revolution was the main reason why Hong Kong leftist films fell behind and became isolated from society, the reality is that even before the intensification of political and ideological control, leftist studios had already found themselves having a difficult time adapting their films to a rapidly modernizing Hong Kong and to a highly commercialized mass culture without undermining their goal of making positive and socially conscious films.[6] They had also failed to appeal to the growing young population, who made up an increasingly significant portion of the film-going public at the time.

A comparison of the martial arts films of leftist companies to those of Shaw Brothers makes these points clear. In 1965, Shaw Brothers launched a campaign for "new school" martial arts films which, unlike the stylized theatrical fighting and supernatural special effects that marked and characterized Cantonese swordplay movies of the time, took their cues from Hollywood and Japanese cinema and embraced, in the name of "realism," a highly sensational style stressing speed, impact, bloody violence, and other forms of sensory thrills (Yip 2017b, 64–74). And paralleling this shift was the emergence of a new male heroic prototype under the rubric of *yanggang* ("staunch masculinity"). Central to this *yanggang* trend, identified most closely with the films of Chang Cheh, were a new generation of young action stars—Wang Yu, Lo Lieh, Ti Lung, John Chiang, Chan Kuan-tai, and others—all of whom were in their mid-20s when they first broke into the scene in the late 1960s and early 1970s. What set apart these newcomers from their predecessors (such as Kwan Tak-hing in the long-running Wong Fei-hung film series from the 1950s and early 1960s) was first and foremost their virile physicality, the ways in which their strong, athletic bodies were put on display for the gaze of viewers. In addition to this heightened corporeal focus, a new subjectivity—a sense of youthful energy and verve, a bold and defiant spirit and a tendency to challenge the established social order, a propensity for violent action—also constituted a crucial element shaping and defining the screen personas of these *yanggang* stars (Yip 2017b, 86–9) (Figure 13.4). These new martial arts films of Shaw Brothers proved hugely popular among the public, especially the young baby boomers craving for more stimuli and seeking to assert their own voices. And with the ascent of Bruce Lee and the transition to the hard-hitting kung fu subgenre in the early 1970s, these trends toward sensory intensification and representations of virile masculinity became even more pronounced.

Figure 13.4 *Yanggang* masculinity in Chang Cheh's martial arts films.

By contrast, the martial arts films of leftist companies were by and large bland and lifeless, their action sequences looking stilted and lacking the sensory thrills and stimulations that made the genre so appealing to young viewers. There were undoubtedly attempts to make the films more fashionable and attuned to market trends; *The Patriotic Knights*, for instance, made use of some interestingly designed (if not well executed) wirework, while *The River Dragon* incorporated various elements—the inn setting, the cross-dressing female knight-errant, the characteristic elliptical editing—associated with the celebrated swordplay films of King Hu. But these efforts were all rather piecemeal and limited, and did little to bring the kind of energy and sensationalism that marked and distinguished Shaws' martial arts films. The struggle here was in part ideological, for given their emphasis on positive and healthy content, no one would expect from the leftist companies graphically violent films like those made by Chang Cheh. In fact, the leftist studios tried to make a point in calling their martial arts films *xiayi pian* ("chivalry films"), presumably to forestall criticisms that they were making mere frivolous entertainment and trying to capitalize on the trend of sensational physical action.[7] At the same time, the problem was not just ideological but also practical; in particular, a dearth of young, athletic actors forced the leftist companies to keep using for their martial arts films the same veteran stars such as Fu Qi, Gao Yuan, and Chow Chong, who were all approaching middle age by the end of the 1960s and whose star personas were built mainly on the gentle, well-mannered roles they had previously played. As a result, the wandering swordsmen, patriotic fighters, and other heroic types in leftist martial arts films look distinctly mature and "soft," a far cry from the *yanggang* heroes in Shaw Brothers' films (Figure 13.5).

On the one hand, it is understandable why the leftist companies wanted—or needed—to make martial arts films, because the genre was dominating Hong Kong cinema in the late 1960s and early 1970s.

Figure 13.5 Soft and mature hero in *The Village of Crouching Tiger* (1969).

But due to both ideological and practical reasons, the companies were not in a position to produce the kind of "sense-sational" and *yanggang* martial arts films prevailing in the market at the time. The inability to keep up with viewer expectations of the genre clearly points to a failure, on the part of leftist filmmakers, to respond and adapt to Hong Kong's drastically changed social environment and film culture.

Conclusion: The End of an Era

To conclude, while it is true that Hong Kong leftist films were losing audiences in the 1960s, this might be due to numerous different reasons. The increasingly stringent political and ideological control that came in the wake of the Cultural Revolution was one of them, but a more complete analysis will have to consider, among other things, the struggle of leftist filmmakers to respond and adjust to a Hong Kong society set on a course of accelerated industrialization and modernization on the one hand, and the rise of a new young generation with distinct tastes and habits of cultural consumption on the other. Also worth noting is the tremendous success of Chor Yuen's *The House of 72 Tenants* (*Qishier jia fangke*) in 1973: with this box-office smash, Cantonese-language films, which had been in a slump since 1970, made a rapid resurgence and were edging out their Mandarin counterparts to become the mainstream of Hong Kong cinema. This further put leftist companies such as Great Wall and Feng Huang, which produced exclusively Mandarin-language films, in a marginal position from which they would not be able to escape. As the Cultural Revolution gradually wound down, Hong Kong leftist films tried, without success, to make a comeback in the late 1970s. In 1982, the three major leftist film studios—Great Wall, Feng Huang, and Sun Luen—merged and formed the Sil-Metropole Organisation Ltd. While the new company continued to engage in film production, the Cold War dynamics in Hong Kong cinema had irrevocably changed in the 1980s and beyond, in part because China itself had adopted the "Open Door" policy and was less interested in ideological warfare than in economic and social modernization. The era of Cold War rivalry in Hong Kong filmmaking—and thus the centrality of leftist filmmaking, at least as it was known in the 1950s and the 1960s—had all but ended.

Notes

1 In 1951, for instance, Li Pingqian's *A Night-Time Wife* (*Jin hun ji*), a Great Wall production, was the highest grossing Mandarin-language film in Hong Kong, followed by three productions (Zhu Shilin's *Should They Marry?* [*Wu jiaqi*] and *Flora* [*Hua guniang*]; Wang Weiyi's *The Fiery Phoenix* [*Huo fenghuang*]) by Loon-Ma and Wushi Niandai, the two companies that would merge to become Feng Huang ("Yi jiu wu ji nian" 1952). Similarly, three films by Great Wall—Yue Feng's *Modern "Red Chamber Dream"* (*Xin honglou meng*),Tao Qin's *Father Marries Again* (*Yi jia chun*), and Li Pingqian's *Honeymoon* (*Miyue*)—held the top-grossing spots in 1952, while Zhu Shilin's *The Dividing Wall* (*Yi ban zhi ge*), a Loon-Ma production, was at the sixth place (Wang 1953).

2 Production picked up a bit—but not by much—in the second half of the 1970s. For instance, nine feature films and one documentary were made in 1978, while the following year saw the release of nine films, of which one was a documentary.

3 Strike was a sensitive issue because it was a labor dispute in a factory, and the strike that followed it, that triggered the 1967 disturbances and riots in Hong Kong.

4 All the figures are calculated from data published in the following sources: *Hong Kong Statistics, 1946–67* (Hong Kong, 1969), *Hong Kong Population and Housing Census 1971: Main Report* (Hong Kong: Government Printer, 1972), and *Hong Kong By-Census 1976: Main Report* (Hong Kong: Government Printer: 1978–79).

5 The success of China-made opera films in Hong Kong can be traced to the release of Sang Hu's *The Romance of Liang Shanbo and Zhu Yingtai* (*Liang Shanbo yu Zhu Yingtai*) in 1954, followed by Shi Hui's *Marriage of a Heavenly Princess* (*Tian xian pei*) in 1956 and Xu Tao's *Searching a School* (*Sou shuyuan*) in 1957. The trend was taken up by Shaw Brothers before long, which made the *huangmeidiao* musicals *Diau Charn* and *The Kingdom and the Beauty*, both directed by LiHanxiang, in 1958 and 1959, respectively.

6 It is worth mentioning in this regard that *The Great Wall Pictorial* would sometimes publish reviews that were critical of the studio's own films. *Those Bewitching Eyes*, for instance, was criticized for its depiction of the female protagonist, whose capricious (*renxing*) attitude was dismissed as mere imitation of foreign films and not something that should be shown in a progressive Chinese film. Besides, the humor in the film was also deemed too Westernized. See Xu (1958).

7 *The Patriotic Knights*, for instance, was advertised as an "outstanding *xiayi pian* from Great Wall shot in color and widescreen," while the publicity materials for *The Village of Crouching Tigers* described the film as a "patriotic, enemy-vanquishing *xiayi* epic" (*xiayi jiandi aiguo juzhu*).

Works Cited

"1950 zhi 1970 niandai xianggang dianying de lengzhan yinsu yingren zuotanhui jilu" (Filmmakers' seminar on the cold war factor in Hong Kong cinema from the 1950s to the 1970s). 2009. In *Lengzhan yu xianggang dianying* (Cold War and Hong Kong Cinema), edited by Wong Ain-ling and Lee Pui-tak, 249–62. Hong Kong: Hong Kong Film Archive.

Bao, Fong. 1999. *Hulu li shenme yao* (What Medicine Is There in the Bottle Gourd?). Beijing: Xiandai chubanshe.

"Bao Fong." 2001. In Monographs of Hong Kong Film Veterans 2: An Age of Idealism: Great Wall and Feng Huang Days, 106–118. Hong Kong: Hong Kong Film Archive.

Chung, Po-yin. 2011. "*Xinlian gushi: zhengzhi, wenyi he yueyu yingye*" (The Sun Luen story: politics, art, and the Cantonese film industry). In *Wenyi renwu: xinlian qiusuo* (Artistic Mission: An Exploration of Sun Luen Film Company), edited by Sam Ho, 35–49. Hong Kong: Hong Kong Film Archive.

Du, Ying. 2017. "Censorship, Regulations, and the Cinematic Cold War in Hong Kong (1947–1971)." *The China Review* 17 (1): 117–51.

Fu, Poshek. 2018. "More than Just Entertaining: Cinematic Containment and Asia's Cold War in Hong Kong, 1949–1959." *Modern Chinese Literature and Culture* 30 (2): 1–55.

Fu, Poshek. 2013. "Cold War Politics and Hong Kong Mandarin Cinema." In *The Oxford Handbook of Chinese Cinemas*, edited by Carlos Rojas and Eileen Cheng-yin Chow, 116–33. New York: Oxford University Press.

Fu, Poshek. 2000. "The 1960s: Modernity, Youth Culture, and Hong Kong Cantonese Cinema." In *The Cinema of Hong Kong: History, Arts, Identity*, edited by Poshek Fu and David Desser, 71–89. Cambridge: Cambridge University Press,

Government Information Services. 1969. "Chinese Press Review No. 44: Festival of Hong Kong." Dec. 18, 1969. Festival of Hong Kong, HKRS70-3-71-1. Public Records Office of Hong Kong, Hong Kong.

Ho, Sam, ed. 2011a. *Wenyi renwu: xinlian qiusuo* (Artistic Mission: An Exploration of Sun Luen Film Company). Hong Kong: Hong Kong Film Archive.

Ho, Sam. 2011b. "Xuyan" (Introduction). In *Wenyi renwu: xinlian qiusuo* (Artistic Mission: An Exploration of Sun Luen Film Company), edited by Sam Ho, 21–31. Hong Kong: Hong Kong Film Archive.

"Hu Siao-fung." 2001. In Monographs of Hong Kong Film Veterans 2: An Age of Idealism: Great Wall and Feng Huang Days, 158–71. Hong Kong: Hong Kong Film Archive.

Law, Kar and Frank Bren. 2004. *Hong Kong Cinema: A Cross-Cultural View*. Lanham, MD: Scarecrow Press.

Lee, Daw-Ming. 2013. *Historical Dictionary of Taiwan Cinema*. Lanham and Plymouth: The Scarecrow Press.

Liao, Chengzhi. 2011. "Guanyu xianggang de dianying gongzuo" (A propos of Hong Kong cinema). In *Wenyi renwu: xinlian qiusuo* (Artistic Mission: An Exploration of Sun Luen Film Company), edited by Sam Ho, 189–95. Hong Kong: Hong Kong Film Archive.

Sek, Kei. 1983. "Gangchan zuopai dianying ji qi xiaozichan jieji xing" (Hong Kong leftist cinema and its petit-bourgeois outlook). In *A Comparative Study of Post-War Mandarin and Cantonese Cinema: The Films of Zhu Xhilin, Qin Jian and Other Directors*, 150–1. Hong Kong: The Urban Council.

Shen, George. 1959. "Tan zhipian de daolu" (On the path to film production). *The Great Wall Pictorial*, no. 100 (November): 4–7.

Shen, George. 2001. "Filmdom Anecdotes." In *Monographs of Hong Kong Film Veterans 2: An Age of Idealism: Great Wall & Feng Huang Days*, 290–319. Hong Kong: Hong Kong Film Archive.

Wang, Zhong. 1953. "Yi jiu wu er nian de xianggang guo pian yingtan" (The Hong Kong Mandarin cinema in 1952). *The Great Wall Pictorial*, no. 27 (April): n.p.

Wong, Ain-ling. 2000. "Tong Yuejuan: The Best of Times in Hsin Hwa." In *Monographs of Hong Kong Film Veterans 1: Hong Kong Here I Come*, edited by Kwok Ching-ling, 38–43. Hong Kong: Hong Kong Film Archive.

Wong, Ain-ling, and Lee Pui-tak, eds. 2009. *Lengzhan yu xianggang dianying* (Cold War and Hong Kong Cinema). Hong Kong: Hong Kong Film Archive.

Xu, Lingyu. 1958. "Mei yue yingping" (Monthly film reviews). *The Great Wall Pictorial*, no. 83 (January): 3.

Yi, Bicai. 1973. "Xianggang jie yu xianggang shehui" (Festival of Hong Kong and Hong Kong society). *Shidai Qingnian* (Youth of the Times), no. 54 (November): 2–4.

"Yi jiu wu ji nian xianggang shangying maizuo chengji zui jia zhi guoyu pian shouru bijiao biao" (The top-grossing Mandarin-language films released in Hong Kong in 1951). 1952. *The Great Wall Pictorial*, no. 12 (January): n.p.

Yip, Man-Fung. 2017a. "Closely Watched Films: Surveillance and Postwar Hong Kong Leftist Cinema." In *Surveillance in Asian Cinema*, edited by Karen Fang, 33–59. New York and Oxon: Routledge.

Yip, Man-Fung. 2017b. Martial Arts Cinema and Hong Kong Modernity: Aesthetics, Representation, Circulation. Hong Kong: Hong Kong University Press.

Yuan, Yang'an. 1950. "Tan dianying de zhizuo" (On film production). *The Great Wall Pictorial*, no. 1 (August): n.p.

Yung, Sai-shing. 2006. "Celebrating Modernity, Dazzling Sounds and Sights: Kong Ngee Films and Urban Media." In *The Glorious Modernity of Kong Ngee*, edited by Wong Ain-ling, 24–39. Hong Kong: Hong Kong Film Archive.

Zhang, Yin. 2010. *Zai jiafeng zhong qiu shengcun: xianggang zuopai dianying yanjiu* (Seeking Survival in Cracks: Studies on Hong Kong Leftist Cinema). Beijing: Peking University Press.

Zhou, Chengren. 2011. "Zhiyou Yueyu pian cai neng zai xianggang shenggen… shi shuo xinlian chgneli Beijing" (Only Cantonese films can take root in Hong Kong: on the establishment of Sun Luen). In *Wenyi renwu: xinlian qiusuo* (Artistic Mission: An Exploration of Sun Luen Film Company), edited by Sam Ho, 53–68. Hong Kong: Hong Kong Film Archive.

14 Who Views Whom through Whose Lenses? The Gazes in USIS Film Propaganda in South Korea

Han Sang Kim

On May 19, 1952, still during the Korean War, the first issue of *Liberty News* (*Ribŏt'i nyusŭ*, 1952–67) was released. It was the third newsreel series produced by Liberty Production, a film studio owned by the United States Information Service, Korea (hereafter USIS-Korea). The launch of the *Liberty News* series was a symbolic event in the history of America's propaganda filmmaking in South Korea. It was not only the core newsreel series of Liberty Production but also an indicator that showed the rise and fall of the film studio. The series represented USIS-Korea's growing incursion into film production. For USIS-Korea, the outbreak of the Korean War in 1950 was a catalyst for a tremendous stride in film production that made the establishment of film studios in Chinhae and Sangnam possible. The film studio in Sangnam, in particular, provided USIS-Korea's film producers with exceptional environments for both technology and techniques since its launch in 1952 (Kim Han Sang 2013, 552). With the Sangnam studio, USIS-Korea's Liberty Production departed from the contract-based production system and hired its own full-time employees. Not a few South Korean filmmakers, including Kim Ki-yŏng, Kim Yŏng-gwŏn, and Pae Sŏg-in, would begin their film careers in Liberty Production (Kim Han Sang 2013, 554–5).

This chapter starts with the premise that USIS-Korea's securing of such a well-organized film production system was part of the historical relocation of the gaze. This relocation was made possible in the newly created historical condition, namely, the end of colonial rule and the emergence of the Cold War system. This chapter examines the fabric of the relocated gazes into which South Korean spectators became woven amidst a barrage of American film propaganda, construing it as a Cold War governmentality that formed in the East Asian context.

The Historicity of the Gaze

In his commentary on the appearance of the sovereign in the parade, Michel Foucault (1995) states that "the 'subjects' were presented as 'objects' to the observation of a power that was manifested only by its gaze" (187–8). Subjectivization is, in other words, a procedure of being observed by a power that reveals itself through its gaze. The sovereign is a "power by the gaze," "power by the spectacle," and "power by discipline"—in other words, the "power of modernity" that is wielded upon every single subject (Chu 2003, 346). Every invisible subject has to be visualized and observed for the sake of such manifestation of power by the gaze. Street management in urban areas, such as cleaning, paving, and lighting, for instance, is a measure of such visualization so that the subjects can be better observed on the sleek surface of the modern streets. However, the locus of the sovereign power in modern society is occupied by "a diffuse and anonymous power whose actual existence soon becomes superfluous to the process of discipline" (Jay 1994, 410). The subjects become subjectivized out of a misunderstanding that they are observed from the vacant locus of the nonexistent sovereign—that is, they confine themselves in the disciplinary, panoptic system of the gaze.

Nicholas Thomas (1994) historicizes these techniques of visualization and the panoptic system by applying them to the understanding of colonial governing strategies (105–42). The authorities in the British colony of Fiji could fully exercise power over the colonial population only after having made the unknown Fijian life and culture visible and recognizable. In this process, the colonial authorities shared certain technologies of government with metropolitan societies as the latter "domesticated and reformed" backward sectors within them (125), which may be seen as a colonial procedure that generated the hierarchy between the colonizers as the authority of the gaze and the colonized as the object of the gaze. "Racial science and anthropological knowledge" produced in colonial Fiji demonstrated such characteristics of the colonial regime of knowledge (107). Considering that visualization of the object of the gaze, according to Foucault, is a matter of not only the visualized subjects but also the visibility of the visualizing authority (Chu 2003, 345–50), the operation of such colonial regime of knowledge was inseparable from the visibility of the colonial authorities that were able to collect and distribute unknown or unseen knowledge.

Seen from this perspective, America's film propaganda toward South Korea, a newly emerging field of Cold War governmentality during and after the Korean War, draws attention to the necessity of rethinking Foucauldian gaze theory in the historical context of Asia's incorporation into the Cold War system. By regarding those American-sponsored film studios and cutting-edge cameras as a means of visualization, we can redefine the Korean War and the postwar period as the time that saw the reshuffling of the authorities of the gaze in Asia. America, unlike colonial authorities, promoted its status as the ally of South Korea and supported the Koreans' path toward postwar recovery and construction of a national identity as an independent nation-state. All this demands a new framework that can explain the entangled historical conditions of the gaze in which the decolonization of the region and the new world order of the Cold War intertwined.

Liberty News: America's Gaze that Visualized the Invisible

Liberty News, a representative product of USIS-Korea's Liberty Production, had found its stable network of exhibition since 1953, in a general practice of cinemas that screened government newsreels before commercial features. This was made possible by the amicable relationship between South Korea's Syngman Rhee government and USIS-Korea in which the latter's public information sector had enjoyed the same level of privileges as its South Korean counterparts since before the outbreak of the Korean War, as Rhee's speech complimenting USIS-Korea's activities in May 1950 showed (*Tonga ilbo*, May 12, 1950, 2). However, the Rhee government was sometimes also an obstructer to USIS-Korea and interfered with the tone and coverage of its films (Chŏng 2003, 35). Especially as a news media outlet, Liberty Production became subject to an uncomfortable relationship with the Rhee administration not a few times during the mid- to late 1950s. In their shared pursuit of pro-American and anti-Communist state-building in the 1950s, Liberty Production was given distribution privileges by the Rhee administration, but there were also times of occasional conflicts in which USIS-Korea would identify itself as an outsider clashing with the South Korean government. This aspect is worthy of examination in that it was related to the unique position of the gaze possessed by USIS-Korea, an American media outlet.

A notable case was the request of the Syngman Rhee government's Ministry of Education to cut certain scenes from *Liberty News No. 164* that contained images of the deceased opposition presidential candidate, Sin Ik-hŭi (*Tonga ilbo*, June 9, 1956, 3). Sin died suddenly on May 5, 1956, during his presidential campaign, and the footage of his successful campaign speech delivered on May 3 was used in the specific issue of *Liberty News* in question. The Ministry of Education demanded deletion of those scenes for the reason that the campaign speech had no relation to Sin's death. This request ignited a social debate, but finally concluded with an uncut release under the condition that the USIS staff members concerned would be censured (*Chosŏn ilbo*, June 13, 1956, e3). This case not only shows the Rhee administration's infringement on freedom of the press as a strategy to "monopolize the nation's attention by repressing any competitive and challenging images against the central authority" (Yi H. 2007, 210); it also reveals the privileged status of USIS-Korea, which the South Korean government could not fully control because of its identity as an American government agency.

A severer case happened at the beginning of 1959, after the Rhee government and the ruling party's railroading of the third revised bill of the National Security Law (hereafter NSL) on December 24, 1958. On January 13, 1959, in the midst of the ensuing "NSL Crisis," a USIS-affiliated

Figure 14.1 USIS-Korea's footage of the NSL Crisis (RG 306.1355, courtesy of NARA).

Korean cinematographer was chased by Korean police officers for filming the rally of the opposition party (*Kyŏnghyang sinmun*, January 15, 1959, 1) (Figure 14.1). Since the officers tried to force into the American embassy building to arrest the cinematographer, the embassy made a formal complaint against the Ministry of Foreign Affairs (*Tonga ilbo*, January 15, 1959, 1). This complaint was basically an extension of the Eisenhower administration's continuous criticism of the Rhee government's suppression of political opponents (Yi C. 2007, 116). However, in terms of the social status of USIS-Korea's film unit in South Korea, the incident was a result of its ambivalent identity—a whistle-blower who filmed and disclosed South Korea's political reality and a foreign diplomatic agency that had extraterritoriality to protect its employees. Those employees, that is, South Korean filmmakers affiliated with USIS-Korea, were also marked with hybridity in their subject formation, identifying themselves as both nation-builders and "Free World" bloc-builders under the umbrella of the U.S. during the post-Korean War period (Kim Han Sang 2013, 560). In the context of the NSL Crisis, the Korean cinematographer's identity as a whistle-blower who belonged to a foreign agency was a reenactment and, indeed, a clear example of this hybrid subjectivity.

Because of this string of conflicts, USIS-Korea's Liberty Production was recognized by the South Korean press as a media outlet that had a tendency to criticize the Syngman Rhee government from the "opponent's perspective" (*Chosŏn ilbo*, December 26, 1960, e4). This view seems to have nurtured certain wishes among the South Korean public that *Liberty News* and USIS-Korea would contribute to democratization after President Rhee's resignation in April 1960. However, USIS-Korea's criticism was in reality an act of the U.S. government that aimed at turning the South Korean political system into a stable, conservative two-party system (Yi W. 2007, 219–20), which would, in turn, protect the "dignity of the US... as an intangible profit" in South Korea as a "showcase for democracy" (Yi C. 2007, 83).

What is worthy of special notice here is that the conflicts between USIS-Korea and the Rhee government are closely associated with the strategy of visualizing the invisible realm of a state hidden by its own government. USIS was not merely a distribution agency that circulated information from the U.S., but more of an intelligence agency responsible for all the information-related functions, including collecting, classifying, and reassigning information in and out of the country of residence. That South Korea's undemocratic political situations were visualized by USIS-Korea signifies that the information of such unseen situations was recognized, collected, and accumulated by the U.S. for its own knowledge.

Films like *Liberty News No. 164* also showed the capacity of USIS-Korea's gaze to capture and visualize the invisible for South Korean audiences, and might have disclosed in the process America as the authority of the gaze. To the audiences outside of Korea, such films provided visual evidence showing whether the Rhee government's internal affairs accorded with the interests of the "Free World" led by the U.S. When the decision of releasing *Liberty News No. 164* was made after the controversy over the scene of Sin Ik-hŭi, a crowd of people surged toward the theaters to see the scene in action, and the issue attracted the largest number of audiences in the history of the *Liberty News* series (Kim W. 1967, 289–95). It was a hit made by the gaze of America that visualized the invisible.

With regard to the historical transition from an imperial-colonial regime to a Cold War regime, this much-debated arrangement of the foreign gaze signified a new governmentality. In the course of USIS-Korea assuming the position as a critic of the Rhee government's undemocratic governance, American-style democracy acquired a representational hegemony that surpassed the legitimacy of the South Korean state. This was a strategy of visualization shared with colonial authorities in building a hierarchy. However, it was accompanied by rather multilayered courses of negotiation, including the competition between a sovereign state and its hegemonic ally, that constituted a new kind of governmentalization of the state in a Cold War setting.

Self-Gazing: The Representation of the Self-Reliant Korean Self

While *Liberty News* and similar newsreels mobilized the Korean audience to the "Free World" led by a supranational power that visualized the invisible information of a sovereign state, some other Liberty Production-made documentaries tended to be more educational and served to construct an ideal model of the Korean. The postwar agenda of "reconstruction" and "self-reliance" in particular resonated with this educational objective and was dealt with in many documentaries and educational features produced by Liberty Production (Kim Han-sang 2012, 244). A frequent narrative seen in many of these films, such as Kim Ki-yŏng's *Ward of Affection* (*Sarang-ŭi pyŏngsil*, 1953), Kim Yŏng-gwŏn's *The Lighthouse on the Street* (*Kŏri-ŭi tŭngdae*, 1955), and Yang Sŭng-nyong's *My 4-H Club Diary* (*Na-ŭi 4 eich'i kwajejang*, 1958), was built upon the growth of a juvenile protagonist. The story of a child who used to be mentally or physically immature but becomes self-reliant through education can be seen as a good means to provide a certain dichotomy between the modern self and the other. Such educational narratives might also have functioned as practical teaching materials for those who were actually in need of rehabilitation.

The Lighthouse on the Street is an intriguing case in that it has a self-reflexive scene of an outdoor screening, at a provisional school, of a *Liberty News* issue depicting children who are educated in rehabilitation programs (Figure 14.2). Considering that the film itself also might have been used in such rehabilitation programs, one can identify a three-layered rehabilitation procedure organized around a repeated structure of gazes involving one rehabilitating body looking at another. It suggests that a certain discipline might be involved in the process through which the juvenile viewers looked at those who, just like themselves, were being trained and educated. I call this process a mechanism of *self-gazing* for the production of the self (Kim Han-sang 2012, 262–3).

It is frequently seen in the history of film propaganda that an object of persuasion and enlightenment is positioned to view characters who are in a similar situation to the object-viewer. This is also the case with

Figure 14.2 A self-reflexive scene in *The Lighthouse on the Street* (RG 306.526, courtesy of NARA).

several colonial Korean films made to promote the agenda of the Empire of Japan. Ch'oe In-gyu's *Angels on the Street* (*Chip ŏmnŭn ch'ŏnsa*, 1941), which is based on an original story of a then existing orphanage Hyangninwŏn and its founder, Pang Su-wŏn, is a film about a social worker relieving and rehabilitating poor children with conviction. The crucial mechanism in the rehabilitation of the children illustrated in the film is to discipline their bodies. Discipline, regulation, and enforced labor relieve and empower the children by making their bodies useful. Several child labor scenes in the film show the aestheticization of discipline and orderly actions. Such aestheticization of collective bodily motions is also observable in other propaganda films of the time. *Japanese Chronicles* (*Ilbon sillok*, 1943), a newsreel series made during the Pacific War, shows a training camp for volunteer soldiers from colonial Korea. One issue of the series shows the rhythmical collective motions of the troops, their well-organized way of life, and their disciplined bodies as attractions. It is obvious that those who were expected to watch this newsreel were either soldiers to be mobilized to the battle front or civilians who would fight on the home front. In other words, the soldiers in the newsreel were a pre-accomplished ideal goal with which many of the audiences were expected to become equated in the end.

However, it might not be easy for the audiences to identify with the owners of the bodies in *Angels on the Street,* who were street urchins and were regarded as abnormal. This might create a problem for the characters being identified as the ideal self. One solution to this problem, as pointed out by Yi Hyo-in (2010), was "to erase the icy stares and cynical attitudes towards the orphans from the film" (271), that is, to close the distance from the children by emphasizing their innocent and pure minds amidst hardships in the film's narrative. Yi argues that this element was added by the director, Ch'oe In-gyu, to the original script written by Japanese writer Nishigame Motosada as a "sign of disobedience" (272). This aspect of the film might have blurred the line between the ideal self and street urchins as the "other." In other words, the immatureness of those urchins may be understood as an emblem of the Korean nation's collective loss, namely, the precolonial Korean self. Even though the film's last sequence includes the "Pledge of the Imperial Subjects" (*hwangguk sinmin sŏsa*) to emphasize the assimilation of Koreans into the Empire of Japan, the ideal self of imperial Japan is necessarily positioned outside the flow of self-gazing within this mechanism of identification.

In this sense, *The Lighthouse on the Street*, a product of USIS-Korea during the Korean War, demonstrates a distinctly different mechanism of self-gazing from that in the colonial propaganda film. While the ideal self of imperial Japan eventually fails to achieve the aim of assimilation within the circuit of self-gazing in *Angles on the Street*, the American-sponsored film does not aim to do anything more than mediating the self-gazing of the Korean audiences. *The Lighthouse on the Street* was not a tool for assimilating Koreans into an American self. America's role as a mediator can also be traced in the post-liberation footsteps of Hyangninwŏn, the real model of the orphanage in *Angels on the Street*. Hyangninwŏn was founded in 1940 and expanded its social efforts during the post-liberation period. A news article from December 1946 reports that Hyangninwŏn organized its mobile screening team to visit schools, factories, institutions, and rural areas (*Chayu sinmun*, December 7, 1946, 2). In September 1947, another newspaper reported that a juvenile drama company consisting of Hyangninwŏn's inmates was established and double-featured a stage play and a child education film (*Chosŏn ilbo*, September 19, 1947, 2). It is noteworthy that Hyangninwŏn's inmates became touring actors and members of a mobile screening team. They can be interpreted as the embodiment of a circulative mechanism in which one is disciplined by gazing at the disciplined body of his/her future self. The Hyangninwŏn inmates had once been virtually exhibited as an attraction of the colonial enlightenment film, and now the *real* disciplined and rehabilitated bodies of the former urchins became the role models who could enlighten the younger ones during the postcolonial period. In this changed condition of gazing, America's propaganda agencies readily took on the role of a mediator for the exchanged gazes. It is remarkable that the U.S. Army XXIV Corps donated a camera to Hyangninwŏn to help its filmmaking activities in January 1948 (*Kyŏnghyang sinmun* January 31, 1948, 2). The U.S. and its agencies were outside the circuit of self-gazing, which means that they remained external to South Koreans' self-identity, but yet they were able to let Koreans see their future self. The films of Liberty Production mediated the gaze that could visualize the yet-invisible future of war orphans and street urchins. Between the lines of the repeated self-gazing in *The Lighthouse on the Street*, the U.S. was displaying its superior capacity for visualization.

The Gendered Gaze and a Christian Landscape

The 1953 USIS-Korea film, *Ward of Affection*, also demonstrates a structure of self-gazing similar to the aforementioned films in that it depicts an amputated child who succeeds in rehabilitation with the support of a nurse who herself was orphaned when young. However, unlike the social worker in *Angels on the Street* and the lieutenant-teacher in *The Lighthouse on the Street*, both of whom serve as a role model for children in the respective films, the nurse named Chŏng in *Ward of Affection* becomes the object of a gendered gaze and stays outside the circuit of self-gazing. This is not unrelated to the ways in which the nursing practice was gendered in media representation. The transition from Japan's imperial rule to a Cold War system spearheaded by the U.S. seems to have rearranged such gendered ways of gazing.

Like the protagonist of Yi Han-gŭn's *Korean Farm Life* (*Han'guk nongch'on saenghwal*, c1948) played by Kim Sin-jae, one of the big stars of colonial Korean cinema, young female figures in American public information films were commonly set forth as role models. This shows a certain gender politics at work in the spectatorship of such propaganda films. Women were usually characterized as highly adaptable to new cultures and thoughts. Such openness allowed them to enjoy the modern American way of life and become good subjects of American democracy. A considerable number of United States Information Agency (hereafter USIA) films during the Eisenhower period featured similar female characters who were both capable and professional in their social lives (Osgood 2006, 257–62). In this regard, it is worth exploring more how nurses were depicted in USIS-Korea films.

As early as August 1946, one year after liberation, the Department of Public Information (hereafter DPI) of the United States Army Military Government in Korea (hereafter USAMIK) produced a film named *The Korean White Angel* (*Paegŭi ch'ŏnsa)* (Commander-in-Chief 1946a). It was one of the earliest films made by the U.S. public information agencies in Korea and one of six documentaries produced in 1946 by the DPI (*Yesul t'ongsin*, December 3, 1946, 1). This unknown two-reel documentary, shown nationwide in September 1946, was said to depict Korean nurses and their services (Commander-in-Chief 1946b). The analogy between nurses and "white angels" had already been commonly used during the colonial period. This "white angel" image not only stereotyped the gender role of nursing but also, in doing so, invested its mission with a political significance. War nurses were widely recruited from the entire territory of the Empire of Japan during the Pacific War. In particular, there were a great number of temporarily employed female nurses from colonies like Korea and Taiwan, who were dispatched to mainland China or Southeast Asia (Sin 2011, 150). While women in general were regarded as part of the rear guard ("*ch'ong hu*") (Kwŏn 2004, 258), many military nurses were actually dispatched to the frontlines. They were sent to battlefields, dressed in white robes, and glorified as brave fighters. They were, thus, enhancing women's social role. However, at the same time, they were thoroughly gendered in terms of their role in the field, not least their *motherly* emotional services offered to the troops (Sin 2011, 167).

Pak Ki-ch'ae's *Straits of Chosŏn* (*Chosŏn haehyŏp*, 1943) captures this double-edged status of military nurses precisely. The wife of a Korean volunteer soldier is taken ill, suffering from lack of news about her husband from the battlefield. She is finally able to get in touch with her husband, and those who connect them together through a phone are nurses. In the final scene of the film, when the injured soldier looks out to the Straits of Chosŏn (currently Straits of Korea) beyond which his wife is waiting for him, a nurse keeps him company, helping him to walk. The strait symbolizes the distance between the battlefield and the home front. While the soldier's wife is at home, working in a clothes factory to supply to the battlefield, the white-robed nurse is beyond the straits, helping the soldier. In this depiction, nurses are rather defeminized in terms of conjugal or romantic roles but, at the same time, are shown as an ideal female companion complementing the male subject who is pursuing a national, sublime mission.

After the liberation from colonial rule and during the anti-Communist war against North Korea, this lofty mission was modified from a national to a broader religious one—the Christian faith. *Ward of Affection* shows this change clearly. The nurse protagonist, Bong-nyŏ, prays to God about a boy, Sun-gil, who lost his parents and a leg during the war. The whole plot of the film revolves around her motherly affection for him. At this point, the representation of nurses had changed completely and gained a quite different meaning from what the representation of military nurses signified during the Pacific War. While Japan's imperial army nurses were depicted as carrying out a grave mission of national triumph, Bong-nyŏ's mission acquires its sublimity from her pursuit of Christian redemption. Though she also mentions the importance of the war against the Communist army, her main concern is more religious than political. She thinks that Sun-gil's late mother would not be redeemed if the boy fails to rehabilitate. After Sun-gil successfully receives rehabilitation treatment and gets a prosthetic leg, she lays flowers on the bed where Sun-gil's mother died and hangs a framed picture of Jesus Christ on the wall behind it (Figure 14.3). Bong-nyŏ's mission gains a spiritual value in this *motherly* way. The changing roles of nurses in the war show how the spirituality of Japanese imperialism made way for the new order led by the U.S. and its Christian values.

The religious life depicted in *Ward of Affection*, along with several other USIS-Korea films, is a fabricated picture rather than a reflection of reality. It is the "landscape" of the new hegemonic religion in South Korea (Kim Hong-jung 2005, 131). Both the rural villages where "millions of believers sincerely worship at over five thousand rural churches every Sunday" in *Korean Farm Life* and the *restored* everyday life in which an entire family goes to church on Sundays in *Building Together* (*Ŭijŏngbu iyagi*, 1955) do not consider whether Christian Sunday worship was actually prevalent in Korea before the Korean War. These pseudo-ethnographies deliver an imagined picture of daily religious lives in Korea and reflect the social and political power structure in religion at the time of the production of these films. They are a way of gazing at the local religious culture, in which the Protestant way of life in New England poses as the universal and the gaze of the camera navigates the local life to confirm its universality (Kim Han-sang 2011, 204).

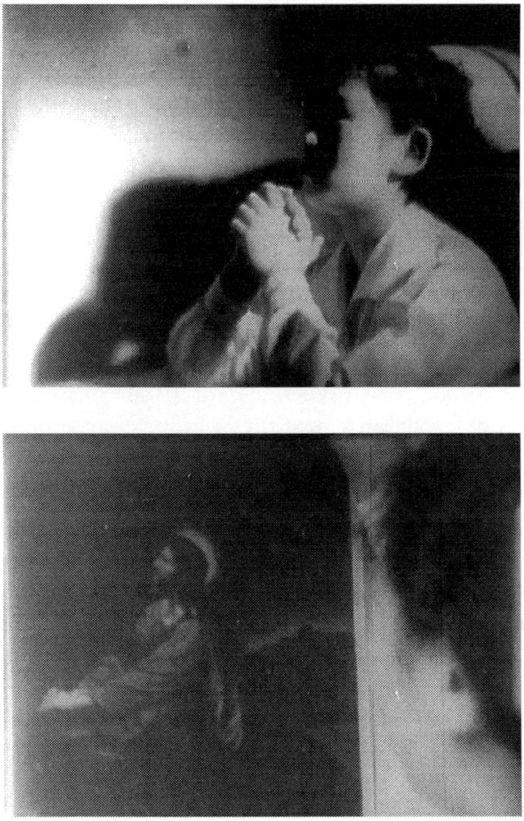

Figure 14.3 The nurse's religious behaviors in *Ward of Affection* (RG 306.3657, courtesy of NARA).

The Recognition of Korean Traditional Culture and Cultural Hierarchy in Asia

Another case of USIS-Korea's strategy of visualization and spectatorship showing the mechanism of gazing can be observed in its representations of Korean traditional culture. Just as Christina Klein (2003) defines the impulse to explore and exchange cultural peculiarities as constituting a "global imagery of integration" during the 1950s (19–60), the USIS was an important tool for integration among allies through mutual understanding. Its representation of local traditional cultures aimed at achieving this very mutual understanding. This project to appreciate and learn obscure cultures of other nations can be understood in terms of the strategy of visualization.

It is particularly significant here to contextualize USIS-Korea's contributions to representing and exhibiting Korean traditional culture in relation to the nation-building project of the Republic of Korea (hereafter ROK), a newly established postcolonial state. In rebuilding the nation-state, the (re)establishment of *traditional cultures* that had been concealed under colonial rule was a very important task. For many Asian countries that had experienced colonial rule and imperialist wars, the process to excavate, assemble, and justify each nation's past was a belated but urgent task. A *nation* was to serve as the strong basis for legitimizing the new regime by providing evidence of origin, genealogy, and history. Cultural elements, which would be resources for such a linear model of historiography, had to be unearthed and reorganized in the early period of nation-building. This was not only a process of decolonization that reinstated elements disavowed and disparaged by the colonial power, but also, inversely, a process of succession which allowed them to reappropriate the pride of a locality given and commercialized by the political economy of the former empire. Therefore, the project of integration driven by the U.S. in the 1950s needs to be understood as a means to interlock Korea's *traditional culture* with the nation-building project of the South Korean state.

An interesting case in point is USIS-Korea's serial filming of the Korean traditional dancer, Kim Paek-pong. Kim personified the superiority of the "Free World," since she defected to South Korea during the Korean War. Her teacher was Ch'oe Sŭng-hŭi, a top star in the imperial Japanese dancing scene for her talent and local identity. While Ch'oe remained in North Korea, Kim, who was born in Pyŏngyang, came down to the South and became "the founder of South Korean traditional dance" (Ch'oe 2009). Liberty Production produced live-recorded films of her first dance recitals in South Korea from November 26 to 28, 1954, and of her original dance drama, *Story of Our Village* (*Uri maŭl-ŭi iyagi*), which was shown from April 12 to 16, 1956. The titles of these USIS-Korea films were *Filial Piety* (*Chi-hyo*), *Fan Dance* (*Puch'aech'um*), and *Story of Our Village*, respectively.

The way in which the introductory parts of these films are organized is worthy of attention. They all show the credits and titles of the performances at first, followed by freeze-frames capturing pages of the playbills with the narrator's brief introduction before the actual performances begin. This organization bears a close parallel to that of films on Western classical music which had been screened many times by the U.S. Army and USIS-Korea since the liberation. *Arturo Toscanini—Hymn of the Nation* (1944), a film distributed by DPI before February 1947 (Noce 1947), also starts in a similar fashion that shows the names of the performers, the title of the performance, a shot of the score, and the performance itself in that order (Figures 14.4 and 14.5). The ways in which the intertitles are illustrated produce an image of a higher art, and the visualization of scores and playbills delivers certain educational impressions that may have introduced the highbrow side of the ideal way of life. Besides *Arturo Toscanini*, American propaganda agencies

Figure 14.4 *Arturo Toscanini—Hymn of The Nation* (1944) (RG 306.197, courtesy of NARA).

Figure 14.5 *Story of Our Village* (1956) (RG 306.7576, courtesy of NARA).

introduced many other similar films on classical music to South Korean audiences, delivering live performances of famous artists and scenes of music festivals.

This parallel between live-recorded films of Korean traditional dance and educational films on the high art of Western classical music makes one reconsider the very function of the former films. Since the Korean dance films were not newsreels but self-contained documentaries, it is obvious that they were not produced merely for reporting purposes.

It is probable that the similarities between these films served to induce audiences to appreciate Kim Paek-pong's performance in similar ways as they received Western classical music. This was a process not only of visualizing Korea's cultural peculiarities but also of displaying the prestige of U.S. authority by stressing its role of recognizing and acknowledging the outstanding characteristics of another nation's culture. Thus, this whole process should be understood as the dual work of South Korean nation-building and the establishment of U.S. cultural hegemony.

In the meantime, a feud between the Eisenhower administration and the Syngman Rhee government arose regarding U.S. strategy toward Asia. The U.S. government's intention to integrate the Asian region economically with Japan as the center of "Free Asia" was in discord with the ROK government's stance to unite militarily with other Asian nations while excluding Japan (No 2002, 207–8). The Eisenhower administration was carrying out its New Look policy, which rhetorically placed an emphasis on "peaceful coexistence" with the Communist bloc under the mutual deterrents of strategic nuclear weapons and pushed forward an economic integration among non-Communist states (Pak 2005, 160). The Rhee government's strong anti-Communist military alliance line, therefore, was difficult to accept (Cho 2008, 215). The Asian Peoples' Anti-Communist League (hereafter APACL), which later would organize two Korean cultural goodwill mission tours, was established in June 1956 in the midst of this disagreement and led by Syngman Rhee. Its first conference was attended by government delegates from five countries (South Korea, Taiwan, the Philippines, Thailand, and South Vietnam), in addition to representatives from Hong Kong, Macau, and Okinawa. APACL was tinged not only with anti-Communism but also with anti-Japanese sentiments, and it was designed to prevent the U.S. strategy of giving Japan a leading role in Asia (No 2002, 210–1). However, the U.S. also pushed to create the Southeast Asia Treaty Organization (hereafter SEATO) in September of the same year, excluding South Korea, Taiwan, and Japan, and in practical terms neutralizing the status of APACL as a regional security alliance (Cho 2008, 235; No 2002, 211).

The Asian tours of the Korean goodwill mission in 1957 and 1958 were the cultural events held after APACL was incapacitated in international politics. The basic anti-Japanese trend had remained up to that time, so the two rounds of touring excluded Japan and involved other member countries and places instead. In spite of the U.S. government's noncooperation with and attempts to neutralize APACL, the mission's tour in 1958 was accompanied and filmed by a USIS-Korea unit. This cooperation should be understood as being conducted on a *cultural* level. In other words, seen from the basic objective of USIS to support mutual understanding among all "free people," its decision to shoot and record the non-governmental cultural interchange by APACL and to help promote international friendship in the Asian region was perhaps not surprising.

However, in the ensuing film, *Korean Cultural Goodwill Mission to South East Asia* (*Han'guk yesul sajŏldan tongnama pangmun*, 1958), USIS-Korea's involvement was more than observing and reporting. According to the intertitles in the introductory opening of the film, the filming was made possible by the "united endeavors" of every USIS branch in the visited countries, and all the events were shot by cameramen dispatched by USIS-Korea. That is to say, the film was a product of a transnational network of USIS branches in the major cities of East and Southeast Asia. This collaborative production was also a process of showing off the prestige of U.S. authority in Asia, by confirming its status and its ability to visualize the cultural peculiarities of various nations and places.

It is worth investigating more closely the narrative structure of *Korean Cultural Goodwill Mission to South East Asia*. The mission's first destination was Saigon, South Vietnam. After depicting the welcoming crowd at the port, the film shows Vietnamese audiences viewing the Korean Products Exhibition installed in the ROK naval vessel LST-810. The next scene shows the mission's audience with President Ngô Đinh Diêm, followed by footage of a performance at the Dai Nam Theatre. A similar narrative pattern is then used for the next destinations: Bangkok, Thailand; Manila, The Philippines; Hong Kong; Taipei, Taiwan; and Ryukyu (Okinawa).

Underlying this recurrent pattern is a repetitive structure used to organize the various parts (corresponding to the various destinations) in the film: a pictured map of the destination, the mission's encountering with the welcoming crowd, the mission's sightseeing of native cultures and/or visits to local authorities, and the mission's performance of Korean traditional arts and Western classic music in the destination city's performance venue (Figure 14.6). This structure mirrors a typical form

Figure 14.6 A repetitive structure in *Korean Cultural Goodwill Mission to South East Asia* (RG 306.3580, courtesy of NARA).

of tourist film that locates the object region on a calculable universe of the map and then panoramically exhibits the region where the object natives represent their ethnicity and the peculiar characteristics of their cultures. The use of this tourist film convention suggests that *Korean Cultural Goodwill Mission to South East Asia* was not only a tool to show the (South Korean) audiences their nation's diplomatic affairs, but also an opportunity for them to experience exotic cultures in the form of virtual tourism, given to people who did not have the freedom to take overseas trips. As seen from the traditional attire of the welcoming crowd and the typical tourist attraction sites where the mission visited, authenticity was staged (MacCannell 1973, 589). These "authentic" features were refined and re-performed via the procedures of film shooting and editing. Furthermore, it is significant to bear in mind that both visitors and natives were performing their own authenticities to each other as a form of cultural exchange. The sightseeing scenes are key examples of this tactic. In these scenes, members of the cultural mission are in Korean traditional clothes and strolling through the downtown streets of Bangkok, Manila, and other cities.

In the mission's performance with which the repetitive structure for each destination ends, three different gazes interacting with one another in the film and/or in theaters suggest an interesting dynamic. First, there is the gaze of Southeast Asian audiences who were watching the South Korean performers in person. Second, the gaze of the South Korean audiences who watched the filmed Korean performers and Southeast Asian audiences, after the film was completed and released, should be considered. They would likely watch the film in theaters before the commercial features or in specifically organized events that had educational purposes. And they would recognize through the logos and intertitles that the film was made by USIS. Lastly, there is the camera's gaze, or the gaze of USIS, on the Korean performers as well as the Southeast Asian audiences. Seen in terms of a strategy of visualization, this interplay of different gazes produces a kind of cultural hierarchy for the Asian region. While the Southeast Asian gaze identifies Korean authenticity and collects knowledge of it, the Korean gaze recognizes and observes the process as a well-planned, ostentatious exhibition of Koreanness. In this process, Southeast Asian audiences are reversely visualized as objects to be comprehended, and the knowledge of them—how they look and live, what their authenticity is, and how they react to Korean authenticity—is collected. Nevertheless, this film, as a product of the "united endeavors" of different USIS branches, proves that the gaze of the U.S. authority is located at the highest rung of the hierarchy. In this view, the camera of USIS filmmakers becomes the gaze of the big Other, which "operates effectively because it is not visible" (Chu 2003, 339). The whole process of Koreans showing off their cultural peculiarity and Southeast Asians appreciating it is, thus, recognized and collected by the camera of USIS as an object of visualization. At the same time, by screening the film in theaters, USIS was showing off its power to see and visualize.

This structure of seeing points to the remarkable positioning of South Korea between the U.S. and other Asian countries. The fact that *Korean Cultural Goodwill Mission to South East Asia* was targeted at a South Korean audience is important. In this exhibition, the South Korean people's self-awareness as second-in-command and their sense of superiority over Southeast Asian people are both cinematically exercised. Following the U.S., a supranational authority that could recognize and collect each nation's cultural peculiarities, South Korea displays the capability to exhibit its *recognized* traditional culture and to perform Western high arts, which were imported and learned through a modern school system. This process corresponds to the Syngman Rhee government's attempted plan to gain leadership in Asia under U.S. hegemony, as second-in-command, by leading APACL and excluding Japan. The exchange of gazes in the film discloses a certain process of disciplining and internalizing of such cultural hierarchy.

Conclusion: The Visualization of Cold War Asia as a Technology of Government

Three focal points for attention are marked in these USIS-Korea films: the recognition of cultural peculiarity by a *supranational* authority, the U.S.; South Korea's positioning as second-in-command in the Asian region; and the Korean people's sense of superiority over Southeast Asians. All of these can be said to have existed in colonial Korea as well. Nicholas Thomas (1994) shows how the process of internalization and self-government had followed a colonial strategy to collect and preserve the knowledge of colonies and visualize an invisible indigenous culture (105–42; also see Foucault 1991, 87–104). This process by which the cultural peculiarities of a colony were discovered and recognized as marketable knowledge, exhibited after rational classification, and then located in a certain cultural hierarchy, can be called the governmentalization of the colonial state.

In this sense, the second-in-command identity in colonial Korea is of importance in that it resulted from a specific combination of the technology of power and the technology of the self. A classic example can be found in the representations of natives of Southeast Asia and the South Pacific, a region that was called the "Southern" (*nambang*). As early as the 1910s, when Japan first reached the South Sea Islands, the perception of this Southern region in colonial Korea changed from both a "savage and barbarous primitive society" and "fertile and natural lands" to "lands and society which must be cultivated by the Japanese Empire." This was a process intended to "schematize the hierarchy of civilizations" (Kim S. 2009, 78). Korean awareness of and interest in the

Southern region were heightened upon Japan's occupation of Singapore in December 1941. Intellectuals in colonial Korea, which was one of the oldest colonies of Japan, regarded Korea as second-in-command in the Pan-Asian region and thought that they had a mission to enlighten Southeast Asia's uncivilized races. According to Kwŏn Myŏng-a (2005), this "Southern fever" originated from "an imperialist fantasy that constituted [colonial Koreans] as a subject of the Greater East Asia Co-Prosperity Sphere—a subject of the Japanese Empire" (357). In this fever and its hierarchical representations, colonial Koreans defined themselves as the subjects who were charged with a mission to civilize and enlighten those "Southerners" (333–6).

There is a similarity between colonial Koreans' self-awareness as second-in-command in the Asian region and that of South Koreans during the Cold War. In particular, the representations of Southeast Asians and Koreans' sense of superiority over them appear to have resulted from the legacy of the colonial period. However, as is evident in the feud between the Eisenhower administration and the Rhee government, the relationships among South Korea, Southeast Asian countries, and the U.S. cannot be inferred from colonial experiences alone, as all of the states in question obviously possessed the status of a sovereign country by all appearances. Then, how could one define the true nature of this seeming similarity between the two different periods?

We can refer to Matthew Hannah's (2000) insight to account for this similarity. Hannah claims that "even quite *benign* governmentality retains a basically *colonial* structure"—a unilateral, coercive collection of knowledge and a consequent legibility, based on "the rule from a distance" (114). USIS-Korea's one-sidedness in collecting information and its coercive "power to see" through filmmaking can be explained using this theoretical framework. In particular, the agency's showing off of U.S. authority through its films signifies that there was indeed governmental power during the Cold War that "differed from panoptic power" in that "the agents of vision traveled to their objects using the same infrastructures available to the objects themselves" (Hannah 2000, 128). In other words, the governmentality of Cold War Asia was formed through a process of inheriting the basic structure established in colonial regimes of knowledge and redetermining the relationship between the newly independent states and the U.S. in the new world order.

Nevertheless, there is a distinct line between colonial governmentality and Cold War governmentality. The visualization of ethnic-national peculiarities that had been represented as the emblem of cultural diversity in the Empire of Japan later became the cultural bases for the nation-building process of politically independent sovereign states during the Cold War. Therefore, the matter of assimilation that had presupposed the confrontation between the Greater East Asia Co-Prosperity Sphere and the external parties now became dissolved and transformed into a matter of alliance and hegemony that entailed the ideological confrontation among each and every sovereign state. The dissolution of imperial world orders at the end of WWII, the new border drawings that emerged within the Asian region, the rise and development of the Cold War system, and the formation of "Free Asia" led by the U.S., all of which were accompanied by the rearrangement of knowledge regimes, are to be examined to determine the governmentality of the Cold War in Asia. The investigation of the mechanisms and structures of gazes in cinematic spectatorship during the Cold War era will be one particular endeavor which historians of Asian cinema can further pursue.

Acknowledgments

This chapter has been revised and developed from the author's original paper, "The Mechanism of the Gaze in the USIS Film Propaganda in South Korea," published in *Yŏksa munje yŏn'gu* (Critical Studies on Modern Korean History), no. 30 (2013): 167–201.

Works Cited

Cho Mu-hyŏng. 2008. "Asia minjok pan'gong yŏnmaeng ŭi ch'angsŏl kwa chwajŏl—yŏkhal iron ŭl t'onghan hanmi kaldŭng ŭi kaenyŏmhwa" (The establishment and decline of APACL: conceptualizing the ROK-US conflict based on the role theory). *Segye chŏngch'i* (World Politics) 10:187–239.

Ch'oe Hae-ri. 2009. "Ch'oesŏn-ŭl tahae ch'oego-ka toeŏra" (Do your best and become the best). *Webzine Arko* 136. Accessed October 29, 2012. www.arko.or.kr/home2005/bodo/sub/forest.jsp?idx=1689&pidx=1365

Chŏng Il-jun. 2003. "Miguk-ŭi naengjŏnmunhwajŏngch'i-wa han'gugin 'ch'in'gu mandŭlgi'" (America's Cold War cultural politics and 'befriending' Koreans). In *Uri hangmun sok-ŭi miguk* (America in Our Academia), edited by Korea Progressive Academy Council, 21–50. Seoul: Hanul.

Chu Ŭn-u. 2003. *Sigak-kwa hyŏndaesŏng* (Vision and Modernity). Seoul: Hannarae.

Commander-in-Chief, United States Army Forces, Pacific. 1946a. "Summation of United States Army Military Government Activities in Korea, No.11 (August 1946)." RG331, SCAP Military & Non-Military Activities, 1945–49, Box 8303. The U.S. National Archives and Records Administration, College Park, MD.

Commander-in-Chief, United States Army Forces, Pacific. 1946b. "Summation of United States Army Military Government Activities in Korea, No.12 (September 1946)." RG331, SCAP Military & Non-Military Activities, 1945–49, Box 8303. The U.S. National Archives and Records Administration, College Park, MD.

Foucault, Michel. 1991. "Governmentality." In *Foucault Effect: Studies in Governmentality*, edited by Graham Burchell et al., 87–104. Chicago, IL: The University of Chicago Press.

Foucault, Michel. 1995. *Discipline and Punish: The Birth of the Prison*. 2nd ed. Translated by Alan Sheridan. New York: Vintage Books.

Hannah, Matthew G. 2000. *Governmentality and the Mastery of Territory in Nineteenth Century America*. Cambridge: Cambridge University Press.

Jay, Martin. 1994. *Downcast Eyes: The Denigration of Vision in Twentieth-Century French Thought*. Berkeley: University of California Press.

Kim, Han Sang. 2013. "Cold War and the Contested Identity Formation of Korean Filmmakers." *Inter-Asia Cultural Studies* 14 (4): 551–63.

Kim Han-sang. 2012. "Chuhan miguk kongbowŏn yŏnghwa sŏnjŏn ŭi p'yosang kwa tamnon" (Re/presentations and discourses in the USIS-Korea's film propaganda). *Sahoe-wa yŏksa* (Society and History), no. 95: 243–79.

Kim Han-sang. 2011. "1945–48 nyŏn chuhan migunjŏng mit chuhan migun saryŏngbu ŭi yŏnghwa sŏnjŏn" (The U.S. film propaganda in South Korea, 1945–48). *Miguksa yŏn'gu* (The Korean Journal of American History), no. 34: 177–212.

Kim Hong-jung. 2005. "Munhwa sahoehak kwa p'unggyŏng ŭi munje" (The sociology of the culture and the problem of the landscape). *Sahoe-wa iron* (Society and Theory), no. 6: 129–67.

Kim Sŭng-ik. 2009. "Ilje kangjŏmgi nambang imiji hyŏngsŏng kwa kŭ ŭimi" (Representation of nambang in modern Korean art during the colonial period). *Han'guk kŭnhyŏndae misul sahak* (Journal of Korean Modern & Contemporary Art History), no. 20: 76–96.

Kim Wŏn-sik. 1967. "Ribŏt'inyusŭ 15nyŏn-ŭi myŏngam" (Light and shade in the 15 year history of *Liberty News*). *Sindonga* (July): 289–95.

Klein, Christina. 2003. *Cold War Orientalism: Asia in the Middlebrow Imagination, 1945–1961*. Berkeley: University of California Press.

Kwŏn Myŏng-a. 2005. "T'aep'yŏngyang chŏnjaenggi nambang chongjokchi wa cheguk ŭi p'ant'aji" (Fantasy of the empire and the ethnography of *nambang* [Southeast Asia]). *Sanghŏ hakpo* (The Leaned Society of Sanghur's Literature), no. 14: 327–361.

Kwŏn Myŏng-a. 2004. "Ch'onghu puin, sinyŏsŏng, kŭrigo sŭp'ai" (The women in the rear guard [Chong Hoo Buin], the new women [Shin Yeosung], and the spy). *Sanghŏ hakpo* (The Leaned Society of Sanghur's Literature), no. 12: 251–82.

MacCannell, Dean. 1973. "Staged Authenticity." *The American Journal of Sociology* 79 (3): 589–603.

No· Ki-yŏng. 2002. "Yi sŭngman chŏnggwŏn ŭi t'aep'yŏngyang tongmaeng ch'ujin kwa chiyŏk anbo kusang" (The development of Pacific Pact policy and the plan of regional security in the Rhee Syngman regime). *Chiyŏk-kwa yŏksa*, no. 11: 186–223.

Noce, Daniel. 1947. "A Letter to Benjamin O. O'Sullivan, 20 February 1947." Textual Records in NARA. RG59, Department of State, Decimal File 1945–49, Box 7398.

Osgood, Kenneth. 2006. *Total Cold War: Eisenhower's Secret Propaganda Battle at Home and Abroad*. Lawrence: University Press of Kansas.

Pak In-suk. 2005. "Aijenhawŏ haengjŏngbu wa 'p'yŏnghwa' ŭi susahak" (Eisenhower's rhetoric of "peace"). *Miguksa yŏn'gu* (The Korean Journal of American History), no. 22: 157–92.

Sin Yŏng-suk. 2011. "Asia t'aep'yŏngyang chŏnjaenggi chosŏnin chonggun kanhobu ŭi tongwŏn silt'ae wa chŏngch'esŏng" (The real mobilization and the identity of Korean military nurses during the Asia-Pacific War). *Yŏsŏng-kwa yŏksa* (Women and History), no. 14: 129–73.

Thomas, Nicholas. 1994. *Colonialism's Culture: Anthropology, Travel and Government*. Princeton, NJ: Princeton University Press.

Yi Ch'ŏl-sun. 2007. "Pusan chŏngch'i p'adong kwa kukka poanbŏp p'adong e taehan miguk ŭi kaeip pigyo" (A comparative study of the U. S. interventions in "Pusan Political Crisis" and 'National Security Law Crisis' in Korea). *Segye chŏngch'i* (World Politics), no. 8: 81–127.

Yi Hwa-jin. 2007. "Kŭkchanggukka rosŏ chel-konghwaguk kwa kinyŏm ŭi kyunyŏl" (The First Republic as "theater state" and the ruptures of commemoration). *Han'guk kŭndae munhak yŏn'gu* (Journal of Modern Korean Literature), no. 15: 197–228.

Yi Hyo-in. 2010. "*Chip ŏmnŭn ch'ŏnsa* wa *migaheri ŭi t'ap* ŭi pigyo yŏn'gu" (A comparative study of *Homeless Angel* and *Tower of Migaheri*). *Yŏnghwa yŏn'gu* (Film Studies), no. 44: 251–79.

Yi Wan-bŏm. 2007. "1950-nyŏndae Yi sŭngman taet'ongnyŏng kwa miguk ŭi kwan'gye e kwanhan yŏn'gu" (President Rhee's autonomy toward the U.S. in the 1950s). *Chŏngsin munhwa yŏn'gu* (Korean Studies Quarterly) 30 (2): 199–229.

Contributors

Hye Seung Chung is Associate Professor of Film and Media Studies in the Department of Communication Studies, Colorado State University. She is the author of *Hollywood Asian: Philip Ahn and the Politics of Cross-Ethnic Performance* (Temple University Press, 2006) and *Kim Ki-duk* (University of Illinois Press, 2012) as well as the co-author of *Movie Migrations: Transnational Genre Flows and South Korean Cinema* (Rutgers University Press, 2015). She recently completed a new book manuscript entitled *Hollywood Diplomacy: Film Regulation, Foreign Relations, and East Asian Representations* (Rutgers University Press, 2020).

Poshek Fu is Professor of History at the University of Illinois at Urbana-Champaign. His research focuses on media history, Cold War cultures, and U.S.-China relations. He is the author of *Between Shanghai and Hong Kong: The Politics of Chinese Cinemas* (Stanford University Press, 2003) and *Passivity, Resistance, and Collaboration: Intellectual Choices in Occupied Shanghai* (Stanford University Press, 1993). He is also the editor of *China Forever: The Shaw Brothers and Diasporic Cinema* (University of Illinois Press, 2008), and co-editor of *The Cinema of Hong Kong: History, Arts, Identity* (Cambridge University Press, 2002).

Namhee Han is Assistant Professor of Korean Humanities at Queens College, the City University of New York (CUNY). Her research interests include theories and histories of Korean and East Asian films, moving image technology, aesthetics and politics, Cold War visual culture, and digital archival practices. Her works have appeared in *Acta Koreana*, *The Journal of Japanese and Korean Cinema*, *Voyage of Discovery* (2017), and *"Postwar" Japanese Cinema* (2012). She is currently completing a book manuscript entitled *Between Screens: Cold War Transnationalism and Widescreen Cinema in Japan and South Korea, 1950s to 1970s.*

Calvin Hui is Associate Professor of Chinese Studies at the College of William and Mary in the United States. He received his Ph.D. in Literature at Duke University in 2013. His first book manuscript focuses on fashion, fiction and documentary films, and consumer culture in the context of contemporary China. He has published in *GLQ: A Journal of Lesbian and Gay Studies*, *Modern Chinese Literature and Culture* (online), *Verge: Studies in Global Asias*, *Journal of Chinese Cinemas*, and *The Changing Landscape of China's Consumerism*, among others. He is a recipient of the 2019 American Council of Learned Societies (ACLS) fellowship.

Han Sang Kim is Assistant Professor of Sociology at Ajou University. His fields of research include visual sociology, Cold War governmentality in East Asia, Korean and East Asian film history, and cultural history of mobilities. He is currently working on a book manuscript on the association between the cinema and modern transportation mobility in twentieth-century Korea. He has published essays in *The Journal of Asian Studies, Journal of Korean Studies, Inter-Asian Cultural Studies*, and several other journals in Korean. He was the inaugural programmer of the Cinematheque KOFA at the Korean Film Archive in Seoul.

Jie Li is John L. Loeb Associate Professor of the Humanities in the Department of East Asian Languages and Civilizations at Harvard University. She is the author of *Shanghai Homes: Palimpsests of Private Life* (Columbia, 2015) and *Utopian Ruins: A Memorial Museum of the Mao Era* (Duke, forthcoming in 2020). Her current book project, *Cinema at the Grassroots*, studies the exhibition and reception of cinema in socialist China, including movie theaters and open-air screenings, projectionists and audiences, as well as memories of revolutionary and foreign films.

Rini Bhattacharya Mehta is an assistant professor in the Program of Comparative and World Literatures at the University of Illinois, Urbana-Champaign. Her research interests include postcolonial theory and criticism, nationalism and religion, globalization, and Indian cinema. She is the co-editor of *Indian Partition in Literature and Films: History, Politics, Aesthetics* (Routledge, 2014) and *Bollywood and Globalization: Indian Popular Cinema, Nation, and Diaspora* (Anthem, 2010).

Michael Raine is Associate Professor of Film Studies in the Department of English and Writing Studies at Western University, Canada. He has worked extensively on Japanese cinema, including essays in *The Oxford Handbook of Japanese Cinema* (Oxford University Press, 2014), *Reorienting Ozu: A Master and His Influence* (Oxford University Press, 2018), *Killers, Clients and Kindred Spirits: The Taboo Cinema of Shohei Imamura* (Edinburgh University Press, 2019), and *The Japanese Cinema Book* (Bloomsbury/BFI, forthcoming). He is editor, with Johan Nordström, of *The Culture of the Sound Image in Prewar*

Japan (Amsterdam University Press), and is completing a manuscript titled *The Cinema of High Economic Growth: New Japanese Cinemas, 1955–1964.*

Jessica Tan is a Ph.D. candidate at Harvard University's Department of East Asian Languages and Civilizations, specializing in modern and contemporary Chinese literature. Her dissertation explores the transnational networks of cultural production between Southeast Asia and East Asia during the Cold War, as well as the ways in which these connections continue to shape literary works and discourses today. Her other research interests include Hong Kong cinema, the history of Chinese in Southeast Asia, and diaspora studies.

Michael G. Vann, Professor of History and Asian Studies at California State University, Sacramento, earned his Ph.D. in history at the University of California, Santa Cruz, in 1999. He has taught at several universities in Northern California and Asia. Vann has been awarded three Fulbright grants (France, Indonesia, and Cambodia), a research fellowship from the Council of American Overseas Research Centers, a Center for Khmer Studies senior researcher fellowship, and fellowship from the Korea Society. His research on the French colonial empire and the history of Southeast Asia during the Cold War has been published in over three dozen academic journals and two books, including *The Great Hanoi Rat Hunt: Empire, Disease, and Modernity in French Colonial Vietnam* (Oxford, 2019). His next book will compare the representations of Cold war-era mass violence in Indonesian, Vietnamese, and Cambodian museums.

Mitsuyo Wada-Marciano is Professor of Cinema and Media Studies, and Transcultural Studies at Kyoto University. She is the author of *Nippon Modern: Japanese Cinema of the 1920s and 1930s* (2008) and *Japanese Cinema in the Digital Age* (2012). She is also the co-editor of *Horror to the Extreme: Changing Boundaries in Asian Cinema* (2009) and *Viewing "Postwar" in the 1950s Japanese Cinema* (in Japanese, 2012). Her latest edited collection is *Rethinking the Media Discourses in Post-3.11* (in Japanese, 2019). Her research interests include: Japanese cinema and media culture, East Asian cinema, queer cinema, and digital film archives. She is currently finishing her book manuscript, *Sayonara, Nuclear Power: Voices from Japanese Filmmakers in the Wake of Fukushima.*

Lanjun Xu is Associate Professor of Chinese Studies at the National University of Singapore. She received her B.A. and M.A. from Peking University, and Ph.D. from Princeton University. Her research interests include modern Chinese literature and culture, cultural history of children and youth in modern China, as well as Cold War politics and Chinese cinemas. She is the author of *Chinese Children and*

War: *Education, Nation and Popular Culture* (in Chinese) (Peking University Press, 2015). She has recently completed an English book manuscript titled *The Child and Chinese Modernity*: *Culture, Nation and Technologies of Childhood in Modern China*. She is currently working on a book project about cultures of the Chinese Cold War in Southeast Asia between the 1940s and 1960s.

Man-Fung Yip is Associate Professor of Film and Media Studies at the University of Oklahoma. He is the author of *Martial Arts Cinema and Hong Kong Modernity*: *Aesthetics, Representation, Circulation* (Hong Kong University Press, 2017) and co-editor of *American and Chinese-Language Cinemas: Examining Cultural Flows* (Routledge, 2015). His work has also appeared in *Cinema Journal*, *Chinese Literature Today*, and numerous edited volumes.

Index

Note: Page numbers followed by "n" denote endnotes.